A CULTURAL HISTORY OF HAIR

VOLUME 3

A Cultural History of Hair
General Editor: Geraldine Biddle-Perry

Volume 1
A Cultural History of Hair in Antiquity
Edited by Mary Harlow

Volume 2
A Cultural History of Hair in the Middle Ages
Edited by Roberta Milliken

Volume 3
A Cultural History of Hair in the Renaissance
Edited by Edith Snook

Volume 4
A Cultural History of Hair in the Age of Enlightenment
Edited by Margaret K. Powell and Joseph Roach

Volume 5
A Cultural History of Hair in the Age of Empire
Edited by Sarah Heaton

Volume 6
A Cultural History of Hair in the Modern Age
Edited by Geraldine Biddle-Perry

A CULTURAL HISTORY OF HAIR

IN THE RENAISSANCE

VOLUME 3

Edited by Edith Snook

BLOOMSBURY ACADEMIC
LONDON · NEW YORK · OXFORD · NEW DELHI · SYDNEY

BLOOMSBURY ACADEMIC
Bloomsbury Publishing Plc
50 Bedford Square, London, WC1B 3DP, UK
1385 Broadway, New York, NY 10018, USA
29 Earlsfort Terrace, Dublin 2, Ireland

BLOOMSBURY, BLOOMSBURY ACADEMIC and the Diana logo are trademarks of Bloomsbury Publishing Plc

First published in Great Britain 2021
Paperback edition published 2022

Copyright © Bloomsbury Publishing, 2022

Edith Snook has asserted her right under the Copyright,
Designs and Patents Act, 1988, to be identified as Editor of this work.

Series design: Raven Design
Cover image: Pallas and the Centaur (Minerva and the Centaur) © Mondadori Portfolio / Contributor

All rights reserved. No part of this publication may be reproduced or transmitted in any form or by any means, electronic or mechanical, including photocopying, recording, or any information storage or retrieval system, without prior permission in writing from the publishers.

Bloomsbury Publishing Plc does not have any control over, or responsibility for, any third-party websites referred to or in this book. All internet addresses given in this book were correct at the time of going to press. The author and publisher regret any inconvenience caused if addresses have changed or sites have ceased to exist, but can accept no responsibility for any such changes.

A catalogue record for this book is available from the British Library.

A catalog record for this book is available from the Library of Congress.

ISBN:	HB:	978-1-4742-3205-0
	HB set:	978-1-4742-3212-8
	PB:	978-1-3502-8554-5
	PB set:	978-1-3502-8751-8
	ePDF:	978-1-3501-2281-9
	eBook:	978-1-3501-2280-2

Series: The Cultural Histories Series

Typeset by Integra Software Services Pvt. Ltd.
Printed and bound in Great Britain

To find out more about our authors and books visit www.bloomsbury.com
and sign up for our newsletters.

CONTENTS

LIST OF FIGURES	vi
GENERAL EDITOR'S PREFACE	x
INTRODUCTION *Edith Snook*	1
1 Religion and Ritualized Belief *Gary K. Waite*	17
2 Self and Society *Anu Korhonen*	39
3 Fashion and Adornment *Carole Collier Frick*	53
4 Production and Practice *Annemarie Kinzelbach*	71
5 Health and Hygiene *Edith Snook*	85
6 Gender and Sexuality *Mark Albert Johnston*	99
7 Race and Ethnicity *Nicholas Jones*	115
8 Class and Social Status *Jana Mathews*	127
9 Cultural Representations *Lyn Bennett*	145
NOTES	156
FURTHER READING	191
CONTRIBUTORS	210
INDEX	212

LIST OF FIGURES

INTRODUCTION

I.1 Band of lace (1640–1680). Needle lace worked in human hair, with thicker outlines possibly in horsehair. © Victoria and Albert Museum, London. T. 150-1963 — 1

I.2 Peter Paul Rubens, *Samson and Delilah* (1609–1610). © The National Gallery, London. NG 6461 — 5

I.3 Martin Luther, *Biblia Das ist, Die gantze heilige Schrifft*, Deudsch (Wittemberg, 1576), fol. 200v. Courtesy Bayerische Staatsbibliothek, Munich. urn:nbn:de:bvb:12-bsb00085706-7 — 6

I.4 After Sir Anthony van Dyck, *Five Children of King Charles I* (1637). © National Portrait Gallery, London. NPG 267 — 8

I.5 *Age* (seventeenth century). Oval wax relief. Courtesy Victoria and Albert Museum, London. A.68-1938 — 10

CHAPTER 1

1.1 Hieronymus Wiericx, *Image or Literal Figure of the Bride of Christ, or the true Restoration or Restitution*, engraving after David Joris, from David Joris, *Twonder-boeck: waer in dat van der werldt aen versloten gheopenbaert is. Opt nieuw ghecorrigeert vnde vermeerdert by den Autheur selue* (n.p., 1551 [Dierck Mullem, 1584?]), part III, fol. iiiv. Courtesy of the Universiteitsbibliotheek van Amsterdam, Kerkelijke Collecties — 21

1.2 Anonymous, *Portrait of the Anabaptist David Joris*, Kunstmuseum Basel, public domain. Courtesty the Yorck Project: *10.000 Meisterwerke der Malerei* [DVD-ROM], 2002 — 22

1.3 Attributed to Albrecht Dürer, *The Demon of Vanity and the Coquette*. From Geoffrey de La Tour Landry's *Ritter vom Turn*, (Basel: Printed by Michael Furter, 1493). Public domain. https://en.wikipedia.org/wiki/File:Vanity.jpg — 24

1.4 Fourteenth-century relief portrait of Mary Magdalene, St. John's Church, Toruń. Photo: courtesy Pko, public domain via Wikimedia Commons. https://commons.wikimedia.org/wiki/File:Torun_SS_Johns_Mary_Magdalene.jpg — 27

1.5 Ulrich Molitor, *De laniis et phitonicis mulieribus* (Concerning Witches and Fortunetellers) (Reutlingen, http://www.ubs.sbg.ac.at/sosa/inkunabeln/WI167.htm). Public domain via Wikimedia Commons. https://commons.wikimedia.org/wiki/File:Ulrich_Molitor_Von_den_Unholden_Teufelsbuhlschaft.jpg — 29

LIST OF FIGURES

1.6 Albrecht Dürer, *Four Naked Women* (1497). National Gallery of Art, Washington, DC. Online database entry 1943.3.3462. Public domain via Wikimedia Commons. https://commons.wikimedia.org/wiki/File:Albrecht_Dürer_-_Four_Naked_Women_%28NGA_1943.3.3462%29.jpg 30

1.7 Albrecht Dürer, *Witch Riding on a Goat* (ca. 1500/1501). Rosenwald Collection. National Gallery of Art, Washington, DC. Open Access. NGA Images. Washington, DC 31

1.8 Hans Baldung, *New Year's Greetings with Three Witches* (1514). Louvre Museum, Paris. Inv.-Nr. RF 1083. Photo: Historicum.net, public domain via Wikimedia Commons. https://commons.wikimedia.org/wiki/File:Baldung_hexen_ca1514.jpg 32

1.9 *Ein erschröckliche Geschicht so zu Derneburg* (A Terrible Event at Derneburg) (1555). Public domain. Central Library of Zurich. Europeana. oai:opac.nebis.ch:EBI01-005347659 32

1.10 *The Naked Runners of Amsterdam*, copper etching after a painting by Barent Dircksz, destroyed in 1652. Lambertus Hortensius, *Het boeck van den oproer der weder-dooperen* (Amsterdam, n.d. [ca. 1600–1650]). Courtesy the Universiteitsbibliotheek van Amsterdam, Kerkelijke Collecties 33

1.11 Jan Luyken, *Execution of Anne Hendricks* (1571). Copper etching in Tieleman van Bracht, *Het bloedig tooneel, of Martelaers Spiegel* (Amsterdam, 1685). Courtesy the Universiteitsbibliotheek van Amsterdam, Kerkelijke Collecties 34

1.12 Francesco Maria Guazzo, *Flying witch*, in *Compendium Maleficarum* (1608). Public domain via Wikimedia Commons. CompendiumMaleficarumEngraving9.jpg 35

1.13 Francesco Maria Guazzo, *Witch takes Flight*, in *Compendium Maleficarum* (1608). Public domain via Wikimedia Commons. CompendiumMaleficarumEngraving13.jpg 36

CHAPTER 3

3.1 *Lorenzo de' Medici* (1478/1521), probably after Andrea del Verrocchio and Orsino Benintendi. Painted terracotta, 65.8 × 59.1 × 32.7 cm. Samuel H. Kress Collection, National Gallery of Art, Washington, DC. 1943.4.92 56

3.2 *Portrait of a Lady in Red* (ca. 1460–1470). Oil and tempera on wood, 42 × 29 cm. Florence. The National Gallery, London. NG 585 59

3.3 Titian, *Portrait of Isabella d'Este* (1534–1536). Oil on canvas, 101.9 × 64 cm. Kunsthistorisches Museum, Vienna 61

3.4 Master of the Legend of Mary Magdalene, *Mary of Burgundy* (1457–1482). Oil on wood panel, 26.5 × 22.5 cm. Musée Condè, Chantilly 62

3.5 Hans Holbein the Younger, *Lady Margaret Butts* (about 1541–1543). Oil on panel, 47.2 × 36.9 cm. Isabella Stuart Gardner Museum, Boston 63

3.6 *Portrait of Henri III before his ascent*, attributed to Jean de Court (1530–1584). Oil on panel, 35 × 25 cm. Musée Condè, Chantilly — 65

3.7 Alonso Sanchez Coello, *Catalina Micaela of Spain* (1585–1599). Meseo del Prado, Madrid — 66

3.8 Peter Paul Rubens, *Self portrait of Rubens with Isabella Brant, his wife, in a Honeysuckle Bower* (ca. 1609). Oil on canvas, 178 × 136.5 cm. Alte Pinakothek, Munich — 67

3.9 Peter Paul Rubens, *Georges Villiers, First Duke of Buckingham* (ca. 1625). Oil on canvas, 65 × 50 cm. Galleria Palatina, Pitti Palace, Florence — 68

3.10 Botticelli, *Young Woman in Mythological Guise (Simonetta Vespucci?)* (ca. 1480–1485). Tempera on wood, 82 × 54 cm. Städelsches Kunstinstitut, Frankfurt am Main — 69

CHAPTER 4

4.1 Self-portrait by Albrecht Dürer (1500). ©Bayerische Staatsgemäldesammlung. http://www.pinakothek.de/albrecht-duerer/selbstbildnis-im-pelzrock. Alte Pinakothek, Munich — 71

4.2 Sandro Botticelli, *Portrait of a Young Woman* (ca. 1480). Tempera on panel, 48 × 35 cm. © Gemäldegalerie Staatliche Museen Berlin, Preußischer Kulturbesitz. Photo: Roberto Contini, http://www.the-athenaeum.org/art/detail.php?ID=34947 — 73

4.3 Samuel van Hoogstraten (1627–1678), *Tromp l'oeil Still Life* (1666–1668). Oil on wood, 63 × 79 cm. © Staatliche Kunsthalle Karlsruhe — 75

4.4 Jeremias Brotbeihel (publishing 1529–1562), Calendar (February 1561). © Creative commons Bayerische Staatsbibliothek VD16 ZV 2544, urn:nbn:de:bvb:12-bsb00087945-0 — 77

4.5 Thomas Murner, *Ein andechtig geistliche Badenfahrt, [...]* (1514). © Creative commons Bayerische Staatsbibliothek Schweinfurt, Bibliothek Otto Schäfer OS 0463, urn:nbn:de:bvb:12-bsb00083105-1 — 79

4.6 Barber-surgeon, from Hans Sachs and Jost Amman, *Eygentliche Beschreibung aller Stände auff Erden [...]* (Frankfurt, 1568). © Wikicommons, File De Stände 1568 Amman 057. https://commons.wikimedia.org/wiki/File:De_St%C3%A4nde_1568_Amman_057.png — 81

4.7 Andreas Schuen, "Master Jurati, elected in the corporation of Barbers and Barber-Surgeons in Ulm" (1637). Watercolor. © Museum Ulm, Ulm — 84

CHAPTER 5

5.1 Pieter de Hooch, *A Mother Delousing her Child's Hair* (ca. 1658–1660). Oil on canvas, 52.5 × 61 cm. Rijksmuseum, Amsterdam. Public Domain. Courtesy Europeana Collections. http://www.europeana.eu/portal/record/90402/SK_A_293.html — 91

5.2	Jane Jackson, *A very shorte and compendious Methode of Phisicke and Chirurgery* (1642), fol. 60v. Wellcome Library, London. Creative Commons License. https://creativecommons.org/licenses/by/4.0/legalcode	93

CHAPTER 6

6.1	Bearded lion being observed by two bearded men, from Thomas Hill, *The Contemplation of Mankinde* (1571), op. p. 187. This item is reproduced by permission of the Huntington Library, San Marino, CA	108
6.2	Woodcut illustrating "The perfite woman" from Thomas Hill, *The Contemplation of Mankinde* (1571), op. p. 148. This item is reproduced by permission of the Huntington Library, San Marino, CA	111
6.3	Mounted fragment of an illustration of unknown origin, purportedly depicting bearded woman Barbara, wife to Michael van Beck, at twenty-nine years of age. Reproduced by permission and copyright the author's private collection	113

CHAPTER 8

8.1	Piero della Francesca, *Portrait of Battista Sforza, Duchess of Urbino* (ca. 1465–1470). Galleria Uffizi, Florence. Photo: public domain via Wikimedia Commons	127
8.2	Piero della Pollaiuolo, *Portrait of Young Woman* (ca.1470). Museo Poldi Pezzoli, Milan. Photo: public domain via Wikimedia Commons	132
8.3	Gian Cristoforo Romano, *Portrait Medal of Isabella d' Este* (ca. 1505). Kunsthistorisches Museum, Vienna. Photo: Mitglied5 (Own work) (CC BY-SA 4.0 [http://creativecommons.org/licenses/by-sa/4.0]) via Wikimedia Commons	134
8.4	Raphael, *The Three Graces* (ca. 1504–1505). Musée Condé, Chantilly. Photo: public domain via Wikimedia Commons	136
8.5	After Barthel Beham, print made by Sebald Beham, *Woman with Two Children in the Bath House* (ca. 1530–1550). British Museum Collection Database 1853, 0709.77. www.britishmuseum.org/museum. Photo: Courtesy British Museum, London	137
8.6	Giuseppe Cesari, *Diana and Actaeon* (ca. 1602–1603). Museum of Fine Arts, Budapest. Photo: public domain via Wikimedia Commons	138
8.7	Peter Floetner, *Allegory of Truth* (ca. first half of the sixteenth century). Graphische Sammlung, Nürnberg. Photo: public domain via Wikimedia Commons	140
8.8	Albrecht Dürer, *The Women's Bath* (ca. 1496). Kunsthalle Bremen. Photo: public domain via Wikimedia Commons	142
8.9	*A Tepidarium with Female Nudes* by manner of French (Fontainebleau) School. CMS_PCF_593145 Collections-Public, National Trust Images	142

GENERAL EDITOR'S PREFACE

A Cultural History of Hair offers an unparalleled examination of the most malleable part of the human body. This fascinating set explores hair's intrinsic relationship to the construction and organization of diverse social bodies and strategies of identification throughout history. The six illustrated volumes, edited by leading specialists in the field, evidence the significance of human hair on the head and face and its styling, dressing, and management across the following historical periods: Antiquity, the Middle Ages, the Renaissance, the Age of Enlightenment, the Age of Empire, and the Modern Age.

Using an innovative range of historical and theoretical sources, each volume is organized around the same key themes: religion and ritualized belief, self and societal identification, fashion and adornment, production and practice, health and hygiene, gender and sexuality, race and ethnicity, class and social status, representation. The aim is to offer readers a comprehensive account of human hair-related beliefs and practices in any given period and through time. It is not an encyclopedia. *A Cultural History of Hair* is an interdisciplinary collection of complex ideas and debates brought together in the work of an international range of scholars.

Geraldine Biddle-Perry

Introduction

EDITH SNOOK

The material culture of the Renaissance includes hair. A substance produced by the body, hair acquired meaning from these visceral origins. That the qualities of a person's hair were in this period thought to be contingent on the body's humoral balance established hair's signifying power as a visible physical marker of the complexion and, thus, of identity. At the same time, hair was infinitely malleable and was dressed, decorated, shaped, cut, colored, and covered in accord with fashion and individual and communal beliefs about morality and the social order. The very intimate association of hair with the self is confirmed by the way that this connection persisted in the creation of beautiful tools for hair care and in the ways that hair circulated apart from the body—used in magical incantations, preserved in jewelry, and stitched into art. Although combs and brushes were first of all practical, used for combing and brushing the hair and for nit-picking, they could also become beautiful gifts. That goldsmiths produced brushes and that combs might be carved from ivory, decorated with scenes of David and Bathsheba and the Judgment of Paris, and engraved with text arises from their affective value.[1] Used as love tokens, boxwood combs were also decorated with textual and visual inscriptions about love, or decorated with inlaid ivory or mirrors.[2] The caskets used to hold these instruments (as well as hair dye, scriminals—used to part the hair—and other cosmetics) might be decorated with relevant mythological scenes, such as Venus at her toilette.[3] Even the protective cases used to secure barbering tools to the belt could be objects of beauty, as with the comb case in the Victoria and Albert Museum's collection that is tooled and stamped and inscribed with "De Boen Amore" (with good love).[4] In magic, hair itself was deployed to break spells or to cast them, to cause harm, or to make a person fall in love.[5] As a love-token, hair symbolized the binding of lovers together, as if with rope. One mid-seventeenth-century ring constructed such a love token as a kind of treasure, enclosing it within a gold-enameled cavity that had been painted with flowers.[6] Hair could also memorialize when it was used to make things. In a narrow band of needle lace surviving in the Victoria and Albert Museum in London, hair is the thread that stitches a hunting scene, possibly as a memento of the person whose hair it was (Figure I.1).

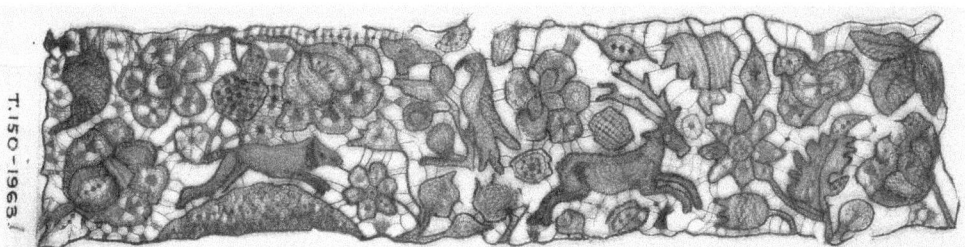

FIGURE I.1 Band of lace (1640–1680). Needle lace worked in human hair, with thicker outlines possibly in horsehair. Victoria and Albert Museum, London. T. 150-1963.

Naturally growing from the body, hair inspired a culture because it was physically meaningful and significant within a range of social and cultural practices.

The chapters in this book attempt to unite a variety of perspectives on hair. Necessarily interdisciplinary, the history of hair in the Renaissance draws together the histories of fashion, political and religious ideas, gender, science, medicine, art, and literature. Sources documenting hair's history are equally wide-ranging and include the Bible and theological treatises interpreting it for Renaissance audiences, conduct books, professional regulations, life-writing, medical texts, calendars, satirical texts, literature, sculpture, paintings and printed engravings, and material objects. The chapters investigate hair's physiological foundations, as outlined by medical thinkers, and explore the spaces, materials, and people (professional and otherwise) dedicated to hair's care. They consider hair's function as a persistent source of multiple cultural anxieties and as a medium to engage with fashion, to perform one's identity as a writer, and to express social identity—including national, gender, class, racial, and religious identities. The primary focus of the volume is on the hair of the head, as it is with many of the Renaissance texts documenting hair's history, but body and facial hair are also considered in several chapters. Hair practices, fashions, and technologies shift across this book's two-hundred-year time span, as they do across Europe's geographical and cultural spaces. Yet some principles do seem to hold. There is a broad attachment to Galenic humoral theory as a means of understanding the body (the challenge of Paracelsian ideas does not appear to have informed thinking about hair to any great degree) and a general commitment to following biblical dictates regarding hair, although doctrinal differences did inform divergent hairstyles. Before the Reformation and after, European dress practices often included a faith-based dedication to rendering women's hair culturally invisible through the wearing of head coverings, a practice which, nevertheless, disappeared for elite women towards the end of the period explored by this volume. Despite these commonalities, however, hair fashions and styles, the anxieties they incited, and its meanings are contextual, informed by particular moments in time, by individual perspectives, and local cultures. An edited collection is for these reasons a productive medium for the study of hair's history, with each contributor bringing a distinct area of expertise to an element of the story of hair in Renaissance Europe.

The chapters in this volume build on existing scholarship around hair. Scholars have written about fashionable hairstyles, the guilds of barbers and barber-surgeons, beards, baldness, and hirsuteness, and about the aesthetic representation of hair in literature, painting, and sculpture. Richard Corson's encyclopedic *Fashions in Hair: The First Five Thousand Years* surveys the multiple styles adopted by men and women across a broad swath of western history.[7] Multiple costumes histories include depictions of headwear and afford some discussion of hairstyles in the Renaissance; Evelyn Welch is notable in particularly highlighting the distinct social functions of hair and head dressings within the fashion culture of Renaissance Italy.[8] Margaret Pelling, Sandra Cavallo, and Annemarie Kinzelbach, among others, have examined barbers and barber-surgeons in England, Italy, and Germany. Pelling's and Kinzelbach's interest is in the professionalization of these practitioners, while Cavallo critiques contemporary distinctions between medical and aesthetic practices related to grooming. Cavallo argues that hygiene customs, such as hair cutting, were regarded as healthful "evacuative therapies" that removed excrements and prevented putrefaction.[9] *Un Idéal Masculin? Barbes et moustaches XVe-XVIIIe siècles* by Jean-Marie Le Gall includes a chapter on sociality of barbers, alongside a broader study of the role of facial hair in European gender, religious, and racial identities.[10] Others have looked at hair itself, and its absence, as in Anu Korhonen's exploration of the complexities of the social stigma around male baldness.[11] Merry Wiesner-Hanks's *The Marvelous Hairy Girls* studies the religious, mythological, and scientific contexts through which the *hypertrichosis universalis* of three sixteenth-century sisters—Maddalena, Francesca, and Antonietta Gonzales—was understood.[12] M.A. Katritzky, also writing about the Gonzales sisters and other hirsute women, argues that in the early modern world representations of satyrs, werewolves, anchorites, and wild men informed thinking about those with unusually abundant hair.[13]

Scholars have also considered artistic renderings of hair. Sefy Hendler, for instance, discusses how for both painters and sculptors in Renaissance Italy representing hair and beards was a "touchstone" for the demonstration of artistic skills.[14] Writing about beards in English literature, Will Fisher argues that beards and hair length materialized gender difference, while Mark Johnston considers the beard as a fetish object that signals attachment to ideological constructs such as a coherent notion of a "natural order," divine authority, and patriarchal privilege. Douglas Biow writes about beards and the professions in Italian literature.[15] Examining European observations about the purported beardlessness of Native American men, Elliott Horowitz argues that Europeans associated beards with whiteness.[16] Sherry Velasco looks at representations of bearded women—a topic also considered by Fisher and Johnston—to argue that in early modern Spain representations of women with masculine traits, such as beards and body hair, were used as instruments of control of nonconforming bodies.[17] Literary critics have also examined the presentation of hair in works by John Milton, William Shakespeare, Margaret Cavendish, and others—essays engaged with seventeenth-century politics, hair discourse's use of nature imagery, and hair's function as a source of imperial power and a sign of identity established by gender, whiteness, privilege, and health.[18]

Because of the parameters of the series, when the hair of people in the world outside of Europe appears in this book, it is for the most part through representations created by Europeans, which reveals more about emerging discourses of race, imperialism, colonialism, and slavery than it does about how non-European peoples viewed their hair. Alf Hiltebeitel and Barbara D. Miller's *Hair: Its Power and Meaning in Asian Cultures* (1998) includes the historical study of hair in Asian culture, while Ayana B. Byrd and Lori L. Tharps's *Hair Story: Untangling the Roots of Black Hair in America* (2001) and Roy Sieber, Frank Herreman, and Niangi Batulukis's collection *Hair in African Art and Culture* (2000) include reflections on African hair in the years of the European Renaissance.[19] Placing African hair in an Atlantic colonial context, Judith Carney shows how enslaved West African women introduced rice to the Americas by hiding grains of rice in their hair, which were then used to grow an important subsistence crop.[20] Much more then can be said about hair in the Renaissance. Not the final word, this book primarily considers England, the Netherlands, France, Germany, Italy, and Spain. It explores how Europeans looked to tradition, especially in medicine and theology, while also engaging with changes in science, technology, fashion, politics, and empire, to forge beliefs and cultural practices around hair and to represent hair and ideas about it in art and literature.

DISTINCTION: THE FOUNDATION OF RENAISSANCE HAIR

Together the chapters in this collection draw attention to a number of particularly influential hairstyles, from royal figures, such as England's King Henry VIII, Queen Anne Boleyn,

Queen Elizabeth I, and the Holy Roman Emperor, Charles V, to other political actors, such as Oliver Cromwell and the Roundheads, to religious ones, such as David Joris, to literary figures, such as Petrarch's Laura, and painted ones, such as Botticelli's young woman. This introduction will explore some of the social values that underpinned how people did their hair. As will be evident across the chapters in the volume, these social values consistently revolve around the maintenance of social distinctions. Key to Renaissance hairstyles is that they were not only fashion: they were regarded as powerful embodiments of social norms and thus as political signifiers of order and disorder.

In this vein, it is impossible to think about Renaissance hair without considering how hair was made to function as a marker of gender difference. In early modern Europe, many beliefs about hair and gender were grounded in the Bible and adjacent beliefs about the natural world. Gary Waite and Mark Albert Johnston explore these at some length in their chapters in this volume. The New Testament proscriptions in 1 Corinthians 11, 1 Timothy 2, and 1 Peter 3 aligned the control of women's hair with their social subordination to men. Pervading early modern culture, these dictates underpinned heteronormative, patriarchal gender ideology and the long-standing fashion preference for covered heads on women and a hair length difference between men and women. The extent to which these regulations—and thus hair itself—were treated as evidence of a divinely ordained, patriarchal social order is exemplified by one of Calvin's sermons on 1 Timothy. Arguing that women are "naturally inclined" to an appetite to show themselves, Calvin explains: "I know how women will decke and trim themselves superfluously, if they follow their own fansie: but this is as filthe before God." From this perspective, hair at once embodies women's suspect moral stature, which goes back to Eve, and their acceptance of patriarchal discipline: controlled hair signals self-abnegation, a rejection of female nature, and submission to the social control which keeps them from "filthe." Class intersects with these gender norms in Calvin's lament that at court there is "horrible confusion" between men and women; if women were truly modest, he says, they would not uncover their heads, "as nowe they have."[21] This belief that men's uncovered hair and beards was evidence not just of their difference from women but of their natural social dominance, secured by women's controlled hair, underpins the discussion throughout this volume, as does the intersection of class hierarchy.

The influence of the Bible on hair in Renaissance Europe was felt beyond its prohibitions, with Bible stories also providing fodder for the exploration of tensions around hair, gender, sexuality, and community. The Bible is replete with hairy men—Esau, Absalom, Nebuchadnezzar, Absalom, and Elijah, and, conversely, Elisha, who was bald—but Samson's tale perhaps most frequently became a site at which anxieties about gender intersected with hair. John Milton resisted the dominance of hair in Samson's story in *Samson Agonistes* (1671) with a Samson who insists that "God, when he gave me strength, to show withal / How slight the gift was, hung it in my Hair."[22] For Milton, Samson's hair and physical strength are less significant than his having been chosen by God, his inward virtues. But the period's visual representations of Samson and Delilah do often evince a special concern with Samson's locks and with the material culture of hair. Crucially, Samson's hair is rarely of a realistic length for a man said in Judges 13 to never have had a razor touch his head. For instance, Peter Paul Rubens's *Samson and Delilah* (1609–1610) shows Samson sleeping in the lap of bare-chested Delilah (Figure I.2). His hair is already short, and he is getting a mere trim, rather than the shave the Bible suggests was his fate, and then from a man leaning over his head with scissors rather than from Delilah.[23] At a historical moment that treated hair length as a visible manifestation of a

FIGURE I.2 Peter Paul Rubens, *Samson and Delilah* (1609–1610). The National Gallery, London. NG 6461.

purportedly natural gender difference, the relatively short locks on Samson's head secure for him an idealized masculinity, also emphasized in Rubens's painting in Samson's muscular, bare back and arm.[24] Moreover, in this picture and others, a man's haircut is not women's work. Rubens shows a man using scissors while an old woman holds a candle to provide light, as if he needed to take care in his trade. Similarly, in the sixteenth-century engravings of Coornhert Dirck Volkertsz and Philips Galle, the male hair cutter appears to have come prepared with a container of tools, both the scissors being used on the hair and other tools in small purses strapped to the waist.[25] Another engraving by Anton Woensam of Worms (1529) shows a man looking upon the sleeping Samson and holding a basin and razor, more tools for barbering.[26] While Delilah has seduced Samson, it is men who remove his power by cutting his hair. Delilah's talents are erotic rather than technical, and the final victory is less hers than the Philistine men's. Yet it is Samson's hair which renders him vulnerable to Delilah's questions, and the implication of the story is that he ought to have managed the threat by remembering that he is a man disciplined to his place in society, a man who can resist giving over his secrets to a voluptuous woman, however attractive she might be. Another biblical paragon of manhood with remarkable hair, Absalom, a man "much praised for his beauty" (2 Samuel 14:25), similarly highlights the importance of masculine control over hair. An engraving in one of the editions of Luther's German Bible translation depicts him as a sixteenth-century knight with a magnificent bushy beard, shoulder-length, thick flowing hair, and armor (Figure I.3).[27]

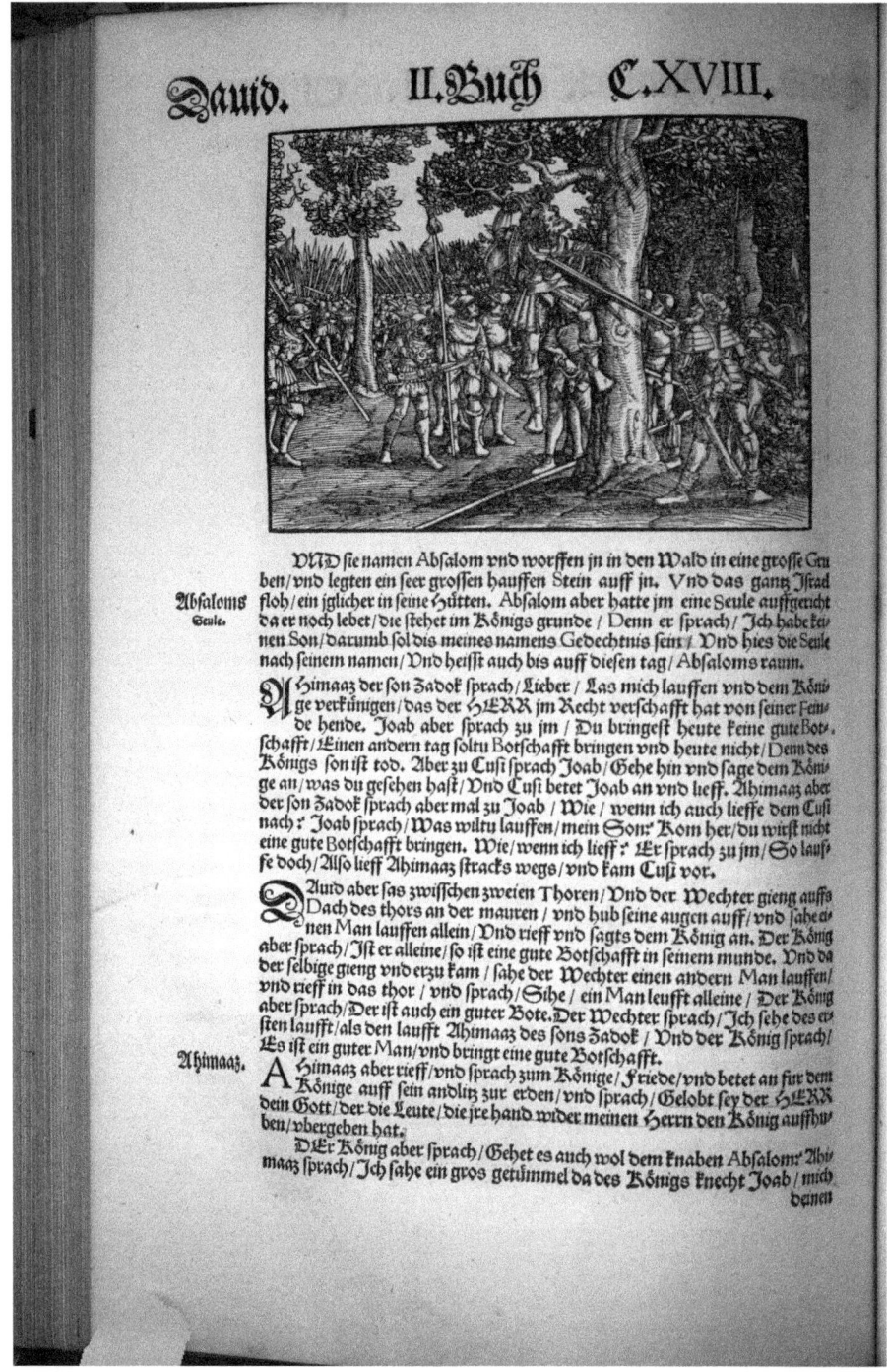

FIGURE I.3 Martin Luther, *Biblia Das ist, Die gantze heilige Schrifft*, Deudsch (Wittemberg, 1576), fol. 200v. Courtesy Bayerische Staatsbibliothek, Munich. urn:nbn:de:bvb:12-bsb00085706-7.

Absalom dangles precariously from a hefty tree branch, entrapped by his thick hair as another knight strikes him through the heart with a spear. For both Samson and Absalom, hair both establishes their manhood and threatens it, marking their beauty and endangering them. The nonconsensual haircut is an egregious affront to identity but so too is the abundant hair that can ensnare a man when he lacks self-mastery.

Moreover, despite how hair length and covering were meant to make visible a heteronormative, patriarchal gender hierarchy, men's hair was not always short—indeed, by the end of the period covered by this volume, men's hairstyles were large and long—and women braided their hair, decorated it, and otherwise displayed it, whatever the Pauline instructions.[28] Not necessarily resistant to dominant ideology, however, such hairstyles were often informed by competing commitments to ideas of order and the distinctions of class, which are explored at some length by Carole Collier Frick and Jana Mathews in their chapters. While they primarily look at the hairstyles of elite people, I want to add here a further note on lower-class people's hair, for which there is much less evidence. The sixteenth-century workman and beggar depicted in Stephen Bateman's *A Christall Glass of Christian Reformation* not only wear aprons and ragged clothes but have untidy hair on their bare heads; by contrast, the rich man from whom the poor man is begging has neat hair, a fashionable forked beard, and a tall hat trimmed with an ostrich feather. The hair on the head and the trim on the beard denote class difference, alongside the clothes.[29] Made in England in the 1640s, Wenceslaus Hollar's engravings of a female servant, the wife of the mayor of London, a merchant's wife, and of Hester Tradescant (the wife of John Tradescant, collector and gardener to Charles I) all show nonaristocratic women wearing head coverings, including a lace-edged hood pinned to the top of the head and a beaver hat over another cap that covers most of the hair.[30] Hollar's engraving of a noblewoman from 1649, in contrast, shows, like most portraits of aristocratic women by this time, a woman with her head uncovered, the hair on the top of her head pulled into a top knot, the hair on the sides in curls.[31] In a culture where ideas of order were grounded, in part, in a class-based social hierarchy, differences of social status were documented on the head and in the hair, for both men and women.

Attached to this investment in class hierarchy are the way that hairstyles marked professional identities. Physicians, for instance, commonly wore some headgear, such as a coif and flat cap, that entirely covered the hair.[32] Some professions regulated beards, thus securing professional distinction through facial hair. Mark Albert Johnston notes that, in London, guilds, universities, and Inns of Court levied fines on boys who failed to shave their facial hair, a move that insisted that they delay the wearing of a beard until such time as they had achieved mastery and citizenship.[33] At Lincoln's Inn, one of the four Inns of Court in London, members were not allowed to dine in the hall while wearing a beard until 1542, with rules on beards being repealed only in 1560. In France, the 1535 "Edict of Beards" forbade anyone from appearing in "the hall of justice" with a long beard, including litigants, and the Sorbonne in 1561 prohibited clerks from having a beard.[34] Neither were Catholic priests supposed to be bearded. Among men, a covered head or the presence or absence of a beard established distinctions among professions, as well as one's position within them. Anu Korhonen's chapter discusses how apprentices and students challenged this system by growing the hair on their head long to resist their elders.

More broadly, hair also marked distinctions of age. Infants and children often wore their heads covered, so younger children before the age of breeching did not have gendered hairstyles, as was the case with dress more generally.[35] As boys and girls grew older, however, they adopted more adult hairstyles which distinguished them from each other and from younger children; for girls that could mean continuing to cover the head with a coif at an age when their male contemporaries were bare-headed.[36] As well, as Carole Frick's chapter discusses, young women of marriageable age marked their entrance into marriage by changing their hair. Portraits of children tend to document the hairstyles of more privileged youngsters, establishing both their class and the differences between younger children and older ones. *Five Children of King Charles I* (1637), for instance, shows a progression of hairstyles at a time when fashionable, elite women uncovered their hair (Figure I.4). The youngest three children—James (b. 1633), not yet breeched; Elizabeth (b. 1635); and Anne (b. 1636), an infant covered only in cloths—all wear white caps on their heads that cover most of their head and permit only wisps of bangs to show. With these very young children, there is little gender difference in hairstyle. The older siblings, however, are distinguished from their younger siblings and from each other because their gender is marked on their heads. The future Charles II, at the center of the frame with a large mastiff dog, and his sister Mary (b. 1631), also a future queen, both wear fashionable adult hairstyles. The prince has straight bangs and long flowing brown hair, while his sister has her hair pulled back at the top with curls at the forehead and on the sides—hairstyles worn by their parents. The connection between parents and children is even more explicit in the 1628 portrait of the Duke of Buckingham and his family, which depicts the duke, his wife Katherine Villiers, their oldest daughter Mary Villiers (b. 1622), and their son George (b. 1628). While the infant George wears a cap which covers all of his hair, Mary, aged six, wears the same hairstyle as her mother: a fringe at the forehead, curls to the side of the head, and a piece of lace covering the back of the head.[37] Because distinctions

FIGURE I.4 After Sir Anthony van Dyck, *Five Children of King Charles I* (1637). © National Portrait Gallery, London. NPG 267.

of age are also distinctions of social power, the hairstyles of older aristocratic children show them moving into the social positions of their parents.[38] Hair is a testament to their belonging, to a family and to a community, an attribute of hair explored further in Anu Korhonen's chapter.

Hair, of course, also marks age through turning gray and disappearing through creeping baldness. Renaissance portraits tend not to display gray hair on the heads of men and focus instead on the head covering and the beard. For instance, a 1555 portrait of John Russell, first Earl of Bedford (1486–1555), shows him with a long white, forked beard and a skull cap, his hair almost entirely covered. Another of William Cecil, first Baron Burghley, painted after 1587 when Cecil was at least sixty-seven years old shows him with a white forked beard and, again, hair covered entirely with a black cap.[39] Jacopo Tintoretto's *Old Man and Boy* establishes an explicit contrast between the beardless boy with short black hair and fashionable clothing and the old man with a long gray beard and a black cap covering his head.[40] As Anu Korhonen writes, "If a growing beard differentiated an adult man from a mere boy, then baldness marked the potential loss of adult manhood, caused by the infirmities of advanced age." Although baldness also had positive meanings—experience, good judgment, wisdom—it had "social dangers," including loss of economic independence.[41] When sparse, white hair is hidden away the danger is mitigated.

Representations of the hair of older women, on the other hand, are often satirical. In literature, as Lyn Bennett discusses in her chapter, women's hair is frequently blazoned by poets, a confirmation of the poet's skill. Older women generally do not figure in such poems as objects of desire. But older female bodies were put on display in visual representations that exposed the body to mockery in the name of moral satire. Albrecht Dürer's *Vanitas* (1507), for instance, depicts Vice in the form of an old woman with a bag of coins. Straight brown hair grows from her armpits, a long breast hangs out of her robe, and she has a toothless smile and thin, straight white hair hanging to her shoulders.[42] Similarly, an oval wax relief in the collections of the Victoria and Albert Museum shows Age in the figure of a topless old woman with sagging breasts, a toothless smile, and sparse gray hair partially covered with a linen cap, her hand resting on a skull (Figure I.5).[43] For these female figures, gray hair and baldness establish the moral turpitude of vice and characterize physical decline as a moral failing.

When older women were allowed more dignity in portraits, their hair was covered, like that of older men. Erin J. Campbell shows that there were representations of old women as moral exemplars that contested these associations of the female body with vice. In Italy in the second half of the sixteenth century, there was a flowering of portraits of old women, paintings that, like portraits of young women, emphasized their virtue. Campbell's examples—Bartolomeo Passerotti's *Portrait of a Seated Old Woman* (ca. 1585), Giovanni Battista Moroni's *Abbess Lucrezia Agliardi Vertova* (1556), Leandro Bassano's *Portrait of a Widow at her Devotions* (ca. 1590–1600), Bartolomeo Passerotti's *Family Portrait* (ca. early 1580s), and Lavinia Fontana's *Family Portrait* (ca. 1600)—all show the women with their heads covered, their hair invisible or nearly so, as in pictures of aged men.[44] Similarly, the triptych of Anne Clifford's "The Great Picture" shows her aged fifty-six with a few brown locks of curled hair just visible around the edges of a black cloth that covers her head. Having inherited the Clifford estates, she covers her hair, setting her age and gravitas in opposition to the picture of her as a beautiful, young woman in the first panel, where she has fashionable brown hair rolled on pads and decorated with pearls.[45] In the dignified representations of age, gray hair does not seem to be shown, as if

FIGURE I.5 *Age* (seventeenth century). Oval wax relief. Courtesy Victoria and Albert Museum, London. A.68-1938.

it could undermine the social status of the wearer. Given that head covering was also used to confirm women's subordination, it emerges with its different uses in the aging process with more than one meaning, depending on the gender and sexual perceptions of the hair beneath the headwear.

In addition to distinctions of gender, class, and age, hair also marked distinctions of race. Race was, in the Renaissance, as Margo Hendricks contends, "an expression of fundamental distinctions." Interwoven with emerging ideas of blackness, race was, as Ania Loomba shows, about blood, a category used to define family and lineage, nation, religion, gender, and class.[46] So not only does hair mark class difference—in the lower-class with messy hair and the elite one with a well-trimmed beard, in Mopsa the daughter of a clown in Philip Sidney's *Arcadia* who has stiff hair like "crapal stone," while the elite Philoclea has waving hair that is of "fine threads of finest gold/in curled knots"—it also distinguishes African men and women, said to have wool, from Europeans, with hair.[47] The moor Aaron in Shakespeare's *Titus Andronicus*, for instance, has "fleece of woolly hair" and "Blood and revenge are hammering in [his] head."[48] The association of African hair with heat seems to come from Galen's contention that people who inhabit hot climates have "black, dry, curly, and brittle" hair—an idea also picked up by

Renaissance anatomists. Helkiah Crooke contends that "hair curleth by reaon of drinesse of the temper; and therefore all Black-Moores have curled or crisped hair."[49] Describing the hair of black people as wool was dehumanizing and situated black bodies adjacent to those of animals. It was also, as I have argued elsewhere, part of a racist medical framework that imagined the black body as essentially excessive and unhealthy, unable to attain the moderation necessary for ideal health, which was implicitly available only to white bodies.[50] For Africans in the period, as Shane White and Graham White discuss, hair was an important social ritual and a medium for communication about identity (tribal affiliation, gender, sex, age, occupation). These practices and values did not disappear in the emerging slave cultures of the Americas but flourished as a medium for resistance against a white culture that continued to derogate African hair as wool.[51] Nicholas Jones in his chapter explores how the resistance of an African woman to this racist context could be imagined in a play about a black woman in early modern Spain through her engagement across racial categories with hair's beauty cultures.

Finally, even as hair signaled and established forms of social distinction, it could also be a means to challenge that order, by being disordered, by growing beyond normative places, and by transgressing boundaries on the body—boundaries that were also social borders. Thus, when women grew beards, Mark Johnston argues, this "was imagined to be the direct result of either a lack of male headship or the female body's refusal to adhere to the patriarchal reproductive imperative."[52] Some pre-Reformation female saints and holy women had this nonnormative hair on their faces, while for others body hair marked them as exceptional: Wilgefortis (also known as Uncumber, among other names), Paula of Avila, and Galla of Rome had beards, while the bodies of saints Agnes, Mary Magdalene, and Mary of Egypt were often depicted as being entirely covered in hair.[53] The story of Wilgefortis's beard, for instance, establishes hair as a form of female resistance, for it grew, a gift from God, because she sought to keep her devout vow to remain a virgin in the face of her father's desire that she should marry; for this, her father ordered her to be crucified. Androgynous, Wilgefortis was often then depicted as bearded and hanging on a cross, which Ilse E. Friesen argues allowed her to be invoked with regard to physical and emotional abuse, health concerns and dying, and by those in prison or otherwise confined. Such images, Friesen argues, "filled an emotional and spiritual need which the official patriarchal Church was failing to provide at the time."[54] While Wilgefortis's excess hair enabled the expression of opposition to oppression, nonnormative hairiness could also be reincorporated into the dominant order. Michelle Moseley-Christian argues that while medieval wild women were associated with negative qualities, "infanticide, sexual promiscuity, ugliness, and violence, traits believed to lurk within the nature of human women," later hairy, wild women in northern Europe were models of virtuous domesticity and motherhood. Such beliefs about wild women also informed contemporaneous visual depictions of the hair of Eve and Mary Magdalene (Gary Waite discusses one of these in his chapter). Thus, Mary Magdalene, who brings Jesus a box of ointment, washes his feet with her tears, and dries them with her hair (Luke 7:38; John 11:2), was also sometimes depicted as being covered in fur. Her loose hair seemingly signifying her status as a fallen woman becomes through her body hair more connected to the wild because, as Moselely-Christian says, of "the belief in humanity's own wild nature in need of redemption."[55]

Beyond these gendered transgressions, the hairiness of Renaissance wild folk and of werewolves also police the boundaries of the human, exposing some ways in which hairstyles embody the period's notions of civility. While the hair of wild folk and werewolves raise the possibility that humans might cross over to the category of animal, that hair might become fur, as Merry Wiesner-Hanks shows, wild folk were in the early modern period somewhat ambiguous characters; they were for some figures of evil, for others of holiness, for some terrifying, and for others figures to be celebrated for their place outside of society.[56] Petrus Gonzales, the hirsute father of the "marvelous hairy girls" at the center of Wiesner-Hanks's study received a humanist education at the court of Henry II of France, and a painting of him records what purports to be his perspective, that a "miracle of nature covered my body with hair" but France, which educated him, "taught me to put aside my wild ways."[57] So although his hair is understood through thinking about wild folk, it does not define him as wild. Alan Stewart writes of the Renaissance that "To be human means not only to be not a beast, but also to subscribe to a specific code of humanity."[58] For Stewart, that code is articulated through education. Thus, through education, Gonzales too becomes more human. Moreover, hair itself seems to undergo a kind of education. To be human in the Renaissance meant on many occasions training and disciplining the hair so that it was not wild. This was, as Annemarie Kinzelbach shows in Chapter Four, the work of professionals with specialized equipment and knowledge in public and private spaces. Hair hygiene and removal, the taming of visible hair growth through shaving and cutting, hairstyles and head coverings all codified an understanding of ideas about nature, hierarchy, and order, about gender and class hierarchy, age status, religious conformity, and professional distinction. However much the uncovered female head, the messy locks, the hirsute body, the woman's beard or the man's absent or unruly one threatened to become disorderly, to move the wearer from civil to the wild, from the reasonable to the mad, the moral to the base, the hair can also be cut, colored, curled, covered, supplemented, and removed. Order can be restored. In hair, historical religious, political, and social ideas converge on human bodies. This history is what these chapters explore.

CHAPTER DESCRIPTIONS

Chapter One, "Religion and Ritualized Belief" by Gary Waite, looks at hair in the Reformation and in magic, the preternatural, and witchcraft. Waite argues that while Luther did not concern himself with particular hairstyles, he did recommend that married women cover their hair at all times and that all women cover their hair in church, in line with Pauline injunctions that linked hair covering to female obedience; Calvin took much the same position. Anabaptists, on the other hand, supported women's subordination but did not require women to cover their hair. More interested in Samson's Nazarite exemplarity, David Joris, a Dutch Anabaptist leader, argued for the need for men to grow beards to honor God and to ensure a spiritual and masculine power. At the margins of this religious culture, hair was believed to retain the life force of its owner and to identify witches, who were often renowned for their wild and uncovered hair. Some images of witches, however, did show them with their hair covered—a result, Waite contends, of the belief that any respectable woman might well be a witch. Others at the margins of society, such as wild men and women with their hirsute bodies and long hair, invoked both lycanthropy and sainthood with their excess hair. In religious discourses, any hair that deviated from the norm of long, covered hair for women and short hair for men could invoke charges of sexual impropriety or insubordination, but hair's association with witchcraft and other forms of magic began to disappear by the end of the period.

Anu Korhonen addresses the topic of "Self and Society" in Chapter Two. Looking both at the physiology of hair and at hairstyles, Korhonen explores how hair was made to function in early modern England as an individual and social signifier, marking both the self and one's relationship to society, within which the self was understood. While medical writers regularly construed hair as a signifier of physiological and psychological complexions and thus established it as a marker of the self, the way that individuals linked their own hair to that of other members of their family suggests ways in which they understood themselves through their kinship networks. For some observers, the hair of individuals, particularly queens, could be made to have meaning with respect to national communities, as well. More broadly, hair could sometimes become an instrument of judgment of others that intersected with beliefs about morality, gender, and race. Korhonen also considers how hair care, a technology of the self, was an important tool with which Renaissance men and women sought to control not just their appearance but also the representation of the self to the world. It afforded a means to police the self according to gendered, class, and religious social norms. For women, this meant disciplining the hair to mark their gendered subordination, faith, and modesty, although women were also cognizant of how hair ought also to mark their rank. For men, hair care often worked to define their difference from women, although young men such as apprentices and students also used their hair as a form of resistance to the authority of their male elders. Finally, Korhonen explores how hair care practices were themselves sociable, with the dressing room and barber shop providing settings in which women and men forged relationships among themselves. Thus, even as hair provided the materials for self-fashioning, people used it socially, to negotiate hierarchies and relationships.

Chapter Three, "Fashion and Adornment," considers hairstyles. Carole Collier Frick focuses first on Italy, the origin of many Renaissance fashions, and then turns to hair fashions in northern Europe. Frick argues that bodily presentation, including hair fashions, were influenced by Renaissance humanism, which placed greater emphasis on the material world, as well as on class and wealth, geography and physical environment, and social attitudes. In the Italian Renaissance, both men and women tended to cover most of their hair with headwear of some kind. On men, hats articulated status and political agendas, while on women, headwear declared women's social place, with headwear and its attendant hairstyle changing with women's changing social place, from maid to wife. While the hair of young women might be partially obscured by a cap, wives covered their hair more fully to indicate submission to a husband's authority and to assert family honor, a particularly important function of hair fashion on one's wedding day. Covering the hair and hiding the body beneath fabric also articulated the dominance of the spiritual over the physical. In this context, hair that was entirely uncontrolled was associated with those outside of social control, such as hermits, the mad, witches, criminals, and prostitutes. Covering the hair was also important in the sixteenth century in northern Europe, where men's hats and head coverings continued to be worn, as in Italy. Suggesting interaction between hairstyles and headwear styles, some hairstyles also copied the shape of headwear. When hair came to be more uncovered in the seventeenth century, hair, as much as hats or other headgear, was a statement of identity, although it was still controlled and disciplined.

Annemarie Kinzelbach's Chapter Four, "Production and Practice," focuses on the work of European barbers and bath-masters and the places where hair care was done, including public spaces, such as bath houses, and private spaces, like the home. Within the household, the evidence of domestic recipe collections suggests that men and women undertook to bathe, comb, and color the hair, to rid the scalp of pests, and to encourage the hair to grow through the use of remedies. Outside the home, hair care was in the purview of barbers and bath masters. While some parts of Europe were suspicious of bathing, in the Holy Roman Empire it was treated as a specialized practice involving technical skills and medical knowledge, a perspective which informed the treatment of hair as an influence on health for which proper timing within the month was essential. Because governors invested in public bathhouses in imperial towns, washing the hair as well as cutting occurred in bath-houses, as well as in shops and homes by barbers. Accessible to a broader range of people, hair care services constituted a significant source of revenue for barber-surgeons and barbers.

Chapter Five, my contribution on "Health and Hygiene," looks at medical writing about hair in early modern England. I consider how anatomy texts, which draw on the classical ideas of Aristotle and Galen, represent hair as a functional part of the human body. Influenced by the body's humors, hair grew from inside the body through the skin to the body's outside. Hair's differences in texture, abundance, curl, and color were all determined by the substance from which the hair was made, the temperature of the body, and the qualities of the skin through which the hair was extruded. An excrement, hair became for anatomists a physiological signifier of essential identity: of gender, age, nation, and character. At the same time as hair was being treated as a substance with a purportedly rational relationship to the body's humors, it was also regarded as mutable and open to the influence of multiple forms of medical treatment. Herbals and collections of medical recipes include remedies for alopecia, hair falling out, baldness, coloring, and lice, among other things. In medical writing, care for the hair is presented as a contribution to the vitality of the body, its overall health, and its humoral balance. Hair's maladies often constituted a form of excess or imbalance, and so hair care became a form of discipline through which a physical and social order could be restored.

Chapter Six, Mark Albert Johnston's contribution on "Sexuality and Gender," explores how bodies and their hair acquire meaning through cultural systems of power. The chapter starts with the foundational premise posited by early modern physiology: that despite a homology of bodies, women were in their humors colder, moister, and inferior to men. In Protestant early modern England, this physiological difference was affiliated with biblical proscriptions against long hair on men and short hair on women, so that God and nature could be aligned in a system where hair supposedly correlated precisely to gender identity and a social order where women were subordinate to men. While men's short hair and beards signified difference, political identity, sexual maturity, wealth, and privilege, women's long hair and hairless faces signified their social subordination. Early modern English writers were, nevertheless, very attentive to the possibilities of semiotic slippage produced by shaving, depilation, cutting, dyeing, and the donning of prosthetic hair, such as wigs and false beards, practices that had the power to disrupt the social order, particularly that grounded in sexual difference and gender hierarchy, and expose the system as contingent rather than natural. Bearded women, too, presented a challenge to notions of the natural, and if they were at first considered lecherous or monstrous, by the end of the seventeenth century, they were thought merely to be natural wonders. In a culture where early modern people were supposed to regulate their hair to conform to their places in the social order, whether that was within the normative construction of their gender, class, or nation, this social discipline had the inadvertent effect of revealing the extent to which the supposed correspondence between hair and identity rested on artifice rather than nature.

In Chapter Seven, "Race and Ethnicity," Nicholas Jones considers the emergence in the early modern period of racialized constructions of hair. Jones's focus is hair in early modern Spain, a major point of contact between Jews, Arabs, Africans, and European Christians. Jones argues that in a Spanish culture that barred Africans from access to important social institutions, the African body was stereotyped and oppressed, with hair treated as fur and likened to a covering for animals. Jones shows that hair was a more important feature of race than has been recognized, citing as evidence that in blackface performances in Spain, not only was the skin of white performers colored with darkening agents, but the hair was transformed with braids as well. To explore the function of racialized and gendered hair in the relationship between Spain and Africa, Jones turns to Lope de Rueda's mid-sixteenth-century play *Comedia Eufemia,* in which an African woman named Eulalla asserts her identity as a black woman, in part through her bleached, blonde hair. Calling Eulalla a "black blonde," and noting that she is knowledgeable about Spanish cosmetic treatments for bleaching hair, Jones argues against the claim that Eulalla is simply and problematically copying white beauty and rejecting blackness. Instead, he contends, she is translating white looks with her body, using mimicry to assert her identity as an African woman.

In Chapter Eight, Jana Mathews considers "Class and Social Status" by comparing the different social functions of head and pubic hair. In cultures across Europe, sumptuary laws attempted to define how people could wear their hair, and while such laws ultimately failed to ensure that the hair on the head was a reliable marker of class, what Mathews calls "complicated hair" emerged instead as a tool of the elite to demarcate them from those of lower social standing. Dyeing the hair blonde, producing hairstyles with complex shapes and elaborate braids and buns, decorating the hair with ribbons, pearls, and other valuables, and changing the hair often were expensive and required the labor of a staff of servants and constant surveillance of the wearer to prevent theft. The wigs and hairpieces that were also part of elite complicated hair also required the physical subordination of lower-class people, whose hair might be sold or taken to be used to supplement the hair of the rich. Such transformations were not accessible to lower-class women. Mathews sets this practice of making class visible on the hair of the head in opposition to the more obtainable transformations of pubic hair. The preferred aesthetic of Renaissance art was for a hairless female pudendum, and evidence suggests that aristocratic women practiced genital depilation. Because the removal of pubic hair was much less difficult to achieve than the complicated hairstyles for the head, Mathews argues, pubic hairlessness had the potential to be a "democratizing agent." Courtesans could use their bald nether regions to perform the role of the upper-class lady, and older women could present themselves as younger through depilation. So while the hair on the head was subject to social discipline because of concern for the maintenance of a visible social hierarchy, pubic hair—less socially visible hair and more difficult to regulate—could constitute a form of resistance to that order.

The final chapter, Lyn Bennett's "Cultural Representations," focuses on representations of hair in English literature. She explores how Petrarch's depiction of his beloved Laura with long, loose, blonde, curling hair was copied and contested in English literary history. Poets from Henry Howard, Earl of Surrey, to Edmund Spenser, to Philip Sidney—and others—represent the female beloved as a woman with Laura's hair, if not always her cold and virtuous heart. In so doing, the poets mark the lady's beauty and social privilege and demonstrate their own wit and virtuousity. Desirable as it is, however, this same hair was also represented as a net, enchanting and entwining the male poet observing the lady's beauty, which can be dangerous or, as for Henry Constable, a source of grief. This rhetorical tradition for representing beauty also inspired a counter-tradition, the anti-Petrarchan mode exemplified by Shakespeare's dark lady, who has hair of black wires. But even here, the representation of hair allows the poet to display his poetic prowess—his mastery of the tropes of Petrarchism and his surpassing of them. For writers, hair also engaged one of the key aesthetic questions of the Renaissance: that of the relationship between art and nature. Just as Philip Sidney drew on Castiglione's notion of *sprezzatura* in his *Arcadia*, he has hairstyles that hide their artful construction—an aesthetic for "sweet neglect" also adopted by his niece Mary Wroth and by Ben Jonson and Robert Herrick. Much of the literary hair of early modern England belongs to women, but some men, most famously Marlowe's Leander, also have beautiful hair, constructed according to much the same aesthetic. In literature, hair is a useful rhetoric that articulates the poet's wit and understanding of tradition, as well as, sometimes, the power of beauty and desire for it.

CHAPTER ONE

Religion and Ritualized Belief

GARY K. WAITE

Hair has always held a range of religious and cultural meanings, and this is particularly true of the early modern period, a period of diverse approaches to religious reform and intense sectarian conflict. It was also the era of the notorious witch hunts. Hair played a role in all of these events, but given the vast array of authors and sources, we will be able to highlight merely a few examples drawn from prominent Reformation-era writers (Lutheran, Calvinist, and Anabaptist) and works relating to magic and witchcraft. It will become clear that hair was regarded as more than a symbol of the era's gendered hierarchy; in popular culture it remained a marker of sexual wildness, demonic affiliation, and witchcraft. Before turning to these aspects, however, we will need to examine the biblical statements about hair since these were viewed as programmatic by both Renaissance humanists and sixteenth-century Reformers.

RELIGIOUS TEACHING AND MORALITY

Attitudes toward hair in the western tradition were shaped by both ancient culture and holy writ as well as by custom. Hair in the Hebrew scriptures had deeply religious significance. For example, in the description in Numbers 6 of the regulations for those Jewish men wishing to take a Nazirite oath to "separate himself to the Lord," the growing of the hair is absolutely essential, along with abstinence from wine and avoidance of dead bodies, and it is only on the completion of the time of separation that the Nazirite must then "shave his consecrated head at the door of the tent of meeting, and shall take the hair from his consecrated head and put it on the fire" which is consuming the other peace offerings. The Hebrew hero Samson was a Nazirite from birth and it was in his long hair where his great strength lay. When Delilah cut off his seven locks, he lost his enormous strength because "the Lord had left him" (Judges 16: 20). Hair, then, could be a ritual sacrifice to Yahweh and a site of divine power or manliness.

In the Christian scriptures the emphasis was twofold. First, the writers cautioned against excessive attention on fashion, and second, they saw proper hair covering as a sign of the hierarchy inherent in Creation. The writer of 1 Peter warns women Christians to be chaste, and "let not yours be the outward adorning with braiding of hair" (1 Peter 3:3). They instead should focus on submission to their husbands rather than on beautification, a common enough sentiment in antiquity. Distinguishing sharply between male and female hair, the New Testament writers no longer identified long hair as a symbol of spiritual purity or holiness for men but as an essential sign of a woman's submission to her husband. This is reinforced by Paul's affirmation that women needed to cover their head while engaged in public worship:

> But I want you to understand that the head of every man is Christ, the head of a woman is her husband, and the head of Christ is God. Any man who prays or prophesies with his head covered dishonours his head, but any woman who prays or prophesies with her head unveiled dishonours her head—it is the same as if her head were shaven. For if a woman will not veil herself, then she should cut off her hair; but if it is disgraceful for a woman to be shorn or shaven, let her wear a veil. For a man ought not to cover his head, since he is the image and glory of God; but woman is the glory of man … That is why a woman ought to have a veil on her head, because of the angels … is it proper for a woman to pray to God with her head uncovered? Does not nature itself teach you that for a man to wear long hair is degrading to him, but if a woman has long hair, it is her pride? For her hair is given to her for a covering. (1 Cor.11:3–15, RSV)

The apostle therefore affirms that proper hair length and veiling are requirements for Christians, and this became a general standard in the Christian West. This was epitomized in the requirement of religious women to be veiled, typically wearing a wimple that surrounded the face, while monks had the center of their heads shaved in a tonsure. Married women were expected to wear a head covering as a signal of their status, while prostitutes were forbidden in many communities from doing so.[1] While Christians did not carry over the Hebrew injunction for men not to touch the corner of their beards (Leviticus 19:27), beards were often considered as signs of manhood or virility.

THE REFORMERS: MARTIN LUTHER AND JOHN CALVIN

The New Testament injunctions about hair and beard therefore remained normative in the early modern era, especially as Protestant Reformers sought to reshape religious and social customs along biblical precepts. None sought to overturn the traditional gendered hierarchy.[2] Here we will survey the perspective of only four major figures: the German Martin Luther, the French-Genevan John Calvin, and the Dutch Anabaptist leaders Menno Simons and David Joris. Catholics did not alter the medieval norms on hair covering, as the Council of Trent increased the claustration of nuns and made no alterations to the wimple and veil as symbols of the nuns' marriage to Christ.

On the subject of hair and hair covering for women, Luther was remarkably restrained. When interpreting Paul's comments in 1 Timothy and 1 Corinthians, Luther moderates what he viewed as extreme applications of the apostle's injunctions about hair. Women, Luther affirms, should dress appropriately, so that what they wear for church would not be the same as for a dance.[3] Certainly "young unmarried women ought not to wear their locks braided but have a veil when they participate in the Sacrament." Yet, he then comments, "I find no fault in our women. I could bear that young women come with their hair veiled, but this is contrary to custom. There should be modesty in dress." He suggests that German women already follow Paul's command, while others do not:

Paul wants women to veil their braids. Here there is no need to prohibit this practice. In France they wear their hair unbound and with open braids so that no one knows who is married or unmarried. Perhaps this is how Greek women wore their hair. Among our people married women veil their hair and braids. When they do this, they veil their locks chastely and modestly, so that it may not become material for watchers to think shameful thoughts.[4]

The expectation that married women would cover their hair to avoid sexually arousing their male neighbors is thus a commonplace that the Reformer believes needed little reinforcement. As to hair coverings in church services, Luther both affirms yet moderates Paul's strictures, noting that, according to Paul's statement in 1 Corinthians 11:5, women could still fulfill the office of prophet, as long as they covered their heads while doing so and kept silent when men spoke, "but if no man were to preach, then it would be necessary for the women to preach."[5]

Elsewhere Luther reflected some aspects of popular culture with respect to hair. For example, in his commentary on the Song of Solomon, Luther pondered the biblical poet's sexual wooing of his beloved. When the poet wrote "Your eyes are the eyes of doves behind your locks," Luther took this to refer to hair hanging down to the eyes, something that "is singularly praiseworthy in a girl."[6] As with most commentators, Luther also pursues a metaphorical meaning, hence "the hair signifies the adornment of the priesthood, for in the church everything must be done decently and in order." As for those who interpreted black hair "to imply a vile outward appearance," Luther points to the positive reference in Song of Solomon 5:11 to show that "black hair was highly praised among them [the Jewish priesthood]." He also quotes Horace as saying a woman is, "worth looking at with dark eyes and black hair."[7] Following his allegorical vein, Luther interprets the long hair of women in Song of Solomon 7:5 to signify the Levite priesthood and government magistracy, the latter "flow from the high priest and king like hair from the top of the head, flowing down the back to the lower parts of the body."[8]

All of this reveals that particular hairstyles for women were not a major concern for Luther, so long as married women wore hair covering in general and all women did so in church. John Calvin's approach was not greatly different from Luther's. In his commentary on 1 Timothy, Calvin advocates modesty and sobriety in dress and style. While "dress is an indifferent matter," Calvin censures superfluity "such as curled hair, jewels, and golden rings." The goal of any virtuous woman should be to distinguish herself from the style "of a strumpet."[9] As for Paul's command about women in 1 Corinthians 11, Calvin agrees with St. Paul that when women pray or prophesy they must cover their heads as a sign of the subjugation of women to men. "Hence, on the other hand, if the woman uncovers her head, she shakes off subjection—involving contempt of her husband." For a married woman to go about with head bare was therefore a form of rebellion against the patriarchal family.[10] It was as if she had a shaven head, something that Calvin found abhorrent to nature, for "to see a woman shaven is a spectacle that is disgusting and monstrous." Hair is certainly a natural covering for women but as a sign of beauty it should be hidden in public out of modesty.[11] Just as a woman covers her head to show her subservience to her husband, he must not cover his head to proclaim that he is the master of the home and his wife. Turning this gender order upside down is what Paul meant about offending the angels: "if women uncover their heads, not only Christ, but all the angels too, will be witnesses of the outrage." For Calvin, then, covering the hair was absolutely essential for pious women.

HAIR IN THE ANABAPTIST TRADITION

While the jury may still be out on the question of whether or not women experienced more freedom to play leading roles in the radical reformation after the early phase of the Anabaptist movement (ca. 1525–1535), which witnessed some women prophets and teachers, male leaders clamped down on further expressions of religious leadership on the part of their women colleagues and reasserted a traditional gender hierarchy.[12] Even so, hair covering was not a major issue in the writings of Menno Simons (ca. 1496–1561), who, after the fall of the infamous Anabaptist kingdom of Münster in June 1535, eventually gained leadership over the peaceable remnant in the Low Countries. For both Joris and Menno, women were to be subservient to their husbands, but neither seemed deeply concerned about hair covering as a symbol of this subservience. Instead, Menno's only published reference to hair referred back to the Samson and Delilah story as part of his argument with the Reformed preacher Martin Micron:

> Dear me, if we poor folk were to abuse the Scriptures one-twentieth part as much as they do ... and would pull the wool over the eyes of simple people as does Micron by his glosses, then (help, Lord) how they would turn up their noses at us ... Nevertheless, however they teach and do; it is a welcome gospel to the poor, deceived world, as was commonly the case from the beginning with all false prophets and their followers. Let him break the bones of the Passover lamb and cut off Samson's hair until the time comes that it is ended with him and he has to give an account before the Lord of his seducing.[13]

Here, then, Menno obliquely compares Micron to Delilah and the cutting of Samson's hair to the persecution of Menno and his followers.

The Samson analogy was far more significant for Menno's spiritualistic competitor David Joris (ca. 1501–1556) who between 1536 and the early 1540s was the major leader of the Dutch Anabaptists until his flight to Antwerp in 1539 and Basel (as Johann van Brugge) in 1544. In exile, Joris moved away from a sectarian identity and developed a spiritualism that depreciated all confessional distinctions in favor of an interiorized religion of the heart. A hunted heretic, Joris wrote dozens of tracts, treatises, and letters to interested parties across Europe. Unconstrained by formal education or theological orthodoxy, Joris allowed his mind to follow "the inspiration of the Holy Spirit" as he read scripture, leading to many unusual theological interpretations (see Figure 1.1).[14]

While Joris, like his male contemporaries, emphasized the subservience of women to men, especially in religious matters, he seemed most concerned about the symbolic emasculation implied when women dominated men, visualized in the cutting of a man's beard and hair. For Joris, then, the Samson story was central, while proper hair covering or styles for women were a secondary concern. Like Calvin, Joris emphasizes that a woman needs to obey her husband, who in turn follows Christ. His advice to his male supporters is to

> let your beards grow and your strength increase in Christ which you, in the first Adam have allowed the woman (your own flesh) to shave off ... By this you have lost the seven Spirits of God, namely, the entire strength and power of God in every manner. You have gone the way of Samson, being bound with bands and straps of darkness, and you will be defeated by death, that is certain [Judg. 16:21, 30] ... Do not let your beard be cut off. Behold your strength and honor, which God has given you to his praise. Do not look upon the beauty of the woman, nor upon her temptation and enchanting, so that you not be softened to her covetousness.[15]

FIGURE 1.1 Hieronymus Wiericx, *Image or Literal Figure of the Bride of Christ, or the true Restoration or Restitution*, engraving after David Joris, from David Joris, *Twonder-boeck: waer in dat van der werldt aen versloten gheopenbaert is. Opt nieuw ghecorrigeert vnde vermeerdert by den Autheur selue* (n.p., 1551 [Dierck Mullem, 1584?]), part III, fol. iiiv. Courtesy of the Universiteitsbibliotheek van Amsterdam, Kerkelijke Collecties.

Elsewhere he warns a follower that if he allows his wife to take spiritual leadership in the family, "he castrates himself and loses his beard," ultimately dishonoring God and becoming "effeminate and is called a woman."[16]

Was this merely metaphorical? It seems not, for he took his advice personally as he was famed for his long red beard, a distinguishing trait that would have been easy enough to remove to reduce the chance of detection but which he maintained throughout his life, despite the risks involved (see Figure 1.2).[17] He may therefore have believed literally

FIGURE 1.2 Anonymous, *Portrait of the Anabaptist David Joris*, Kunstmuseum Basel, public domain. Courtesy the Yorck Project: *10.000 Meisterwerke der Malerei* [DVD-ROM], 2002.

that male potency and/or spiritual power was linked to hair, despite his proclivity to find the true significance of things only in their inner reality rather than their external form. Even after his death in 1556, his beard identified him as the notorious heretic. Although buried in St. Leonard's churchyard in Basel, Joris's body was rumored to instead be residing in the family chateau where his followers awaited his resurrection. Basel's magistrates ordered his remains exhumed and a barber surgeon cut off a piece of Joris's beard to appease the crowd.[18] Once Joris's postmortem trial began in 1559, it was again his red beard that, even after nearly three years in the grave, gave proof of the heretic's identity.

BEARDS AND MALE POTENCY

Joris was expressing the typical male perspective of his day, that facial hair marked adult men as mature and distinct from adolescents. Mark Johnston in Chapter Six below pursues in greater detail the issue of hair and masculinity, but here I will consider some of the religious dimensions of this association. Since Catholic priests were not allowed to wear a beard, they were often derided as effeminate, and for this reason some clerics, such as the Italian Piero Valeriano Bolzani, wrote pleas for this regulation to be overturned, since it unnecessarily raised doubts about their masculinity.[19]

Concerns over hairstyles and implicit fears of emasculation continued to haunt many Protestant sectarians; English Puritans seemed especially susceptible in the seventeenth century as hairstyles became increasingly ornate for men. In 1628, the prolific Puritan writer William Prynne (1600–1669) warned against "Effeminate, Proud, Lascivious, Exorbitant, and Fantastique Haires, or Lockes, or Love-lockes" that have become so fashionable. The danger to gender clarity was obvious in these "Degenerous, Unnaturall, and Unmanly times," when women wore short hair that "Hermophradited" them. The unnatural cutting of their hair removed their "Naturall vaile, their Feminine glory, and the very badge, and Character of their subjection both to God, and man." Similarly, "divers of our Masculine, and more noble race, are wholy degenerated and metamorphosed into women" through their "Crisping, Curling, Frouncing, Powdring, and nourshing of their Lockes, and Hairie excrements."[20] Such fashions, he asserted, were a sign of the sad decline of England and went against the English tradition of faithfulness to Christian scripture. Spending more time with their barber than with their minister, English men had "degenerated into Virginians, Frenchmen, Rustians, nay Women," in their fancy hairstyle.

HAIR AND THE SUPERNATURAL: LIMINALITY, MYTH, MAGIC, FETISH

These concerns about beards and emasculation allow us to turn to preternatural and supernatural aspects of hair. Facial hair for men was more than normative; for example, in 1600, one English writer published a treatise assisting readers to spot potential witches. He advises them to beware of those who have some deformity, "and especially of a man that hath not a beard."[21] Similarly, writers often expostulated that witches were more often than not old and "with a wrinkled face, a furr'd brow, a hairy lip, a gobber tooth, a squint eye, a squeaking voice, or a scolding tongue." It was, as Keith Thomas wrote in his classic *Religion and the Decline of Magic* of 1971, "proverbial that bearded women were likely to be witches, and physical ugliness or deformity could thus awaken suspicion."[22] Hair was therefore part of the criteria separating normalcy from deviance that was often utilized by villagers when expressing suspicion toward a neighbor for magical malfeasance.

For early modern writers, hair was an important element of female beauty, yet some, such as the late fifteenth-century German Dominican Inquisitor Heinrich Kramer (Institoris) and the early seventeenth-century French judge Pierre de Lancre, went further in their linkage of hairstyle with morality. For example, in his infamous witch-hunting manual of 1486, the *Malleus Maleficarum*, Kramer argued that incubi (demons who have taken the form of a man) harassed some women more than others due to their quality of hair:

> William [*Bees* 2.3.25—William of Paris] also notes that incubi seem to harass woman and girls with beautiful hair more because such women pay more attention to caring for or grooming their hair or because it is their wish or habit to inflame men with their hair or because they vainly glory in it or because the goodness of God permits this so that women will be deterred from inflaming men by the means by which the demons too wish men to be inflamed.[23]

Precisely because St. Paul described hair as the glory of woman, celibate priests and monks such as William of Paris and Kramer feared its implicit powers of seduction. Hair was, in this schema, a medium of sexual temptation, hence the vice of vanity was often depicted as a woman admiring her hair in a mirror, and in some of these a demon is seen in the glass (Figure 1.3). In others, such as Hans Baldung Grien's *Three Ages of the Woman and Death* of 1510, the woman is too preoccupied with admiring her glorious locks to notice Death's warning. The hair of women was thus both a blessing and a curse, and in the clerical mind, a symbol of sin and temptation.

Despite being a secular judge rather than a cleric, Pierre de Lancre made similar association between women's hair and sexuality when he describes the women of the Labourd, where he had been sent to oversee trials for witchcraft. In his published account of his heroic efforts to eradicate demonic witchcraft from the region, de Lancre seeks to explain why the people of the Labourd were so inclined to witchcraft. Among the many factors, such as being "hasty" and "hot-headed," naturally violent and lovers of dancing, he also included that "they also hate hats for some reason." He then turns to the subject of female fashion, which he describes as extremely immodest, especially among the lower classes, and this included "their hairstyles." Some, he continues,

> are shaved except for the tips of their hair, which are very long. Others, of a slightly higher standing, have their hair covering half their cheeks, flowing down over their shoulders and complementing their eyes in such a way that they seem much more beautiful in all this innocence, and they are more attractive than if one were to see them in the open field. With such beautiful hair they show themselves to great

FIGURE 1.3 Attributed to Albrecht Dürer, *The Demon of Vanity and the Coquette*. From Geoffrey de La Tour Landry's *Ritter vom Turn* (Basel: Printed by Michael Furter, 1493). Public domain. https://en.wikipedia.org/wiki/File:Vanity.jpg.

advantage and are so well armed that the sun shines its rays on these tresses as it would on a cloud. The sheen of their hair is so striking and forms highlights as brilliant as those appearing in the sky when one witnesses the birth of Iris. This gives them their bewitching eyes, which are as dangerous in love as in witchcraft, although for them to wear a head covering is a sign of virginity. And in certain areas common women who wish to marry wear certain spiked headdresses in a shape that is so indecent that one would say they are more the weapons of Priapus than of the god Mars. Their hair seems to testify to their desire, for the widows wear the headdress without a point, indicating that they lack a husband.[24]

These women prefer to eat apples, the "fruit of transgression," and "with their heads bare," they live in this mountainous region "in total freedom and innocence just as Eve lived in the earthly paradise. They listen to men and to demons, and pay attention to every serpent that wants to seduce them." Uncovered hair, then, implied sexual freedom and the breakdown of gender norms, a point to which we will return when we discuss images of witches.

HAIR'S PRETERNATURAL PROPERTIES

Natural philosophers of the fifteenth and sixteenth centuries conceived of the cosmos in broadly neo-Platonic terms in which the universe was in effect a macrocosm of the human body (the microcosm) and in which all things were interconnected like a living being. There flowed through the universe "occult sympathies and vital spirits" that practitioners of the occult sciences sought to utilize for healing or for gaining knowledge, while university-trained physicians consulted astrological charts as part of their diagnoses. As Thomas again put it, in this worldview "One could harm a man by manipulating his hair, his fingernail parings, his sweat or his excrement, all of which contained his vital spirits."[25] It was widely assumed that hair, like fingernails, continued to grow after death, hence it retained elements of the person's life force postmortem. We see this, for example, in Emmanuel LeRoy Ladurie's classic study of the fourteenth-century French Cathar village of Montaillou. Ladurie notes how deeply connected were the homes with their resident families, so that the "bits of fingernail and hair belonging to the deceased head of the family" were kept inside the domus, since these "were regarded as bearers of especially intense vital energy" and through which "the house 'was imbued with certain magic qualities belonging to the deceased,'" qualities which could be passed on to other family members.[26] In this village culture, it was essential that bits of the nails and hair be clipped and retained as soon after death as possible to ensure that the residual life force be as strong as possible. One village woman, Alazaïs Azéma, reported to the inquisitor that she had been asked by the widow of Pons Clergue, father of the priest, to "cut some locks of hair from around the forehead of the corpse ... so that the house of the dead man might remain fortunate." As another villager, Brune Vital put it, "I have heard that if you take locks of hair and bits of finger- and toe-nail from a corpse, it does not carry away with it the star or good fortune of the house." To avoid rinsing away "some precious qualities attached to the skin and the accumulated dirt," they did not wash the body before clipping the hair and nails.[27] The procedure had to be a surreptitious one, of course, since it went against church custom.

This practice was likely common across rural Europe, since we know that hair was also one ingredient among many derived from the human body that were utilized in magic and love potions. Locks of hair were also kept by a lover or spouse both as a keepsake and as a means of maintaining contact with the beloved, in ways very similar to the workings of a saint's relic which a supplicant could touch or hold (inside a reliquary or not) in order to gain the attention of that particular saint in heaven.[28]

REVENANTS

The belief that a deceased's physical remains retained some of the person's original *"vis vegetans*, or 'invigorating force,'" lay behind not only the Catholic cult of saints, but also widespread beliefs about revenants.[29] Other hair-related signs were important too, such as body hair in unusual parts of the body, such as along the spine; in Romania, persons with blue eyes and red hair were immediately suspected of revenantism.[30] The placement of sharp objects in the urns of cremated revenants, including hair needles, was believed in some locales to prevent the return of the dead, while in Serbia lit candles may have been placed next to corpses to singe the hair and thus prevent their rising from their graves.[31] As Paul Barber reveals, misunderstanding the processes of decomposition of human remains lay behind a wide range of popular beliefs and fears about the dead rising from their graves.

WILD MEN AND WOMEN

Excess body hair was similarly imbued with special preternatural characteristics as stories of wild men and wild women covered in hair proliferated across Europe but especially in the German-speaking regions, where artistic images of wild men "grew increasingly positive in the sixteenth century."[32] Some citizens of Basel even created a *Zur Haaren* club decorated with images of wild men and which celebrated "hairiness" as a sign of manly strength and "freedom from the rules of society." Extra hair on the body could be indicative of lycanthropy, of course, but also of sainthood. As Merry Wiesner-Hanks has observed, this was particularly true for women, for whom facial hair was regarded as unusual. One of the most popular stories of a hairy saint is that of Mary Magdalene whose medieval legend had her landing in France, preaching to the locals, and living in a cave as a hermit (Figure 1.4). During this time her body became covered with hair, which transformed her into a saintly wild woman whose cult became a favorite of women seeking to protect their honor against lascivious men.[33]

Another popular hairy saint was St. Wilgefortis (or St. Uncumber) whose miraculous growth of facial hair saved her from an arranged marriage, and she was the subject of prayers from women seeking freedom from abusive husbands.[34] Cases of women suffering from *hypertrichosis universalis*, a condition that results in hair covering most of the body, were also a great spectacle, although the famed sixteenth-century Basel physician Felix Platter concluded from his diagnosis of one of these, Antonietta, daughter of Petrus Gonzales, that her condition was just one of excess hair and not indicative of monstrosity.[35] Given the popularity of stories of the monstrous, his voice was clearly not in the majority.

FIGURE 1.4 Fourteenth-century relief portrait of Mary Magdalene, St. John's Church, Toruń. Public domain. Photo: courtesy Pko, public domain via Wikimedia Commons. https://commons.wikimedia.org/wiki/File:Torun_SS_Johns_Mary_Magdalene.jpg.

HAIR IN MAGIC

We see the preternatural power of hair implied frequently in confessions of accused witches and again we can return to our German Inquisitor Kramer's manual of witch-hunting. In a first-hand account of a soothsayer seeking to heal the Dominican from bewitchment that had led to lameness in his foot, Kramer reports that the unlearned peasant healer held a ladle of molten lead over the afflicted foot and then poured it into a bowl of water in which various shapes, such as thorns, hairs, and bones, suddenly appeared. The soothsayer explained that he knew this was witchcraft since Saturn, the god of lead, revealed it through his process of detection. Of course Kramer was suspicious that there had instead been demonic agency in the procedure, but the peasant's reference to learned alchemy reassured him that it relied upon natural forces. The peasant's ministrations healed the Inquisitor, who then expostulated, "hence, sorcerers through no natural power and merely with the assistance of demons on the one hand, and demons by themselves with the help of some object like thorns, bones, strands of hair, pieces of wood or the like on the other, bring about the effects of sorcery when they insert or deposit some device."[36] Hair was one of the frequently used ingredients in harmful magic but one that was potentially more powerful than mere wood or thorns due to its possession of the residual life force of the former wearer.

This can be seen in further references to the use of hair in magical spells such as the case of a Parisian girl reported by the French legal expert Jean Bodin in his defense of witch-hunting, *On the Demon-Mania of Witches* of 1580. According to Bodin, this girl apparently confessed that one day while praying at the grave of her father, Satan came to her in "the form of a tall black man" who continued to harass her into giving him a sign of her subservience, "even asking her for some of her hair. She gave him a lock of it."[37] Clearly Satan, whose knowledge of the workings of creation was far superior to that of mere mortals, believed that possessing a lock of this girl's hair would grant him a special connection to her that would in effect be the seal of a diabolical pact.

One sign of demonic possession or bewitchment was the vomiting up of unnatural objects, such as, "iron fittings, hair, pieces of cloth, broken glass."[38] In another of Bodin's examples, a German ploughman in 1539 was bewitched so that when a barber surgeon pulled out an iron nail that had lain under his skin but without any obvious entry point, he was so beset by pain that he "cut his throat in desperation." According to Bodin's version of the story, which he garnered from his Protestant opponent the medical practitioner Johan Wier (Weyer), the locals performed a version of an autopsy and discovered in his bowels "a rod, four steel knives, two horseshoes, and a ball of hair." For Bodin, this was evidence that diabolical witchcraft had been utilized on this unfortunate man, so that the foreign objects were inserted magically into his body to cause him pain. For the more skeptical Wier, however, the iron objects, nail, and "a roundish tangle of hair" had been placed surreptitiously by a demon postmortem in such a way that the barber surgeons were unaware of the sleight of hand during their autopsy.[39] The hair of animals was also utilized in magical spells; in 1569, Bodin himself spoke to an imprisoned witch in Paris who claimed to be able to cure horses through the magical use of horsehair: "he was found in possession of a great book full of hairs from horses, cows, and other animals of every colour. When he had cast the spell to kill some horse, people came to him, and got it cured by bringing him some hair, and he gave the spell to another animal."[40]

Such usage of hair in magic remained a commonplace in the early modern era across Europe, as the numerous references to it in eighteenth-century witchcraft trials in Scandinavia attest.[41] Here knots made of hair were a particular magical specialty. As Jacqueline Van Gent comments,

> If hair was found somewhere on a person's clothing or within their farmstead, they had to be careful. If the hair was bound in a *trollknot*, one could be almost certain that there was harmful intent behind it and that misfortune could be expected. The victim would quickly employ causal logic to make links between the use of hair, harmful intent, and misfortune.

Those who discovered that they were the object of such magical manipulation of hair feared that this would adversely affect their life force, since hair, like other body parts, represented personal power in popular culture.[42] This was particularly true in love magic, for in the effort to impel a man to fall in love with a woman it was essential that some part of her body or hair—especially that from her "secret part"—be ingested by the intended to effect the desired attraction.[43] In other examples, such as those provided by the Spanish Belgian Jesuit Martin del Rio in his *Investigations into Magic* (*Disquisitiones Magicae*) of ca. 1599, the hair required for love magic was regular human hair, along with some of the following: nail pairings, the Host, menstrual fluid, semen, excrement, herbs, leaves, roots, and bits of material that had touched the intended object of bewitchment.[44] According to the learned del Rio, these do not work on the basis of their own properties alone but due to the intervention of demons. Given the dominant belief in sympathetic forces that linked everything together in the cosmos, the ingestion of pubic hair would necessarily have an effect on the sexual feelings of the one consuming it.⁴⁵

LOOSE HAIR, SEXUAL ABANDON, AND WITCHES

With its strong association with sexuality and magic, it is no surprise that female hair could be linked in very powerful ways with witchcraft. Since covered or bound hair was a sign of female piety and submission to male religious authority, loose hair was a sign of sexual abandon and female nonconformity. Undone hair could signal eroticism, or sadness, or mourning.⁴⁶ Most significant, however, is Charles Zika's discovery of a development in artistic representations of witches in the late fifteenth and early sixteenth centuries: an emphasis on wild hair as a signal of sexual wildness and malign intent.⁴⁷ In these popular images, unbound and wild hair became a signature of a witch, especially in Hans Baldung Grien's famous woodcut studies of witches in the second decade of the sixteenth century, all of which have unrestrained gestures and "the flying hair with its traditional magical and sexual associations" serve not only to identify the subjects as witches but "to create a sense of turbulent energy."⁴⁸ In the images included in the various reprints of Ulrich Molitor's *De Laniis* (*The Witches*) of 1489, the woman with a bow and arrow has loose hair, signifying "her wild and dishevelled nature, a common visual cue increasingly employed in the sixteenth century." ⁴⁹ Zika also notes

FIGURE 1.5 Ulrich Molitor, *De laniis et phitonicis mulieribus* (Concerning Witches and Fortunetellers) (Reutlingen, http://www.ubs.sbg.ac.at/sosa/inkunabeln/WI167.htm). Public domain via Wikimedia Commons. https://commons.wikimedia.org/wiki/File:Ulrich_Molitor_Von_den_Unholden_Teufelsbuhlschaft.jpg.

a manuscript image of a witch and Death from ca. 1500 that has changed the witch from "a traditional sorcerer, with a head covering" of the original 1491 edition into one with long, dishevelled hair, so that in a few years "the loose unbridled hair of the sexually dissolute had begun to be considered an appropriate visual cue for identifying the social and moral threat of witchcraft."[50] In other images in Molitor, such as the one of a witch and demon caught in an embrace, the woman has a head covering (Figure 1.5). Zika speculates that this suggests that the embrace occurred before the consummation of the demonic pact and also indicates that she is married, hence this is a scene not only of demonic seduction "but also of adultery."[51]

Depictions of witches by early sixteenth-century artists such as Albrecht Dürer, his student Baldung, and Albrecht Altdorfer, further developed such tentative steps toward a new iconography of witchcraft into a "new visual vocabulary" through the depiction of cues such as cauldrons and wild hair.[52] Dürer's 1497 *The Four Naked Women* provides subtle clues that these are in fact witches (Figure 1.6). Along with the demon peeking out from behind a doorway on the left and the skull at the women's feet, the woman with her back to the viewer has her hair escaping from her head covering. Dürer's later image of a witch from 1510 is much more obvious (Figure 1.7).

FIGURE 1.6 Albrecht Dürer, *Four Naked Women* (1497). National Gallery of Art, Washington, DC: Online database entry 1943.3.3462. Public Domain via Wikimedia Commons. https://commons.wikimedia.org/wiki/File:Albrecht_Dürer_-_Four_Naked_Women_%28NGA_1943.3.3462%29.jpg.

FIGURE 1.7 Albrecht Dürer, *Witch Riding on a Goat* (ca. 1500/1501). Rosenwald Collection. National Gallery of Art, Washington, DC. Open Access. NGA Images. Washington, DC.

In Baldung's *New Year's Greetings with Three Witches* (Figure 1.8), of 1514, the women are identified as witches by a flaming vessel and their wild hair and are also associated with "the fiery lusts of Venus."[53] Similarly, the figures in Baldung's *The Weather Witches* of 1523 have their hair flying in different directions, representing their "unbridled lust."[54]

In many other images, wild hair served as a warning that all magic was potentially demonic and that latent within women was a powerful sexuality that could burst forth in maleficence. While most prominent in the early sixteenth century, this iconographic device appears in many images thereafter. It is visible, for example, in the woodcut of the burning of the witches at Derneberg in 1555, in which the wild hair of the witch who is being raised out of the fire by the demon identifies her as the ringleader who had made the pact with the devil and had had sexual congress with him, while her two compatriots have their hair covered (Figure 1.9).[55]

At the same time that artists were depicting female witches with wild hair, representations of wild women became more positive. Wiesner-Hanks suggests therefore that images of "destructive hairy women did not disappear from the sixteenth-century imagination, but emerged in a new form: as witches." Witches could be bearded, as in Shakespeare's *Macbeth*, although most woodcuts did not portray them as such, since the wild hair was a sufficient device to indicate their malice.[56]

FIGURE 1.8 Hans Baldung, *New Year's Greetings with Three Witches* (1514). Louvre Museum, Paris. Inv.-Nr. RF 1083. Public domain. Photo: Historicum.net via Wikimedia Commons. https://commons.wikimedia.org/wiki/File:Baldung_hexen_ca1514.jpg.

FIGURE 1.9 *Ein erschröckliche Geschicht so zu Derneburg* (A Terrible Event at Derneburg) (1555). Public domain. Central Library of Zurich. Europeana. oai:opac.nebis.ch:EBI01-005347659.

THE HAIR OF ANABAPTISTS AND WITCHES

The period in which Dürer and Baldung were creating their images of witches was one in which there were relatively few witch trials, at least those involving groups of accused. Instead, the attention of courts and inquisitors was focused on suppressing the Protestant and especially Anabaptist reformations, and there were efforts to associate the latter with diabolical heresy.[57] From 1533 to 1535, the Anabaptists in the Netherlands and northern Germany were caught up in a highly apocalyptical movement that resulted in the Anabaptist kingdom of Münster and efforts to spread this militant form of Anabaptism elsewhere, such as Amsterdam, before the imminent return of Christ. In 1535 or 1536, the city magistrates of Amsterdam commissioned the artist Barent Dircksz (Doove Barent) to complete a series of painted panels to warn against such heresy. While the originals have been lost, the scenes were recorded in several engravings, including those in seventeenth-century editions of Lambertus Hortensius's (ca.1500–1574) *Tumult of the Anabaptists*.[58] One of the scenes depicted was the so-called *Naaktlooper* incident when, on the evening of February 11, 1535, a small group of eleven Anabaptists, four of them women, removed and burned their clothes and then ran through the streets of the city, proclaiming the coming wrath of God and the "naked truth" (Figure 1.10).[59]

FIGURE 1.10 *The naked runners of Amsterdam*, Copper etching after a painting by Barent Dircksz, destroyed in 1652. Lambertus Hortensius, *Het boeck van den oproer der wederdooperen* (Amsterdam, n.d. [ca. 1600–1650]). Courtesy the Universiteitsbibliotheek van Amsterdam, Kerkelijke Collecties.

The woman on the left foreground is depicted with hands folded in pious prayer, yet her flying hair reveals that her pious gesture is insincere as does the hair of one of the background runners which is flying in the opposite direction.[60] This image implies that Anabaptist piety was a mere cover for forbidden sexuality and malign intent. Yet such efforts to associate Anabaptists with diabolical intent failed, and most images of Anabaptist women, even those being martyred, had their hair contained in the bonnets that Mennonites had mandated as a sign of female modesty. This is clearly apparent in the many engravings performed by the Mennonite artist Jan Luyken (1649–1712) for the Mennonite *Martyrs' Mirror*, images that intentionally oppose the unfettered sexuality hinted at in Hortensius's engravings (Figure 1.11).

In all of his pictures the women's hair is under control and modestly contained within a bonnet, even in the flames. As the prosecution of Anabaptist heresy had, in most places, ended or become less severe by the 1560s, judicial attention related to demonic heresy returned to the witch, now conceived of as a member of a large conspiracy of women and men who had made pacts with the devil and performed harmful magic upon their neighbors.[61] Meeting regularly in the infamous witches' Sabbaths, images of the witch now could retain the wild hair. Many images, however, have the hair of the witch carefully covered or bound. A good example is provided by the 1608 treatise on witchcraft, the *Compendium Maleficarum*, by the Italian priest Francisco Maria Guazzo, which contains a number of woodcut images. In all but one of these, the female witches have their hair nicely tied up on their heads, even when engaged in the witches' dance or kissing the devil's posterior. The only exception is Guazzo's image of a witch flying on a demonic animal (Figure 1.12), for which he has clearly drawn on the earlier iconographic tradition,

FIGURE 1.11 Jan Luyken, *Execution of Anne Hendricks* (1571). Copper etching in Tieleman van Bracht, *Het bloedig tooneel, of Martelaers Spiegel* (Amsterdam, 1685). Courtesy the Universiteitsbibliotheek van Amsterdam, Kerkelijke Collecties.

RELIGION AND RITUALIZED BELIEF 35

FIGURE 1.12 Francesco Maria Guazzo, *Flying Witch*, in *Compendium Maleficarum* (1608). Public domain via Wikimedia Commons. CompendiumMaleficarumEngraving9.jpg.

such as Dürer's image from 1510. Even so, in another image of a witch taking flight on a demonic goat, her hair is tied up in a bun (Figure 1.13).

Evidently Guazzo wished to indicate that witches were not easily identifiable and instead could be any respectable woman, not just those obviously wild or cantankerous. Guazzo wrote at the height of the witch-hunts when accusations were often leveled against women and men of higher social standing than the typical old peasant woman of earlier imagination. While retaining the sexual wildness and power of the traditional image, the demonic witch of the late sixteenth and seventeenth centuries was often portrayed as in many respects normal looking, with hair contained, while other iconographic devices were used to portray demonic agency. This artistic strategy helped elevate the level of fear, since now seemingly normal neighbors could be in truth members of the witch sect and in league with the devil.[62]

THE HAIR OF WITCHES IN THE COURTROOM

Given its association with magic and witchcraft, the hair of accused witches was regarded by judges and inquisitors as problematical, to say the least. It was frequently believed to be hiding a magical object, or more often, covering the location where the devil had branded his adept with his mark. In one case at Brindisi in November 1590, Guazzo notes that a Claudia Bogarta was about to be tortured, "she was closely shaved, as the custom is, and so a scar was exposed on the top of her bare brow. The Inquisitor then suspecting the truth, namely that it was a mark made by the devil's claw, which had before been

FIGURE 1.13 Francesco Maria Guazzo, *Witch takes Flight*, in *Compendium Maleficarum* (1608). Public domain via Wikimedia Commons. CompendiumMaleficarumEngraving13.jpg.

hidden by her hair, ordered a pin to be thrust deep into it." Since she felt no pain, this was presumed to be the devil's mark.[63] The shaving of accused witches was therefore commonplace in trials. The procedure was a deeply humiliating one that helped to break down the suspect's resistance to confessing what her interrogators wanted to hear. In his how-to manual, Kramer had earlier suggested that interrogation of suspects should begin with the removal of their clothing (if a woman, by "women of good reputation") in order "to remove any device for sorcery that may have been sewn into his clothing."[64] In order to protect the judge and others in the courtroom, it was also necessary to shave the accused to find their "hidden devices for sorcery," especially when the accused refused to confess, for "the sorcery of silence they sometimes keep superstitious amulets consisting of certain objects in their clothing or in the hair of the body or sometimes in the most secret places, which cannot be named."[65] At this point Kramer notes that the shaving of the genitalia was regarded as a shameful practice in Germany where

> this sort of shaving, especially around the secret places, is considered very degrading, and for this reason we inquisitors also make no use of it. Rather, we shave the hair on the head, and then we put a drop of Blessed Wax in a chalice or cup of Holy Water and give it to them to drink three times on an empty stomach in the name of the Most Holy Trinity. By the Grace of God we have removed the sorcery of silence from many in this way. In other kingdoms, however, inquisitors order this shaving to be carried out over the entire body. The Inquisitor of Como in fact told us that last year, which was 1485, he ordered forty-one sorceresses to be burned to ashes after the hair was shaven off over their entire bodies.[66]

If such procedures do not work, then the demonic silence could be overcome only through the prayers and fasting of the devout.

Resistance to the practice of shaving accused witches broke down first in the Protestant Swiss Cantons in the 1530s, while Catholic regions avoided it until around 1600. Zika confirms this by referring to the available Swiss images of witch burnings: all of the five execution scenes showing the victims with shorn heads were from Protestant cantons, while the four with hair untouched were from Catholic territories. As he concludes, "while the stripping of witches and cutting their hair was a formal act of degradation and humiliation, the shorn heads may also refer to the practice of searching for the devil's mark," an action that preoccupied both Protestants and Catholics.[67] Thanks to the association of unbound hair with sexual license and witchcraft, later religious nonconformists, such as Dutch Mennonites, English Puritans, and the Quakers, to name just a few, strongly emphasized the need for their women to contain their hair to avoid such connotations.

CONCLUSION

Hair in the early modern era held multiple meanings. It was, of course, also a matter of style, but even the decorative elements carried with them religious or preternatural significations. Anything other than the norm—long hair neatly covered for women (married) and short hair but with face bearded for men—could lead to suspicions of sexual wildness, gender crossing, disobedience of the divinely ordained hierarchy of the sexes, or even of monstrosity, witchcraft, and revenantism. As fashions changed in the seventeenth century the moralists cried out even louder than before, but they were unable to turn the tide of fashion. After the witch hunts had died down after the middle of the seventeenth century in most locales, anxiety over unorthodox hair seems also to have decreased. This was likely one of the side effects of the havoc caused by the large-scale witch-hunts, as scholars rethought aspects of the nature of the preternatural world, including magic, witchcraft, and the devil.[68] In this learned discourse, hair became less magical, although it retained many of its preternatural aspects in popular culture and retained its function as a marker of gender difference and hierarchy into the modern era.

CHAPTER TWO

Self and Society

ANU KORHONEN

For men and women of the Renaissance, hair was among the primary identifiers of individuality. What one did with one's hair every day—a ritualistic, performative production of identity—was involved in the constitution of a gendered, classed, and racialized self. At the same time, the cultural regulations that either hid hair or allowed it to be seen further enhanced hair's representational power.[1] When outward appearance was described, hair featured prominently and its characteristics, whether color, length, or curliness, intimated personality traits as well as social differentiations. Hair embodied connections between people of similar rank, gender, or political opinion and was especially useful for expressing familial relationships. Hair was a physiological attribute of one's self that also contributed to, and drew upon, a range of social practices and meanings, and it is the cultural mapping of these connections that this chapter focuses on.

Hair mediated between self and society in many different ways. It allowed Renaissance individuals to create a sense of both their personality and ancestry and worked as a distinguishing feature when people remembered or recognized others. Hair was a system of signification: it was legible through a set of cultural codes, but those codes also formed a grid of power, against which individuals could define both themselves and others. To make use of these interpretative registers, Renaissance people drew on several discursive frames and conceptual categories simultaneously. Like any other constituent of identity, hair was a malleable sign that functioned linguistically, visually, and performatively at the same time.

The context in which hair as a symbolic constituent of the self will be discussed in this chapter is English society, and my focus is on English language materials. How hair is made to embody ideas about class, gender, race, morality, and health are my concern—as they are the concern of other chapters—but this discussion focuses more particularly on how they informed the construction of the self and one's relationship to society. If identity is constructed in an ongoing negotiaton of changing identifications, we need to consider the early modern self, too, as a set of relationships that are in constant flux but also governed by cultural and social codes and conceptualizations. I will concentrate especially on bodily materiality (which influenced ideas about families and nations) and hair care which were informed by social relationships, patriarchal governance, and religious ideology, and influenced early modern constructions of selfhood and society in different and overlapping ways.

HUMORS

A wealth of scientific and practical literature testifies to the fact that early modern people associated different looks and qualities of hair with their wearer's identity, status, and bodily constitution. Basic questions such as why women have longer hair than men, why some people have soft hair and others hard, why some people's hair is curly, and why some people turn gray earlier than others were most often answered with reference to humoral theory, the influential framework for interpreting almost all aspects of the human body, including psychological traits and mental states.[2] Indeed, medical treatises explaining how humoral theory worked typically used hair qualities to differentiate between different complexions.

Humoral constitution, in turn, suggested methods for interpreting selfhood and interiority. Color in particular worked as an indication of one's physical constitution and inspired judgments about age, beauty, health, and emotional self-control. According to the Dutch physician Levinus Lemnius, for example, a humorally balanced body produced hair that was of a nice auburn or chestnut color, whereas differences of heat in one's constitution could generate either blacker hair, in the case of hot complexions, or blonder hair, in the case of cooler temperaments.[3] Choleric, melancholic, phlegmatic, and sanguine complexions all had distinctive hair, and, conversely, certain characteristics of hair could be read as signs of a particular corresponding temperament.

Gender and age were also manifested directly in the material conditions of one's hair. Women and young boys had less body hair than men because their bodies were governed by moistness but since the moist vapors inside their bodies ascended towards the head, they grew more head hair than men. Women's hair especially grew very long because of their moistness, whereas the heat that made men's bodies hairier overall also made them stronger and more courageous, Lemnius suggested.[4] For those well versed in humoral theory, knowledge of temperament could also suggest everyday therapies such as dietary restrictions, sleep patterns, or control of emotions, believed to counteract imbalances of humors. Such technologies of the self were intimately linked with how one understood one's identity to be humorally constituted and managed. There was no clear separation between physiological states and mental states, as both depended on the humors, and one's understanding of oneself as a person was informed in a profound way by the idea that the materiality of the humoral body, made evident in traits such as hair, governed the creation of selfhood in a physical sense.

Moreover, humoral theory offered a ready framework for reading other people's constitutions and making assumptions of their particular humoral selfhood for purposes of interaction, whether those people were complete strangers or among one's nearest and dearest. It is this understanding of the shared humoral basis of individual variation that allowed hair to mediate meanings of material selfhood and locate them in a social network of personal relationships. Hair gestured towards a fundamental physiological constitution at the heart of identity that could be used in understanding and describing both oneself and others.

Families

To an extent, humoral materiality was a product of family lineage and suggested characteristics inherited from one's parents and ancestors. Renaissance elites, in particular, seem to have taken pride in their hair when it joined them visibly together with family members and strengthened ties across generations. In early modern autobiographies, people often seem to delight in belonging to a long line of similarly colored heads.[5] For example, Edward Herbert, born in 1583, remembered his father "to have been black haired and bearded as all my Ancestors of his side are said to have been."[6] This is also the context in which Lady Anne Clifford, one of the few women of the period to comment on her own hair, introduced the subject: "never was there child more equally resembling both father and mother than myself," she wrote, adding that "the hair of my head was brown and very thick, and so long that it reached to the calf of my legs when I stood upright, with a peak of hair on my forehead."[7] While this description carries a whiff of pride that many Renaissance people could have found objectionable, Clifford mentioned her aristocratic hair as an aspect of her familial heritage, as proof or her lineage, and credit to her parents.

For other memoirists, descriptions of hair simply created textual portraits of family members. Even though we tend to assume that historical hairstyles and colors were primarily of interest to women, early modern men too were emphatically categorized through their hair: Ann Fanshawe recorded that her father had "hair dark brown and very curling, but not very long."[8] Oliver Heywood noted that his eldest brother had red hair and his youngest flaxen.[9] Hugh Cholmley, remarkably interested in ancestral hair patterns, reported that his sixteenth-century great-grandfather Richard was known as "the great blacke knight of the North" for having "his haire and eies blacke and his complection very browne." He also mentioned the flaxen and chestnut heads of his grandmother, mother, and wife, but the most intricate description Cholmley reserved for his father: "the haire of his head was chestnut browne and the end of his locks curled and turned up very gracefully, with out that frisling which his father Sir Henrys was inclyned to, his beard a yellowish light browne and thinne before upon the chinne as was his fathers."[10] While Cholmley undoubtedly aimed for accurate descriptions, the chestnut heads of his father and wife happily call to mind the superior coloring of balanced complexions in humoral theory. In this way, a family tint could suggest favorable personal characteristics and lineages fortunate not just in status but in the humoral advantages of their members.

The descriptions of family members almost always started with hair, while other features and characteristics followed after. In the Renaissance, it was customary to list human features from the top down, whether we look at depictions of actual persons or the more impersonal blazons of female beauty. But something more is going on here: hair and character were intimately linked, and few human features were as infused with affect, virtue, and power as hair. These meanings could be used to highlight the affective ties and identifications produced by family and lineage. Situating oneself within a family network was the primary context for Renaissance understandings of selfhood, and hair could work as a marker of these connections. But the emphasis on the familial meanings of hair also points to the fact that, for Renaissance people, hair was not primarily a matter of individuality but of interpersonal and kinship relations.

For Renaissance men and women, then, golden tresses and chestnut manes functioned as outward signs of both interpersonal relationships and inner humoral qualities, suggesting conceptual categories that directly informed one's understanding and presentation of the self. These qualities of hair were not just accidentally created by God and inherited from parents but also social and personal signs that needed to be deciphered and worked on. Humoral materiality, family, and selfhood were intimately linked. In this way, hair carried a much deeper meaning for Renaissance identity construction than descriptions of outward appearance would at first imply.

Nations

As discussed in Chapter Five of this volume, humoral theory was linked to climate theory. Renaissance anatomists believed hot climates would heat up people's bodies so that those living under the southern sun generated darker and curlier hair than those living in the north. While hair could delineate bloodlines, it also had wider meanings that reflected local, national, ethnic, and racial identities. Here I want to consider how women's hair particularly functioned as an indicator of national difference. In England, as in many other nations in Europe, the local climate was understood to produce especially attractive hair. This meant, for example, that English hair represented both climatically temperate and humorally balanced qualities that easily tied together with other desirable feminine traits, presented with the kind of local pride that is evident in this quotation from a play by Nicholas Breton: "for a flaxen or a browne hayre, for a chaste eye, and an honest face, for a good complexion, and a gratious disposition, I thinke all the worlde is not better prouided for good Wenches then our Countrie."[11] When national identification was negotiated through the visible medium of hair, it stressed the moderate blondness of white Englishwomen, steering clear of both the darker hues of southern people and the excessive paleness of people in cold climates. In fact, although there were national variations of these value judgments around Europe, most countries managed to explain their own typical coloring as not only the fairest but also the fittest. For some, however, hair also registered a state of decline in one's own nation. Reading signs of a moral downturn in every change of fashion, a moralist pamphleteer like Leonard Wright could lament how England was "most wildely corrupted with intollerable pride" that showed itself in new-fangled hairstyles and curled beards.[12]

The most significant carrier of hair's national meanings was the monarch, especially if she was a woman. Queen Elizabeth's reddish gold hair, which she maintained in her old age with numerous wigs, initiated a national fashion for red hair that came to be considered a typically English characteristic. Elizabeth deliberately used and manipulated her appearance, as is well known. Several foreign ambassadors reported on her hair and looks and gave the impression that the queen herself habitually joked about her appearance, thus making it a tool of international politics. Moreover, discussing the styles and colors of hair in various countries was standard diplomatic small-talk. Sir James Melville of Halhill, a Scottish diplomat visiting England in the 1560s, discussed with the queen the fashions of the countries he had traveled in, all of which the queen was familiar with. Melville described Elizabeth's own looks when reminiscing about a conversation where the queen cross-examined him not only about her own beauties but those of Mary, Queen of Scots—a diplomatic game of courtly love that Melville fortunately mastered:

> Her hair was more reddish than yellow, curled in appearance naturally. She desired to know of me, what colour of hair was reputed best; and whether my Queen's hair or hers was best; and which of the two was fairest. I answered, The fairness of them both was not their worst faults. But she was earnest with me to declare which of them I judged fairest. I said, She was the fairest Queen in England, and mine the fairest Queen in Scotland. Yet she appeared earnest. I answered, They were both the fairest ladies in their countries; that her Majesty was whiter, but my Queen was very lovely.[13]

A female monarch's hair, as indeed her whole body, signified the beauty of the nation, not just the beauty of her person.

While feminine hair on one's home turf denoted safe national values, the gaze directed at foreign parts called forth sexual undertones that seemed to color the locations with desire and danger. We can see this especially clearly in the accounts of male travelers, who recorded their impressions of foreign countries and categorized inhabitants as more or less pleasing, often hinting at the sexual components of exotic female beauty. Visited places were frequently assigned a value on the basis of the human sights they offered. German women, for example, were known to be beautiful because they all had yellow hair and were in the habit of "washing it weekly with one kind of lee and drying it in the sunne," sitting outside their doors and spreading their hair on the brim of a straw hat.[14] Venice, the sex capital of Renaissance Europe according to many observers, boasted similar pleasures, providing travelers with the sight of voluptuously blonde women who were also known to bleach their hair publicly.[15] National hair fashions played an important part in the European geography of gendered experience.

The idea that women's bodies embodied local or national character had its most curious manifestation in men's apparent habit of traveling to foreign parts expressly to gaze upon far-flung beauties. Some accounts of such practices also show significant awareness of and curiosity about women's coiffures. Edward Herbert, for example, recounts in his autobiography an episode at an inn in France, where he went deliberately to see the innkeeper's daughter, reported by his friend to be "the handsomest Creature that euer they sawe." Herbert's description of her eccentric hairdo is surprisingly exhaustive, down to the last reddish ribbon that adorned her shining black hair:

> I shall touch a litle of her discription, her haire being of a shining Black was naturally curled in that order that a Curious woman would haue drest it, for one Culre rising by degrees aboue another and euery Bout tyed vp with a small Reband of a Nackarine mixture while it was bound vp in this manner from the Poynt of her shoulder to the Crowne of her head; her Eyes which were round and black seemed to bee a Modell of her wholle beautye and in some sort of her heyre while a kynde of light or flame came from them not vnlike that which the reband which tyed vp her hair exhibited.[16]

Herbert's encounter reveals the importance of hair for experiencing places and nations. While different hair colors typified different nationalities, real-life encounters made use of a more personal and varied set of characteristics, weaving in local peculiarities and class inferences when explaining how hair was dressed and decked.

Without ever acknowledging it directly, these exchanges were racialized as strictly white and equated European hair unquestioningly with beauty. If hair could signify belonging through family allegiances, national characters, and notions of origin, it also necessarily worked as a racial marker, allowing the long and sleek hair of Europeans to manifest social power.[17] The racial import of hair becomes even clearer if we turn our gaze towards Europeans' descriptions of other racialized peoples. Travelers to sub-Saharan Africa, for example, designated the hair of locals as black, curled, and woolly and sometimes reported this in their writings.[18] Even if European visitors usually evaded direct value judgments of African hair, their descriptions resemble the ways in which disagreeable or unhealthy hair was imagined in Europe.[19]

Hair could, then, reflect national and local identities in various ways but it did so most often through displaying difference to the gaze rather than suggesting a national identity directly related to one's own hair. In a sense it was a weak signal: there was too much variation in hair color and texture within every nation to elevate it to the same level with the bodily traits that carried strong national meaning, such as skin color, a primary racializing marker in the Renaissance. Sporting the same kind of hair as others could certainly nurture some sense of belonging, and hair could help evaluate typical local appearance, but in fact Renaissance people of many nations were quite interested in foreign fashions and emulated imported new styles in order to gain social recognition. National characteristics of hair were used to construct national communities rather than national selves; here hair was a social rather than an individual marker.

HAIR CARE: TECHNOLOGY OF THE SELF AND SOCIABLE PRACTICE

Within the humoral framework, hair was seen as excess matter that was expulsed from the body through the scalp, a protective shield and a gateway between the body's inner substances and outside air. Many of the hair practices Renaissance men and women engaged in originate in these functions and they all have implications for thinking about the self.[20] It was a common opinion that combing of hair opened the pores in the skin and let out harmful vapors. Plentiful hair could stop these vapors from exiting, but hygienic practices could moderate bodily discharges. Hair offered physical protection for the self, and its manipulation created and protected the social self too. Even though hair practices could be motivated by physiological and medical knowledge, the aim of Renaissance hair care was also pointedly social and moral: the way in which hair was manipulated and cared for had much to do with good manners, and it contributed to people's sense of the status and place they occupied in the world. Hair care can be understood as a bodily technique that Renaissance men and women employed to control both their outward appearance and their sense of self. After all, in the Renaissance imaginary, the self seems to have been called into being primarily in the negative sense, as a capacity to self-discipline one's body and mind.[21] Hair routines produced the ideal gendered and self-policing body-subject, on which social status, gender structures, and Christian belief systems were continually inscribed.[22]

Femininities

While both men and women were to take care of their hair, women's hair practices were especially keenly observed, appreciated, and criticized, making femininity uniquely dependent on outward appearance and its manipulation. Feminine hair practices were viewed through a strict gender hierarchy which demanded that women display their subjection to men and to God through their disciplined hair, while it was precisely that discipline that further confirmed their need for subordination. This idea that dressing of hair was emphatically a feminine activity had a long and venerable history that went back to the Bible and the church fathers, who often equated women with decoration—women naturally decorated themselves but were also by nature decorative—and focused on female hair as a site of pride and display.[23]

Because of this ideology, teaching women the difference between socially prescribed self-care and sinful concentration on and display of the self was crucial. Juan Luis Vives emphatically defined this boundary when he argued that women were not to dye their hair but should only comb it "cleanly" and remove any "scurf." They were not to perfume their hair but only keep it from stinking, and they were not to look in a mirror in order to dress their hair but only to see "if any foule thing or vncomly be on her head that she coude nat els se."[24] Women who changed their hair through other means not only disregarded

God's wishes but were clearly displeased with themselves. Thomas Tuke in his *Treatise against Painting* (1616) mused: "she is alway miserable, that pleases not her selfe, as she is. Why is the colour of the haire changed?" His answer was that women suffered from lack of self-knowledge, or, as we would perhaps express it, of low self-esteem. Women attended to their hair in the hope that they could become someone else, someone better: "And after al this, why doth she consult with her looking glasse, but because she is afraid, lest she should be she, which she is indeed?"[25] Others thought hairdressing just took up too much time, which could have been spent more profitably in prayer; women opted for "spending an houre rather in righting the tresses of their haire, than a moment in bending their thoughts to deuotion," wrote Robert Greene.[26] According to Phillip Stubbes, late sixteenth-century tall hairdos were even a source for criminal activity: the fashion-conscious elite bought poor people's hair for a pittance or stole the fair hair of defenseless children.[27] Thomas Bentley's prayers for women asked for preservation from all occasions of sin, including "pranking, pricking, pointing, painting, frisling, & decking of my self to appear piked, feate, gorgious, & gaie in the eies of men." Arthur Dent's denunciation of pride laid special blame on women who spend "a good part of the day in tricking and trimming, pricking and pinning, pranking and pouncing, girding and lacing, and brauing vp themselues in most exquisit manner."[28]

The repetitive vehemence of these warnings may express misogynist suspicion of how women spent their time, but hair care practices did represent a real danger to the souls of the tricking, trimming, and frizzling women, according to Christian thinking. Any attempted change in one's appearance was conceptualized as deceit that hid one's true God-given identity and thus jeopardized one's salvation. God would not recognize people who had altered his creation when they came knocking on heaven's door. "Some cannot be content as God made them," wrote James Cleland, "but as though they were hudled up in hast, and sent unto the world not fully finished"; using cosmetics, brushes, and curling irons were misguided efforts to improve on God's work.[29] In this view, changing the hair betrays the deeply held, yet contradictory, Christian notion of a core self, which is at once fashioned by God and unchanging and yet implicitly unstable and vulnerable, for the smallest outward alteration could destroy it.

The sixteenth-century shift to uncovered hair, when even married women gradually started to reveal their hair when venturing out of their homes, was a key moment in hair care history, one not met with universal approval, since freely flowing hair was at this time still insistently coupled with intimate relationships between husbands and wives or the dangers of illicit sexuality. In Lewis Wager's 1560s morality play *The Life and Repentaunce of Marie Magdalene*, Mary Magdalene is tempted by Vices, who advise her on various fashion choices, including best hairstyles. Carnall Concupiscence sets her hair about her face, recommending "That all your hair for the most part may be in plain sight; To many a man a fayre haire is a great delight." Infidelitie teaches her to curl her hair with a hot needle, Pride suggests that fashionable trinkets worn in the hair will allure young men, and Cupiditie reminds her that if her hair color ever starts to fade, she could use certain waters to dye it back to yellow.[30] The potent relationship between visible hair and sexuality is brought forth here, signaling the anxieties women's hair fashions could raise in the more religiously minded. Covered hair continued to indicate modesty and chastity, whereas the new open styles could be thought to call these qualities into question, even though the bare hairstyles were not worn loose either. Braiding and gathering the hair in place could in fact be seen as representing control as much as the veiling fashions of the early decades of the period did, only in a new form.

The social and ideological significance of women's beauty was naturalized in both the substance of hair and the performative rituals of hairdressing, informing how women saw their hair. When Alice Thornton, whose own hair fell out during an illness in the mid-seventeenth century, saw her daughters Kate and Alice too lose their crowning glory as an effect of smallpox, her language stressed hair's significance for assessments of female beauty. Kate had been characterized by "her faire haire on her head" and her "beautifull complection" before her illness, and her mother interpreted changes in her appearance as a loss of that beauty. In Alice's case, she formulated her hair loss as a "favour cleane taken from her."[31] For women, long hair was a sign of both health and femininity, but femininity itself was intimately linked with the idea of bodily beauty as a predominantly female quality—or indeed a characteristic of womanhood in general.[32] The ideological nexus of long hair, beauty, and femininity constituted a base for women's identity work, then, allowing both assessments of one's own relative position in the hierarchies of beauty and practices and relationships that could advance that position.

Women clearly seem to have internalized warnings against women's hairstyling issued in pamphlets, treatises, and sermons, despite the social importance of women's beauty. Rose Thurgood's conversion narrative from the 1630s uses exactly the same vocabulary as the moralists do to condemn the women who "Crispe and Curle & Cutt their heare, buylding Towers on their heads."[33] Grace Mildmay, too, called for women to dress themselves with shamefastness and modesty, avoiding "braided hair or gold or pearl"—invoking the language of 1 Timothy 2:9.[34] Such counsel not only repeated well-known admonitions but attempted to shield women's honor and sense of self in a religous culture, where fashion was treated as a threat to both salvation and psychological health. For many Renaissance women, it was the Christian framework that guided body practices, hair practices included, and provided the self with a meaningful frame of expression. Particularly towards the end of the Renaissance, which saw ever smaller headgear and uncovered, elaborately coiffed hair,[35] adopting a modest style and hiding the hair under coifs and hats would have consciously communicated women's religious convictions and modest aspirations.

Yet some women did adopt more ostentatious styles and used hair as a vehicle for fashioning their public selves and inviting attention. Some fashionable path-breakers, such as the sixteenth-century Italians Isabella d'Este and Lucrezia Borgia, chose to display loosely bound flowing hair as a mark of their youthful purity. Even though they risked being identified as immoral, they created new possibilities for women's self-presentation by their choice of hairstyle.[36] In northern and western Europe, however, such styles were associated with the sinful sensuality of southern Europe and generally frowned upon. For an honorable lady there, control of hair was paramount: loose hair signified immorality and availability and was insistently associated with courtesans and women of ill repute. Yet Renaissance writers did acknowledge that hair fashions were also a necessary sign of rank, wealth, and family.[37] Some complained that wives cost their weight in gold—their hair needed to be adorned with pearls, aglets, and flowers—but those same ornaments also functioned as testimony to the wealth and status of the wearer's husband and family, and husbands could have strong views about how they wanted their wives to wear their hair.[38] It was legitimate for women to cherish their hair to signal their proper position, in relation to both their menfolk and their God, even if that also allowed them to display their creative talents within limits.[39] Hairstyles were meant to be socially legible, displaying and enforcing social hierarchy. Beauty, whether natural or achieved by artifice, was systematically presented, particularly, as an aid to women's social success, suggesting that improving on one's looks could result in greater emotional well-being, a significant component of a sense of self.[40] We are here dealing with a twofold notion of what a Renaissance self may have consisted of: in a theological sense, a person's self was tied to the soul and its relationship with God, while the social notion focused on one's relationship with other people and one's place in the various hierarchies of human society. Both ideas were current in the Renaissance mind-set, although individuals could and did emphasize one or the other. But in gaining social visibility and marking rank, women, particularly, risked losing their moral standing—according to moralist writers, at least. Finding the right balance between fashion and modesty would have demanded knowledge, expertise, and an acute sense of propriety.

Masculinities

Carefully drawn boundaries between the sensual and decorative meanings of long feminine hair and the physical valor and strength associated with masculine hair growth were in constant danger of collapsing when men tended their own heads of hair. To police these boundaries, male and female hair practices were insistently contrasted in Renaissance discourses, and men needed to steer clear of hair practices that carried feminine implications—as was the case with the especially piercing scorn heaped upon lovelocks, long extra curls falling over the shoulder.[41] The *Schoole of Good Manners* presented it as "clownish and unholsome" for men not to comb their hair for the sake of cleanliness, but it was quite another matter to start "crisping, curling, and laying out lockes like wanton yong women."[42] Excessive hair care threatened to effeminize men, a charge that presumed the fundamental vanity of women. In Castiglione's *The Courtier*, too, curling one's hair and picking of one's brows were womanly tricks, not to be engaged in by the proper male courtier. One of the characters states, not without irony, that it was a feminine conceit to

> carrie a mans heade very stedfast for feare of ruffling his haire, or to keepe in the bottom of his cappe a looking glasse, and a combe in his sleeve, and to have alwaies at his heeles up and downe the streetes a Page with a Spunge and a Brush.[43]

These guidelines, of course, point towards the fact that men, too, could make a show of their fine heads of hair, but it also indicates how instrumental modest hair was to the ideals of masculinity. When this started to change and men's long hairstyles came into fashion in the later sixteenth century, the gendered aspects of the newest fashions were eagerly debated.[44]

The use of hair care practices to mark gender difference intersects with ideas about age. In his 1530 conduct book for children, Erasmus delineated the bare minimum of hair care for little boys: one needed to keep one's hair clean, comb it regularly, and remove nits and lice, as scratching of one's head was not becoming. Shaking and ruffling one's hair were not courteous behaviors, and one should not keep tossing one's head to cast it back but rather discreetly use one's hands for this purpose.[45] Erasmus's advice to boys is the same as that expected of adult men. Young men, however, may have used hairstyles as a way to express generational tensions.[46] Sporting the newest cuts was a way to gain attention and emphasize their newly found manliness. When men's long hair became fashionable, it was first identified, and satirized, specifically as young men's folly.[47] "Make not a foole of yourselfe in disguising or wearing long haire or nailes," King James I counselled his growing sons in *Basilikon Doron*, "whiche are but excrements of nature."⁴⁸ Thomas Dekker's satirical conduct manual *The Guls Hornebooke*, in turn, advised aspiring young men never to comb their hair and to grow it "thick and bushy like a forrest" and as long as possible—indicating that rather the opposite would be honorable. In Dekker's humorous opinion, long hair frightens enemies and looks manly to one's friends, functions as a shield against sword strikes, warms the head like a nightcap in winter, and cools it like a feathered fan in summer. Long hair was for him a thoroughly ridiculous fashion that could be satirically justified with reference to young men's martial exploits and their attempts to gain prestige within their homosocial friendship circles.⁴⁹ Both these rather different texts were written within the conduct genre and addressed the younger generation, exposing the adult suspicion that young men were adopting hair fashions that potentially endangered the masculine, patriarchal political structures.

The challenge to the social hierarchy represented by young men growing long hair was also apparent in criticisms of apprentices and students. Authorities in the early seventeenth century tried to curb apprentices who grew their hair long by issuing various ordinances, among them the Common Council Act of 1611 which decreed that no apprentice was to "weare his haire with any tuft or lock but cut short in decent and comelie manner" or they would be imprisoned.⁵⁰ Much the same happened within the universities, where students, too, could be required to wear humble cuts, as signs of their serious scholarly status and as markers of group identity but also as a control device wielded against the young and fashionable. This could annoy the young men greatly. Edmund Verney wrote to his brother Ralph from the University of Oxford in 1635, complaining about new strictures demanding that students wear their hair short. At a time when fashionable youths boasted long hair and lovelocks, young Edmund clearly felt his fashion sense violated by the order. He hoped for an escape and asked his brother to call him away.⁵¹ Hair had great power of signification in the identity games an individual played within his community, showing the rebellion of young and subordinate men against their elders' values through their fashionable hairstyles and allowing them to use the mastery of current styles to acquire informal status among their peers. The seventeenth-century attempts at control of male hair could even suggest an emergence of a youth subculture where both belonging and difference were expressed through men's growing hair length.

Despite all of the moral and social anxieties expressed about hairstyles, the huge number of formulae in books of household recipes that contain guidance for making products related to hair suggest that many Renaissance people were profoundly attentive to their hair, or its lack. People seem to have been far from satisfied with the heads they had and fashioned their selves by changing what emerged from under their hats into blond, brown, or even black. Darker hues may have been targeted at men and women with graying hair, a sign of unwanted aging in the Renaissance period too. Perhaps even more important, however, at least in terms of the number of recipes, were concoctions for keeping hair from falling off or making it grow back when it had been lost. A number of these recipes were directly addressed to men and mentioned beards as well as hair. Both head hair and beards contributed to early modern notions of manliness; as Will Fisher has shown, facial hair in particular was "insistently mapped onto social roles like father and soldier," tying together masculinity and the wider sphere of social meanings and identifications.⁵² Baldness was seen as primarily a male problem, and so, even when male heads were not expressly mentioned, we may take most of the hair growth recipes to be providing answers for men's beauty problems rather than women's.⁵³ Depilatory creams, in turn, were suggested primarily for women, as ways of removing unwanted body hair and for raising the hairline on one's forehead. Recipe collections also gave advice on lotions that made hair curly and suggested special perfumes for hair.[54] Clearly, there was a significant demand for such recipes, emphasizing the social importance of hair as a visible and changeable sign of identity that could be fashioned to one's liking. What is articulated in the recipe literature is not just Renaissance expertise in preparing hair care products but the ways in which the materiality of the self was made meaningful for Renaissance constructions of the self. Although it is difficult to say whether the products were actually widely used, recipe collections offer a completely different view of hair care than many other sets of source material. Where moralistic texts, for example, link hair dyes and dressing to cosmetics and condemn both as pure feminine vanity, recipe collections address both genders and give no hint that the products would have been morally questionable.

Sociability

Hair could build an explicit link between oneself and others through its emotional power. Like any form of beauty, attractive hair was believed to provoke a positive affective reaction, often labeled love.[55] When Renaissance people felt drawn to each other, hair was mentioned among the special features of the beloved that incited passions.[56] Demonstrating the intricate link between hair and the self, the practice of exchanging hair as a love token showed that even when they were severed from their wearer, locks could be caressed, kissed, and dreamt about. Hair as a physical token allowed the beloved to be recalled, but it could also carry the characteristics of the person, mental as well as physical, in its texture and color.[57] Some even suggested that women combed their tresses deliberately into a shiny trap that reeled in love-struck suitors.[58] For Jane Anger, defending women against the misogynist attacks penned by Joseph Swetnam, it was clear that while women's hair invited sexual attention from men, women had little control over men's hairy desires. "If we cloath our selves in sackcloth, and trusse up our hair in dishclouts, *Venerians* wil nevertheles pursue their pastime," she wrote, hinting that women's tying up their hair or hiding it under hoods and hats worked as a conscious form of sexual control.[59] Nor was the idea of hair as an agent of emotions restricted to men's desires. Lucy Hutchinson credited her awakening love for her future husband partly to his nice head of hair: "she was surpriz'd with some unusuall liking in her soule when she saw this gentleman, who had haire, eies, shape, and countenance enough to begett love in any one at the first."[60]

Hair care practices themselves, the daily interactions of combing, dressing, and cutting hair also forged social relationships. For women, these practices were situated within the home and involved intimate relationships between women of the household, both between mistresses and servants and between women of similar status. Sociability was clearly an important aspect of these daily encounters: women had fun by curling, braiding, and setting each other's hair and shared their attempts at new styles. While men thought these pursuits an insignificant waste of time, for women they represented a way of sustaining friendships and intimate networks.[61] The vocabulary of such practices was indeed deemed so important that it was even expressly taught in language manuals. Peter Erondell's guide to the French language instructed Englishwomen on how to survive their daily hair care sessions with maidservants in a different language, providing them with expressions for dandruff and combing cloth as well as impatient commands and reproaches.⁶² For the lady, Erondell seems to have thought, the everyday ministrations of maids could present many reasons to be dissatisfied, even when traveling to the allegedly elegant neighboring nation, but his model sentences also testify to the importance of hair care's beauty routines in Renaissance social life. Setting of a lady's hair by a servant was an occasion in which her rank was performed and made manifest. It also represented an intimate episode in which her bodily needs were catered for and her social persona created. Such scenes were also depicted in Renaissance art and drama.

Although a mistress of the house was expected to act as its well-groomed representative, not all women treated their appearance as a constituent of their identity. Some shunned practices of care and aspired to what they thought were higher goals. The biography of Elizabeth Cary, Lady Falkland, paints an almost comic picture of a woman whose carelessness over her appearance was remedied only by affectionate and helpful maidservants. For Lady Elizabeth, "dressing was all her life a torture," although she endured it to please her husband. Yet

> she was not able to attend to it all, nor ever was her mind the least engaged in it, but her women were fain to walk round the room after her (which was her custom) whilst she was seriously thinking on some other business, and pin on her things and braid her hair; and while she writ or read to curl her hair and dress her head.⁶³

Even for Lady Falkland, braided and curled hair worked as proof of her high status, so her own disregard for her appearance made her maidservants try that much harder to provide what was expected. One wonders whether Lady Falkland actually used her impatience with hairdressing rather cunningly to express herself and manipulate her husband, for whom it seemed to matter greatly what she looked like. What is more important for us here, however, is the portrayal of her servants, ever vigilantly guarding her appearance and making her look presentable. Lady Falkland herself was also represented as picking and choosing her servants so that they would be experts on fashion practices while also complicit in her eccentric reading habits.⁶⁴ For working women, expertise in hair could be a marketable professional skill.

The barbershops where men had their hair done in fashionable styles offered other health and beauty services, attending to nails, teeth, and blood-letting, and acted as centers for male sociability. Margaret Pelling suggests that one could enjoy "music, drink, gaming, conversation, and news" in the barbershops which sometimes even doubled as brothels.⁶⁵ Men frequented these establishments especially in larger towns, even though they were also much satirized for it. The figure of the "carpet knight" was evoked to describe them: as the chief care of these gallants was to trick themselves up, they wasted time consulting their mirrors and their barbers who curled, powdered, and perfumed them to rectify their "native nasty sent."⁶⁶ According to critics, "barbing" was a "noble science" that spawned such brave innovations as the French, Spanish, Dutch, Italian, and the new cut, all different shapes for fashionable beards.⁶⁷

Although depictions of everyday bodily practices often reach us in a somewhat distorted form, through censure and ridicule of religious moralists, people needed to pay attention to their hair, if not for the sake of their appearance, then for health reasons. Whether performed by servants, personal barbers or the professionals of a barbershop, the shaping of hair offered a possibility to fashion both one's inward self, implicit in the health effects of hair care, and one's outward appearance, a manifestation of a desired personality. For men and women both, the persona called forth through hairdressing was always created within a social network that made reference to age, status, and fashion. Hair was a key ingredient of both cleanliness and beauty and allowed Renaissance people to manipulate their outward appearance to suit the identities they aspired to. Hair was not simply recognized by others as belonging to a specific person, it was actively treated by both individuals and groups as a means to express identity and achieve or retain status. Observing the Roundhead fashion for short hair, for instance, Lucy Hutchinson thought the Puritan style "ridiculous to behold" and completely ill-suited for her Parliamentarian husband Colonel John Hutchinson, who had a fine head of thick hair that she much appreciated.[68] He was not fully recognized by his own party, however, as "the godly of those dayes, when he embrac'd their party, would not allow him to be religious because his hayre was not in their cut."[69] Haircuts worked both as willingly chosen signs of social belonging and as a control device a group enforced on its members. Individual negotiation of these meanings could be challenging, even if the ideological content referred to by the cuts remained much more important than its outward signs. Signifying several identity categories at the same time, hair materialized gender, age, and status, and even political loyalties, and allowed them to be performed and articulated in everyday life.

CONCLUSION

The categories we should think about when trying to grasp the social significance of hair are various and sometimes conflicting. Hair was a religious and moral issue, with slightly different implications for men and women. Renaissance people acted as innovators or followers of fashion, when they wanted to gain visibility or merge into their surroundings, and they could display their ideological and religious leanings through their hairstyles. Hair materialized gender in a physical way and allowed men and women to perform gender in their everyday lives, but hair also extended its reach of meanings to the very heart of the gendered structure of the social. Beauty practices allowed men and women a different set of spaces and relationships, and hair care also represented an area of expertise and knowledge. Hairstyles were relentlessly policed by other people, particularly in the case of women appearing in public. Hair embodied status, both through the style one adopted and the choice of ornaments.

People often would have negotiated many of these social categories at the same time when dressing their hair, but they also help us outline how social categories themselves were upheld and reshaped with the help of hair practices and ideologies. The meanings of hair were both individual and social. Hair functioned as material for self-fashioning for Renaissance men and women, but it was also cultural material that was used to negotiate hierarchies and relationships between different kinds of people. Often these social hierarchies, relationships, and allegiances were deemed to have overriding importance, while individuality was only an emerging concern, mediated through the complex set of more fundamental social and cultural discourses, such as patriarchal ideology, humoral theory, and Christian symbolic practice. On the other hand, if indeed there was a slow but profound shift in perceptions of individuality on the way during the Renaissance, as many have suggested ever since Burckhardt, perhaps hair could be seen as one of the many sites in which contestation over the issue occurred. The appeal of hair fashions and practices points to an acute awareness of how a sense of self could be fashioned through manipulation of the material body. The vigorous attempts to curb fashionable hair practices, in turn, work as evidence of an intense campaign to control self-presentation and self-fashioning, often taking its cue from religious teaching and viewing individuality as potentially threatening to the Christian community. Both stances suggest the problematic nature of the self in the Renaissance. Hair practices and discourses represent a grid of social power that both conditioned Renaissance selves and provided techniques for the cultural construction of bodies and identities.

CHAPTER THREE

Fashion and Adornment

CAROLE COLLIER FRICK

When charting a coherent path through the historical fields of material culture, one must proceed mindfully as most practices are local and dependent upon custom, class, and geography. Therefore, generalizations can be tricky. For example, due to climate, hair and headwear in northern Europe were more covered than in the south, and because of closer human interaction, fashion innovations were seen first in the cities of western Europe and appeared at a slower pace in the less-populated areas of the east. Between 1450 and 1650, new styles were introduced, influenced by dramatic changes in society and culture during the Renaissance, including New World contact, the ascension of Charles V as Holy Roman Emperor and King of Spain (thus combining both areas under one powerful ruler), and a middle class that was growing throughout Europe. The effects of Protestantism and the edicts of the Council of Trent were also strong forces in reining in fashion flamboyance and replacing opulent jewelry for the hair with veiling and lace.

The Renaissance saw some fashions highlighting the hair, but the primary focus of fashion was on covering up one's unruly hair, which made headwear the key to an individual's fashionable identity. Plucking a woman's hairline back can be seen all though this time period and in the early to mid-fifteenth century in the north, women of fashion could shave their foreheads and even their eyebrows, while the rest of their head remained covered. These practices allowed more skin to be seen, which perhaps was part of the allure of such artifice, when human flesh among the elites was not generally visible. Toward the 1480s young women wore chin-length sections of hair ironed into loose waves or curls at the sides of their faces, a style that would inspire hair fashions in the early seventeenth century. Strawberry blonde hair was considered the most desirable color in Italy and elsewhere, and images from the time period show Venetian women (especially courtesans) lightening their hair (with lemon juice) by sitting out in the sun with their hair spread out on a large straw "*solana*" worn like a crownless hat, this lightened hair would be twisted up into the stylishly coiled horns (or *corne*).[1] Yet much more than having a particular hair color or hairline, to have fashionable hair meant hair that was under measured control and covered by a variety of forms of headgear that functioned with the hair. Although studies have been done on the history of hairstyles sans hats, hoods, and headdresses, the actual look of a person's head would have been dominated not by the length or appearance of their hair but rather their fashionable headwear.[2] A range of hairstyles was worn in this time period which allowed for the realities of individual hair types, but for women, two general trends that can be identified are the center part as well as the fashion for decorative braids. For men, fashionable hair was cut above the collar and beards and mustaches were rare.

Given the wide diversity of social and cultural influences in hair and head adornment, in this chapter, I will move from a discussion of covered hair, where fashion focused instead on the head *coverings*, to uncovered hair, where fashion was more about adorning the visible hair itself. Here, I will take a broadly chronological/geographical approach to discussing fashion innovations and overall trends in this era, beginning in Italy with the universal *cappuccio* in the 1450s and ending in 1650s Britain.

RENAISSANCE ITALY

By the last quarter of the fourteenth century, the cultural changes in late medieval society that had incubated in the city-states of the northern part of the Italic peninsula beginning with Petrarch would become what is now known as the Renaissance, defined by its appreciation for the urban values of classical civilization. While Petrarch had expressed his passion for the world of ancient Rome in his dogged collecting of antique pre-Christian manuscripts, the more secular European society that followed saw the advent of the *studia humanitatis*, or the study of the humanities. This new focus on human beings as part of the natural world had an impact on how people conceived of their identities, less through the "*vita contemplativa*" of the medieval period and more through the "*vita attiva*." In the city-states of Italy, echoing the influence of the ancient values of proportion, balance, and moderation, men and women would express their physical appearance differently from their predecessors in the medieval period as well, creating a newly engaged, less exaggeratedly-dressed "civic" populace.

On the Italian peninsula by the mid-1500s, an urban elite had emerged alongside the noble ranks with the money and relative freedom to sport their own style of adornment from head to toe. Hair and headwear now suited a person's social and political agenda. If clothes "made the man," then his *head* allowed him, briefly, to speak. Hair on men was worn neatly cut above the shoulders and turned under in a "pageboy" shape, whereas curly hair was trimmed up even shorter. A bowl haircut with the hair shaved at the back of the neck for men was considered stylish. Shorter hair and shaven faces signaled male engagement in human society; therefore, by 1450 in artwork beards denoted foreigners from the East. Distinctive hats and headwear were important in all Renaissance cities, where some scholars have located the signs of a nascent early individualism.[3] In Milan, a ruffian (or an enemy) could be fined five lire for pulling a man's hat off his head ("*pro descapuzando*").[4] In Rome, the papal tiara was a metonym for overarching power, while in Venice the doge was distinguished sartorially by his unique humped cap. In Florence, which presented itself as a merchant republic, hats were meaningful for politically active men as distinguishing marks of subtle individual style, as on their bodies they all dressed as one, wearing an unadorned dark toga in public.[5] Hats were also symbols of power for those costumed for specific professional office. The *pileus rotundus* was a round cap edged with ermine (sometimes called a *rolled hood*) that served as the identifying badge of a graduate in law or medicine as university statute required.[6] The four-cornered hat worn by clerics was known as "*a quattro canti*," while the "*tondo*" was a round, flat-brimmed red beret worn by *condottieri* in power, and the slashed hat "*a tagliere*," was sported by the doge (like the ambassadors of Venice) when at home.[7]

Hair, especially for men, looked remarkably egalitarian—a simple covering for the head upon which to place ones identifying headgear. Giorgio Vasari, the first Renaissance art historian, tells a story about the importance of hats over uncovered hair in the early sixteenth century. He writes that Botticelli played a practical joke on a student, one Biagio, who had painted a copy of his life-size tondo of a Madonna and eight angels. Botticelli had already brokered its sale for six florins, and the student was bringing a buyer to Botticelli's workshop to see it. As a prank, Botticelli and another student "made several paper hats (like the ones the citizens wore) which they stuck with white wax over the heads of the eight angels that surrounded the Madonna." When Biagio and the buyer came in

> Biagio looked up and saw his Madonna seated not in the midst of angels but in the middle of the councilors of Florence, all wearing their paper hats! He was just about to roar out in anger and make excuses when he noticed that the man he was with had said nothing at all [being let in on the joke beforehand] and was in fact starting to praise the picture ... so Biagio kept quiet himself.

The student subsequently accompanied the buyer to his house, where he received his six florins for the painting. When he got back to the shop, Botticelli and his other students had removed the hats, "and he found [to his amazement] that the angels he had painted were angels after all."[8] Evidently in Renaissance Europe, hats, not hair, conveyed male identity and were thought to be powerfully transformational.

The new currents in Italian urban society eventually worked to convert fundamentally functional objects of material culture into newly individuated personal expressions for men, and a clear declaration of societal place for women. In this society still favoring covered hair, at least a dozen varieties of headgear were fashionable, and no adult was considered completely dressed without their headwear in any European city of the time. While politically important adult males wore the same formal cloak or *cioppa* in the public streets over their sleeveless mid-calf or shorter *"lucco,"* a plethora of creative headgear was generally available. Various head coverings for men, which for example appear in family log books, were the *berretta, cappello, cappellone, cappuccio,* and *ghirlanda*. The hats "like the ones citizens wore" in Vasari, were undoubtedly *cappucci* (also known as *chaperone* in the north).

It has been observed by students of dress that male costume in a republic (such as Florence declared itself to be) tends to be similar to one other, for fear of otherwise resembling a hierarchy.[9] When everyone dresses more or less alike, they publicly proclaim their allegiance to whatever group's uniform they are wearing and also declare sartorially to share in its beliefs.[10] This carefully crafted image of an egalitarian society was eloquent in its intended message of the underlying unity of the merchant elite. However, citizens were generally anxious to eschew too strict a limitation on this uniform. The faces of men depicted in paintings are clearly portraits of individuals and many of them have further distinguished themselves by wearing headwear of different types.[11] One writer on dress has suggested that covering the body completely with clothes, in essence hiding the body, has the effect of authorizing the mental over the physical, the upper regions of the body (the brain) over the lower corporeal concerns, the spiritual over the physical.[12] While dressed essentially alike, any localized element (such as a hat and accompanying hairstyle) would serve to draw attention to itself or to that part of the body. Thus, subtly, both individual style and distinctive headwear could highlight the particular male citizen's face and such hair as was visible.[13]

Uncovered hair in public was viewed as a state of incomplete dress. From the fourteenth to the fifteenth century in Europe, the *cappuccio* was the style of headwear that acted as a transitional piece in fashions for the head. Figure 3.1, a terracotta bust of Lorenzo de'

FIGURE 3.1 *Lorenzo de' Medici* (1478/1521), probably after Andrea del Verrocchio and Orsino Benintendi. Painted terracotta, 65.8 × 59.1 × 32.7 cm. Samuel H. Kress Collection, National Gallery of Art, Washington, DC. 1943.4.92.

Medici, probably after a model by Andrea del Verrocchio (1478/1521), shows the de facto leader of Florence in the republican toga and *cappuccio*.[14] With his somber eyes and chin-length, blunt-cut, straight hair and headgear, he is portrayed as the quintessential male power of the city. Verrocchio's depiction of Lorenzo also clearly shows the three discrete parts that composed the *cappuccio*. First, there was the *mazzocchio* (in France the *bourrelet*), a cork roll padded with cloth that circled the head and was closed and lined on the top, providing the wearer with a basic head covering. The second part was the *foggia* (or *gorget*) the piece of fabric anchored under the left side of the *mazzocchio*, which hung to the shoulder, slightly shielding the whole left side of the face. The *foggia* was a new feature of asymmetrical style which had been unseen in the public costume of the previous century. It certainly added a bit of *élan* which relieved the monotony of the long plain cloak. The third aspect of the *cappuccio* was the *becchetto* (in the north the *liripipe*), a doubled strip of the same cloth on the *right* side of the face, which reached all the way to the ground. Lorenzo winds the *becchetto* around his toga, to hang down on the right side.

Both men and women of the upper ranks could wear the *cappuccio*, which most often was fashioned of the same fabric as the toga or cloak, so as to create the unified ensemble look of the earlier hooded cloak (but with more panache) and still completely cover the hair. As one upper-class woman wrote to her husband, she needed a new *cappuccio* if she was going to have a new cloak made, because one could *not* wear an old *cappuccio* with a new cloak.[15] This leads one to believe that, early on, the fashion was for the two garments to match; perhaps this is why this type of headwear was made by the same tailors who would be crafting the cloaks, instead of hat-makers.[16] Decorative paintings on mid-fifteenth-century marriage chests literally bristle with *cappucci*.[17] Narrative scenes show the various elements of this head covering being worn in a variety of ways. One young man pictured at a wedding party (in an apparently festive state of *joie de vivre*) has tied the end of the hanging *becchetto* of his yellow *cappuccio* in a large imposing knot in front of him. Another has casually tossed his blue *becchetto* over his shoulder.[18] Some men wound and tucked the long *becchetto* and shorter *foggia* around the hat form, creating a turban-like hat which allowed ease of motion and greater convenience. Covering the hair in such a way certainly made a powerful statement that highlighted the head in an exotic manner and conveyed a sense of activity and motion about him. Other less active folk wore the *becchetto* or *liripipe* casually folded over a bent arm in front of themselves, or threw it over their left shoulder. The multiple ways of wearing this element thus afforded the wearer a certain sense of personal style, which would have immediately conveyed individuality to the viewer.

Cappucci had practical social functions as well. In the urban realm, to salute a person of superior rank on the street a man pushed the *cappuccio* slightly up on his forehead with a deferential gesture, without actually raising it.[19] The *cappuccio* was also worn differently in public by women. A woman of the upper ranks could *shield* herself visually in a rapid veiling technique when encountering a man in the street, if need be, by pulling the *foggia* on the left side across her face with her left hand. Thus, this element could serve as a public cover. For a fashion statement, a rich woman's *cappuccio* could also be decorated with delicate gilded metallic ornaments, like the "*tremolanti d'ariento dorati*" recorded in a family log book.[20] The *becchetto*, hanging long from the right side of the *cappuccio*, eventually got in the way of expediency. It was too fussy for the "active life" increasingly valued in the urban milieux, so accommodating tailors detached its long drape from the *cappuccio*, instead providing the wearer with a *becchetto* that was essentially a separate stole to be worn thrown over the shoulder for a bit of urban sophistication.[21] This did reveal a bit of the hair; however, the volume of this luxurious hat still dominated ones look.

Theorist of costume Quentin Bell has written about the desire of important people wanting to command public space with garments and headwear that are large and imposing, and we do see this extravagance on portraits of kings and military leaders. Hair was not considered able to accomplish this end on its own. But there are always limiting factors as to how far fashion can go (imposed by the dimensions of the human body) before becoming ludicrous, and therefore the small *beret* and the Spanish *toque* will have their sartorial moment beginning in the first third of the 1500s, as we shall see.[22] These styles of hats would reveal the hair more than had the *cappuccio*, but the emphasis in fashion was still firmly on the hat. Italian sumptuary legislation from 1625 put limits on headwear, allowing a person to possess no more than twelve hats, and they could not be embroidered in gold, silver pearls, or silk. What was permitted was felt or wool. Also permitted were feathers, plumes, and flowers on a headband but worth no more than ten scudi, still a good amount of money.[23]

Throughout the Renaissance in Italy, headgear for women covered the hair to reflect their social role as the chaste wives and daughters of powerful families crucial to the reputation of the lineage. For a married female member of the elite ranks in this period, hair in general was visually absent in a proper ensemble, part of the moralistic dictum for the "good wife" to remain invisible while in the public realm; hair was completely covered and under social control. Variations of the *cuffia* (Juliet cap), *sella* (saddle-shaped headdress), and *balzo* (bulbous headdress) are testament to that. These types of headgear could be worn in a wide range of combinations as well, depending upon the inventiveness of one's tailor (for *cappucci*) or headdress maker.

A wife covering her hair signaled discipline and the understood acceptance of her husband's authority. Therefore, perhaps, women of the upper ranks were given even more styles of headwear from which to choose, including the *balzo*, *berretta*, *cappellina*, *cappuccio*, *corne*, *cuffia*, *ghirlanda* (or *chaplet* in the north), *hennin*, and *sella*, and later the *gable hood* and *French hood*. The *sella* was a padded, large headdress that could sit atop veiling or even a *cappuccio*. It had been popular in the late medieval period not only in Italy but France and Germany as well and was considered an outlandishly shaped style of headwear. The *sella* prompted San Bernardino of Siena to berate women with devilish comparisons to their inner natures, and he took issue with the twisted up conical "horned" hairstyle (*corne*) popular with women of rank, with courtesans, and later with women identified as witches, likening all these women to owls.[24]

Uncontrolled or unkempt hair was seen as a symbol of outsider status or of being less amenable to social norms than the good, dutiful citizen or wife. Only those partially or wholly excluded from acceptable human contact—hermits, the mad (or those crazy with grief), witches, criminals, and prostitutes—would have long hair and a bare head, all associated to differing degrees with animals or uncontrolled emotionality. But children's hair was also more visible than adults, for they were legal outsiders due to their tender age. Throughout Europe, boys and girls were dressed in smaller versions of their elders' head ornaments, headdresses, and caps, so headgear for children lent a degree of control to the hair while still leaving it visible to the viewer. The hair on young women was partially obscured with sheer veils or small caps. Popular in Lombardy, for instance, was the *coazzane*, a long single plait of hair wrapped in ribbons worn down a young woman's back … one long braid, only seen on nubile girls.[25] These hairstyles were then displayed in profile or three-quarter-view portraits, to gaze at, at one's leisure.

The role of the hair and headdress in establishing a young woman's wealth, status, and desirability is visible in Figure 3.2, *Portrait of a Lady in Red*. Here, the severe profile portrait of a serious young woman in her late teens with a very stylish plucked hairline pictures her wearing an elaborate pearl-embroidered *cuffia*. The overall red-flowered design created by the embroidery is spectacular in enhancing her gown of the most expensive crimson dyestuff of kermes.[26] Fifteenth-century profile portraits of young women often depict such exquisitely embroidered *cuffie* with pearls and wound thread, gilded or silvered. With a basic cap that would have been fashioned by a female *cuffiaia*, her hair is covered but enticingly still partly visible.[27] Headwear also included beaded tiaras, hair extensions, and the head brooch ("*brocchetta di testa*"), tiara or diadem.[28] Craftswomen could specialize in headdresses for special occasions, the magnificently embroidered *cuffie* and *balze*, and complicated hair and head treatments such as the *vespaio* (an intricate hairpiece that could be interwoven with pearls, beads, ribbons, and braids) and the head garland, or *ghirlanda*.

FIGURE 3.2 *Portrait of a Lady in Red* (ca. 1460–1470). Oil and tempera on wood, 42 × 29 cm. Florence. © The National Gallery, London. NG 585.

The sartorial and hairstyling presentation for elite women from prominent families became particularly important on their wedding day and intimately involved the approval of the patriarch of the family, as parading the women gloriously outfitted accrued to familial honor. A woman of the upper ranks on her wedding, the *one* day she assumed a vital public role in visually representing her family, was also allowed headwear that was individuated. As this link was new and therefore fragile, brides were permitted to wear their finery for a limited time after their wedding as well, but in general, distinguishing hats/headdresses on women were reserved for public ceremonies celebrating rites-of-passage only and then immortalized in paintings from the era. In general, however, these wedding-day hairdos were not "fashion"; they were costume. The formal hair treatment for public display on unmarried girls often took the place of a hat or headdress and was loaded with artifice. The young woman was turned into someone else on her wedding day, a symbol of the unity of two lineages. This was not about expressing herself. This was a sartorial duty call.

Nuptial hairdos often highlighted the young woman's head by adorning the top of her central hair part with the large head brooch which could include other single strands of pearls (*frenelli*) draping over her hair. The *frenello* could also be worn as a headband around the top of the forehead, formed of pearls and woven with gold or silk "hair," often forming a point at the middle of the forehead. Another style was a woven braid of small pearls set in gold, then worked back into the hair, or worn around the border of a *cuffia*. From the 1490s, the *ferronnière*, that consisted of a simple headband of thin leather or cord with a small jewel such as a garnet set in the center, was popular in Lombardy. The portrait in the Louvre known as *La belle ferronnière*, attributed to Leonardo da Vinci (1493–1494), shows this fashion. In addition to a young woman's own hair, false hair pieces (*cappelli morte*) could be added, giving the wearer an extra volume of hair at the back of her head, all of which would then be completely covered with decorative nets of silk and false braids set with precious gems.[29] Nothing was too extravagant for the public display of the nubile women from families of the upper echelons of society.

Women did not abandon head fashions upon marriage. In the 1550s, Eleonora da Toledo, the style-setting Spanish noblewoman and daughter of the Viceroy of Naples, brought her own personal hairdresser with her when she married Cosimo I of Florence. As she matured and had children, her hairdresser created hairstyles for her that were always simple and elegant and influenced Florentine style, with her center-parted, shoulder-length hair held back in a metallic, pearl-embroidered snood.[30] Meant to keep long female hair under control, the snood was a bag-shaped hair covering that could be made of net or fabric and be worn beneath a hat. Depending on social rank, the snood could be very plain or highly decorated. This hair device came in many styles and was also known as a "*caul*." Eleonora's head jewelry included earrings, which were seen on Gentile women beginning around 1525 and could have been part of the larger "ispano-moresco" trend in influential Italian dressing practices.[31]

Coming to terms with the ongoing phenomena of new styles in hair and headwear (that is, the emergence of "fashion") had the sumptuary police continually on alert, as the acceleration of change in dressing practices was a new development. A very elegant style headdress (the *balzo*) was popular from the first half of the fifteenth century (when it completely covered the plucked-back hair) to the mid-sixteenth century (when it moved back on the head to show curled hair around the face). Titian painted such a headdress in his *Portrait of Isabella d'Este* (1534–1536) (Figure 3.3).[32] The *balzo* foundation was formed of a light willow frame, then covered with silk and embellished with braids of hair, either real hair or colored silk, and often further adorned with pearl trims, ribbons, or a brooch. The inventiveness of shape, material, color, and detail in these formal hats and headwear can be seen in a wide variety of visual evidence from Renaissance Europe. These basic shapes could be combined with others to form unique head coverings. Europe-wide, the shapes of headwear for women reflected their public role: while the *cuffia* was girlish and coy, appropriate for nubile young women, the *balzo* could resemble a halo, perfect for the wife and mother whom humanists saw as the moral exemplar for the family.

NORTHERN EUROPE

If coverings for the hair were essential in Italy, the same was even more true of northern Europe, where everyone wore a hat in public. In England it was against the law for men or women to appear without their heads covered; hatless folks could be fined up to a week's wages for an infraction. For women in Burgundy, France, and England, a version of the head covering called the *vespaio* in Italy was known as a *crespine*, originally a thick hairnet or snood. This then evolved into a mesh of jeweler's work that confined the hair at the ears on the sides of the head and was worn by women of the upper ranks.

FIGURE 3.3 Titian, *Portrait of Isabella d'Este* (1534–1536). Oil on canvas, 101.9 × 64 cm. Kunsthistorisches Museum, Vienna.

The *crespines* would have been attached to a narrow headband of fabric or metal that could sit on the head like a small crown. This headband was known as a *fillet* or *coronet*, and extended to the *crespines* on either side at the ears.[33] The practice of symbolically protecting a woman's ears from loose talk in public was common from the medieval period until about the last thirty years of the sixteenth century, with ear coverings that were more constructed in the north and diaphanous in the south.

The court of Burgundy was considered the *sine qua non* of sophisticated European elegance and the dramatically extravagant headdress known as the *hennin* was associated with this court, as well as that of France, Poland, Hungary, and even Britain in the mid-fifteenth century. The *hennin*, which had many shapes, could completely conceal the hair. Embroidered with pearls or covered in brocade to match or complement the gown, it could be a twelve- to eighteen-inch cone, or a flat, truncated cone such as we see on Mary of Burgundy in Figure 3.4, a rounded beehive shape, or a divided design such as the butterfly or horned *hennin*.

The hat foundation was made of wire mesh or heavy paper. Divided *hennins* often looked similar to the *sella* seen in Italy and France. Trailing from the top-most point, called the "steeple," gossamer veil or veils covered the ears and could be further elevated by wires extending from the tip of the hat in an inverted "L" shape. On Mary we see the

FIGURE 3.4 Master of the Legend of Mary Magdalene, *Mary of Burgundy* (1457–1482). Oil on wood panel, 26.5 × 22.5 cm. Musée Condè, Chantilly.

padded roll (called a *"bourrelet"*) encircling her head and adorned with *crespines* that cover her ears and are held in place by three decorated fabric strips that match her gown of expensive crimson silk. A diaphanous veil frames her face, and a long, light-red ponytail of hair hangs loose down her back from the top of the hat. There was often a cloth *lappet* or *frontlet* at the center of the *hennin* covering part of the brow.[34] This short loop on the forehead was used to move the *hennin* forward or just keep it on one's head. Later *hennins* featured brims that turned back, or were worn over a hood with a turned-back brim.

Linen veils that framed the female face and covered the hair were ubiquitous in all ranks of society in northern Europe, especially in the Netherlands and the Germanic lands of the Holy Roman Empire. The wide variety of veils available would have signaled social class immediately to the viewer by the quality and quantity of cloth and value of the pins anchoring it. The finest linen available to the rich was from the city of Rheims. From thick and concealing (the neck-covering *wimples* of lush, heavy linen) to almost transparent in quality, veiling provided not only warmth but also a flattering light color of cloth next to the face. Headbands, head circlets, head brooches, or simple pins were all used to hold veils in place. Veiling often was semi-circular in shape, with the straight edge falling on either side of the face and the curved edge brushing the top of the shoulders.

FASHION AND ADORNMENT 63

The veil could be made of two layers of white translucent material; one could be short, ending at the back of the neck, while the other fell onto the shoulders. As well, a head veil could fit over the crown of the head or be wired to stand up stiffly in a horned shape ("*a corne*") similar to the divided *hennin* that extended the shape of the head, and draped from the back. As we have seen, veils could then be combined with more structured head coverings like *cuffie* and *hennins*, to cover the ears.[35]

In Britain, the small and compact *gable hood* or headdress, the *French hood*, and the heart-shaped *attifet* covered women's hair, and appear in portraits from the sixteenth-century court of Henry VIII and later. The *gable hood* or headdress was a stiff, close-fitting headpiece with a raised border at the front hairline and a point in the center (like the gable of a house). It was popular at the British court (1480–1550) for women of all ages. The decorated side panels over the ears could be shaped into *crespines*. Figure 3.5 shows the *gable hood* on Lady Margaret Butts, painted by Hans Holbein the Younger in about 1541–1543. This style had a veil at the back and over time became a complex box-shaped structure stiffened with buckram that could have two conical veils hanging on either side of the face, as seen in a portrait of Elizabeth of York by an unknown artist from around 1500, now at the National Portrait Gallery in London. The *French hood*, on the other hand was a small hood on a stiff foundation worn on the back of the head, revealing a bit more hair.[36] Anne Boleyn is credited with introducing the *French hood*

FIGURE 3.5 Hans Holbein the Younger, *Lady Margaret Butts* (about 1541–1543). Oil on panel, 47.2 × 36.9 cm. Isabella Stuart Gardner Museum, Boston.

into England. During her stay at the French court in Paris as a girl, she had adopted this continental style, and continued to wear it upon returning home. The front border, fitting close around the head, was curved forward on either side to end over the ears, the hair being exposed above this limit only. The back of the crown of the *French hood* was shaped into a horseshoe-shaped curve over the head. Pearls or jewels that decorated the edges of these hoods were known as *"billiments"* and could match the ornamented borders of a woman's gown.[37] Anne's forerunner, Catherine of Aragon, painted by Hans Holbein as a young woman in 1520, also wore the *French hood*. *French hoods* were seen in portraiture for about sixty years, from 1520 to 1580 and were one of the longest-lasting types of headwear of the sixteenth century. With these headdresses, hair tended to be very plainly arranged: parted in the middle and smoothed to the sides of the face with rigid control. Even curly hair was pulled tight to the head. Here too, only "loose" women were portrayed with loose hair.

Later in the century, as hair began to again emerge in public, middle-part hairdos mimicked the shape of the *attifet*, with the hair that framed the face rolled tightly to each side of the part and pinned back under a hat or head ornament. The *attifet* was similar to the *French hood* but was heart-shaped rather than rounded, having a point in the middle that came down onto the forehead. *Attifets* worn by widows were usually black. This taste for shaping various female parts into heart shapes can be seen in corseted dresses of the time as well.[38] The *attifet* appears in portraits of Elizabeth I of England. A portrait of the very blonde Anne of Austria, Queen of Spain, by Coello from 1571 shows her wearing a small velvet *toque* with ostrich plume over her heart-shaped, center-parted hair, and a 1575 portrait (after Clouet) of Louise of Lorraine, pictures this wife of Henri III of France with her center part adorned at the hairline by three large tear-drop pearls, part of a rich jeweled headpiece.

For European men during the High Renaissance and the Baroque (1500–1650), the ups and downs of contemporary politics were apparent in new ways of dressing that became popular and were depicted in paintings of the powerful. King of Spain and Emperor Charles V's personally conservative taste in clothing and hair favored sober black velvet or woolen cloaks and felt hats, his dark hair cut very close to the head, with neatly trimmed beard and mustache—undeniably influencing male dress in this time of conflict, especially in the popularity of the color black among the elites of the military and the professions.[39] After 1524, men in power wore a trimmed beard (*barba*) or goatee and mustache (*pizzo e baffi*) to accentuate male virility (newly in vogue in dress), which was also signaled by the appearance of the prominent codpiece in the first full-length portraits of state.[40]

Beards varied in shape, from the "square beard" worn by Henry VIII in England to the full "bush" beard, the long and rounded "sugar-loaf" beard, the "forked" or "swallow-tail" beard, and the full "cathedral" beard associated with clergymen and sported by Scottish reformer John Knox. Beards in general were under regulation in northern Europe, with long beards not allowed in courts of law. The truly fashionable man trimmed his beard short. One especially short beard was the French "marquisette," cut close to the face. A short beard that came to a point could be called a "spade," a "stiletto," or in France a "pique devant." Short beards required upkeep and could be dyed, waxed, powdered, or even starched and curled, perfumed beards becoming current among urban men of fashion.[41]

For the head, it was the *beret* that found favor with those men in power, a style that exposed the hair, kept short and closely clipped.[42] The combination of short hair and

FASHION AND ADORNMENT   65

small hats is evident in the many portraits of Henry VIII of England among others. In Figure 3.6, the future Henri III of France wears the *beret*, which was also prominent on the Swiss Guard at the Vatican. By the first third of the sixteenth century *berets* became popular among the rich bourgeoisie as well. At the beginning of their popularity, sumptuary legislation from Brescia in 1503 had attempted to squelch this style by limiting the fabric of which they were constructed to wool and the style to the local. Eventually, however, the *beret* became popular Europe-wide and came to be made of felt due to the impermeability of this fabric. In 1515, even a small *beret*, however, still needed roughly 1½ yards of cloth to fashion.[43] Even though hair was exposed to sight, it was not the focus of visual display. In Henri III's case, the ostrich plume and jeweled trim on his velvet *beret* captures the viewer's eye, while his high tight ruff obscures his short beard. The fashion of the early to mid-sixteenth-century demanded tight styles of clothing and close-fitting headwear to enclose and contain one's physicality.

The Protestant Reformation made itself felt with changes to hair fashions, headwear, and dress rather dramatically in the last decades of the sixteenth century, changes that continued well into the first half of the seventeenth century. The influence of the Council of Trent (1545–1563), Catholicism's response to the Reformation, altered dressing practices with the repression of bodily display that came to characterize the period. Female fashion became totally enclosed, in keeping with the new orthodox principles set

FIGURE 3.6 *Portrait of Henri III before his ascent*, attributed to Jean de Court (1530–1584). Oil on panel, 35 × 25 cm. Musée Condè, Chantilly.

out by the church, and hair in general was pinned into submission and much less adorned except in royal portraits—a little hat on the back of the head serving as decoration. Formal female attire in portraits was now rendered in strikingly independent parts. Women in painted depictions became geometric images, with cone-shaped skirts held rigidly in place by the *guardinfante*, an understructure of wooden circles connected with laces or wire. Flat bodices, tight sleeves, and high-ruffed collars (called *lattuga* or *gorgieri* in Italy) were closely fitted, as seen in portraits of the Spanish upper nobility.

Figure 3.7, the portrait of the Spanish infanta Catalina Micaela by Coello (1585–1599), shows how ruffs originally prompted the balance of smaller headwear. The small Spanish *toque* sat atop a pinned-up mass of exposed curly hair echoing the fussy design of the ruff.[44] For older women, stiff linen head coverings with lace (to go with large ruffs or wide lawn collars) which exposed curly lightened hair became the height of fashion in the early 1600s, whereas younger women had the little velvet *berets* and *toques* often with feather plumes.[45] In Protestant Europe, the jewels in the hair seen in the Italian Renaissance were replaced with lace (*pizzi*) and embroidered linen as ornamentation, demonstrating the virtue of the "substitution of the dignity of handiwork for the luxury of jewels."[46]

Eventually, fashions in hair and headwear changed for both men and women. The tight-fitting fashions and closely cut hair and beard for men of the earlier sixteenth century were loosened. Women in general still covered most of their hair with headwear and veils in their portraits, and eventually for both genders, neck ruffs were supplanted by simpler lawn collars (sometimes trimmed with lace), which led to the appearance

FIGURE 3.7 Alonso Sanchez Coello, *Catalina Micaela of Spain* (1585–1599). Museo del Prado, Madrid.

of the "pilgrim look" in portraits. Hair for men was left longer, beards and mustaches less rigidly trimmed. Large hats with upturned brims ("*a falde*") were favored by some, especially in informal settings. Initially characterized by a rounded crown, this headwear was also known as a *cockel hat* or traveler's hat. Some were worn cocked at an angle, whereas others sat squarely on the head. The wide brim was used to keep the sun off ones face and could be adorned with a shell to denote the traveler's pilgrim status. At mid-century these hats assumed the form of a tall and rigid dome or were round and soft, known in Burgundy as "sugarloaf hats."[47] The large hat later became known as the *capotain*, worn by both men and women.[48]

In Figure 3.8 we see a stylish young Rubens who has painted himself and his wife Isabella Brandt from ca. 1609; she sports the *capotain*, which almost completely covers her hair, and he a goatee and mustache with short curly brown hair. From the end of the sixteenth into the mid-seventeenth century in England and Protestant Europe, the *capotain* became a tall-crowned, narrow-brimmed, slightly conical hat with a flat crown at the top (sometimes called a "flat-topped hat") often black and was worn by men and women.

The later *capotain* and the term "roundhead" were especially associated with Puritan Oliver Cromwell in England in the years leading up to the English Civil Wars and during the Commonwealth. The term "roundhead" came from the style of hair worn by some Puritan men. Cut close to the head in front and on the sides, parted simply in the middle, hair was left longer in the back. This distinctive hairstyle set them immediately apart from

FIGURE 3.8 Peter Paul Rubens, *Self portrait with Isabella Brant, his first wife, in a Honeysuckle Bower* (ca. 1609). Oil on canvas, 178 × 136.5 cm. Alte Pinakothek, Munich.

the noblemen, who had begun to wear their hair longer and curled. "Roundhead" appears to have been first used as a pejorative term at the end of 1641, when parliamentary debates incited riots between the Puritans and the noble "Cavaliers." An anonymous primary source from 1611 noted that most of the Puritans had their hair cut short, above their ears, and therefore were given the pejorative nickname of "roundheads" when they demonstrated in the streets of Westminster.[49]

In the latter part of the sixteenth century, in northern Europe and to a lesser extent in Italy, very curly or even frizzed light reddish-blond hair became commonly seen in paintings. The hair itself became fashionable, perhaps influenced by the stylish leader and most-depicted woman of this century, Elizabeth I of England. By the end of the century, shoulder-length loose curly hair, seen here in a Rubens portrait of the dashingly handsome First Duke of Buckingham from ca. 1625 (Figure 3.9) became stylish for men and women, a trend that would continue into the seventeenth century. Hair for women was seen uncovered in portraits and continued apace with wildly curly updos and jewels set within or hats perched jauntily atop. Both men and women were wearing their hair long and flowing, hair again emerging as its own strong statement of identity. By the 1630s, long curled hair with the *capotain* was worn casually for hunting and riding by everyone but also was seen in formal portraits, such as Anthony van Dyke's portrait of Henrietta Maria of England (1633). The so-called "Van Dyke" beards or goatees and mustaches became the arresting symbols of the age for hair, as seen in Van Dyke's painting of Charles I of

FIGURE 3.9 Peter Paul Rubens, *Georges Villiers, First Duke of Buckingham* (ca. 1625). Oil on canvas, 65 × 50 cm. Galleria Palatina, Pitti Palace, Florence.

England at the hunt from two years later (1635). In the eighteenth century, wigs replaced hair for those of the upper ranks—the ultimate in hirsute artifice.

CONCLUSION

Fashionable hair had the potential for transformation and re-invention during this period of change, where some have seen the emergence of the individual. Hair went from covered to uncovered, straight to curly, under strict control to gently tousled by the breeze in portraits "al fresco." But what did this mean? Where one *had* been privileged to view female hair in abundance and unconstrained by a headdress throughout this entire period was in depictions of iconic biblical figures or in imagined mythological figures, such as Botticelli's *Young Woman in Mythological Guise (Simonetta Vespucci?)* ca. 1480–1485 (Figure 3.10). Here a young female in three-quarter view is shown with her wild, exotic strawberry blond hair in an elaborate hairdo composed of false hair interwoven with red velvet ribbons at the crown that extend to the nape of her neck. A loose net of braids and pearls is fitted over the top of her head, thicker braids interwoven with more pearls, and knotted tassels (*nappe*) of false hair adorning her hairline to frame her face. Flamboyant hair displays in artwork were also seen on crazed or disgraced biblical woman, such as a distraught but penitent Mary Magdalene or a frenzied Judith decapitating Holofernes

FIGURE 3.10 Botticelli, *Young Woman in Mythological Guise (Simonetta Vespucci?)* (ca. 1480–1485). Tempera on wood, 82 × 54 cm. Städelsches Kunstinstitut, Frankfurt am Main.

(as in Artemisia Gentileschi's *Judith* [ca. 1620] in the Pitti Palace in Florence). Such hair was emotional, pictured uncovered, flowing, luxurious, and sometimes adorned. In these fascinating images, an array of hairpieces, extensions, and adornments such as head brooches could be viewed in detail. One can only imagine a viewer's affective response and even amazement at such images. However, in the real world, hair and headwear could not be extracted as separate pieces of the fabric of material culture. Only by donning headwear on top of the hair did fashionable people regard themselves as dressed and able to participate appropriately in society. Hair with headwear signaled the wearer's civic engagement and political or religious allegiance, class status, family lineage, and cultural attachments. Cultural practices were organic, and changes, including the uncovering of the hair, came only gradually. The Renaissance arguably injected a new energy of individualism into European society; however, this interest in the all-too-visceral world of humanity needed to be cloaked in a palatable manner in order to be accepted by all. Hair was too potentially disruptive to be completely freed from convention just yet.

CHAPTER FOUR

Production and Practice

ANNEMARIE KINZELBACH

The previous chapter has shown how Renaissance art suggests that hair mattered. Portraits of kings and dukes, queens and duchesses document a variety of hairstyles, while portraits ornamenting books and manuscripts, the side altars and niches in churches, and the walls of castles, palaces, and city houses reveal the hair shaping the faces of gentry or established burghers.[1] All these pictures imply that such hair—from the precise cut of the beard and hair to ornamental styling—cannot have been achieved without effort and experience. In this chapter I will trace European sources providing clues to the related hair-styling practices and practitioners, explore the professional work offered by bathmasters or barbers, and survey places where hair was done, while considering attendant issues of public and private space.

In 1500, the self-portrait of Nuremberg citizen and artist Albrecht Dürer (Figure 4.1) depicted his hair with artful curls and layers of golden color and his face adorned by a twirled mustache and a well-trimmed beard.[2] Comparable works of art suggest that in large parts of Renaissance Europe, the creation of such elaborate hairstyles was neither a

FIGURE 4.1 Self-portrait by Albrecht Dürer (1500). ©Bayerische Staatsgemäldesammlung. http://www.pinakothek.de/albrecht-duerer/selbstbildnis-im-pelzrock. Alte Pinakothek, Munich.

specifically male activity nor limited exclusively to artists but involved both sexes. Artists may have adorned the hair and hairstyle in portraits intentionally in order to follow conventions, fulfill representative functions, or to satisfy their patrons.[3] Yet written sources from totally different contexts provide proof that the techniques they represented were used throughout the early modern period. Despite the prevailing plainness of shorter haircuts for men in many English portraits during the century following Dürer's self-portrait, ornate beards continued to prevail in England and Europe. Indeed, the pamphleteer Phillip Stubbes's criticism of English women suggests that strenuous endeavors to improve their natural hair continued for women as well:

> Then followeth the trimming and tricking of their heades, in laying out their hair to the shew, wich of force must be curled, frizled and crisped, laide out, (a worlde to see) on weathers and borders, from one eare to another. And least it should fall down it is vnderpropped with forks, wiers, and I cannot tell what … Then on the edges of their bolstered hair (for it standeth crested round about their frantiers and hanging ouer their faces like pendices or vailes, with glasse windowes on euery side) there is laide great wreathes of gold and siluer curiously wrought, and cunning-applyed to the temples of their heads. And for feare of lacking any thing to set forth their priede withall, at their haire thus wreathed and crested, are hanged Bugles, (I dare not say Bables) Ouches, Ringes, Gold, siluer, glasses and such other childish gewgawes, and foolish trinkets besides, which for that they be innumerable, and vnskilfull in womens tearmes.[4]

At the end of the sixteenth century, this moralizing critique lists the manifold ways of manipulating the hair of women in order to display it artfully, including the volume-extending use of supporting devices and the often complicated interweaving with decorative objects. Stubbes mentioned, for example, wreaths made from gold or silver, brooches, and black pearls. His written description even outclassed the artful hairstyle of earlier decades shown in the "Portrait of a Young Woman" in Figure 4.2.

Clues to elaborate work with hair can be found in this portrait of an Italian woman (Figure 4.2) depicted by Sandro Botticelli in the latter fifteenth century: braiding, binding, and adorning with pin-pearls, laces, combs, and hairpieces are obvious. During the sixteenth and early seventeenth centuries, even artists who often depicted women with covered hair or plain braids still reserved for female members of the nobility representations with elaborately adorned hair.[5] No woman would have been able to achieve such a complicated hairdo by herself; it must have been the result of cooperation with others. This conclusion corresponds with the results of recent research underlining how the everyday cooperative work of women ranged from daily chores, such as caring for children or preparing precious food, to arrangements directing future politics. The localities identified for such activities were bedrooms, chambers, or closets, places where hair care took place.[6] The following section will provide evidence for homes functioning as space for practices of hair care.

DOING HAIR IN THE HOUSEHOLD

Stubbes's moralizing pamphlet on manners in late sixteenth-century England provides clues to the household as a place where women engaged in work particularly focused on hair. His critical remarks even imply the fabrication of hairpieces or wigs in the

FIGURE 4.2 Sandro Botticelli, *Portrait of a Young Woman* (ca. 1480). Tempera on panel, 48 × 35 cm. © Gemäldegalerie Staatliche Museen Berlin, Preußischer Kulturbesitz. Photo: Roberto Contini, http://www.the-athenaeum.org/art/detail.php?ID=34947.

household.[7] According to Stubbes, English women had several ways of acquiring the necessary additional material: they bought hair from animals and dyed it, and richer women convinced the poorer to cut and sell their beautiful, "fair" hair. Stubbes even accused "nice Dames" of luring children with "verie fair hair" into their houses in order to deprive them of their natural gift for the promise of a penny.[8]

The early modern household as a space for practices of hair care and hair styling also comes to the fore in recipes gathered by women (and men). Current studies highlight the contribution of gentlewomen and female members of the high aristocracy to the practice of early modern medicine in activities such as gathering recipes and preparing remedies by various techniques.[9] Moreover, early modern women have become renowned for their knowledge of beauty secrets.[10] Men also were interested in such know-how. This is underlined by the manuscript recipe collection of Count Palatine Ludwig VI, written between 1570 and 1572 and containing twenty-four prescriptions referring to hair.[11] Here, men and women contributed: the first ten formulas, for instance, name Countess Palatine Katharina, Countess Juliana Nassau-Dillenburg, Count Palatine Ludwig VI, and Count Palatine Richard Palatinate-Simmern as sources of information.[12] The processes suggested, of course, include the preparation of substances for washing and swathing (i.e. wrapping with a damp cloth) the hair and head. Instructions for regular bathing and rubbing with ointment extended the care to the whole body. Other recipes connected the body's outside and inside by combining washing and drinking. More specific amelioration for hair can be found in prescriptions for changing the color or shape through cooking, distilling, and burning of herbal substances, and mixing herbal liquids, dairy products, animal, and inorganic substances. This is illustrated in the way the count's compilation establishes basic expectations, such as regaining a healthy scalp and getting rid of pests in the hair. Healing the *erbgrind* (lit. inheritable dandruff, scab, scurf) was a main concern. One of the treatments suggests, for example, applying an ointment prepared from alant roots and butter, after washing the head and hair in a decoction from oak and elder leaves.[13] The suggestion to dissolve alder-ash in water as a means of getting rid of "hair mite" is described as a traditional remedy, coming from "old art fiches" (i.e. paper slips containing ancient medical advice).[14] The fight against head lice was to be won by anointing the hair with rue crushed in oil in a mortar.[15] Aesthetics were a concern as well: to make hair grow on bald patches the Countess of Nassau-Dillenburg suggested a succession of local applications, first a mixture of "foam from small fishes" with honey, then onion water.[16] Other prescriptions from other information sources served to speed up hair growth, to curl hair, or to change the color. The color-focus was on *"Gelb Haar"* (yellow hair). One easy-to-prepare mix contained nettle-roots in detergent as a coloring washing fluid, while an alternative more time-consuming method recommended cooking the roots of burdock in detergent, washing the hair in this liquid, drying it, and then wetting the hair several times a day with a brush moistened in the washing liquid.[17] The beauty recipes also included concoctions that removed hair. A simple one advised the individual to mix the seeds of nettles with vinegar and rub the mixture on the hairy skin; the result was described as "hair comes off."[18]

A preoccupation with healthy and beautiful hair was not limited to the noble household. This is illustrated by the manuscript of a German school teacher named Johann Bützel from Augsburg. In 1565 he compiled his notes, which contained information similar to the duke's manuscript. Bützel even started with recipes against similar vexations of scalp and hair, but he delved deeper into questions of making hair grow thickly or beautifully and described more methods of coloring by adding blackening and browning substances.[19] Moreover, authors of published vernacular medical advice books promised help for similar and even more hair-related concerns. The latter becomes obvious in popular herbals.

Hieronymus Bock's (1498–1554) books, for example, described the effects of herbs and included among them the hair-related properties of plants. This botanist, physician, and minister's herbal was reprinted and edited copiously throughout the sixteenth and seventeenth centuries.[20] Some of Bock's prescriptions differed from the count's collection, as illustrated by the following examples: sage cooked in water and used as washing lotion was said to blacken the hair, banish mites, and heal scabs, and a plaster made from mustard seeds and vinegar, Bock suggested, would eliminate white scab, a sign of leprosy.[21] The nobility were still addressed in his dedication to a Palatinian countess—Elizabeth (1503–1563), wife of Palatinian count Ludwig II of Zweibrücken and count Georg Simmern—despite such plain ingredients, and Bock did not refer explicitly to other readers, unlike Lonitzer, writing one generation later. Adam Lonitzer (1528–1586), physician and high-school teacher in Frankfurt, published his first German herbal in 1557. For more than two hundred years (until 1787) a continuous flow of new editions and reprints appeared.[22] These books provided more details on hair, which could be found easily because he listed thirty-five references to hair-related content in the index. In his sixth revised edition of 1578, Lonitzer aimed at a broad public and named explicitly the *"gemeinen Mann"* (common man) as recipient.[23] This fits nicely into what recent studies have found more generally for medical advice literature.[24] Bookplates reveal that, indeed, citizens acquired such books. In 1579, shortly after appearing in print, a copy was marked by a juridical doctor and his wife for "domestic use."[25] The household of a jurist, however, did not represent exactly the common lot but was part of the elite in cities.[26] The social exclusiveness represented by the owner of this copy is no coincidence. Among the published procedures for preparing herbal remedies, including the ingredients for hair care, quite a number required refined equipment, complex chemical procedures, or even a garden full of exotic plants.[27]

PROFESSIONAL EQUIPMENT AND KNOWLEDGE

Many processes concerning hair and beards suggested in advice books consumed a great deal of time and energy. Additionally, recipes required expensive substances, such as cinder of asphodel roots, or equipment, such as distillers, not to mention the basic provision of water and heating material.[28] It then was a general advantage to live in cities and towns, where water supply was an essential part of politics. Nevertheless, high costs for having a water tap in the house forced poorer people to carry water from public fountains to their homes.[29] An increasing demand for heating material, especially for wood, caused prices in the sixteenth and seventeenth century to rise.[30] These factors limited the number of persons who could heat water at home. Moreover, costly objects could represent precious everyday commodities for the most basic practices such as combing, cutting hair and beard, as illustrated in Samuel van Hoogstraten's (1627–1678) *Tromp l'oeil* in Figure 4.3.[31] Here Hoogstraten depicted scissors, a razor, a comb, and a lice comb on the same level as a precious medallion, the book he had authored, a gold chain of honor, the

FIGURE 4.3 Samuel van Hoogstraten (1627–1678), *Tromp l'oeil Still Life* (1666–1668). Oil on wood, 63 × 79 cm. © Staatliche Kunsthalle Karlsruhe.

gold coin he had received from Emperor Ferdinand III for his artistic achievement, and other things of specific personal value. I do not suggest that the artist wanted to depict things that were equally cost intensive but rather that his intention was self-representation and an allusion to vanity.[32] What I want to underline is that scissors and razors were expensive items that not everybody could afford to own. Obviously, neither were ordinary items, such as nails and knives, because they were not included in the early modern lists of fixed prices. Their processing demanded even more skillful labor than the production of a good hunting knife, for which a *"Tax-Ordnung"* (list of fixed prices) set a value worth eleven days of a workman's wage in the 1620s.[33] Since a workman spent almost all of his income on food, for him buying these devices was beyond reach.[34]

It was not just elaborate styling and procedures that had to be mastered, nor that costly equipment had to be acquired. Discourse concerning hair was related to specific knowledge and experience—expertise increasingly claimed by emerging professions. As illustrated above in the case of Lonitzer, medical doctors published compilations covering relevant items. Yet their offer of guidance went further and resulted in cooperation and competition with the "artisans of the body."[35] The transcendental meaning of hair is discussed in previous chapters, here, I wish to show that even basic practices, like washing and cutting hair, were seen as complicated processes which demanded specific skills and medical knowledge.

The precise instructions in early modern calendars illustrate how general rules were constructed as a cultural frame for everyday life. They assisted or were intended to assist the forming of individual behavior and social and communal life.[36] Figure 4.4, which is part of Jeremias Brotbeihel's calendar for February 1561, illustrates the traditional and complex interrelation between macrocosmos and microcosmos in such prognostic devices.[37] The small symbols accompanying each day included advice for political and economic practices and personal relationships as well as suggestions for common chores, like changing clothes and clipping fingernails. Text and signs for February 5, for example, indicate that there will be wind and that this will be a good day to send messengers, to start as a journeyman, to render accounts, and to do business in general. In addition to such general rules, scissors opened downwards or upwards signal how to handle hair. Hair cut on February 5 (scissors pointing down) would grow slowly, with the same prognoses for two other days, February 9 and 11. The tips of the scissors pointing up on February 19 signaled a day which was ideal for a cut, when men or women wished that hair should grow fast again. Brotbeihel also recommended eight specific days for taking a bath. Practices in baths, for example soaking or sweating, usually included the washing of the hair at the end of the procedure.[38] The suggestions for bath days reveal the tight intertwining of body and hair care with prophylactic health measures. The author generally combined taking a bath and cupping, this method of removing small quantities of blood was considered an important means to achieve a balance of humors. Moreover, on February 3 and 19, Brotbeihel augmented these procedures with prophylactic bloodletting and suggested another seven occasions for therapeutic bloodletting. Seven bath days in February, additionally, were associated with a positive prospect for taking medication.

Brotbeihel's combination suggests that this calendar was aimed at a diverse public. Only wealthy readers could afford the procedure in their homes, usually in separate building facilities for bathing, which included an attending barber (and a medical doctor). Among particular communities, the inmates of monasteries definitely resorted to such private services as diaries reveal and so did inmates of hospitals.[39] Governors in

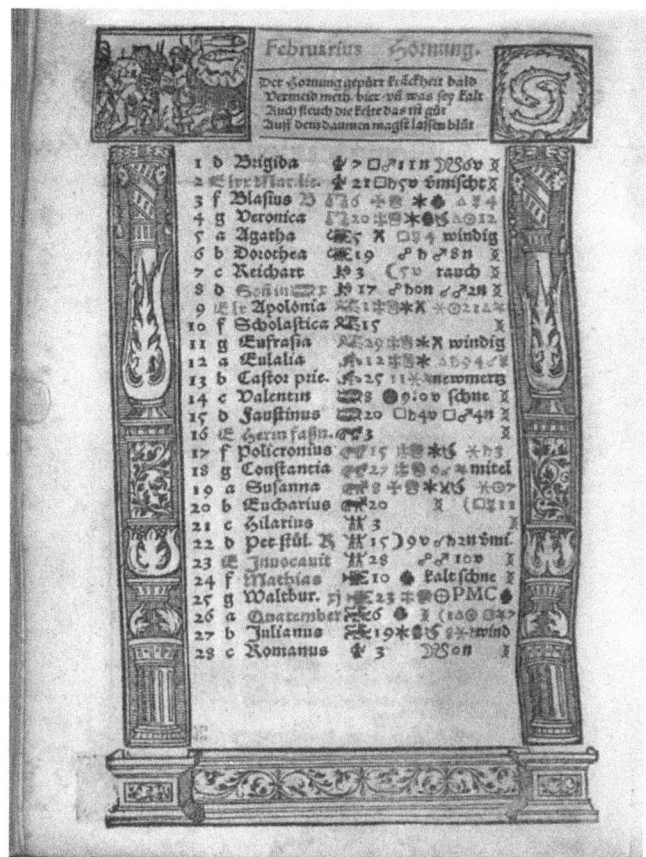

FIGURE 4.4 Jeremias Brotbeihel (publishing 1529–1562), Calendar (February 1561). © Creative commons Bayerische Staatsbibliothek VD16 ZV 2544, urn:nbn:de:bvb:12-bsb00087945-0.

cities, however, were rather reluctant to allow the construction of private baths because governors anticipated fire hazard and competition with public baths.[40] Owners or tenants and visitors of public baths represented another part of the intended readership of the calendar. Cheaper and much simplified versions of the discussed booklet were printed on broadsheets. While the making of Brotbeihel's calendar was directed towards a literate public, the system of signs could also serve for instructions of illiterate persons. A reduced number of the signs (as shown in Figure 4.4) was used in calendars which presented the prognosis for one whole year in just one sheet. The printers of these broadsheets explicitly addressed persons who "did not understand to read."[41]

These reduced calendars may have been hung in public baths where they could have helped patrons to memorize the prohibited and sanctioned days at a glance, though such recommendations seemed to vary. Often sheet and booklet calendars were written by specifically appointed physicians, and, therefore, they represent a tendency to provide information in parallel with an attempt to shape cultural habits.[42] Moreover, for physicians who often produced whole series of calendars, these offered excellent opportunities for self-promotion.[43] A comparison over time and regions suggests that recommendations for bathing (and, therefore, washing hair) and for cutting hair varied. For example, only fifteen years after Brotbeihel's calendar appeared, a medical doctor in Zürich suggested three days less bathing for February 1577 and also reduced the recommendations for cutting hair. In Bohemia the prognosis for February 1605 limited the monthly bathing frequency to two days. At the same time, the author suggested more days—three, rather than two—for cutting hair that should grow fast and limited those aimed at slow growing hair to two.[44] By the later seventeenth century, the differentiation between fast and slow re-growing hair or even the topic of hair generally began to vanish from calendars.[45] In many cities this change in published prognosis for hair is accompanied by severe conflicts between bath-masters, barbers, barber-surgeons, and surgeons, which ended in their corporative separation even where they had continued to represent a joined art. The "artisans of the body" offered all hair-related services in noblemen's and citizens' homes, in hospitals, or in their barbershops and public bathhouses or spas. Most of those living in cities and bigger towns and owning a workshop or running a bathhouse were organized in guilds, in the Holy Roman Empire they had to belong to a corporation even if it was that of painters, butchers, or merchants. The history of (forced) reunion and repeated separation between these artisans is accompanied by evidence for a crisis of public bathhouses. The crisis was one of an established profession and, of course, did not develop uniformly in Europe.[46]

PROVIDING HAIR CARE IN PUBLIC BATHHOUSES AND BARBER SHOPS

Public bathhouses had become abundant in late medieval cities and towns; very low fixed prices for services and the habit of giving *"Badgeld"* (bath-money) to servants, journeymen, and paupers suggest that even poor people could afford to visit these public facilities.[47] Contrary to generalizations, bathhouses did not disappear but remained important in towns and cities of the early modern Holy Roman Empire. Jeremias Grienewaldt (1581–1626), historian and Carthusian monk, exemplifies how imperial citizens took pride in "their" public bathhouses. In his description of the imperial city of Regensburg he mentioned "six beautiful and much frequented public bath-houses, which all are vaulted, the floor and benches built from beautiful smooth and polished white stones, to which no blood, sweat, or filth will adhere."[48] Members of the elite and the poor continued to participate in ritual and hygienic practices.[49] Governors felt responsible for these spaces because they ritually united potential adversaries in local politics. Moreover, they bridged private and public spheres by rituals such as the *"Hochzeitbad"* (marriage bath) to which groom and bride, separately, invited their families and friends as part of the wedding ceremonies.[50]

The set prices for services offered in bathhouses suggest that early modern contemporaries did not distinguish among washing and cutting hair or practices like cupping; though today we might consider the latter more medical or cutting more refined, in this period the respective compensation was set equally. Despite continuous price increases during the sixteenth and seventeenth centuries, hair care in these facilities was affordable for a town's or city's more humble inhabitants, such as the *"bettelvogt"* (beggars' officer) and his family; even paupers and orphans were provided with access to such services.[51] No information on place and practice, which are related to hair, are given in such and other governmental rules or the statuaries for the trade.

Questions concerning settings and spaces for practices of hair care have to be answered by drawing from other sources far flung from those of the profession. They come from chronicles or from texts produced within varying contexts of civil life, such as contracts, inventories of baths, governmental interventions, or publications on health-related properties of bathing.⁵² In 1514 the Elsassian Franciscan, humanist, and poet Thomas Murner (1475–1537) published a pastoral text in which he described Christ as bath-master/barber and the penitent sinner as his client.⁵³ In illustrated poems that explained each step in a bath, Murner transformed each detail in the mundane scene into a specific scene of penitence. The work starts with the call of the master who announces that the bathhouse was ready, then describes the arrival of the client, his disrobing, and so on, and ends with his dressing, resting, and returning to the family's home to have a festive meal. Comparable to Figure 4.5 Murner confronted seemingly real procedures with Latin quotations from the Bible in the margin. In Figure 4.5 Murner set a quote from Judas Maccabeus, "*Et imposuerunt cineres capiti suo*" (the origin of the proverb, "to wear sackcloth and ashes"), parallel to German rhymes under the heading "washing the head." The link between the Bible and practice in the bathhouse was ash, for in Maccabeus's version, penitents put ash on their heads (1 Macc. 3: 47).⁵⁴ Ash is used for making soap and lye water, which in this woodcut is standing in a tub at the client's right leg and has been prepared in an earlier scene by

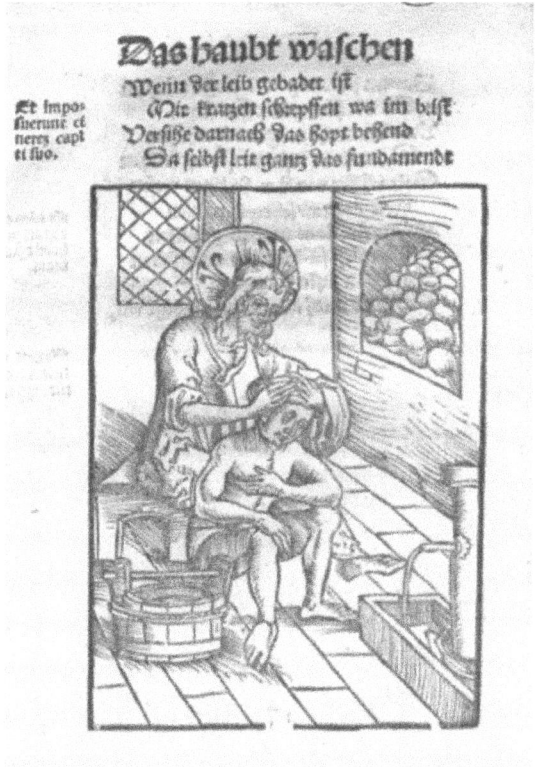

FIGURE 4.5 Thomas Murner, *Ein andechtig geistliche Badenfahrt, [...]* (1514). © Creative commons Bayerische Staatsbibliothek Schweinfurt, Bibliothek Otto Schäfer OS 0463, urn:nbn:de:bvb:12-bsb00083105-1.

Christ, the bath-master. Cleaning was the main concern of such preparations. We have seen above that contemporaries expected additional effects from mixtures of different ashes and other ingredients; these included making hair grow, repelling mites or lice, and healing diseases.[55] According to the illustrated and rhymed German text, washing the head with water and lye was a fundamental procedure which followed bathing the body, rubbing and slashing the skin, and cupping.

The standard for a bathhouse, though seemingly simple in Murner's image, would require rather high initial investments. Despite scarce evidence of exact values, sources such as chronicles, transaction minutes, or other public records in local archives suggest the investment of 5,000 florins, which in 1597 amount to an equivalent of about five estates with houses, stables, sheds, and planted gardens or vineyards in the Swabian region.[56] In Figure 4.5 the stones in the oven allude to a steam bath, and the running fountain underlines how provision with fresh water was important for these facilities, a need that hardly was met by a drawing well. Moreover, building a fountain was expensive, as illustrated in a contract for the renovation of a brazen standpipe and lead water pipes between the plain water bathroom and the steam bathroom in 1581. The eighty-five florins for the plumber come up to a quarter of the price paid for the house in which the *"Steinbadstuben"* (room for a stone or steam bath) was installed.[57]

Some physicians and moralists, especially in France, underlined the danger of prostitution in bathhouses and wanted to get rid of them.[58] Yet in other parts of Europe public bathhouses were regarded as prestigious facilities. What is said above about calendars underlines the health-preserving effects attributed to what was later considered as mere hygienic and aesthetic services.[59] Where bathing was judged as a means of prophylaxes or cure, the governors were ready to invest. A large number of cities and towns proudly offered bathhouses with specific health-related qualities inside the walls or in territories close by. Often physicians received remuneration in money or an appointment when propagating these houses.[60] From the sixteenth to the eighteenth centuries, various contracts, inventories of baths, fiscal requests, and advice literature document premises which encompass big gardens and either several buildings or multistoried houses. Even in rather small imperial towns several public bathhouses offered their services inside the walls. During the second half of the sixteenth century, the government of Überlingen, for instance, had all facilities renovated or rebuilt, including steam and tub baths for just about 4,000 inhabitants. The water flowing in the biggest public bath was tested, and a published medical certificate testified positive effects on the kidneys, bladder, and stomach. This property included a tree and herb garden and buildings which integrated a steam bathroom, two water bathrooms, and three boilers to fill fifty bath tubs. A separate story and four heated rooms were furnished with rocking chairs for slow adaptation to lower temperatures and for relaxation after bathing. The buildings also housed the barber and his family.[61]

During the early modern (and late medieval) period, barber-surgeons offered to cut hair and beards outside bathhouses—in their own shops or in the clientele's homes. So, in German-speaking regions the topic of hair occurs in ordinances in the context of professional differentiation: "shearing dry" could become exclusively the right of barbers in shops or in private homes, whereas bath-masters were allowed to provide the services of cutting hair and beards only in bathhouses. Such differences, though part of the trade's *"Ordnung"* (statuary), were not fixed but negotiated again and again.[62] In 1568 a seemingly fixed professional differentiation is given in the illustrated description of all *Stände auff Erden* (ranks and professions on earth) by Hans Sachs and Jost Amman.[63]

PRODUCTION AND PRACTICE

The pictorial representation of the *Bader* (barber or bath-master) showed this character in a bathroom wearing a bath cloth and applying cups. The rhyme describing his offer to "rich and poor" included washing hair and body and most practices aimed at cleaning the humors, such as slashing the skin in order to open the pores, sitting on an oven bench to provoke sweating, and finally letting blood.[64] In the same book, the *Balbierer* (barber, barber-surgeon, or surgeon) was depicted in fashionable breeches and doublet, a man cutting hair in a pleasant, flower-decorated, big-windowed room, while in the background his apprentice was washing the hair of a customer. Figure 4.6 shows additional allusions to medical tasks: the wall and table display basins, a knife indicates bloodletting as a prophylactic and therapeutic measure, various bandages in the window would treat wounds and bone injuries, and instruments and pots on a shelf point to other medical practices. These are directly announced in the rhymed text (Figure 4.6): "I ... can make many beneficial ointments, [can] heal fresh wounds ... fractures and injuries [ulcers], [can] heal the French disease, remove the cataract, cure gangrene and extract teeth. And of course, barber [i.e. shave], wash hair and head, and cut hair, and I like to let blood."[65]

FIGURE 4.6 Barber-surgeon from Hans Sachs and Jost Amman, *Eygentliche Beschreibung aller Stände auff Erden [...]* (Frankfurt, 1568). © Wikicommons, File De Stände 1568 Amman 057.https://commons.wikimedia.org/wiki/File:De_St%C3%A4nde_1568_Amman_057.png.

The inclusion of the French disease in the list in Figure 4.6 is misleading because persons suffering from disease which contemporaries considered as transmittable were excluded from public shops.[66] Barber-surgeons (and physicians) cured these in separate houses.[67] Since the Middle Ages, the exclusion of diseased persons from public manipulations with hair is explicitly mentioned. In 1463 the statuaries of barbers in Frankfurt, for example, determined that "no master or his servants should shear [shave the beard or cut hair of] lepers" but should rather denounce those who transgressed the rules of separation. Lepers were provided with their own bathhouses equipped with separate instruments; the governors appointed barbers, barber-surgeons, or surgeons for their services. During the sixteenth century, imperial cities in general also banned persons suffering from the French disease and "open sores" from baths and defined instruments used for them as contaminated and not fit for public use. Increasingly, rumors spread that persons had been "infected" with diseases in public baths or in barbershops by contaminated cups, knives, or benches. Generally, hair was considered to be a dangerous waste material comparable to blood. The same paragraph of the mentioned statuaries in Frankfurt required that blood and hair should be carried outside the city walls each evening and dumped into the river.[68]

LEARNING AND WORKING AS AN "ARTISAN OF THE BODY"

In general, a multitude of statuaries, rules, and ordinances for barbers and barber-surgeons testify to the public interest in their practices. Comparable to the governance of other artisans and trades, most regulations for barbers and barber-surgeons concerned the relationship between barbers and governors, hierarchy and interrelation in corporations, differentiation and quality control, other professional standards, and issues of social security.[69] In some places, public safety, especially fire hazards, was a specific point: the barber guild provided water vessels for drenching fires.[70] Early statuaries and ordinances often provide no information on education and training of barbers. Most details come from later ordinances, from biographies, contracts, court records, testimonies, and so on. Mobility was a main precondition for gaining professional knowledge. Individuals and governors agreed that the art was learned by observing what other masters did in other places and by participating in their work.[71]

Where guilds influenced the trade, as for example in imperial cities and towns, the minimal number of years for apprenticeship varied between two and three years, not ruling out that individual apprentices contracted for seven years. There, apprenticeship was always only the first step towards the profession and a precondition for service as journeyman. In northern Italy, in contrast, the apprentice stage was less precisely defined and fused with the status of journeyman. A fusion of services as apprentice and as journeyman is documented for England, as well. In 1605 in Norwich an ordinance set "the space of seven yeares at the least" as service time for an apprentice before he was allowed to open a shop, the same was stipulated in 1671 in Newcastle. Unlike the practice of training a future master locally, trainees in the Holy Roman Empire were obliged to travel. And, in fact, there is evidence of barber-surgeon journeymen traveling several thousand kilometers and serving masters in many parts of central Europe. In the second half of the seventeenth century, such traveling journeymen contracted in three professional stages: beginner (immediately after the ceremony of *"Freisprechen"* confirmed completion of apprenticeship), middleman (after half a year of service), and, half a year later, full journeyman. The number of years in service as an apprentice and journeyman fluctuated a great deal. Written regulations existed during the sixteenth century, but guild members and governors constantly negotiated the terms. In Ulm in 1534 a survey of armed men in the barber guild listed the youngest master aged twenty-two years; compared to this young master, the journeyman working with the guild master was senior by seven years. Similar age differences—with first approbation as master occurring between age twenty-two and thirty years—can be observed during the second half of the seventeenth century and seemed to increase later on. Carrier inequalities were biggest in Turin where licenses were acquired between ages eighteen and thirty-four. The years spent as apprentice and journeyman depended very much on family networks and knowledge transferred among kin. Very young masters, for example, often had an opportunity, provided by the family, to integrate learning the trade and attending school.[72]

Political and social opportunities for bath-masters and barbers in public baths oscillated between members of the council and almsman, wealthy citizens and paupers. Thorough, comparative studies on this specific group are still missing. What is known so far instead focuses on barber-surgeons and surgeons, often in their medical functions. We have evidence for the wealth of the corporation of barbers and barber-surgeons in the middle of the sixteenth century. By the seventeenth century, barber-surgeons and surgeons had become wealthy and influential citizens of the Holy Roman Empire and Switzerland and demonstrated their improved status by associations with economically and intellectually influential families and corporations. Yet this status was not shared all over Europe. It changed during the eighteenth century and was altered dramatically in the nineteenth century, when the artisans of the body lost their medical function. Differences seem to result from the variety in political-juridical practices and in European political systems and from the fundamental changes in those systems. On a smaller scale, comparable to other Renaissance artisans, the individual barber's destiny was also shaped by changes in the local environment caused by climate, warfare and troop movement, and by economic and agricultural development.[73]

In Italy and the Holy Roman Empire surgeons embodied a status similar to that of physicians.[74] Pictorial representations in books of guilds and in printed books underlined this achievement from the sixteenth to the first decades of the eighteenth centuries.[75] The 1637 group portrait in Figure 4.7 presents the "Geschwornen Maister der Wundtartzneij" (Master Jurymen of Surgery) and is one of seven representations of masters elected from the guild of barbers, barber-surgeons, and surgeons in Ulm between 1574 and 1766. The seven pictures were attached to handwritten copies of proceedings concerning forensic and surgical matters over which the depicted men presided. In this watercolor the masters proudly sit in a room in which instruments and equipment of their trade are used as decorative elements. Most details—the seating, gestures, outfits, books and sealed letters, the hourglass, and coins symbolizing legal charges and costs—are statements that associate barbers and barber-surgeons with judges and physicians.[76]

Despite such claims to represent a medical profession, further evidence points to a continued economic value in the business of shaving and cutting hair at the turn to the eighteenth century. A surgeon and his wife in the imperial city of Ulm claimed the right to have a barbershop in addition to an appointment for specific surgical tasks. They argued that without this business the family could not be kept. Moreover, in a fiscal survey of thirteen barber-surgeons and barbers in public bathhouses in the imperial city of Nuremberg the *"Barbier-Verdienst"* (income from shaving and cutting hair) varied

FIGURE 4.7 Andreas Schuen, "Master Jurati, elected in the corporation of Barbers and Barber-Surgeons in Ulm" (1637). Watercolor. © Museum Ulm, Ulm.

tremendously. A comparison of their declarations suggests that compared to cupping, bloodletting, and surgery, the portion of income provided by hair care varied between about eighteen percent and sixty-six percent for individual practitioners.[77] The aesthetic (and medical) practices of barber-surgeons also seemed to play an important role at royal, papal, ducal, and comital courts; their service in monasteries has been mentioned above.[78]

CONCLUSION

In Renaissance Europe, practices focusing on hair and beards received much attention because hairstyle mattered, and washing, cutting, and shaving were seen as influences on health for which proper timing was essential. The skills necessary to maintain healthy and stylish hair and beards demanded complex know-how. Handwritten compilations of such knowledge by members of the nobility and by citizens and the increasing interest in pertinent printed publications point to the spread of related practices in households. A number of techniques for styling and relevant preparations for hair care demanded costly equipment and complicated procedures; together with difficult access to basic resources this limited such processes to wealthy family-homes. At the same time, governors continued to invest massively in public baths, at least in middle Europe, which made care for the hair and body more accessible to all social ranks within the urbanised zones of the Holy Roman Empire. In cities of all sizes, governors increasingly regulated bath-masters, barbers, and barber-surgeons who relied heavily on an income from services offered for the care of the hair and beard. At the end of this period, barber-surgeons presented themselves primarily as a medical profession, despite evidence that a considerable part of their earnings was made from "barbering," styling hair and beards.

CHAPTER FIVE

Health and Hygiene

EDITH SNOOK

In early modern medical thinking, hair had a physiological function. It was both an excrement and an ornament, a natural outgrowth of the body and a site for artful intervention, and a physiological signifier of an essential identity and a body part subject to change and external influence and open to transformation. This chapter focuses on the construction of hair in medical discourses, largely in England. Knowledge about hair's physiology was created by anatomy texts, which theorized how and why hair emerged from the skin on the head and the body, the rationale for aging and baldness, and hair's role in marking gender and geographical difference. Considering hair as a part of the body's exterior, surgical texts pondered diseases that prevented hair growth, such as alopecia, while herbals and collections of remedies also attend to cures for a range of problems with hair, including baldness, the removal of excess hair, hair coloring, and lice. Despite this interest, early modern medical writing about hair appears to have been deeply informed by tradition, particularly by the writings of Aristotle and Galen, and was not a major focus of innovation and debate; thinking about hair did not see the equivalent of William Harvey's *De Motu Cordis* (1628) and its challenge to existing knowledge of the circulation of the blood.[1] But Thomas Winston's 1659 *Anatomy Lectures* do turn to a more observational investigation of the body with his contention that hair was not round, as was believed, but square, which "you may observe with a perspective glasse."[2] Still, Galen and Aristotle remained preeminent in thinking about hair's function. An outcome of the body's humors, hair was a functional part of the body that merited serious consideration by medical thinkers, practitioners, and patients, and as such required intervention and care to secure good health.

THE PHYSIOLOGY OF HAIR

While not the only sources on hair for early modern English anatomists, Aristotle and Galen crucially construct the hair as an excrement, as a functional component of the body that was an outcome of essential sexual difference and the humoral complexion. Written in the fourth century BCE, Aristotle's *History of Animals* and *On the Generation of Animals* explored differences of thickness, fineness, length, and color, explained these differences according to the location of hair on the body, the quality of the skin, and the body's relative heat (harder hair will grow in hot places and soft in cold ones), and distinguished between congenital hair on the head, eyelids, and eyebrows and the hair that develops on male and female bodies at sexual maturity.[3] Proposing that hair is formed from substances inside the body, *On the Generation of Animals* uses the notion of evaporation to explain the material quality of hair, suggesting that hair is not formed from skin but "out of the skin moisture evaporating and it becomes solid and earthy as the moisture evaporates." The quality of the hair changes with the thickness of the skin, the size of the pores, and how quickly the moisture dries.[4]

Galen's *Mixtures* (also called *Of Temperaments*)—written in the second century and one of several of his works to consider hair—extends Aristotle's ideas about the formation of hair. Galen contends that hair depends upon the humoral complexion, the skin, and the pores. Within the body, "heat draws to itself a considerable amount of moisture from within." This transpiration informs the substances that are excreted through the skin to become hair, whether "pure vapour or pure moisture," with the vapor passing easily, moisture, or "sooty, thick, and earthy" vapor, which is more likely to be obstructed. The skin's pores inform how the hair moves through the skin. In cold, soft skin, "like cheese," the paths of egress close, while in hard skin, "like well-set cheese," the pores are "unable to come together because of the dryness" and are more open.[5] This expulsive process produces the multiple forms of hair, including black (produced when the excretion, black bile, is roasted by heat in the body) and fair (yellow bile is excreted with less heat), as well as white hair, produced by phlegm, and red, which is "half way between the phlegmatic and bilious." Curly hair results from the "dryness of the mixture or because of the pore in which it is rooted."[6] In this framework, skin is like earth—ideally the earth in spring or the beginning of summer—the pore is like "the root of a blade of grass or other plant, while that which protrudes from the skin is like the plant itself."[7]

Hair's status as an excrement affects Galen's thinking about hair's color, curl, and abundance, as well. A hot, dry complexion produces "extreme hairiness," a balanced complexion a moderate degree of hairiness, and a cold complexion baldness.[8] In *Art of Medicine*, Galen further explains that the particular complexion of an individual's brain, heart, liver, and genitals influences the hair on the body's surface above the part. Thus, a brain disposed to heat results in a head prone to baldness, but the hot and dry brain produces fast-growing, vigorous, black, and curled hair; the hot and wet brain produces straight and "blondish" hair, while, conversely, the cold and dry brain underpins premature graying, slow hair growth from birth, and "insubstantial and red" hair.[9] Importantly, this causal relationship between the complexion and hair gives hair a signifying power: "The state of the brain as a whole is taken from its size and shape and from the nature of the hair."[10] Ideally, hair that grows above a well-balanced brain complexion will be "genuinely fair hair ... halfway between straight and really curled."[11] Likewise, the complexions of the heart, liver, and genitals affect the hair on the contiguous surface of the body, with excess heat in the organs producing more hair on the skin and cooler complexions less.[12] Throughout the body, hair aids in establishing the body's humoral balance by drawing inward excesses out. As a result, hair is not only functional but evidentiary, revealing the body's complexion, as if hair, like wine, had a *terroir*.

Galenic humoral theory was influential throughout Renaissance Europe, informing the view that hair was a significant and functional part of human anatomy. In England, vernacular medical texts—Thomas Elyot's *The Castle of Health* (1537), Levinus Lemnius's *Touchstone of Complexions* (1576), Thomas Vicary's *A Profitable Treatise of the Anatomy of Man's Body* (1577) and *The English Man's Treasure* (1596), and Helkiah Crooke's *Microcosmographia* (1615), for instance—all reiterate Galenic constructions of hair's physiology and function, the significance of its presence or absence, and its relationship to aging and disease. Hair's status as a functional body part is evident in the common listing of hair's purpose. One of the first English anatomies, Thomas Vicary's *A Profitable Treatise of the Anatomy of Man's Body*, lays out hair's four functions: to defend the brain from excess heat and cold; to make the head seem "more seemelyer or beautyfuller"; with the color of the hair, to make known the complexion of the brain; and last, to allow the "fumosities of the brayne" to "assend and pass lyghtlyer out by them."[13] Even eyebrows and eyelashes are functional. Vicary contends that eyebrows are to beautify the face and to "defende the Eyes from noyaunce without foorth." He also assesses the function of eyelashes: "by them is addressed the formes or similitudes of visible things unto the apple of the eye."[14] Hair's expulsive function is crucial, for hairs all over the body "are but a superfluitie of members, made of grosse fume or ... passing out of the viscoues matter."[15]

Vicary is not alone in his emphasis on hair's physiological utility, part of which depends on hair's work as an excrement. Giving hair the same four purposes as Vicary does, Crooke's *Microcosmographia* (1615) outlines the usefulness of the eyebrows, eyelashes, body hair, and the hair of the head. In Crooke's words, besides cover, defense, and ornament, hair should "consume and waste away the thicke and fuliginous or sooty excrements."[16] Explaining how hair grows with reference to Hippocrates and Galen's *Book of Temperaments*, Crooke contends it requires heat, matter out of which the hair can be generated, a place to grow, and nourishment to grow and persist. Hair's matter is superfluous moisture and "sooty, thicke and earthy vapour," which "when the aliment is turned into true nourishment of the parts" is elevated by heat and "passes through the pores of the skin." The skin, which is full of pores, is "fit for breeding" when it is moderately dry and hard to hold the root of the hair.[17] The anatomist and the personal physician of Marie de Medici, Jean Riolan, wrote (in the English translation *A Sure Guide, or, The Best and Nearest Way to Physick and Chyrurgery* [1657]) that "the internal cause" of hair "is a sooty Excrement, which thrusting it self forcibly by the small Pores, gains the form of a thred."[18] As a thread of excrement, hair is physiologically functional, contributing to the body's balance and health.

Socially functional, as well, hair's ability to make the complexion known—that it is excreted from inside the body to its surface, its features determined by the body's humors—establishes hair as a mark of identity, particularly with respect to age, gender, and ethnicity. On age, Galen had argued, like Aristotle, that small children do not have hair because there is no passageway for it in the skin, but as children grow, their heat and the number of pores increase, and hair growth is stronger. As men age further, however, they can grow bald because of increased dryness, and the hair turns white due to insufficient nourishment, which makes the hair's substance, "somewhat like a mould, the phlegm having undergone putrefaction over the year."[19] Levinus Lemnius in *Touchstone of Complexions* (1576) answers the question of why children have no body hair in much the same way as Galen does: either children have no pores in their skin to enable the exhalation to the bigness of hair, or they want the "fuliginous excrement, where withall the small threads of the hayres, are wont to be drawen and produced out."[20] At a more "lusty and flourishinge" age, however, the hair will be bushier and black, growing on the head, chin, armpits, and "privities" for "the pores and passages then beginne to be opened and enlarged."[21] The hair on the chest, arms, and thighs also appears in puberty, for they "be seene to be rough and hayrie, yet do those hayres grow, neither so copiouslye nor to anye great length."[22] Because the body's humors alter with age, the excrement from which hair is made changes, and hair's appearance shifts, too.

Closely related to its revelation of sexual maturity is the work hair does to reveal what was regarded as an essentialized sexual difference. Galen had argued that women, like children, do not have beards because "this animal does not have an august character as the male has and so does not need an august form;" neither, he says, do women have body hair as protection from the cold because they stay indoors.[23] Likewise construing women as relatively hairless, Helkiah Crooke treats hair as nature's evidence of sexual difference and a patriarchal social order:

> For it is a venerable sight to see a man when he is come to the yeares fit for it, to have his face compassed about with thicke and comely haire. Nature therefore hath made the upper part of the cheek and the nose without haire, least the whole face should be wilde and fearce, unbeseeming a milde and sociable creature such as a man is. In women the smoothnesse of their face is their proper ornament; they needed no ensigne of majesty because they were borne to subjection. And Nature hath given them such a form of body as is answerable to the disposition of their minde.[24]

From this perspective, hair signifies supposed fundamental humoral differences not only between men and women but also between humans and animals. The beard shows that men rule where women do not, but the normative demarcation of where hair should be from where it should not ensures that man will not be "wilde and fearce," that his civil identity is secure. Hair shows, in Crooke's view, the mind of the man, the fundamental basis of his purportedly natural superiority.

Hair's physiological origins in the body's humors also meant that it was treated as a signifier of ethnic difference. Again, the idea has its source in Aristotle and Galen. Like Aristotle, Galen argued that climate had a crucial influence on hair. In *Mixtures*, Galen observes that Ethiopians are curly-haired because of the hot climate.[25] He adds:

> The hair of Egyptians, Arabs, Indians, and in general all peoples who inhabit hot, dry places, has poor growth and growth and is black, dry, curly, and brittle. That of the inhabitants of cold, wet places, conversely Illyrians, Germans, Dalmatians, Sauromatians, and the Scythian types of people in general has reasonably good growth and is thin, straight, and red.[26]

On the other hand, those who live in a moderate climate, he says, have hair "with extremely good growth, which is strong, fairly black, moderately thick, and neither completely curly nor completely straight."[27] In the early modern period, Helkiah Crooke develops these ideas. He allows, for example, that climate is one of the influences on hair's thickness/thinness, hardness/softness, length/shortness, straightness/curliness, and multitude/scarcity.[28] And he asserts that as a result of a dry climate, "haire curleth by reason of the drinesse of the temper; and therefore all Black-Moores have curled or crisped hair," while those that inhabit cold, wet climates "have soft haires which grow moderately, are small or fine, straight and reddish, as the Illirians, Germans, Sarmatians and all the cost of Scythia, as Galen sayth."[29] In a context that saw the emergence of global trade and colonialism, this medical perspective seems to have been based less on new, supposedly scientific observations arising from cross-cultural contact than on Galenic tradition. Crooke re-deploys Galen's geohumoralism to explain ethnic differences in hair, which, as I have argued elsewhere, makes moderate, slightly curled hair contiguous with health. Crooke is not alone in this, and as a result, early modern medical writing establishes a privileged form of hair that will align with a politicized, imperial construction of whiteness that supports the emergence of racial hierarchies in the early modern period.[30]

Finally, hair's physiological function as a humoral excrement contributed to the construction of hair as a sign of character. This approach is evident even in the eyebrows, for as Thomas Vicary argues, "Aristotle sayth, that over measurable Browes betokeneth an envious man: Also high browes and thick betokeneth cowardnes: and meanly signifieth gentlenes of hart."[31] Thomas Elyot's *The Castle of Health* (1537), in perhaps the most extended analysis of hair as a signifier of character, precisely charts the character and physical features, including hair type, that belong to each of the humoral complexions. The sanguine complexion thus produces hair "plenty and red" and a character that is "Angrie shortly"; one with a phlegmatic complexion, marked in "much and plaine hair," experiences "dullnesse in learning" and cowardice. One of a choleric complexion, "blacke or darke, aburne, curled" hair, "sharpe and quicke" wits, and is "hardy, and fighting"; and the melancholic complexion, "plaine and thin" hair and is "Stiffe in opinions" and "timorous and fearefull."[32] Systematically revealing the body's complexion, hair purports to document how one will behave in the world.

Similarly, *Touchstone of Complexions*'s description "Of a complexion, perfectly and exactly temperate" lays out the moderate ideal for the complexion in relation to both hair and character. The further from moderation "that any man is, in worse case of health is hee, and a great deale readier to fall into diseases of body, & perturbations of mynde."[33] The exactly temperate man, however, has a steadfast memory and honest manners and conversation; he is also quiet, courteous, calm, discerning, and affectionate to his wife and children.[34] Because the gifts of nature reveal themselves in "outward shew, shape and behaviour of the bodye," the body of the temperate man is proportionate, his hair is "of fayre aburne or chesten colour," and his eyebrows are "comely."[35] The best pattern of a man, the text concludes, is Christ.[36] Digressing from this healthy and moral mean are all the excessive complexions, each made visible in hair. For instance, the hot complexioned person has "rough & hayrie" skin, a fair and comely beard, and black hair on the head, for "hayres being generated of a fuliginous & grosse excrement" turn black. Curled hair is the result of a dry complexion or "the straiteness and narrow issue of the pores … for then have they much ado to peep up."[37] From this perspective, hair that departs from the ideal is not just a departure from health but also a falling away from a social ideal for character and civility.

That hair's physiology reveals character can also encompass a person's presumed sexual character. While Lemnius connects thick hair on women's heads to their sexual maturity and their difference from men—"For young damselles and Maydens, being anye thinge grown in lustie age, have their heads thick heyred and longer then Youngmen have"—he also connects women's pubic hair to their sexual ethics; women with "verye roughe and thick growen with hayre" in their "privities" "be greatlye desirous of carnall lust and copulacion" and are "more lecherous, the more hayrie & fruictfuil."[38] This view is also evident in midwifery books, which are particularly interested in genital anatomy. While *The Complete Midwife's Practice* (1656) says of women merely that the lower part of the belly is hairy because "of the heat and moisture of the place," it proposes with respect to men that those with hotter testicles "are more salacious and prone to venereal actions, having the places neer about much more hairie."[39] Jane Sharp writes in *The Midwife's Book* (1671) of women's pubic hair that "when maids are ripe they are full of hair that grows upon them, but they are more curled in women than the hair of Maids. They that have much hair and very young are much given to venery."[40] Wherever it grows on the body, hair is a powerful physiological marker. Functioning to secure the body's humoral balance and appearing on its surface, hair is in anatomical writing a signifier of the body's complexion and, as a result, of identity—of age, gender, sexuality, ethnicity, and even character. As an excrement, hair assumes physiological and social functions, working both to secure the body's healthful humoral balance and to articulate the wearer's identity.

REMEDIES AND CURES

While anatomists strove to construct hair as a stable signifier of an essential identity, other medical writing shows that hair's signifying power was ultimately unstable. Early modern medical writers were keenly aware that hair could be changed, and remedies recommended multiple ways of transforming it, usually but not always for reasons of health. Writing about barber-surgeons, Margaret Pelling argues that "human beings were seen as continuously interacting with their environment, so that health, even if attained, was a matter of a carefully preserved equilibrium rather than a state of permanency;" as a result, emphasis was placed on "cutaneous appearances which might now be regarded as superficial" and "a good appearance and health itself must have been seen partly as interchangeable."[41] This sense that the exterior of the body was essential to maintaining its health and equilibrium is foundational to thinking about medical treatments of early modern hair. Indeed, disputing contemporary distinctions between medical and cosmetic practices, Sandra Cavallo argues that "The cleansing of the body was deemed to have an effect on health, rather than just being a matter of personal decorum. It was conducted with the aim of enabling the processing of waste products which lurked within the body and preventing these substances from becoming blocked and rotten inside, thus provoking pathologies of different kinds."[42] She adds, "the cutting of hair is ... a procedure necessary for maintaining health given that a 'bushiness of hair' does not only produce a proliferation of 'vermin and filth' but the blocking of poisons to be expelled from the body."[43] Thus, while other chapters in this volume address how both men and women (but particularly the latter) could be called to account for excessive attention to their hair, grooming could be regarded as essential to health and bodily balance. Galen had written in *Of the Usefulness of Parts* that "Nature has made sufficient provision to keep man from being greatly troubled about his body and from being a perpetual slave to its necessary services. For I think it fitting for a wise, civilized animal to have moderate care for his body." Galen is critical of those who abandon friends in need to instead "in private pluck their hair with plaster of pitch, adorn themselves, and spend their whole lives in unnecessary attention to their bodies, not understanding at all that they have something better than the body."[44] But moderate attention to the body is necessary. Indeed, it defines civility, marking a position between vanity on the one hand and animality on the other. The healthy maintenance of the body's surface, including its hair, is a means to facilitate a healthy humoral equilibrium.

One starting point in bodily care is combing the hair, a hygienic practice essential to health. William Bullein's *The Government of Health* (1595) allows that it is "reasonable but to keepe himself cleane;" keeping clean includes washing the hands with cold water, rubbing the body, and combing the hair:

> kembing of the head is good in the mornings, and doth comfort memorie, it is evil at night and openeth the pores. The cutting of the haire, and the paring of the nailes, cleane keepeing of the eares, and teeth, be not only things comely and honest, but also holsome rules of Phisicke for to be superfluous things of the excrements.[45]

Cleanliness, then, did not necessarily include washing the hair. Histories of English hygiene have focused on Renaissance antipathy to bathing, which was believed to open the pores to allow pestilential vapors to enter the body and to thus dangerously disrupt the balance of the humors.[46] Although as Annemarie Kinzelbach shows in Chapter Four, other European cultures did have a bathing culture, there, too, people might sponge scented waters on the hair or rub it with a powder that could be combed out instead of washing it.[47] Cleansing was more invested in orderliness, as Douglas Biow contends in his work on Renaissance Italy.[48] That figures here as well. Combing the hair dealt with superfluous excrements securing the body's overall humoral balance.

Combing was also a component of the treatment of lice, a major concern in hair care. Delousing by picking the hair with a comb or fingers featured repeatedly in the domestic scenes of seventeenth-century Dutch painting.[49] Many paintings showed mothers delousing children (Figure 5.1), while Michael Sweerts' *Sleeping Old Man and Girl* shows a young girl looking for lice in the hair of a man, sleeping on table with his head resting on his arms (ca. 1650).[50] Not surprisingly, then, multiple medical remedy collections include remedies for lice. Crucially, lice were not treated as parasitic insects but things created by the body as a result of the humoral imbalance of excess moisture. William Drage included "the Lousie-Eveil" in his list of "Diseases and Affects of the Hair," where he describes the causes of lice, which are incident, he says, particularly to children. Lice are made "from a putrified,

FIGURE 5.1 Pieter de Hooch, *A Mother Delousing her Child's Hair* (ca. 1658–1660). Oil on canvas, 52.5 × 61 cm. Rijksmuseum, Amsterdam. Public Domain. Courtesy Europeana Collections. http://www.europeana.eu/portal/record/90402/SK_A_293.html.

but not sharp Humour, and hot and moist distemper of the part" and caused by "Putrid Humours collected 'twixt the Cuticle, and true skin not very sharp, and residing most in the Emunctories, and hot moist places that have hair to cover them"; figs, when eaten, also turn to the "excrement that Lice are bred of."[51] Lice can be remedied by keeping the clothes clean, by avoiding the immoderate use of waters and contact with others who have lice, and by using "internal dryers" and topical remedies that open the pores so that the "matter of which Lice are made, will breath forth."[52] Riolan's *A sure guide* includes among its analysis of diseases of the head, "the Louzie Evil," which occurs when "instead of thicker Excrements, or together with them, Lice are bred in the top of the Skin, or deep in the same." The curse, he adds, is a "hot and moist distemper of the Skin, with a putrified humor not very sharp; which makes this Disease commonly subject to Children, and old Flegmatick Persons."[53] "A Chapter of Lice" in Giovanni Vigo's surgical text recommends to cure lice the use of purgation, diet, and the application of topical remedies. For diet, the patient needs to abstain from foods that "engender corrupt or rotten mattier, as Figges, Chestnuts, Coleworts, &c." and in topical medicines, Vigo recommends juices of broom or wormwood, oil of aloes, or gum of yew tree, white and black beets, and cods of "sene"; lice in the privy members can be "killed" with a cloth gilded in silver.[54] Women's recipe collections also address this malady. Lady Frances Catchmay's recipes has a recipe "To kill lyce on Childrens heads" that recommends the use of honey and ivy berries stamped together: "rubb the head therwith it will kill the lice."[55] *A Right Profitable Booke for all Diseases, called the Pathway to Health* (1632) has several recipes to kill lice on the head, one with frankincense and barrows grease and another with stavesaker (stavesacre is a plant native to southern Europe and Asia). Nits can be killed with the gall of a calf and worms with calamint.[56] Culpeper's *English Physician* has several recommendations for remedies that kill lice: the bark of black alder boiled in vinegar; broom boiled in oil; the oil of hyssop; mustard seed mixed with honey or applied as a wax; the juice of English tobacco; and the bark of the tamarisk tree decocted.[57] His translation of *Pharmacopoeia Londinensis* takes a more preventative approach, recommending cottonweed, "of a drying and binding nature," which "keeps the head from nits and lice."[58] Preventing that which engenders corruption or rottenness, including lice, is a component of the body's overall good order and health.

Domestic recipe collections suggest that remedies for hair loss, hair removal, and hair color and curl can also be framed by this concern with the complexion's balance. Remedies for hair loss are perhaps the most prevalent. *A Very Shorte and Compendious Method of Phisicke and Chirurgery*, signed by Jane Jackson and dated 1642 (Figure 5.2), indexes several recipes for the amelioration of baldness: three "for the sheding of haire" and others "To make heare to growe where there is none," "To restore haire againe," and "To make hayre never to growe."[59] Another domestic collection, *Receipts Approved by Persons of Qualitie and Iudgment collected by Elizabeth Digby: 1650*, has a recipe to "doe away haire" that recommends combing the hair with the blood of a male lamb. The recipe to "take away haires from any place" uses horseleeches burned to a powder, and "To make haires growe where none bee" employs mallows root and ale.[60] Such remedies for hair's maladies, along with other medical remedies, are part of a culture of knowledge creation, investigation, and experiment.[61] Physicians and surgeons wrote many similar remedies for hair. The physician William Drage considers hair systematically in "Of Diseases and Affects of the Hair, and of outward Eruptions," written he says in 1658 and 1659 and drawn "from the best of the Moderns;" Drage identifies hair's diseases: ophiasis, alopecia, *defluvium*

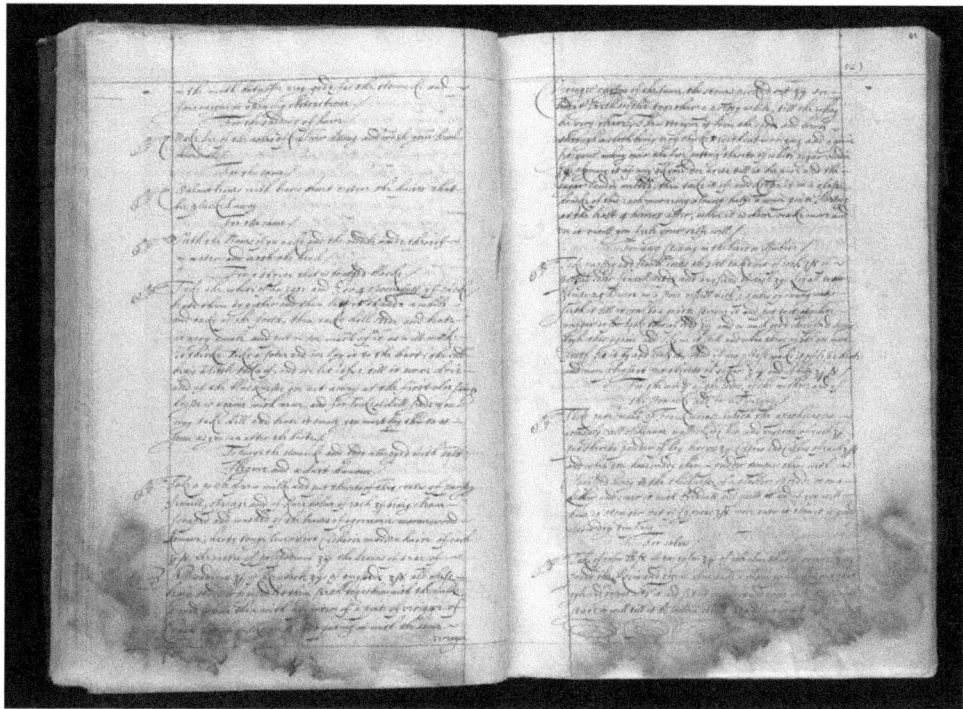

FIGURE 5.2 Jane Jackson, *A very shorte and compendious Methode of Phisicke and Chirurgery* (1642), fol. 60v. Wellcome Library, London. Creative Commons License. https://creativecommons.org/licenses/by/4.0/legalcode.

capillorum (the "general falling off of Hair"), baldness, scurfiness, and "the lousie evil." Along with defining these maladies and their causes and symptoms, he offers cures for them, as well as for superfluous hair, gray hair, plaiting, cleaving, and worms in the hair.[62] Just as Helkiah Crooke had written that when the humors are "well fed, and with lawdable aliment, they [hairs] encrease apace," Drage links a general falling of hair to "want of nourishment."[63] Baldness is caused by "the want of good humours," plica (the folding of hair into tufts) by "a matter unprofitable to nourish the Hairs," and alopecia by "corrupted Humours, eroding the roots of the Hair."[64] In this analysis, hair loss is the result of humoral imbalance and insufficient inward nourishment for the hair.

The relationship between hair loss and the body's humoral balance is equally visible in herbals, where the virtues of plants (as hot, dry, cold, or wet) can be used to aid hair growth. John Gerard's famous herbal includes among the virtues of herbs causing the hair to grow and to keep it from falling, as well as hair colorings.[65] Gerard claims that maidenhair, for instance, is drying and will cause the hair to grow, while a thistle called euphorbium (which is very hot) will cause hair to grow again on a scalded head.[66] The pharmacopoeia of the College of Physicians, *Pharmacopoeia Londinensis*, records remedies approved by the college and was printed first in Latin in 1618 and then translated by Nicholas Culpeper in 1649. It indicates that plants, including asphodeli (hot and dry), the ashes of golden maidenhair (drying), and ladanum (heating), as well as animal products, such as the roasted brains of a hare and bear's grease will aid hair growth.[67] "Froath of the sea," hot and dry, helps baldness and "trimly decks the head with hairs," which suggests that a full head of hair is both attractive and healthy—and a concern fully authorized within medical culture.[68]

It is possible that hair remedies—both for hair loss and for excess hair—might be drawing on hair's identity as an excrement by using excrement, as well as ashes, in the cure. Among the several cures for baldness in *The Treasury of Health*, there are waters to rub on the head that have ingredients such as ashes of culver dung, ashes of goat's dung, and "hogges pisse."[69] Peter Levens begins his collection with remedies for all parts of the head, including cures promising hair growth that turn often to burned ingredients and excrement. One suggests burning "mollwarpe [moldwarp is a kind of mole], skin and all," then laying the ashes in a cloth and burning that, then burning the dung of a doe and laying that in a cloth and burning it, then mixing these two powders with honey and anointing the place where hair is desired.[70] A remedy to keep hair from falling suggests the ashes of burned frogs or goat's dung or culver-dung, while another to remove hair recommends using a powder of cat's dung.[71] Other recipes addressing excess hair also treat it with excrements. Culpeper's *School of Physick* recommends pigeons' dung or bay-salt mixed with fasting spittle applied as a plaster to any place where excess hair grows.[72] Through the principle of propriety, excrement might treat the hair, itself excremental.[73]

Hair loss remedies also rely on cleansing, which addresses the problem of putrefaction, seemingly caused by the blockage of transpiration between the inside of the body and its outside. *The Marrow of Physick* recommends restoring hair by frying the yokes of one hundred new laid eggs, "until they turne reddish and yeeld a fatty moisture" which should be put hot into a "haire bagge" and the oil pressed out, which is "good to cleare the skin, and restore haire, and to cure maligne and fistulous ulcers."[74] Honey is a frequent, cleansing ingredient. According to Charles Butler, honey is used "to open, to cleanse, to dry, to digest, and to resist putrefaction."[75] Salvator Winter's *A Pretious Treasury* (1649) recommends taking a little aqua mellis (honey water) every morning, warming it in a saucer, dipping a sponge in the water, and moistening a "fine Boxe Combe" and "therewith moysten[ing] the very Rootes of your Haire in combing it, and it will grow long, thick, and curled in very short space."[76] *The Queens Closet Opened* (1655) has two recipes that focus on the cleansing power of honey. One entitled "Hair to grow thick" recommends putting honey on the bald spot, and another "to make Hair grow" recommends, exactly as Winter does, combing aqua mellis through the hair, promising hair will "grow long, thick, and curled in a very short time."[77]

Depilatories and concoctions to prevent hair from growing back in collections of remedies likewise construe the treatment as a remedy for a humoral disorder. *The Treasurie of Health* contends that, like baldness, excess hair is the result of humoral excess, "the multitude of incorrupt humours and thickness of the skin of the head, with straightnesse of the holes through which the haire groweth."[78] Drage similarly treats superfluous hair as a disruption, "where they grow indecently and out of due order and place," and *Natural Magic* explains the logic of hair removal from a body part "deformed with abundance of Hair, or for lack of Hair."[79] Remedies to remove excess hair thus restore order. *The Path-way to Health* suggests that excess hair can be removed by shaving the head and then anointing the place with stamped nettles. After this treatment, however, "you must sweat and when that you are hote, then annoynt your head therwith and doe this three daies, and there wil growe no more haire."[80] The purpose here seems to be to affect the body's overall complexion.

Although remedies for hair growth and removal are the most common recipes found in recipe collections, there are cures for other supposed maladies, which include rough, short, or overly straight hair. The herbal *The Garden of Health* (1598), for instance, indexes in addition to remedies that would prevent hair growth, remedies to cause hair to grow, to inhibit hair loss, to color or curl the hair, and to prevent it from "Standing up."[81] To curl the hair, the herbal includes among the virtues of "milfoyle"—alongside explaining its use in salves to "cleanse, drie, and heale" and its effectiveness in curing the patient of other diseases—the recommendation that "the juice with oyle rubbed, causeth curled haire, & with hony it causeth haire to grow."[82] Dandelion juice, "often applied, layeth downe the flaring of the haire of the eybrowes, and causeth newe haires to grow."[83] *Natural Magic* indicates that to make the hair softer, "Augustus was wont to burn his Legs with a burning Nut, that the Hair might grow softer," while another remedy provides details on how hair can be made to grow longer. Curled hair "seems no small Grace and Ornament to the Head" and can be produced not with a curling iron but by anointing the head with maidenhair boiled in wine with smallage seeds (from Pliny), with camel dung, with oil and the ashes of rams horn, with the ashes of chestnuts or hedgehogs, or with the roots of daffodils boiled in wine poured onto a shaved head.[84] A collection of medical and cookery receipts belonging to Sir Peter Temple contains multiple recipes for the hair, including to curl it, to "breed in bald places," to grow thick, and to dye red or gray hair a darker color; another is for "Hayre taken off as in Italy."[85] Temple is interested in medical authority and establishes in the beginning that "Although I often have these receits from women, yet men of judgment make them … & such are usually harmelesse, & certaine."[86] He thus offers a recipe "To make Hayr grow Thicke and Curle" which recommends washing the head with sack and combing the hair with another water, "the better keepe yor head not too hot." It ends with the assertion, "This I am confident will make it curle. P.T."[87] In these remedies, curled hair, like other types of hair defined as healthy, is a result of humoral balance. Remedies that address what we might see as hair's aesthetics—its curl, for instance—are regarded in the early modern period as a component of health, as well as a component of hair's natural function as an ornament.

Even hair color could be made to function as a sign of health, with hair dye the focus of some attention in medical sources. The chapter "To black the haire," by the French barber-surgeon Ambrose Paré, whose works were translated into English in 1634, recommends that the hair must first be prepared with lye in which alum has been dissolved before "fitting medicines" can be applied. These medicines, he says must be "aromaticke and cephalicke [pertaining to the head], and somewhat stiptick [having a binding effect], that by their odiferous and astringent power they may strengthen the animal faculty."[88] He then includes after four recipes to make the hair black, two medicines to make it fair, and more "Medicines to fetch off hair."[89] Even when hair dye is not named a medicine, dyes are regularly included in medical recipes books. *The Garden of Health*, *The English Physician*, and *The Path-way to Health* have multiple recommendations on how to make the hair yellow.[90] Blonde is a preferred color, in line with dominant aesthetics, but other colors are also addressed. A red dye is included in *The Path-way to Health* because there are those who have a ruddy complexion for whom to make the hair yellow would "not agree with their Complexion," while the black hair dye is for "those such as are ashamed to seem old."[91] In suggesting that the hair and beard, if gray, can be dyed black with "froth of silver" and burned brass in such a way that it will not be discerned, Levens reveals both that men use these hair dyes and that it is important that the coloring be concealed—surely more a social concern than a medical one.[92] *The Precious Treasury* says that hair can be dyed black with lye and leaves of beer, sage, bay, and walnut, although one must take care not to get the dye on the face; that men used these dyes is confirmed here too by a recipe recommending coloring the hair black by dissolving a groat or six-pence in aqua fortis and using the water to "wet your beard or hayre therewith, but touch not the skin."[93] While William Drage distances hair coloring from medical practice when he suggests that it is normally achieved by the topical application of paint, he adds that "Medicines that are taken inwardly to restore and conserve the Youth, and keep off the gray Head" can also be effective, a reminder that hair color remains a symptom of the body's complexion.[94] That hair color is meant to work to hide one's age appears to be behind the complaint in the Italian Lucrezia Marinella's *The Nobility and Excellence of Women, and the Defects and Vices of Men* about the deception in men's use of hair dyes and lead combs.[95] Altogether, however, the rational for the inclusion of hair dyes in collections of medical remedies seems less that coloring hair is itself healthful than that a youthful appearance is also a healthy one and a health body also has the moderate complexion of the ideal, civil man.

While a desire for youth may be behind men's use of hair dyes in Marinella's assessment, the need to be beautiful informs perceptions of women's use of them—a logic that construes hair's ornamental function as a contributor to the wearer's social position, to their social health, as it were. In a section on "How to adorn Women, and Make them Beautiful," *Natural Magic* explains the rational for recipes to make the hair yellow: "Women hold the Hair to be the greatest Ornament of the Body; that if that be taken away, all the Beauty is gone: and they think it the more beautiful, the more yellow, shining and radiant it is."[96] Medical writers certainly do regard hair as a natural ornament consistently identifying it as one of hair's four primary purposes. According to this logic, if hair is to function ornamentally, blonde coloring most perfectly fulfills that natural, physiological function. Female beauty, moreover, is necessary to social order:

> I did not write these things for to give occasion to augment Luxury, and for to make people voluptuous. But when God, the Author of all things, would have the Natures of all things to continue, he created Male and Female, that by fruitful Procreation, they might never want Children: and to make man in love with his Wife, he made her soft, delicate and fair, to entice man to embrace her. We therefore, that Women might be pleasing to their Husbands, and that their Husbands might not be offended at their deformities, and turn into other womens chambers, have taught Women, how, by the Art of Decking themselves and Painting, if they be ashamed of their foul and swart Complexions, they may make themselves Fair and Beautiful.[97]

Here the inclusion of hair dyes with medical remedies is constructed as natural on the grounds that dyes, like other cosmetics, allow women to secure for themselves a place within a patriarchal, racialized social order where privilege comes from being "fair." If excess or insufficient hair is disorderly, blonde hair, which allows women to attract a husband, is orderly; hair dye from this perspective ensures the stability of the social order by fortifying women's attractiveness to men. If *Natural Magic* is exceptionally assertive about the merits of cosmetics, it is not the only work to be concerned with hair's appearance. Hair's structure and function is of theoretical interest to anatomists, and remedies that ensure its continuing effectiveness in these functions are ready concerns for physicians, surgeons, and other medical practitioners. What the early modern constitution of knowledge about hair's physiology, its maladies, and the purported remedies for them show is that hair is a legitimate medical concern and its health a component of the well-being of the whole body.

CONCLUSION

Hair is an excrement. Hamlet's mother Gertrude evokes this physiological fact in *Hamlet* when she exclaims that his "bedded hair like life in excrements, / Start up, and stand an end" (3.4.121–2). Hair emerges to the body's exterior from its inside, with its qualities determined by the balance of the body's humors and its health. It is an excrement treated as a signifier of identity, even character, and one subject to multiple medical interventions. As an excrement, hair occupies a conflicted social place, constantly mediating between human and animal, civil and wild. On the one hand, hair evokes Bakhtin's grotesque body, which shows how "the limits between the body and world are weakened"; in its hair, the body is never fully closed off from the world because hair is constantly crossing the body's boundary, from inside to out. Hair is a protrusion, a body part as Bakhtin says of noses and other appendages, that "seeks to go out beyond the body's confines."[98] In this respect, too, hair is grotesque and unruly, going beyond the body's borders. On the other hand, hair is an ornament, naturally and properly beautiful, physiologically functional, and socially revelatory. It marks civility when it grows where it should. Medical thinking about hair is constantly negotiating these polarities. Discussing the discipline of the excremental (the body's urine, feces, mucus, saliva, and wind), Stephen Greenblatt argues that in the Renaissance "Proper control of these products, along with the acquisition of the prevailing table manners and modes of speech, mark the entrance into civility, an entrance that distinguishes not only the child from the adult but the members of a privileged group from the vulgar, the upper classes from the lower, the courtly from the rustic, the civilized from the savage."[99] Greenblatt neglects hair's status as one of the body's excrements—perhaps because it has lost this status today—but early modern hair is as subject to discipline as other excrements are. Hair may emerge from the body already disciplined, the result of a balanced complexion and physiological moderation, the result of health; this hair is treated as civil, privileged, and mannered. But for hair that does not emerge as moderate—the hair in the wrong place, the hair that is too abundant or too thin—its social acceptance depends not just on being tucked, parted, tied, and covered, on being fashionably under control, but also on an array of medical remedies that restore order. Remedies for baldness, depilatories, and treatments for lice aim to produce humoral balance in the body, aiding the production of hair where it is desired and removing it where there is too much, where it is disorderly. Even hair dyes can aid order. In early modern England, order is documented in the hair, and medicine is interested in manners, in defining the civilized body.

CHAPTER SIX

Gender and Sexuality

MARK ALBERT JOHNSTON

This chapter interrogates how, during the Renaissance in England, hair was loaded with cultural significance confirming normative codes of sex, gender, and sexuality.[1] Although early modern English culture was both patriarchal and patrilineal, gender stratification was more complex than simply all males exerting power over all females: birth order, title, wealth and inheritance, marital and professional status, age, and myriad other factors besides sex influenced a person's relative social standing. As Alexandra Shepard notes, patriarchy and manhood are not identical and should not be conflated by gender historians, since women as well as men wielded power over subordinates of both sexes.[2] In this highly nuanced sex and gender hierarchy, hair played a vital role by signaling relative status; because hair (unlike clothing, which was also systematically regulated in the period) was taken to be a "natural" product of the body, it was considered a highly reliable index of an individual's essential, ineluctable condition and station. On the surface, this view seems to ignore the fact that hair can be manipulated in countless ways, through cutting, coloring, styling, accessorizing, shaving, falsifying, and so forth, but early modern writers themselves acknowledge this potential for manipulation, generally in order to condemn excessive or inappropriate modifications and to approve modest, status-appropriate maintenance, removal, and/or provision. This chapter considers a wide variety of early modern English discourses on hair that intersect directly with contemporaneous sex and gender politics, focusing specifically on their shared interests in promoting "natural" social hierarchies and discouraging abusive social mobility. These discussions of hair's significance, which range from historical accounts, medical texts and diaries, to literature, drama, and polemics, all share in common the basic assumption that hair is an inherently meaningful medium "naturally" equipped with the power to expose essential truths about the individual sporting it.

THE RENAISSANCE OF HAIR VALUE

Hair's intersections with sex and gender in Renaissance England are grounded in traditions inherited from antiquity and widely disseminated through the translation and printing of both scripture and classical texts. Three inherited stratifying systems influenced early modern conceptions of hair in relation to sex and gender hierarchies and proprieties: the *scala naturae*, which imagines a vertically organized cosmos, in which God's authority over all creation models the king's rule over his subjects and the patriarch's rule over his household; Galenic humoral theory, which construes women and boys as corporeally colder, inferior versions of hotter, superior men; and the Bible, which both establishes men's divinely ordained authority over women and legislates conventions governing acceptable displays of male and female hair.

For early modern English culture, microcosm and macrocosm were imagined in terms of a *scala naturae* or "natural scale"—a vertically stratified, top-down social hierarchy that orders all creation below God and Nature and (among other relations of power) affords men God-given primacy over women. In the early modern imagination, the *scala naturae* represented a divinely ordained system of super- and subordination, according to which the patriarch's governance over his family (like a master's authority over apprentices, or a schoolmaster's priority over students) mimics monarchic dominion over subjects, which in turn mirrors God's absolute authority over creation. Since any subversion threatened the stability of the entire system, insubordination required immediate, punitive correction. Thomas Laqueur's *Making Sex* influentially reiterates the pervasive early modern humoral notion—derived from the classical works of Galen and his followers—that the sexes are essentially homologous, sharing identical parts and vital liquids but differing calorically, in varying degrees of an essential, male heat.[3] Basically, in those bodies that are colder (women, boys), the penis, testicles, and beard are internalized and/or imperfectly developed. By contrast, those bodies that are sufficiently hot perfect and externalize these parts, thereby confirming the attainment of manhood. Sexual differentiation is thus literally a matter of degrees of difference, materially expressed via hair. After the Reformation in England, scripture in the vernacular became not only widely available but essential reading for the salvation of the Christian soul. Setting the precedent for assessments of hair and gender normativity throughout the early modern period by demanding obvious specular sex and gender differentiation, scripture forbids men to shave off their beards and also to either grow long or shave off the hair on their heads but, rather, enjoins men to crop short the hair on their heads, and women to grow long and never to cut the hair on their heads.[4] Long hair, in this rubric, displays submissive obedience in women, while short hair blazons dutiful devoutness in men. These biblical injunctions are often reiterated in the arguments of mid-seventeenth-century hair moralists, who petition for clear tonsorial distinctions between men's and women's hair, condemning long hair on men and short hair on women and demanding beards solely on the faces of men.[5] In light of humoral theory, the *scala naturae*, and scripture, the normatively sexed and gendered early modern body materially confirms the belief that corporeality betrays divine order—that outer appearance reveals essential, integral truths that, in turn, confirm the validity of the social hierarchy. The absence and presence, location, quantity, and qualities (length, color, texture) of hair were thus all loaded with meanings, each of which contributed to a complex semiotic through which hair could be read as an accurate gauge of "natural" status, or *degree*.

SEXING AND GENDERING HAIR

For theorists like Judith Butler, bodies acquire meaning or *matter* solely through cultural systems of power. Early modern gender critic Valerie Traub dubs the same process *psychomorphology*: the attribution of social value to object, bodies, and parts.[6] Both Butler and Traub insist that physiological sex distinctions create a false dichotomy grounded in differences that materialize or matter solely through discourse, suggesting that hair's meaning is always a product of culture. We might further consider the overdetermination of hair as a sex/gender/sexuality signifier through the lens of fetish, a phenomenon that, for both Karl Marx and Sigmund Freud, invests material objects, bodies, and parts with (religious, economic, erotic) values that are not integral but psychologically, socially, and culturally produced. In this light, fetishism construes hair as material evidence of ideological values like sex, gender, and sexuality, thereby obscuring the social origins of those values. Renaissance hair polemicists do not distinguish between sex and gender in terms of embodied traits versus cultural influences but, rather, regard bodies, activities, functions, and tendencies as mutually confirming predetermined manifestations of *degree*. Despite fetishizing hair by lending it signifying power, early modern writers simultaneously betray a keen awareness of the potential for semiotic slippage by attacking abuse, deception, and disguise. Shaving and other depilatory techniques remove hair; trimming creates variations in length; styling affects qualities like volume and texture; dyeing alters hair's hue; while prostheses like wigs and false beards permit people (particularly stage actors but also citizens with sufficient means and desire) to sport an endless variety of artificial hair types, styles, colors, and so forth. Not surprisingly, these activities are all condemned by seventeenth-century hair moralists like Thomas Hill and John Bulwer in their defenses of what they regard as the "natural" semiotic.

Although hair constituted just one corporeal signifier among many, the conspicuous character of its occurrence made it highly visible, thus lending it considerable interpretive weight. Thomas Hill's seventeenth-century physiognomy text, *The Contemplation of Mankind*, explicitly calls "the eyes, the forehead, the head, and the face" the "principallest places" to look for the "more open and manifester signes" of a person's true condition—all places in which the absence, presence, and appearance of hair are most apparent.[7] Hill's prefatory epistle construes all creation, including the body and its parts, as direct indexes of God's perfect order—as legible signifiers that can be exegetically read, discerned, and interpreted to ascertain the higher truths toward which Nature reliably points. Championing physiognomy's power to translate correspondences between material form and spiritual significance, Hill insists that "if a man diligently beholde, not only the sundry and variable forms and shapes of living creatures, but also the forms & fashion of man himself, [he] shall wel perceive ... the great providence and will of almighty GOD, which extends it selfe unto the numbring of the heares of mans head."[8] Hill's invocation of scripture here articulates a principle of divine intent that early modern medical moralists took literally: hair serves a revelatory function, materially verifying God's stratifying both sexes (reproductive bodies) and genders (proximities to power). French barber-surgeon Ambroise Paré, in his instructions for sexing hermaphrodites, advocates a thorough examination of corporeal signs, including "le visage, et si le cheveaux sont déliés ou gros" (the face, and whether the hair is fine or coarse).[9] In a 1588 appendix to his essay "On a Monstrous Child" (1580), Michel de Montaigne sexes an ambiguous figure he describes as "A shepard at Médoc, of thirtie yeares of age, or thereabouts, who had ne signe at all of genetorie parts: But where they should be, are three little holes, by which his water doth continually trill from him. This poor man hath a beard, and desireth still to be fumbling of women."[10] Despite the shepherd's lacking genitalia, Montaigne calls the figure a "man," evidently due to the shepherd's occupation, facial beard, and erotic desire for women. Since early modern humoral theory suggested that beards—like sperm—were produced by viable testicles, the shepherd's beard implies his body's production of sufficient heat, first to eject and then to perfect the testicles. If the beard is fetishized as evidence of male virility, then the shepherd's facial hair effectively stands in for the missing genitalia. Theatrically, wigs and beards served a similarly metonymic fetish function—particularly in children's drama, wherein men and women were played by boys in prostheses—by constituting or materializing manhood and womanhood.

In *Anthropometamorphosis*, John Bulwer's concerns about the semiotics of hair and its potential alteration clearly revolve around a desire to conserve proper rank, order, and place. The title page of Bulwer's book advertises its intent to catalogue and condemn practices altering the body "from the Mould intended by Nature" and champion instead "the Regular Beauty and Honesty of Nature."[11] Bulwer's introduction deploys biblical precedent both to praise the "natural" condition of the human body and to denounce any who "find faulte with" or "question the wisdom of *God* in the contrivance thereof" by taking "upon them an audacious Art to forme and new shape themselves, altering the humane Figure, and moulding it according to their own will and arbitement."[12] Referring to the "natural" order as "Gods chaine," Bulwer repeatedly warns against mankind's tendency to sever that divine hierarchy through intentional transgression: "All other creatures keep their ranks, their places and natures in the world, onely man himself disorders all, and that by displacing himself, by losing his place."[13] Bulwer devotes to hair in all its variety five of his twenty-four chapters anatomizing the human body and its potential alterations, thereby confirming not only the centrality of hair to early modern notions of corporeality and identity but also the considerable anxiety caused by hair's manipulability as a means of disrupting the "natural" semiotic.

In his book's prefatory epistle, Thomas Hill seeks "to obtayne and purchase the truth" by drawing direct "comparisons, between the bodily formes & lineaments, and between their [possessors'] dispositions, courage, and wit."[14] Attaching significance to the presence and absence of hair, as well as its location, quantity, qualities (color, texture, curl), and so forth, Hill disseminates an interpretive index for reading value outside in, and hair as an accurate gauge of degree. Since high levels of heat were supposed to signal masculinity and virility, hirsute men with wiry hair are considered especially volatile, prone to quick tempers, bravery in battle, sexual potency, jealousy, and so forth. Conversely, "Those bodies naturally cold" Hill associates with "heares thinne and slowe in the growing" along with weakness, sleepiness, witlessness, and little reproductive power.[15] "Those bodies naturally moyst" Hill characterizes as producing "thinne heares on the head, and but little in quantitie," together with weariness, fearfulness, and intelligence, whereas "Those bodies naturally drie" he describes having "much heare on the head and in the other places: and that rough, and curled," along with health, strength, and endurance.[16] Generally, for Hill, abundant, thick, coarse hair, regardless of its location, denotes superiority, strength, courage, and vitality, while sparse, fine, or absent hair signifies inferiority, weakness, cowardice, and lethargy. Hot and dry bodies, following this logic, are "bushy of heare, and the heare on the heade, thick and blacke," while cold and moist bodies and the sluggish simpletons who inhabit them are "naked of heare" and have "gentle and soft heares on the head."[17] Since the ultimate objective of humoral medicine was the avoidance of excess and attainment and maintenance of perfect balance and moderation, Hill associates bodies of temperate condition with "heares on the heade in the forme appearing a meane" or average, and proceeds to link specific humoral temperaments and complexions, intellects, tendencies, and inclinations with specific quantities, qualities, and locations of hair.[18] Analyzing degrees of sexual difference, Hill notes that "The wyse and skilfull Physiognomers, in their examinations, doe divide mankinde into two forms, as into the Masculynitie and Femini[ni]tie, according to the propertie of the spirite. For man naturally, except his procreation be hindered, is perfiter than the woman, both in conditions and actions": women are comparatively lacking in heat, strength, intellect, honesty, morality, self-control, constancy, and so forth.[19] Although "femininitie hapeneth to man by accidence of the depriving," generally man is "hotter and drier than the woman," who tends to be cold and moist, and so men inherit both heat, the abundance of body and facial hair it produces, and the ideals associated with it.[20] Like Bulwer, Hill entertains the possibilities of both the effeminate man and the masculine woman, associating these deviations with wilful manipulation rather than "natural" causes. The apparently neat and tidy formulas that Hill advances, however, have limits that betray the semiotic's contradictions. Hill, for example, attributes some hair colors to environmental climate rather than to embodied degree, and although abundant hair generally signifies virile masculinity, "The whole bodie covered with heare, both thicke and rough: doth denote such a person to be of a more brutish will and nature, than manly."[21] Hill suggests that at an undefined point, hairiness not only fails to signify masculinity but threatens to undo civility and humanity by denoting brutish animalism. Since the sex and gender categories and hierarchies that hair is supposed to materialize "naturally" are historically and culturally discontinuous, the exceptions and deceptions that vex early modern hair polemics ultimately expose the contingency of the entire semiotic.

EARLY MODERN ENGLISHMEN AND HAIR

The biblical injunction against men growing long hair on their heads typifies a problem central to early modern attributions of "natural" value to hair. Bulwer initially cites Pliny's observation that "Men by the Donations of Nature, have as long Haire on their Heads as Women," but he subsequently decides that "For Men to nourish long Haire is quite contrary to the intention of Nature," quoting St. Paul's judgment "that long Haire in a Man is a shame."[22] The logical dilemma arising from such judgments—that Nature intends men to have short hair on their heads but inexplicably bestows on men hair that will grow long—forces Bulwer to justify the very artificial manipulations he otherwise deems "unnatural." Bulwer thus contradictorily argues that Englishmen's maintaining short hair functions as a sign of their civility, "just moderation," and comeliness, not only distinguishing them from women but also differentiating them from the filthy Irish and "Barb'rous Indians," both of whom Bulwer condemns "for never cutting nor regulating their Haire, as suffering themselves to enter into a nearer alliance with Beasts then ever Nature intended." Paradoxically, Bulwer thus approves tonsure (from the Latin *tondēre*, meaning to clip, shear, or shave) as "made by Art, although for a Naturall end."[23] The "natural" result—sex and gender differentiation and stratification—is ironically a product not of "nature" but of human intervention. Accounting it shameful that "one Sex cannot be known or distinguished from another," Bulwer appeals to "the Counsell of the best Physitians," who advise that men's "Haire should descend no lower than the Eares."[24] Artifice, in this deeply flawed system, is thus not only acceptable but paradoxically necessary in order to obtain "natural" sex and gender distinctions. So, Bulwer wants it both ways: on one hand, unadulterated hair reflects Nature's perfect order but, on the other, Englishmen must trim their excess hair in order to differentiate themselves from women, foreigners, and beasts.

For William Prynne, in *The Unlovelinesse of Love-lockes*, the effeminacy of men with long, curled hair not only impacts the individual but, by extension, also compromises national masculinity:

> Is it not now held the accomplished Gallantrie of our youth, to Frizle their Haire like Women: and to become Womanish ... even in the very length, and Culture of their Lockes, and Haire? Are not many now of late degenerated into Virginians,

Frenchmen, Ruffians, nay, Women, in their Crisped-Lockes and Haire? ... and shall they yet professe themselves to be English-men?[25]

At stake in the individual's tonsorial conformity or transgression is the integrity of the entire system. Prynne uses biblical precedent from Leviticus and 1 Corinthians to assert that men who grow their hair long "expressely oppose, and contradict the word of God" in an act "directly contrary to the Law of Nature," since long hair is "naturally a Womans glory."[26] Prynne (like Bulwer and Hill) further denounces men who pay excessive attentions to their hair, warning that by "Crisping, Curling, [and] Frouncing ... of their Lockes and Hairie excrements," men will become "wholly degenerated and metamorphosed into women."[27] In Phillip Stubbes's *Anatomy of Abuses*, Amphilogus

> cannot but marvell at the beastlinesse of some ruffians ... that will have their haire to growe over their faces like monsters, and savage people, nay rather like mad men than otherwise, hanging downe over their shoulders, as womens haire doth: which indeed is an ornament to them [i.e. women], being given them as a signe of subjection, but in man, it is a shame and reproch.[28]

Thomas Hall declaims *The Loathsomnesse of Long Haire* worn by men, insisting that it "is unlawful ... not onely by mans Law ... but by the Law of God ... [and] contrary to that order which God hath set in nature."[29] Hall cites biblical precedent to condemn shaving the head or growing its hair long, advocating only polling, tonsuring, and "even rounding of the head."[30] As Will Fisher notes, the reiteration of these scriptural directives carried potent political charges in the mid-seventeenth century, when "hair became the principal way of distinguishing between the two political factions of the English Civil War. Parliamentarians ... supposedly had close-cropped hair and came to be known as "'roundheads' ... [while] Royalists ... were known for their long flowing tresses and were labelled 'cavaliers.'"[31] Since most early modern treatises on hair were written by Puritans (who also tended to be Parliamentarians) during the height of the conflict, they predictably associate men's short hair with godliness and propriety and long hair with effeminacy and vice, thereby exposing their political and religious motives for maintaining a traditional, conservative stance on hair conventions in relation to sex and gender normativity.

According to Hill, hair color signified variously gendered degrees, with darker shades like black and red signaling high masculine heat, middling shades like brown and blonde signaling moderate heat, and pale colors like gray and white signaling low or dwindling heat.[32] Different quantities and qualities of hair also manifested gendered degrees: Hill contends that few hairs denote coldness, while many hairs confirm heat, citing Aristotle's assessment that "very thinne" hairs on the head "doe indicate an effeminate minde" since the brain's heat and moisture determine the quality and quantity of hair that the scalp produces.[33] Generally, thin hair is a product of low and thick hair of high heat, while straight hair stems from a cold, moist humor and curly hair from a hot, dry complexion. Bulwer judges any cosmetic process that colors or dyes hair a "trespasse against nature," "a foolish and ridiculous affectation," and "a sinful vanity" justly derided upon discovery, thereby approving only "natural" hair coloration.[34] Bulwer specifically attacks "old Leachers, who knowing grey haires in the Beard to be a manifest signe of decay in the generative faculty, and an approaching impotency incident to Age, vainely endeavour to obliterate the naturall signification thereof" and derides "old Coxcombs" who attempt to alter the semiotic, calling such manipulations "a terrible thing, and not to be endured."[35] Men who are advanced in years, or those with "the beard discerned soone hoarie," Hill reminds his reader, "their nature then is knowne, to draw neere unto the womans."³⁶ As men age and their vital heat and moisture begin to dwindle, their hair whitens and thins in direct proportion to their declining reproductive virility, so graying hair and beards signaled waning masculinity. Elderly men were thus the most likely purchasers of hair dyes that would allow them to maintain the semblance of youth and vitality.

Bulwer and Hill unanimously condemn all such artificial hair manipulations, but both also allow exceptions to their rules. In his discussion of eyebrow hair, for example, Bulwer asserts on one hand that plucking, shaving, dyeing, and so forth are unnatural but, on the other, that some management is requisite: "when they [i.e. the eyebrows] prove overgrown in old Men ... they stand in need of clipping," and "The regulating of the Haires of the Eye-brows when they chance to grow out of orders, and the reducing them with Pinsers or Scissors to conformity, is but a Cosmetique elegancie."³⁷ Like the hair of the head, Bulwer suggests, the hair of the eyebrows is best in its "natural" state, unless "Natural Law" (common sense) suggests that the hair must be forced to conform to Nature's original intent. Thomas Hill similarly devotes a chapter of his treatise to considering "The forme and judgement of the overbrowes," which he contends "expresse the affections of the minde" but must also "of necessitie, and for comelynesse sake ... be clypped" when they grow too long.³⁸ Contradictorily, Bulwer calls hair removal by Greek and Roman men the "effeminate plucking and pulling of their bodies, and abusing it with depilatories," which he judges to be "unmanly practices" performed by "effeminate Men ... [who] are to be pitied."³⁹ Bulwer ultimately insists on the evils of depilation by concluding that

> Man is perfect when he wants none of those things which he ought to have, for that is his perfection ... Whatever Haire is in the body, whatever it be (so nothing happen besides Nature) it is necessary, which we ought to be persuaded of, and that by a reason, no way contemptible, taken from the dignity of Nature, who always whatsoever she doth, shee doth for some end.⁴⁰

But Bulwer's parenthetic caveat, which suggests that fallen Nature relies on human intervention to signify correctly, again exposes the speciousness of the entire semiotic: men must alter their hair in conformance with "natural" sex and gender ideals.

THE EARLY MODERN ENGLISH MALE BEARD

Beards in Renaissance England have a rather storied history: throughout the fourteenth and early fifteenth centuries, the beard was popular among Englishmen, but that trend was apparently curtailed when Henry V was struck by an arrow in battle and underwent surgery to remove it. Suffering permanent and extensive facial scarring, Henry determined not to hide his injury beneath a patchy beard but instead proudly to display his war wound as evidence of his martial valor, thereby establishing a fashion for beardlessness that lasted for more than a century. From Henry's reign (1413–1422), a succession of English monarchs remained unbearded: Henry VI (1422–1461), Edward IV (1461–1470 and 1471–1483), Edward V (who reigned a mere seventy-eight days), Richard III (1483–1485), and Henry VII (1485–1509) are all depicted without facial hair—as was Henry VIII (1485–1509) in the early decades of his reign. The beard's popularity as a signifier of virile manhood in post-Reformation England can, in part, be attributed to Henry VIII, who insisted on allowing his beard to flourish despite both the objections of his first wife,

Catherine of Aragon, and the long-standing fashion for beardlessness. In a display staged at court on May 8, 1535 and subsequently immortalized in John Stowe's *Annales*, the king "commanded all about his court to poll their heads, & to give them example, he caused his own head to be polled, and from thenceforth his beard to be notted and no more shaven," thereby modelling ideal masculine authority to his court as short-haired and bearded.[41] Henry also appears on the title page of the first English translation of scripture, the Great Bible of 1539, distributing bibles with short hair and a beard, further exemplifying Protestant masculinity for male emulation.

In humoral terms, beards signaled male testicular viability and semen production, and so "naturally" appeared solely on the faces of males who had achieved what the culture construed as manhood. Thomas Hill devotes a chapter of his text to "The condicion, and judgement of the Beard," claiming that "The bearde in man ... beginneth to appear in the neather Jawe, which so ascendeth towarde the Temples, through the heate and moisture, carried unto the same, from the forepart of the genitours: which draw to them especially, the sperme from those places."[42] Bulwer cites Ulmus's *De fine Barbae Humane* in order to assert that "Nature gave to mankind a Beard, that it might remaine as an Index in the Face, of the Masculine Generative faculty."[43] Men who shave their beards thus essentially castrate themselves. Bulwer relates the story of "*Clisthenes* ... branded in the Proverbe, *Clisthenes rasura*; who to seeme young ridiculously suffered himself every day to be shaved," thus justly earning himself "scoffs" and "infamy."[44] While Clisthenes' smoothness gains him the appearance of youth, it simultaneously earns him the social inferiority and derision appropriate to that low degree. Hill claims that "As touching the womans testicles [ovaries], in that these are but weake, for the same cause [as fertile men have beards] are they [women] knowne not to be bearded," citing ancient wisdom to set "after xiiii yeares of age" as the time when beard growth begins to occur.[45] But early modern London guilds and fraternal institutions like the universities and Inns of Court levied fines on boys who failed to shave their facial hair, thereby delaying the display of beards by males until after they had achieved mastery and citizenship. Since apprentices were not permitted to engage in "the honourable estate of [procreative] marriage" until completing the terms of their indenture, beard growth and reproductive fertility were linked in both medical theory and social practice.[46] Beardless boys were thus considered (sexually/socially) impotent, even though many males would, in reality, have reached puberty well before achieving mastery. In early modern English parlance, the terms "boy" and "man" referred not to age per se but rather to relative degree, so while some "boys" might physically be capable of growing beards, some "men" might not. Such is the case with Abel Drugger in Ben Jonson's *The Alchemist* who, although he has achieved the requisite status to become "free of the Grocers" (1.3.5), is not physically able to grow facial hair and so has gullibly purchased "A receipt, to make hair come" (1.3.39).[47] In Shakespeare's *Much Ado About Nothing*, Beatrice reasons, "He that hath a beard is more than a youth, and he that hath no beard is less than a man" (2.1.36–7).[48] Despite the apparent logic of her claim, Beatrice's assumption is actually syllogistic: what she regards as a "natural" distinction (beardedness/beardlessness) differentiating men from boys is actually a product of systematic social practice instead.

Beards also signified status in economic terms, functioning as a symbol of wealth, prestige, and privilege. Robert Greene's *A Quip for an Upstart Courtier* depicts Clothbreeches complaining that his barber affords affluent men like Velvetbreeches preferential treatment and an array of beard styles, while offering only one basic cut to poor men like Clothbreeches.[49] Since small, meticulously manicured styles required regular maintenance, they were favored by the elite as visual confirmation of their possessing disposal time and wealth. Benjamin Rudyerd's "A Commendation and Censure of Beards" perpetuates the fantasy of the beard's "natural" occurrence by concluding, "But the beard I commend / Is no Barbers friend, / Where nature acts his part, / Which grows on the face / In due form and place, / And scorns the help of Art" (lines 91–6).[50] Rudyerd implies that beards assume their "due form" without any artificial assistance—but even Bulwer and Hill concede that beards require the barber's intervention in order to materialize status accurately.

Every quality of the beard (color, style, length, thickness, etc.) was taken into account in early modern assessments of male degree. For Hill, beard color "doth sometimes express the qualities & quanityes of the humors," though he admits that the system is not infallible. Men with red beards, for example, "are knowne to be luxurious, deceavers, and lyars: and in them ... does the principall heape of vices rest: unlesse that grace & godly education, seeme otherwise to contrarie the abovesayde."[51] Hill also reads the shape, style, and thickness of beards as indicative of male virtue:

> The bearde discerned comely, and well fashioned: doth innuate [i.e. intimate] such a creature to be of a good nature, of reasonable conditions, congruent to all thinges, and mannered after his bringing up. Contrariwise judge of them, which have the beard not seemely formed, or evill fashioned in the length: as appeare thin the gelded persons, which after they are depryved of their genytours, be then greatly changed, from the nature of men, into the condition of women.[52]

Despite the fact that beard fashioning entails artificial manipulation, Hill maintains that there is a "natural" correlation between the appearance of the beard and the relative masculinity of the male who sports it. The anonymous author of "The Ballad of the Beard" pauses near the conclusion of his poetic catalogue of beards and the occupations characterizing them to praise the exemplary beard of Henry VIII: "But oh! Let us tarry for the beard of King Harry, / That grows about the chin, / With his bushy pride, and a grove on each side, / And a champion ground between" (lines 53–6).[53] Here, the anonymous author describes Henry's beard—which featured not only on the title page of the Great Bible but also on the faces of a set of gold coins minted in 1544 and in a great deal of contemporary portraiture—in martial terms, associating it with military victory.[54] Since the beard symbolized virility, many period styles were named after and cut to look like phallic weaponry. As "The Ballad of the Beard" confirms, particular shapes and colors were also strongly associated with specific occupations. The spade beard, for example, was typically worn by soldiers and associated with martial fortitude, taking the shape of the spade or shovel that would dig an enemy's grave. In this light, beards materialized not only sex, by distinguishing men from women, but also gender status, by disambiguating men from other males.

Symbolizing both the relativity and the mutability of sex and gender designations, early modern barbers constituted a necessary evil: on one hand, they profited by marketing the latest (detestable, foreign, improper) hair fashions to the highest paying customers but, on the other, they were crucial for maintaining the visibility of the social order that hair in all its variety made manifest. In Phillip Stubbes's *The Second Part of the Anatomy of Abuses*, Amphilogus derisively lists the many beard styles available in barbershops in Ailgna (*Anglia*, or *England*, backwards) but ironically concludes that "barbers are verie necessarie, for otherwise men should grow verie ouglisom and deformed, and their hair would in process of time overgrowe their faces, rather like monsters, than comlie sober

Christians."⁵⁵ Without barbers to wash, trim, groom, and style their hair, Amphilogus suggests, Englishmen might not only appear less beautified but also corporeally degenerate from godly, civilized humans into pagan foreigners or wild animals. By this logic, hair possesses the ability to fashion the individual who sports it by either materializing or nullifying crucial categorical qualities, but Amphilogus's comment also exposes a rhetorical contradiction pervading early modern discussions of hair's constitutive, creative, transformative power: on one hand, hair signifies innate status "naturally," as part of a divine semiotic code, but, on the other hand, hair is crucially reliant, requiring the barber's tending, maintenance, supplementation, and removal services in order to signify status correctly.

As Bulwer insists, men who shave their beards undo their manhood, becoming beardless and "therein not men."⁵⁶ Bulwer calls the beard the "naturall Ensigne of Manhood" and condemns its removal "as unseemely as to shave the Crest of a Lyon" (Figure 6.1), ultimately comparing shaving to castration. "Shaving the Chin is justly to be accounted a note of Effeminacy," he contends, "For what greater evidence can be given of Effeminacy than to be transformed into the appearance of a woman, and to be seen with a smooth skin like a woman, a shamefull metamorphosis!"⁵⁷ Despite listing several reasons why men might want to remove their facial hair—its interfering with mastication, its drooping into food and beverages, its catching spit and snot, hindering elocution, and so forth—Bulwer ultimately defends the utility of the beard and mustache, insisting on their "being placed there for certain uses and ends," though he is less forthcoming about what these "uses and ends" might be.⁵⁸

FIGURE 6.1 Bearded lion being observed by two bearded men, from Thomas Hill, *The Contemplation of Mankinde* (1571), op. p. 187. This item is reproduced by permission of the Huntington Library, San Marino, CA.

Although he advocates trimming and keeping beards "regulated at ones pleasure and arbitrement," Bulwer warns that "to shave or pull up" the beard "Nature never meant he should."[59] Beard tugging, pulling, and plucking were considered direct attacks on a man's status, a principle Bulwer also applies to self-inflicted depilation or shaving. In Shakespeare's *King Lear*, Regan defies gender convention by plucking hair from the traitor Gloucester's beard as an act of ritual humiliation before her husband Albany plucks out the old man's eyes. Bulwer reports how "the *Turkes*, who shave their slaves, do justly scoffe at such Christians, who cut, or naturally want a beard, as suffering themselves to be abused against Nature," thereby implying that even heathen nations recognize beard shaving as a punitive act that removes male status along with the hair.[60] To remove the beard that God intended is "a willingnesse to evert the Law of Nature," Bulwer claims, "the Beard is a singular gift of God, which who shaves away, he aimes at nothing than to become lesse man. An Act not only of indecency, but of injustice, and ingratitude against God and Nature, repugnant to Scripture."[61] Bulwer offers examples of exotic, foreign beard removal practices, implicitly condemning them as heathen and barbaric, while extolling the English beard as "natural" sign of godliness and civility. Bulwer's rhetoric here, like Prynne's likening men with long hair to foreigners, partakes in a pervasive early modern racial gendering, which regarded beardless, unbarbered "New World" native men as effeminate barbarians and inferior, ungodly sodomites, thereby justifying English seizure of their lands and suppression of their languages, religions, and cultures. Bulwer repeatedly emphasizes the "natural honesty" of the beard, its reflecting "as in a Glasse" or mirror the qualities of the man who sports it, but his anxious tendency to vilify any excessive manipulation that might alter the "natural" correspondence between signifier and signified tacitly confirms not only how easily beards can be altered through shaping, styling, dyeing, depilation, or prosthetic supplementation, but also how vigilantly the semiotic equating hair with sex and gender status must be regulated, policed, and managed in order to correctly obtain.[62]

EARLY MODERN ENGLISHWOMEN AND HAIR

Asserting that Nature "hath granted [women] by a peculiar indulgence, as an Ornament and beauty, the increase of long Haire, even down unto the Feet: Nature having allowed them in recompence of their smoothnesse and want of a Beard, prolixe Haire," Bulwer construes women's long hair as compensation for their lacking beards, thereby implying that lengthy tresses were as constitutive to properly submissive femininity as beards were to divinely entitled manhood.[63] This claim certainly holds true in period drama, wherein boys wore long wigs in order to play the parts of women and beards in order to undertake the parts of men. In Ben Jonson's *Epicoene*, Dauphine hires a boy actor to impersonate a woman and marry his wealthy uncle—a part the boy assumes by wearing a peruke, or wig. When that peruke is removed in the dénouement, revealing the short hair of the boy actor beneath, the moment immediately and completely undoes Epicoene's womanhood. Early modern Englishwomen who defiantly cropped their hair short thus opened themselves to accusations of being unnaturally masculine. The anti-cross-dressing pamphlet *Hic Mulier* (1620) decries "Masculine-women" who exchange "the glory of a faire large hayre, to the shame of amost ruffianly short lockes," insisting that "The long hayre of a woman is the ornament of her sexe, and bashfull shamefastnesse her chiefe honour: the long haire of a man, the vizard for a theevish or murderous disposition."[64] The title page of the pamphlet depicts a pair of women being tended by a scissor-wielding barber and his boy beneath the caption, "Mistris, will you be trim'd or truss'd?" Women who crop their hair short, the pamphlet implies, assume male prerogative and so constitute monstrously unnatural aberrations. Hill's and Bulwer's mid-seventeenth-century polemics, considered alongside the *Haec Vir* and *Hic Mulier* pamphlets, not only confirm the prior popularity of the conservative hair fashions for which they all advocate but also imply that fashions in hair were in a state of transition. Indeed, Corson contends that by the middle of the seventeenth century, the popularity of the beard was waning, and longer hairstyles for men, including the love-lock and powdered wig, were quickly coming into vogue.

In the late seventeenth century, Thomas Wall published a defense of sexual differentiation entitled *God's Holy Order in Nature*, in which he focuses on the gender propriety of hair length. Wall asserts that since woman was intended to be the glory of man, "it was therefore a pleasure of God to give unto Woman a sign in nature differing from Man, to teach her subjection to Man whose Glory she is, namely long hair; and that Man was created with short hair, is also clear."[65] In the Third Eglogue of a section of pastoral dialogues called "The Shepheards Tales," Linus complains about his beloved Lesbia's tendency to follow the latest fashion:

> Though ill it seemes a country Shepheardesse,
> Such harsh fantasticke fashions to professe:
> One day vnto a *Barber* she'de repaire,
> And for what end but this, to cut her haire,
> So as like to a *Boy* she did appeare,
> Hauing her haire round cut vnto her eare.
> ...
> So strangely clipt she seem'd, and in disguise,
> So monstrous ougly, as none could deuise
> To see one clad in lothsomer attire:
> And this she knew was farre from my desire,
> For I did euer hate it.[66]

Linus's rhetoric here condemns short hair on women as strangely boyish, monstrous, ugly, loathsome, and wholly undesirable. Similarly, the introduction to William Prynne's treatise *The Unlovelinesse of Love-lockes* castigates women who cut their tresses short, bemoaning the "Degenerous, Unnaturall, and Unmanly times: wherein as sundry of our Mannish, Impudent, and inconstant Female sexe, are Hermaphrodited, and transformed into men ... even in the unnaturall Tonsure, and Odious, if not Whorish Cutting, and Crisping of their Haire, their Naturall vaile, their Feminine glory, and the very badge and Character of their subjection both to God, and Man."[67] Prynne continues by chastising "our Immodest, Impudent and ... mannish Viragoes, or audacious Men-women, [who] doe unnaturally clip, and cut their Haire; wearing their Lockes, and Fore-tops (as they stile them) in an odious, and shamelesse manner, as if ... they were really transformed, and transubstantiated into Males, by a stupendious metamorphosis."[68] Although he lists some exceptions to the rule, Prynne ultimately insists that cutting or clipping her hair "is the most infamous, unnaturall, and shamefull thing, that can befall a woman." For Prynne, women's long hair functions as "a Badge, or Embleme of their subjection to their Husbands," so any alteration of that ensign signals a defiance of the "natural" order, which threatens the entire socio-sexual hierarchy.[69]

Thomas Hill directly associates the "naturally" smooth hairlessness of women's faces and bodies with the cultural ideals of female silence and submissiveness: "The perfite woman, is knowne to be sufficiently naked of heares, especially about the mouth: suche a creature ... is reported and judged to be of a good qualities: that is to say, bashefull, fearefull, honest, weake of courage, gentle of behauiour, and obedient."[70] Hill further contends that women ought to have "long comely heares on the head, yet little and small [i.e. few and fine] heares on the breast, belly, hands, and feete, through hir cold complexion" (Figure 6.2).[71] For hair moralists, the ideally submissive, obedient woman has long, unadorned hair on her head and no hair at all on her face or body. Attempting to explain why men should have beards and women none, Hill suggests that Nature made women beardless in order to make her less independent, unable to bear the "bitter colde weather" or "suffer greateer stormes on the bodye, than she maye, without harme to insue."[72] Women's lacking beards is thus Nature's way of keeping them dependent on men for survival, so bearded women embody independence and autonomy—qualities in a woman that early modern patriarchal culture found deeply disturbing. Bulwer asserts that "Woman by Nature is smooth and delicate; and if she have many haires she is a Monster," nevertheless admitting, "yet such Monsters have appeared in the World," and subsequently enumerating several "monstrous" women who have been reported to possess facial beards. By conclusion, Bulwer remarks that "women through discontinuance of the Company of men, and defect of their Courses, have grown Bearded, and passed into virile

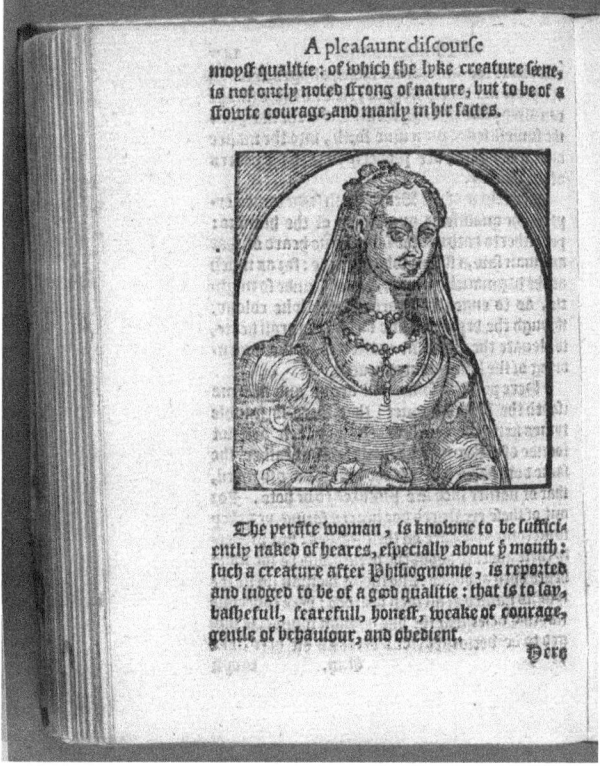

FIGURE 6.2 Woodcut illustrating "The perfite woman" from Thomas Hill, *The Contemplation of Mankinde* (1571), op. p. 148. This item is reproduced by permission of the Huntington Library, San Marino, CA.

appearance, not without danger to their health and life."[73] Alexander Read, in a series of lectures delivered to the London barber-surgeons, similarly asserts that "in women their courses being stopped, vapours ascend to the chin, from whence a beard doth bud out. As Hippoc[rates] ... doth report of Phaetusa the wife of Pytheus, who got a beard by reason of her husbands absence from her."[74] Thomas Hill's book of dream interpretations tells of a woman who "dreamed, to haue a halfe a bearde, who after lyued separate from her husbande, so that if she had thought to haue a whole bearde, then after to be a wydowe."[75] According to this logic, women who fail to serve the patriarchal reproductive agenda by living single, without male headship (such as spinsters or widows), or by surviving past childbearing years, run the risk of growing beards by existing outside the "natural" order prescribed by God and Nature. Such women, Bulwer suggests, are dangerous—to themselves, to others, and to the social hierarchy—and so must be corrected or eradicated.

Women with extremely hot testicles (or ovaries), Hill reasons, not only grow facial hair but are also excessively prone to "coeating," or copulating (*OED*): "suche women which are found to have these [testicles] hoter than the common sort, have also somewhat of the refiered matter ... [which] draweth with it the moisture, of which in them [women] are engendred the thinne and small heares of the Bearde: and thys especiallye verified in them, which use often and verye much coeating."[76] "Out of these creatures," Hill continues,

> doe heares spring, yea they sometimes appear on their Jawes: but properly these appear about the mouth, where the more heate doth abounde: and such a woman ... is named of all men bearded: here conceive ... that the like woman founde, is judged to be verie luxurious through hir hote, and moyste qualitie: of which the lyke creature seene, is not onely noted strong of nature, but to be of a frowte courage, and manly in hir factes.[77]

Hill's concluding synopsis on beards includes a succinct analysis of women and facial hair: "The woman bearded, to be leacherous. The women having no bearde at all, to be honest conditioned."[78]

Despite their evoking concern about sex, gender, and erotic transgressions, bearded women were both depicted and displayed in Renaissance England, apparently evoking a mixture of fearful hostility and anxious curiosity. Most images of bearded women, like that of the bearded Venus gracing the Italian and French editions of Vincenzo Cartari's collection of classical myths, were of foreign provenance, but Catholic legends of bearded female saints—St. Paula of Avila, Spain, and St. Wilgefortis or Uncumber, who reputedly unencumbered wives of their unwanted husbands—may have remained familiar to English readers after the Reformation. Witches were also frequently depicted as bearded, as are the *weird* (or wayward) sisters in Shakespeare's *Macbeth*: Banquo tells them, "You should be women, / And yet your beards forbid me to interpret / That you are so" (lines 3.45–7).[79] Some women with beards were displayed as attractions in late seventeenth-century England. John Evelyn reports in his diary entry for September 15, 1657 going to see "the hairy Maid, or Woman who twenty years before I had also seene when a child ... [S]he had ... a most prolix beard, & *mustachios.*"[80] Evelyn describes the lady's having a hairless breast, being married with one child, and playing well on the harpsichord. In his edition of the diary, William Bray concludes that the woman Evelyn viewed was Barbara van Beck, an image of whom appears in the 1824 edition of Rev. J. Granger's *Biographical History of England* as Barbara Urselin/Urselerin, wife to one Michael van Beck (Figure 6.3). In that illustration, a girlish but hirsute Barbara plays the

FIGURE 6.3 Mounted fragment of an illustration of unknown origin, purportedly depicting bearded woman Barbara, wife to Michael van Beck, at twenty-nine years of age. Barbara stands beside a pipe organ—a symbol of her domestic propriety that symbolically defuses the subversive power of her facial beard. Reproduced by permission and copyright the author's private collection.

virginals, a musical instrument considered particularly appropriate for young maidens. In his commentary, Granger compares her appearance to that of "a monkey. She has a very long and large spreading beard, the hair of which hangs loose and flowing like the hair of the head. She is playing on an organ. Vanbeck married this frightful creature, on purpose to carry her about for a show."[81] A later image of Barbara appears in the 1869 edition of Henry Wilson's *Wonderful Characters*, wherein she is identified as Barbara Urslerin, the hairy-faced woman and is again compared to a monkey.[82] In his edition of Evelyn's diary, William Bray claims knowledge of three portraits of Barbara, including a representation in "some German Book of Natural History."[83] A third illustration of Barbara depicts her at a still later date standing beside a pipe organ that, together with her conventional attire and claims of her being a good wife and mother, help to situate her within the realm of female domestic propriety that offsets and defuses her beardedness.[84] Samuel Pepys records in his diary that on December 21, 1668 he went "into Holborne, and there saw the woman that is to be seen with a beard ... bushy and thick. It was a strange sight to me, I confess, and pleased me mightily."[85] By the late seventeenth century, with the rise of the two-sex model and the centrality of genitalia as primary sexual signifiers, beards no longer materialized manhood as they had in humoral theory, so bearded women no longer posed the profound threat to the socio-sexual order that they once had. Displayed together with reassurances of their domestic propriety, male headship, and dutiful reproduction, bearded women could constitute "natural" wonders, whose conformity to cultural norms of femininity ultimately confirmed, rather than threatened, the social order.

CONCLUSION

Early modern English writers imagine a close alliance between God and Nature, arguing that whatever Nature produces generally reflects God's will. Early modern English treatises attempting to read the body thus champion a "natural" correlation between appearance and sex/gender status and commend those members of society who uphold the normative ideal by appearing precisely as God/Nature intended, thereby confirming the "naturalness" of the sex and gender hierarchy. Of course, this reasoning is ultimately specious since, on one hand, complete failure to attend to one's outer appearance might blur the boundaries distinguishing human from animal or civilized from barbaric, while, on the other, excessive manipulation might lead to the blurring of boundaries distinguishing aristocrats from commoners, boys from men, men from women, and so forth. The solution, then, is for individuals conscientiously to regulate their own appearances with honesty and integrity, to vigilantly style and maintain their outer selves in conformance with the semiotic system, by knowing their proper station and strictly obeying its codes of appearance and conduct, while also policing their neighbors. This reliance on human compliance to validate a supposedly "natural" order, which in turn validates a putatively divinely ordained social hierarchy, renders the semiotic far from self-sufficient or stable, and Renaissance writers express considerable anxiety about potentials for error or transgression. That Nature must rely on human effort to maintain its integrity ultimately suggests that Nature is ironically not "natural" at all—that Nature, like the hierarchies it validates, is an artificial, historically and culturally contingent construct. Since hair is not intrinsically meaningful and possesses no history of its own, it freights instead a cultural history, a record of the significances socially and historically attached to it. Early modern English assertions of hair's "natural" or "unnatural" occurrences thus reveal far more about the culture's ideological sex and gender presumptions than about any inherent, fixed correspondences between hair and any predetermined *degree*.

CHAPTER SEVEN

Race and Ethnicity

NICHOLAS JONES

This chapter explores cultural and literary representations of black Africans' hair in sixteenth- and seventeenth-century Spain. Described alongside skin color, lips and the nose, and genitalia, hair powerfully signals the racial otherness of blacks in early modern Spain.[1] The image of blacks in Iberian early modernity, often constructed by white dramatists, poets, and prose writers, reflected black Africans' condition as slaves. "Images of Africans, whether in erudite ethnology or poplar caricature," explains Jeremy Lawrance, "constantly retraced a vicious circle in which the insidious link between body and culture identified black nudity as an allegory of unbridled lechery, giving rise to an image of Africans as noisy, feckless children of nature prone to unrestrained physicality."[2] To have dark skin and the hair of a black African was indicative of a social mark of difference. In the pages ahead, this chapter will examine the contradictory and paradoxical ways in which white Spanish writers depicted black Africans' cultural and racial difference through their hair. While the first part of this chapter defines and describes the term "race" in early modern Spain—thus illustrating how white Spanish writers who represented black Africans in their works often denigrate them—the second half will provide a close reading of an intermission skit—referred to as an *entremés* or a *paso*—inserted within Lope de Rueda's larger play *Comedia Eufemia* (1542/1554) that features a black woman character named Eulalla and her white male suitor Polo. This short-skit play serves as a case study to highlight Rueda's representation of Eulalla's blackness and performative challenging of whiteness through her hair. These two parts converse with one another in order to underscore this study's larger contention that early modern Spanish depictions of sub-Saharan Africans' hair reveal black African hair not only as aesthetically abject but also the corporeal site where—through the mimicry of white European hair—blacks can articulate and perform their resistance to colonizing disempowerment and dehumanization. Eulalla and the theatrical performance of her being blonde ultimately furnish a fascinating interlude to see hair as a cultural artifact that empowers the analysis of race in Renaissance studies.

RACE IN EARLY MODERN SPAIN

In early modern Spanish literature, the word "race" (commonly *raza* in Castilian, *raça* in Portuguese, and *race* in French and English) seldom appears directly to describe black African bodies. During the medieval and early modern periods in Europe, the definition of race designated lineage or genealogy along the lines of a shared ancestry. The Spanish lexicographer Sebastián de Covarrubias y Horozco (1510–1579), in his *Tesoro de la lengua castellana o española* (1611), defines *raza* in terms of horses, textiles, and lineages in the following manner:

> La casta de caballos castizos, a los cuales señalan con hierro para que sean conocidos. Raza, en el paño, la hilaza que diferencia de los demás hilos de la trama. Parece haberse dicho *quasi* reaza, porque *aza*, en lengua toscana, vale hilo, y la raza en el paño sobrepuesto desigual. Raza, en los linajes se toma en mala parte, como tener alguna raza de moro o judío.
>
> (The caste of purebred horses, which are branded with iron, so they can be recognized. *Raza* in woven fabric is the thread that differentiates other threads in the weave. It appears to be said also as *reaza*, for *aza* in the Tuscan language, means thread, and that the *raza* on the fabric represents an unequal appliqué. *Raza* in lineage is understood to be bad, such as having the *raza* of a Moor or a Jew.)[3]

For Covarrubias, *raza* operates interchangeably with lineage, echoing John Florio's Italian–English 1598 dictionary *A Worlde of Wordes*, which defines "razza" as "a kind, a brood, a blood, a stock, a pedigree."[4] But Covarrubias complicates his definition of *raza* as lineage with his own anxieties about the mixing among different racial groups. Although Covarrubias uses his definition of *raza* to refer to horses, his insistence on referencing this specific animal is noteworthy. His idea of *raza* as "*casta*" (caste) changes from "*linaje*" (lineage) into explicit anxieties concerning racial mixing that will alter the cleanliness, or purity, of one's blood, or *limpieza de sangre*.

Covarrubias's Hispanic-oriented lexical constitution of *casta* complicates the meaning of *raza*, especially in the eighteenth-century *Diccionario de Autoridades* (1726–1739), which threads a definition of *raza* similar to that of Covarrubias published a century prior.

> RAZA. Casta o calidad del origen o linage. Hablando de los hombres, se toma mui regularmente en mala parte ... Defin. de Cal[atrava]: "Ordenamos y mandamos que ninguna persona, de qualquiera calidad y condición que fuere, sea recibida a la dicha Orden ... sino fuere Hijodalgo ... y de legitimo matrimonio nacido, y que no le toque *raza* de Judio, Moro, Herege, ni Villano."
>
> (RACE. Caste or quality of one's origin or lineage. Speaking of men, generally understood to be bad ... [By the knightly brotherhood] of Cal[atrava]: "We order and command that no one, of whatsoever quality and condition, be received into the said Order ... unless he be a Gentleman ... born of legitimate matrimony, and not of Jewish, Moorish, Heretic race, nor commoners.")[5]

The early modern understanding of race bleeds over into Spanish Enlightenment constructions of the term, which are not mutually exclusive from one another. Each definition from Covarrubias and the *Diccionario de Autoridades* reveals its inheritance of Castilian politics of race ca. 1492, which hinged on the purity or impurity of one's Christianity. María Elena Martínez in "The Language, Genealogy, and Classification of 'Race' in Colonial Mexico," suggests "that Spain's late medieval nobility was not a closed caste did not temper its belief in the superiority of its 'blood' and its use of the concept of *raza* to distinguish itself from commoners. Indeed, some of Spain's military orders only granted habits to persons whose ancestors had been of noble blood and without the 'race or mixture of commoners.'"[6] In addition to discourses of ethnicity and race in relation to blood and social and religious institutions such as military order, we can also include the relationship between hair and race in Inquisition trials in both Spain and its colonies in the Americas and the Pacific. Concerning both inquisitors and nosey neighbors, for example, was the idea that hair embodied a complex and racially gendered association with Catholic morality and an individual's social status. I have found that the Inquisition racialized hair, as evidence and grounds for heresy, along the lines of seduction, temptation, prostitution (or rather transactional sex), and, more broadly, anti-cosmetic sentiments.

In the early modern Castilian lexicon, *casta* sheds light on other cultural and social issues that directly relate to the category of race, racial difference, and the mixing of different groups of people. For the linguist, *casta*:

> Vale linaje noble; y castizo, el que es de buena línea y decendencia, no embargante que decimos es de buena casta y mala casta. Díjose casta, de *castus, a, m*, porque para la generación y procreación de los hijos, conviene no ser los hombres viciosos, ni desenfrenados en el acto venéreo; por cuya causa los distraídos no engendran y los recogidos y que tratan poco con mujeres tienen muchos hijos.
>
> (Equals a noble lineage, and *castizo* means one that is of good stock and descent; despite the fact that we say of good stock and bad stock. Caste is said from the root *castus, a, m*, due to the generation and procreation of offspring, it is better for men to be neither given to vice nor unbridled in the sexual act; for this cause distracted men do not engender children, while moderate men, who deal little with women, have many children.)[7]

The idea of a "lexicon of blood" best describes how the language of *raza* shifts to that of *casta*. The conception of "lexicon of blood," as Martínez explains, "had been influenced by common understandings of how reproduction functioned in the natural world (especially in the realm of horse breeding)."[8] While both *raza* and *casta* could refer to breed, species, and lineage, the two terms at times were, in fact, also used interchangeably to describe groupings of animals, plants, or humans.[9]

Casta, however, had a series of other connotations. If as a noun it was usually linked to lineage, as an adjective it could allude to chastity, nobility ("good breeding"), and legitimacy, and more generally to an uncorrupted sexual and genealogical history.[10] *Casta*, notably in the above-cited passage from Covarrubias's *Tesoro*, was thereby able to give way to the term *castizo*, which referred to a person of notable ancestry and legitimate birth.[11] When applied to humans, the language of race operative within Covarrubias's sixteenth-century definition of *casta* alludes to a system of social order centered around procreation and biological parenthood, one in which reproducing the pure and noble group was mainly predicated on maintaining the chastity of its women.[12] Whether in the "Old" or "New" World, as the above passage clearly insists, notions of caste purity and their privileging of endogamic marriage and legitimate birth were never separate (because of women's role in reproduction) from discourses of gender and female sexuality, from a sexual economy constituted by gendered notions of familial honor.

THE BLACK AFRICAN'S HAIR: HEGEMONY, RACE, STEREOTYPE

Europeans inhabiting the Iberian Peninsula had contact with sub-Saharan Africans for centuries. The Jews and Arabs living both within and outside of the Iberan Peninsula, for example, knew about dark-skinned Africans, and the scholarly attention Hispano-Arab and Jewish thinkers once gave to sub-Saharan Africans grew out of the development of African slavery in the Islamic world as far back as the eighth century.[13] From 711 until their expulsion in 1492, Muslims controlled a significant portion of the Iberian Peninsula. At the height of Islamic rule in Iberia, the Muslim world extended east to China, where wide-ranging Islamic influences had profound effects on the thinking of Iberians and, in many respects, charted the course of emerging racial hierarchies. And for these precise reasons, early Islamic racial ideologies theorizing black Africans' denigrated racial inferiority was codified through hair, skin color, and other cultural differences that ultimately codified a corpus of racialized knowledge about sub-Saharan Africans. Regarding the backdrop of African slavery in Spain, the intersection of racial, cultural, and religious animus was manifest most clearly during the medieval period in the writings of the Castilian king Alfonso X "the Learned." Generally believed to have fostered a thirteenth-century intellectual and spiritual renaissance in Castile, Alfonso X promoted a subtle philosophy of racial hostility and xenophobia.[14] Most of Alfonso's rancor was expressed in religious imagery by attacks on Jews and Muslims (as witnessed in his *Siete Partidas* for example), where he reserved his strongest antipathy for the black Moors of Africa.[15]

Since the medieval period in Iberia, Muslims from Toledo published treatises—oftentimes with extremely racist and disparaging sentiments—explaining the climatic theories for black Africans' hair and dark skin. A treatise by Sa'id al-Andalusi, an eleventh-century historian from Toledo, describes the status of the sciences and learning among various nations. Sa'id commended all countries but those of the far north and far south for their impressive scholarly achievements. He held black Africans in particular contempt:

> For those peoples ... who lived near and beyond the equinoctal line to the limit of the inhabited world in the south, the long presence of the sun at the zenith makes the air hot and the atmosphere thin. Because of this their temperaments become hot and their humors fiery, their color black and their hair woolly. Thus, they lack self-control and steadiness of mind and are overcome by fickleness, foolishness, and ignorance. Such are the blacks, who live at the extremity of the land of Ethiopia, the Nubians, the Zanj and the like.[16]

Sa'id's environmental explanations for black Africans' skin color and sensibilities were applied to black slaves in the Muslim world. By the time the historian wrote this, both climate theory preceded and informed black slave stereotypes and vice versa.

In medieval Iberia, Alfonso X "The Wise" became acquainted with the Muslim system of black slavery and adopted similar sets of symbols and myths, with additional arguments. Not only were blacks not Christians, they were the Muslims' servants, the heathen, doubly cursed by their status as nonbelievers and by their servile condition. In this regard, the emerging climatic theories in Spain about the somatic Blackness of sub-Saharan Africans substantiated racialized discourses that sought to distinguish their contrasting dark skin and hair with white Iberians and tawny-colored Muslims. The invidious perception of difference, expressed in language that suggested black inferiority, became refined and sharpened by Muslims, Jews, and Christians of Iberian origin.

When Spain began to establish its empire during the Renaissance, most blacks in Spain and its colonies were slaves. They contributed to early modern Hispanic imperial expansion by serving as cartographers on long-distance transatlantic voyages, building urban infrastructure, and producing crops and material goods. In the seventeenth century to have the hair texture, dark skin color, and phenotype of a black African constituted a social mark of difference and subordination. Society barred blacks from access to guilds, religious confraternities, the army, the church, and the convent. Slavery was something more than the misfortune alluded to in the *Siete Partidas*, where it was defined not as a natural institution but as a social one. The practice of slavery impressed on its victims and their descendants a stigma that was intimately connected to the racialization and hypervisibility of their hair and skin color. To be a black African was synonymous with being a slave. The Spanish Baroque satirist Francisco de Quevedo, in his poem "Boda de negros" (1643), links the perceived inferiority of black African's hair to references of velvet as a means to animalize the black body with the texture of animal fur, thereby transforming one of the text's characters, and his "manos de terciopelo" (velvety hands), into a furry animal or beast.[17] To that end, hair and hairiness for Quevedo—just like his other poetic examples of large, phallic Jewish noses—operate as proxies for launching xenophobic critiques against blacks.

Based on Aristotelian and Galenic thinking, early modern Spanish medical theorists such as Juan Huarte de San Juan in his *Examen de ingenios para las ciencias* (1575) reference hair and hairiness through the figure of the manly woman commonly referred to as the *mujer barbuda* (bearded woman). Although cold and moist liquids predominate in all women, not all have the same levels of these humors, which are assessed by observing different categories such as intellectual capacity, habits and behavior, voice tenor, body fat and musculature, coloring, facial hair, and physical beauty or ugliness.[18] According to Huarte de San Juan's classifications, the woman with the lowest level of coldness and moisture, which would indicate a proximity to the hot and dry composition of most men, is more intelligent but such a woman is also more disagreeable and has an aggressive and combative personality.[19] Likewise, since a strong, deep voice is common to the hot, dry nature of men, a woman with a "masculine" voice and excessive facial hair also has the lowest level of coldness and moisture: "tener mucho vello y un poco de barba es evidente señal para conocer el primer grado de frialdad y humidad. Porque, sabida la generación de los pelos y barba, todos los médicos dicen que es de calor y sequedad" (having a lot of hair and a bit of a beard is an evident sign to know the first level of coldness and humidity. Because once the generation of the hairs and beard are known, all doctors say that the cause is due to heat and dryness).[20] Moreover, these hot, dry women are rarely beautiful and frequently display a more muscular physique: "por maravilla sale la mujer hermosa; porque, estando seca la simiente de que se formó, fue impedimento para que no saliese bien figurada ... La mucha humidad pone las carnes blandas, y la boca, ásperas y duras" (by a miracle she comes out beautiful, for dryness of the seed that formed impeded her ability to turn out well. The excessive humidity makes the legs soft and the mouth rough and dry).[21] In addition to the characteristics delineated by Huarte de San Juan, Jerónimo Cortés in his 1601 treatise *Libro de fisionomía natural* connects lasciviousness with hairy women: "La mujer que tiene muchos pelos en las quixadas y junto a la barba, es de fuerte naturaleza, y de condición terrible, y es calida en sumo grado, por lo qual es muy luxuriosa y de varonil condición" (hairy, bearded women are strong by nature; of fearsome condition. She is extremely hot, which makes her lustful and manly).[22] These examples of women with excessive facial and body hair illustrate the way in which early modern Iberian tracts animalize them as monstrous others. The above-cited passages, further, express racialized thinking and anti-woman rhetoric in the early modern period. And as these treatises highlight, male-dominated scrutiny over women's hairy bodies constitutes a racialized imagery ascribed to these denigrated women as departures from a male-defined biological and medical "norm."

Like treatises on physiology, blackface performance, or the racial "blacking up" used in the Renaissance to mark Africanness and the black body, also makes visible the racialization of hair. In early modern Spain, for example, actors practiced blackface by staining the skin with darkening agents consisting of burnt cork or soot—and on the opposite end of the spectrum, in the practice of whiteface, they applied flour to whiten the skin. Although scholarship on blackface performance has mainly focused on skin color, this chapter seeks to bring into focus not only the material presence of African hair in blackface performance but also the imagined ideation of the foreign quality of black African hair on early modern Spanish stages. Evidence of the use of hair in blackface performance comes from the *Cuenta del libro de gastos del año 1525*. It appears on the last page of *Archivo que fué de la Obra de la cal de Toledo—Papeles de Barbierz*. Emilio Cotarelo y Mori's *Colección de entremeses, loas, bailes, jácaras y mojigangas desde fines del siglo XVI a mediados del XVIII*, describes this Toledan document as: "La más antigua descripción completa de estas danzas que hemos hallado, es una que en 1525 presentación en Toledo Bautista de Valdivieso y Juan Corica, en la fiesta de la Asunción (15 de Agosto)" (The oldest and most complete description of these dances we have found is one that appears in Bautista de Valdivieso and Juan Corica's 1525 presentation in Toledo during the Feast Day of the Assumption on August 15).[23]

The text consists of nine short entries that explain the cost and use of masks, paints, threads, and other materials utilized in blackface performance to portray its black actors. With respect to hair, the archival document's brief fourth entry uses the word "trenzas" (braids) to describe the theatrical representation of the braided hair texture, or style, of an African's head. We are told that the cost of thread to make such braids is one *real* and nine *maravedí*. Although scant information is provided on treatment of hair in blackface performance, it is important to be aware of the salient role material culture played in the racialized performance of hair. A well-organized and prepared commodification of goods, materials, and objects determined the value and the extent to which the representation of not only black bodies but also so-called "savage" bodies were dressed up. The institutionalized and specialized manner employed to dress, paint, and mask the black African's body takes form in the economic exchange and investment of sixteenth-century coins: the *real* and the *maravedí*. With respect to "blacking up" the bodies, since the sixteenth century, theatrical blackness required a lot of money, time, and training for it to be portrayed well on Spanish stages. In relation to blackface performance, African hairstyles, wigs, and props were required to perform the African and are pertinent to the study of race and the cultural history of hair across Renaissance Europe. By directing our scholarly attention to the understudied presence of hair in the racial impersonation of blacks, Renaissance scholars of race studies and performance studies can then expand upon the valuable role hair plays in the construction of staging the racial difference on non-white theatrical characters.

PERFORMING THE BLACK BLONDE: HAIR, RACIAL IDENTITY, AND RESISTANCE IN RENAISSANCE SPAIN

One of the most suggestive and vivid depictions of hair appears in the sixteenth-century Spanish dramatist Lope de Rueda's *Comedia Eufemia* (1542–1554) through the black female character, Eulalla. Eulalla is fascinating because she speaks with witty verbal puns and exhibits audacious bodily performances representative of Renaissance self-fashioning. To assert her racial identity and to resist the socially constructed confines of her gender and race as a black woman, Rueda has Eulalla rely on material culture (e.g. books and letter writing, hair and makeup, and foreign exotic animals) to contest racial stereotyping. A close study of Eulalla's cosmetic alteration of her hair allows for a holistic understanding of intersectional fluidity between gendered and raced constructions of the black body.

The *scena séptima*, a freestanding interpolated dramatic entity known as a *paso* or *entremés* (short-skit play), is the intermission act where Eulalla first appears in *Comedia Eufemia*. Her costar, the *lacayo* (valet or footman) Polo, pursues Eulalla as his future wife. In the middle of the night Polo stands anxiously, yet earnestly, in front of Eulalla's house expressing his love: "Acá me quiero andar siguiendo mi planeta, que, si aquesta mi Eulalla se va conmigo como me tiene prometido, yo soy uno de los bienaventurados hombres de todo mi linage" (Here I want to tread cautiously following my planet, for if this love of mine, Eulalla, goes off with me as she has promised I'm one of the luckiest men of all my lineage).[24] A close reading of Polo's monologue illuminates a more legible framework for unpacking the thorny issues of social class and race—for example, as foreshadowed by the word "linaje" as an encoded reference to race, or the Spanish "raza," that groups people together according to filiations and lineage. Polo's social status, or lineage as he articulates it, belongs to the servant class. Even more suggestive is Lope de Rueda's usage of the name Polo, or pole, as a symbolic gesture to astronomy, planets, and astronomical axiological alignment. I read Polo's relation to planets and planetary axes as figuratively symbolic of the amorous relationship he seeks to establish with Eulalla: a heteronormative-racial binary where opposites, theoretically speaking, bond. On one end of the axis we have Polo—white and male—and on the other end of that axis we have Eulalla—black and female.

Two short passages reference Eulalla's hair in the *scena séptima*: (1) "Siñor, preséntame la siñora Doñaldoça, un prima mía, una hojetas de lexías para rubiarme na cabeyos y, como yo sa tan delicara, despójame na cabeça como nas ponjas" (Sir, on my behalf, show Lady Doñaldoça, a cousin of mine, some bleaching patches to bleach my hair; and since they're so delicate, strip my head of these sponges),[25] and (2) "Tráigame para mañana un poquito de moçaça, un poquito de trementinos de la que yaman de puta" (For tomorrow, bring me a bit of mustard and a bit of turpentine that's said to come from the whore).[26]

What I glean from Eulalla's obsession with cosmetic recipes for altering her hair and skin operates at the level of Rueda's meta-appropriation of blackness and whiteness. Rueda's racial appropriation of Eulalla is layered: on the one hand, it operates as Rueda's white appropriation of Eulalla's Africanized Spanish and cosmetic adornments, and, on the other hand, Eulalla's own appropriation of European medieval and Renaissance standards of female beauty as she interpellates herself into the discourse of makeup. In this interpellative gesture, Eulalla declares her subjectivity and authority, which is then further constituted in epistemological terms. Eulalla is a repository of knowledge. She embodies a lavish, shrewd, witty woman who knows what she wants in life thereby refusing to defer her dreams to Polo. Throughout the act, Polo flirts with Eulalla, lauds her beauty, and repeatedly begs that she does not alter her hair and skin. The skit opens, in fact, with Polo exclaiming: "¡Ah, señora Eulalla! No te alteres" (Oh, my Lady Eulalla! Don't get mad / change yourself).[27] According to Miguel de Cervantes Saavedra in his prologue to *Ocho comedias y ocho entremeses* (1615), the highly acclaimed playwright Lope de Rueda blackfaced and cross-dressed as a black woman in his own theater company. I interpret the performative acts in the *scena séptima* as possible modes of destabilizing Spanish (mis)understanding of black Africans' racial difference and position in society.

Critics have insisted on reading Eulalla as tragic and devoid of any agency and racial identity, a critical reception of her bleach-blonde hair—as well as of other black women who colored and straightened their hair—that subordinates black women to a white beauty culture.[28] Characteristic of a diva, Eulalla is lavish, shrewd, witty, and knows what she wants in life. She refuses to defer her dreams for any man. Also well-read, if not at least up to date on the cosmetic trends readily furnished by Fernando de Rojas's 1499 bestseller *La Celestina*, Eulalla knows the natural world and its ecological benefits.[29] Eulalla, as a practitioner of cosmetic alteration and adornment, requires a rethinking of the concept of hegemony. Her beauty politics destabilize the notion that black women's objectification as the so-called "Other" is so complete that they become willing participants in their own oppression. Eulalla's black beauty is multifaceted in its approach and execution. Her racial politics, or racialized self-awareness and self-perception, silently resists the norms against which black women are judged. Eulalla disavows whiteness even though she attempts to cosmetically fashion her body to embody it. Whiteness for Eulalla is *not* the only central focus of black beauty norms. It operates as a multivalent form of her racial appropriation of whiteness whereby she inserts herself into the discourses of hair and makeup that dialogue more broadly with European medieval and Renaissance standards of female beauty.

To invoke the words of Frantz Fanon in "The Fact of Blackness," Eulalla captures how Blackness is an object in the midst of other objects.[30] The evidence of visual representation of blacks in the early modern period suggests that long before both Spain and later England gained a foothold in the Atlantic slave trade, blacks played an important role in the symbolic economy of elite culture. Black Africans were brought to Spain not only as slaves with the absolute objectification of the state but also as curiosities who represented the riches that could be obtained by European travelers, traders, and collectors in the Atlantic world.

I assign Eulalla to the category of "black blonde." Lope de Rueda's text tells us that she is, in fact, a black blonde when she uses "hojetas de lexías para rubiarme na cabeyos" (bleach pads in order to dye my hair blonde).[31] As a "black blonde," I do not aim to connect Eulalla to a white iconic "original," but instead to call into question and facilitate the term's location on the black female body. Through the process of Stuart Hall's conception of translation as a process of cultural change in which cultural practice becomes translated, Eulalla's black female body becomes *different* from what it once was because of the impact of new spaces and times. This is particularly plausible for Eulalla's case if we are to imagine her being removed coercively from western sub-Saharan Africa as a slave and then placed in a sixteenth-century Iberian metropolis such as Lisbon or Seville. Black beauty, and especially Eulalla's black beauty, can be seen as something that has "evolved" and has become *different* from what it once was. Translation involves critique, deconstruction, and reconstruction that emerge as she inscribes beauty on her body's *surface* through stylization. Eulalla's stylization operates at the level of appropriation, and it is worthwhile recognizing her ability to translate, with her inscription on her body, what are taken to be "white looks."

Eulalla's obsession with power and sociocultural/racial upward mobility is reflected in José Antonio Maravall's idea that material wealth governs the *pícaro*'s (rogue, swindler) desire for upward social mobility. Eulalla also fits in the literary tradition of characters who please the audience by behaving badly. As a bad girl, Eulalla relies on cosmetic alteration and adornment to legitimize her cultural capital. Pierre Bourdieu sees "cultural capital" as a set of knowledge, skills, and various forms of cultural acquisitions, such as educational or technical qualifications.[32] Eulalla acquires and negotiates her cultural capital through *hojetas de lexías* (cosmetic hair bleaching pads) and the application of *afeites*, ranging from *mudas* (cosmetic balms or ointments), *mostaça* (mustard), and *trementinos* (turpentine). For Eulalla economic capital is constituted by material wealth in the form of money and luxurious objects. So that the self-perception of her honor will not be compromised and forfeited, she demands that her white male suitor Polo, should he be lucky enough to marry her, bestow on her foreign tropical animals—"una monas, un papagayos" (a monkey and a parrot).[33] She also requests of her white female patrons—"la monja Santa Pabla" and "la señora Doña Beatriz" (Saint Pabla the nun and Lady Doña Beatriz)—aristocratic fineries: brocade for her blonde hair and a "ventayos" (*ventalle* or fan).[34] These objects in return represent a symbolic capital—accumulated prestige or honor—readily associated with aristocracy. As a result, Eulalla is then able to crystallize her own self-awareness through their symbolic power.

Beauty, as much as race and the representation of black people's blackness, is performative. Black women across the ages of time have acted out their racial politics and subjectivity through stylizing their bodies—particularly their hair and face/skin—through cosmetic manipulation. What can we glean from Eulalla's obsession with cosmetic recipes for altering her black body? Her approach is a meta-appropriation of whiteness; she appropriates medieval and Renaissance white female standards of beauty and cosmetic concoctions by inserting herself into the discourse of makeup or *afeites*, which she then uses to assert her subjectivity and authority.

Although Lope de Rueda's literary portrayal of Eulalla is a specific case, the representation and treatment of her hair demonstrates how the categories of race, gender, and social class are not necessarily acquired but in fact *learned* without obvious teaching or conscious learning. Citing theorists Omi and Winant's *Racial Formation in the United States*, black feminist critic Patricia Hill Collins reminds us that: "Black women are not simply grafted onto existing social institutions but are so pervasive that even though the images themselves change in the popular imagination, [their] portrayal as the Other persists. Particular meanings, stereotypes, myths can change, but the overall ideology of domination itself seems to be an enduring feature of interlocking systems of race, gender, and class oppression."[35] Hill Collins's remarks capture not only Eulalla but in fact an array of other black women's impetus for using cosmetics in order to alter their bodies. For both blacks and whites, the conception and ideation of black beauty is complex. Eulalla, and her sisters of African descent in the African Diaspora, are not dupes of white male patriarchy and racism, devoid of agency and an awareness of their strategic self-positioning. Black beauty is multifaceted in its approaches and goals. Black women's racial politics—or rather their racialized self-awareness and self-perception—manifest in Eulalla's challenging of whiteness, even though she attempts cosmetically to fashion her body to embody it. Eulalla challenges whiteness by treating it as a commodity whose value is directly related to both its scarcity and its use to black Africans of her time—ultimately a thought-provoking, subversive act that Rueda probes through Eulalla's articulation of agency and personhood in the *Comedia Eufemia*. It is, in sum, her commodification of whiteness—the bleaching of her blonde hair—that disrupts the way it has been constructed as an exclusive category connected to racial purity and superiority as it is codified in the categories of beauty and power.

I want to show that hybrid mimicry is a viable discourse for rereading Eulalla's desire to whiten her skin and bleach her hair. In *Location of Culture*, Homi Bhabha had conceptualized mimicry as one of the strategies of colonial power and knowledge, wherein to obey the colonizer's demands, the colonized other—in this case Eulalla—must adopt the colonizer's values and norms. Developing Bhabha's idea of mimicry in *Black Beauty: Aesthetics, Stylization, and Politics*, Shirley Anne Tate explains: "Bhabha also speaks about another aspect of mimicry when he looks at hybridity as being a displacement of the eye of surveillance through mimicry. The hybrid mimicry of which Bhabha writes is speaking back that produces something other than was entailed through colonial discourse's construction of the other."[36] For this chapter's purposes and treatment of hair, race seeks to read "speaking back," not as a literal action but as a *translation* and inscription onto bodies through race-ing stylization which reproduces black beauty as what Tate calls an "un-decidable."[37] The un-decidable resists oppositions, she contends, such as "Black/white, Black anti-racist aesthetics/white beauty as icon, Black as ugly/white as beautiful without ever constituting a third term once and for all."[38] Similar to the hairstyles and beauty practices of black women described by scholars such as Ingrid Banks and Noliwe Rooks, Eulalla's stylization operates at the level of appropriation and an inscription onto the surface of her body.[39]

In a larger context, it is important to recognize the cultural history and practice of black women's ability to translate what are taken to be "white looks"—blonde hair and white-facing makeup—onto their bodies in a way analogous to Bhabha's treatment of mimicry: "a way imitating, but in a mischievous, displacing sense—imitating an original in such a way that the priority of the original is not reinforced but by the very fact that it can be simulated, copied, transferred, transformed, made into a simulacrum and so on."[40] Practicing this kind of mimicry, Eulalla's cosmetic imitation is anchored in her desire for upward social mobility as constituted by symbolic capital. It is easy to underscore the theme of self-hatred in Eulalla's desire to bleach her hair and whiten her skin. Many may even indict her for aligning herself ideologically to whiteness and regard her as a "sell-out" for drastically altering her skin and hair. This view is in line with some feminist thought. "A system of oppression," claims black feminist activist Pauli Murray, "draws much of its strength from the acquiescence of its victims, who have accepted the dominant image of themselves and are paralyzed by a sense of helplessness."[41] Yet regarding Eulalla as a practitioner of cosmetic alteration and adornment can rethink this concept of hegemony. Her beauty politics destabilize and rupture the notion, in a broader sense, that black women's objectification as the so-called "Other" is entirely complete, that they become willing participants in their own oppression.[42]

CONCLUSION

In this chapter I have discussed textual representations of hair in sixteenth- and seventeenth-century Spain. Primarily concentrating on the depiction of hair on the head of sub-Saharan Africans, the chapter also has linked racialized discourses on hair to the hairy body of manly women in Renaissance Spanish medical treatises. In the second half of this study, the unique theatrical case study of Lope de Rueda's black female character Eulalla served to demonstrate the contradictory and paradoxical ways in which a white Spanish playwright from the Renaissance could explore the subversive potential of black women's cultural and racial difference through their (blonde) hair. Whether codified racially as braids as a prop used in blackface performance, or in terms of Eulalla's blonde hair, this chapter closes by reiterating that hair cannot be detached from the racial ideologies that construct it. As a racial signifier—as informed by early modern Spanish definitions of the term "casta" and "raza" and the variety of textual fragments herein—hair marked and produced political and social power. Functioning as a sign of one's blood and lineage (or "raza," as previously defined by Covarrubias), hair sets the black African apart from other ethnic and racial groups in the European Renaissance culture and imaginary. As in the case of Eulalla in Lope de Rueda's *Comedia Eufemia*, we learn that hair transcends its seductive roots for authority and power.

CHAPTER EIGHT

Class and Social Status

JANA MATHEWS

A vigorous and protracted battle for dominion over hair and its signifying powers was waged in Europe between 1450 and 1650, a period characterized by unprecedented social upheaval and change. Profile portraits, such as Piero della Francesca's late fifteenth-century portrait of Battista Sfroza (Figure 8.1), participate in the campaign to preserve long-standing social hierarchies by using their subjects' hair to stake claims to the most privileged positions on the socioeconomic spectrum. If this portrait says one thing with unabashed confidence, it is that the Duchess of Urbino really liked her hair. Notably absent of makeup and self-consciously expressionless, Sforza's facial features are rendered strategically in such a way as to draw maximum

FIGURE 8.1 Piero della Francesca, *Portrait of Battista Sforza, Duchess of Urbino* (ca. 1465–1470). Galleria Uffizi, Florence. Photo: public domain via Wikimedia Commons.

attention to her carefully sculpted locks.¹ Parted down the center and drawn into two sections, the duchess's elaborate coiffure is comprised of coils of interlocking hair and ribbon connected by a jewel-encrusted headband and held together by a sumptuous veil and bedazzled brooch. The case that the Sforza portrait makes for the duchess's social exceptionalism is buttressed by the force of a new breed of law whose guiding principle is, in Frances Elizabeth Baldwin's words, "to preserve class distinctions, so that any stranger could tell merely by looking at a man's dress to what rank in society he belonged."² Enacted in massive quantities by nearly every type of legislative body in the fourteenth, fifteenth, and sixteenth centuries, so-called sumptuary law was, as Kim Phillips aptly puts it, "a must-have" form of legislation.³

In this chapter, I show how sumptuary legislation mobilizes head hair as an instrument of social and economic control by dictating in excruciating specificity what individuals belonging to various social stations could and could not do with their tresses. Through its vigorous defense of long-standing social hierarchies inherited from the Middle Ages, sumptuary law makes an ambitious but ultimately failed attempt to convert hair into a reliable marker of class and social status. The rise of informal and arguably more effective sumptuary codes emerge as a strategy to both fill in the gaps in the letter of the law and extend its authoritative scope. Specifically, I argue that the creation of a new type of hairstyle—what I call "complicated hair"—constructs a powerful social barrier that restricts access to everyone except the most socially and economically privileged.

Either through the law or the culture that buttressed it, individuals from lower classes were stripped of the ability to determine the style, color, and length of their own locks. As a result, they were forced to seek out alternative vehicles through which to communicate messages about themselves. In the final sections of this chapter, I suggest that one of the most natural and accessible surrogates for head hair is the pubic hair that is hidden from public view and thus lies outside the jurisdictional domain of law and popular culture. Attention to the female pudendum is widespread in early modern Europe and manifest primarily in the preoccupation with cleaning up the zone. While removing hair from any part of the body during the reign of sumptuary legislation has the potential to signal submission to its ideology, I argue that pubic baldness has the capacity also to signal the opposite. Using examples from contemporaneously produced art and literature as cases in point, I argue that the hairless pudendum constructs a narrative of individual and group identity that competes with and attempts to overwrite that articulated by sumptuary law-curated head hair. Anthony Synnott has argued that "to control the pubic hair, is to control the person."⁴ If this is true, then the process of carving out an authoritative space for oneself and ascending the socioeconomic ladder in early modern Europe may require taking it all off.

TANGLED: OR HOW THE LAW AND HEAD HAIR GOT INTERTWINED

Hair's insurgent potential had been a source of hand-wringing for the church and moralists for centuries, but the object did not evolve into a significant enough threat to the social and moral order to require formal and sustained legal intervention until the later Middle Ages. The post-Plague economy of the late fourteenth century upended the existing social hierarchy in unprecedented ways by tipping the economic scale in the peasants' favor, enabling them to demand higher wages and increased access to opportunities for class mobility. By the mid-fifteenth century, the traditional requirement for high social standing—property ownership—was under tremendous pressure by the emergence of a category of individuals who were not members of the landed aristocracy but had enough money to masquerade openly as them. An anonymous fifteenth-century chronicler records a scene where

> builders, blacksmiths, pork-butchers, shoemakers, and weavers dressed their wives in crimson velvet, in silk, in damask and finest scarlet; their sleeves, resembling widest banners, were lined with satin or with marten, fitting only for kings, on their heads pearls and the richest crowns glittered, crammed with gems; I myself saw wives of shoemakers wearing stockings of cloth of gold and dresses embroidered with pearls, interwoven with gold, silver, and silk with marvellous skill.[5]

The problem with dressing in clothing and wearing headgear that is "fitting only for kings" is that it creates a culture where individuals who do not have royal pedigrees can be assumed—based on their appearance—to have them. The anxiety that underlies the passage—that it is possible for a hair accessory to blur the line between the highest and lowest members of the kingdom—illuminates why sumptuary law was embraced so enthusiastically by the ruling classes.

Attempting to preserve the traditional social order, sumptuary law adopts a unique structural framework. While other modes of jurisprudence cast a wide jurisdictional net that lumps all of society under the rubric of "subject," sumptuary law partitions its subjects into discrete categories that sometimes look a lot like feudalistic boxes. Claire Sponsler cites an Edwardian petition from 1483, for example, that lists its subjects from top to bottom. Starting with the king, the document moves systemically downward through dukes, lords, and knights until it reaches the bottom, where common laborers and their wives are located.[6] The purpose of segregating one's subjects serves both ideological and practical ends. As Maria Muzzarelli notes, the construction of precise social categories enables the law to signal "proximity to power as well as distance from it."[7] It also creates a mechanism by which it can assign different versions of its dress code to each group.

In his seminal history of European sumptuary law, Alan Hunt demonstrates how hair and headgear serve as a kind of professional resume for the laboring classes. At the equivalent of early modern job fairs, people seeking employment would advertise their professional skill sets using braids tied to their hats fashioned out of discipline-specific materials: whip cords for wagoners; cow-hair for cowmen; flowers for gardeners; and so on.[8] Once individuals entered into a profession, they would wear clothing and hairstyles that were practical for their field of work and adapted to the needs and demands of their jobs. For women, this often meant wearing their hair pulled back, in a tight braid that was then wrapped up at the nape of the neck and covered by a simple kerchief or contained in a bag fashioned out of cloth or inexpensive crepe netting.[9] Men's headgear of the working classes was similarly designed to serve as a form of protection—wide-brimmed hats to keep the sun out of one's eyes or more narrow brimmed ones to keep hair out of one's face. Within the apprenticeship model of professional training, facial hair was used to signal one's status within the ranks. Mark Albert Johnston notes that in sixteenth- and seventeenth-century London, "the presence of a beard advertised the completion of apprenticeship and the acquisition of freeman status."[10] Since individuals could not marry until they had graduated from their apprenticeships, a bearded face also heralded "both the socioeconomic and sexual viability of its host to the early modern English imagination, mapping sexual prerogative over economic privilege."[11]

If professional guilds created and enforced informal sumptuary codes, the bulk of the formal legislation predictably targeted individuals who had the most to profit literally and symbolically from "dressing up." Many of those targeted by such laws were individuals whose work did not require a specific uniform or whose field of employment garnered them enough resources to purchase a second wardrobe outside that dictated by their profession. The form this took in 1457 Scotland, for instance, was an edict that forbade merchants' wives from wearing any headdress other than a short kerchief.[12] In 1485, the town council in Ratisbon Germany enacted a law that restricted the wives and daughters of prominent men to "2 pearl hair bands not to cost more than 12 florins, one tiara of gold set with pearls, not more than three veils costing 8 florins each."[13] In fifteenth-century Nürnberg, veils were not allowed that contained over six folds or with attachments that cost more than six gulden. Women were allowed to wear tiaras, pearl fringes or fillets, but the cost of all of the materials comprising each object could not exceed forty gulden.[14] A similar ordinance included a rule that burgher women could not wear headdresses with more than a certain quantity of material and could not wear them in such a way "that the ends in front lie upon the head."[15]

While the level of specificity manifest in the letter of the law presents sumptuary legislation as a solid juridical vessel, the sheer number of laws in existence (over three hundred sumptuary laws were enacted between 1200 and 1500 in Italy alone) reveals the mode of legislation to be more of a leaky ship.[16] By nature, the law has the capacity to regulate what currently is in existence, but it lacks the ability to imagine what has yet to be invented—or imported. As a result, the law is almost always one step behind current fashion trends and, by extension, the individuals who are imitating them. The losing cat-and-mouse game that sumptuary law plays with fashion is illuminated in a royal proclamation issued in England in 1542 that whines about the number of sumptuary laws that "have not been observed & kept, but neglected & contemned."[17]

Although ambitious and bold, the letter of early modern sumptuary law does not always match up with reality. Indeed, Julia Emberley claims that the model of social relations articulated in this genre of law is more legal fantasy than fact in that it "does not describe what people actually wore or, indeed, what they were necessarily expected to wear," but, rather, records a vision of what legislators wanted individuals to wear and how they wanted them to wear it.[18] Examples of individuals who violate the terms of sumptuary law pervade early modern literature, reaching one of its fullest and most comedic expressions in Ben Jonson's social satire *Cynthia's Revels* (ca. 1601). Act Two finds socialites Philautia and Phantaste fretting over the knock-off headdresses worn by other women:

> PHILAUTIA Ay, good Phantaste. What? Ha' you changed your head-tire?
> PHANTASTE Yes, faith; th' other was so near the common, it had no extraordinary grace. Besides I had worn it almost a day, in good troth.
> PHILAUTIA I'll be sworn, this is the most excellent for the device, and rare. 'Tis after the Italian print we looked on t'other night.
> PHANTASTE 'Tis so. By this fan, I cannot abide anything that savours the poor overworn cut, that has any kindred with it. I must have variety, I. This mixing in fashion I hate it worse than to burn juniper in my chamber, I protest.
> PHILAUTIA And yet we cannot have a new peculiar court-tire, but these retainers will have it, these suburb-Sunday-waiters, these courtiers for high days, I know not what I should call 'em-
> PHANTASTE O aye, they do most pitifully imitate.[19]

In an attempt to categorize their social imitators, the women test out a series of nomenclatures, but despite coming up with several creative options, none of the candidates stick. What is intended to be an act of erasure—Philautia's insistence that she does not know what to call her social imitators is a way of denying their existence—ends up functioning as an act of inscription. By putting her social imitators in a kind of nominal purgatory—she is not willing to classify them as upper class, but she cannot in good conscience put them into a lower social grouping either—she creates a hermeneutic space where they can fit just as easily into either group, or slide fluidly between them.

In Jonson's *Volpone* (ca. 1607), the realization that hair can open doors is not lost on Lady Would-Be, an appropriately named social climber. After discovering what she thinks might be an insurgent lock in an otherwise perfect hairdo, she calls two chambermaids into her room for a second and third opinion: "Come nearer. Is this curl / In his right place? Or this? Why is this higher / Than all the rest?"[20] When her suspicions are confirmed, Lady Would-Be barks out a command to repair the curl and then chides her servants for their negligence:

> Besides, you seeing what a curious nation
> Th' Italians are, what will they say of me?
> "The English lady cannot dress herself."
> Here's a fine imputation to our country![21]

Lady Would-Be humorously casts the location and placement of the curls on her head as a threat to international diplomatic relations. While her claims of self-importance are exaggerated, and hair may not be a matter of national security, there is some truth in what Lady Would-Be says: having good hair is critical to her own personal social security. Specifically, hair serves as the designated vehicle by which she will attract a favorable husband and, through marriage, graduate from her social apprenticeship and be allowed to drop the "would-be" suffix from her name. As fashion's power increased and law's fortifications began to crumble, members of the upper class devised increasingly creative mechanisms to keep the masses from breaking down the proverbial door to their privileged social space. The ladies in *Cynthia's Revels* identify one strategy to be to simply abandon a hairstyle the instant that someone outside the social circle imitates it. The next section examines another, namely the construction of a hairstyle so complex that it cannot be copied.

IT'S COMPLICATED: THE POSSIBILITIES OF AND PROBLEMS WITH INTRICATE HAIR

We do not know the identity of the woman in Piero del Pollaiuolo's *Portrait of a Young Woman* (ca. 1470), yet her likeness is one of the most recognizable within the corpus of Renaissance art (Figure 8.2). Like many other profile portraits, what is on display—more than any other body part—is the subject's hair. The woman's tresses are notable for many reasons, including their color. While most Venetians (then and now) are natural brunettes, artists like Pollaiuolo, Botticelli, and Titian, whose paintings commonly feature high-ranking women and goddesses with golden locks, are credited with making blonde the must-have hair color of the century.[22] Having fashionable hair, however, comes with a hefty cost. As sixteenth-century fashion chronicler Cesare Vecellio reveals, the process of dyeing one's hair is a multi-day affair. The event takes place on rooftop loggia, where women spend

FIGURE 8.2 Piero della Pollaiuolo, *Portrait of Young Woman* (ca. 1470). Museo Poldi Pezzoli, Milan. Photo: public domain via Wikimedia Commons.

as much time in the altana (as they call the wooden building mentioned previously) as in their bedrooms, or else keep their heads exposed to the sun for days at a time. For this process, in which they are both the served and the servants, they sit on these altane when the sun is the hottest and wet their hair with a little sponge attached to a wooden handle and soaked in a liquid that they buy or make at home themselves; and over and over again, as they wet their hair, they let it dry in the sun, and in this way they turn their hair blonde so effectively that we think it is natural.[23]

The time and effort it takes to dye hair to the ideal shade of blonde served as an effective form of social segregation in that only individuals with copious amounts of free time had the ability to create and maintain the look.

The labor required to acquire the right color of tresses is rivaled only by the work involved in arranging it into its desired shape. Pollaiuolo's model dons a hairdo that is comprised of a complex maze of interwoven braids, buns, and loops. The intricacy of its design makes the hairstyle impossible to create on one's own. According to sumptuary law historian Katherine Killerby, this is precisely the point. Along with expensiveness and novelty, she names ineptitude as a requisite principle of signifying wealth. "The ideal," she says, "is to consume without producing."[24] Etiquette manuals like Peter Erondell's *The French Garden: for English Ladyse and Gentlewomen to Walke in* (ca. 1605) teach that an upper-class woman's head hair requires a multi-person staff to wash and dress it every day. Through a fictional high society woman named Lady Rimelaine, the text offers up a template grooming ritual that a reader of equal social caliber might follow. Not surprisingly, this routine involves the lady of the house remaining completely stationary throughout the laborious process and calling out orders to her servants from her chair.

Another way that complicated hair signaled social status was through the decorative accessories that often were attached to or inserted into it. The hairdo of the woman profiled in Pollaiuolo's portrait is meticulously fastened together and held in place by strategically placed netting, ribbons, clips, strings of pearls, and other valuables. Lady Rimelaine similarly instructs her chambermaid to gather up an assortment of materials to be used as decoration for her daily hairdo:

> Set vp then my French whood and my Border of Rubies, giue me an other head attyre: take the key of my closet, and goe fetch my long bore where I set my Jewels (for to haue them out) that I use to weare on my head, what is become of my wyer? Where is the haire cap? Haue you any ribans to make knots? Where be the laces for to binde my haires?[25]

For Lady Rimelaine, a ruby-encrusted hood is not a fashion accessory to be reserved for special occasions but, rather, is a component of her everyday dress. As kinds of portable and open treasure chests, complicated hairdos such as these necessarily needed to be under constant surveillance and monitoring to guard against theft. But being rendered essentially homebound by one's hair was not as much a punishment as an aspiration, for this condition served as a way for upper-class individuals to pull rank within their own social groups. Specifically, the number, kind, and quantity of special accommodations that one's hair required worked to create a gated community within a gated community, with the wealthiest and most privileged of the bunch signaling their exceptionalism by requiring the most special treatment.

Given the energy and effort required to create, maintain, and protect complicated hair in the early modern era, it should come as no surprise that men and women alike sought out ways to immortalize their hairstyles. One vehicle was the commissioned profile portrait. Another was its portable cousin—the portrait medal. Fashioned out of silver or gold and typically round and worked on both sides, these objects self-consciously resemble coins but were never designed for monetary exchange. Specifically, commemorative medals like that produced for Isabella d' Este, Marchesa of Montua in 1505 (Figure 8.3) bore an embossed profile likeness of a wealthy individual and were distributed to and traded with friends, romantic interests, colleagues, and relatives as a kind of "Renaissance calling card."[26] As in profile portraits, hair takes center stage.[27] In homing in on this attribute, portrait medals make complicated hair a defining and requisite feature of the social groups who make and exchange these objects. A material representation of an individual's social network, the portrait medal collection communicates one's proximity to power by literally putting one's alliances, allegiances, and relationships on full display.

The popularity of profile portrait medals in the sixteenth century was due in part to their ability to make a permanent copy of a status symbol that is, by nature, temporary. In the seventeenth century, prosthetic hair emerged as a more flexible and adaptable alternative. While portrait medals had the ability to immortalize a single complicated hairdo, wigs offered individuals access to a stable of complicated hairdos, which they could show off in daily succession. Like other fashion trends of the era, wig-wearing

FIGURE 8.3 Gian Cristoforo Romano, *Portrait Medal of Isabella d' Este* (ca. 1505). Kunsthistorisches Museum, Vienna. Photo by Mitglied5 (Own work) (CC BY-SA 4.0 [http://creativecommons.org/licenses/by-sa/4.0]), via Wikimedia Commons.

was popularized by celebrities. Queen Elizabeth, Catherine de' Medici, and Mary Queen of Scots all were noted for their indulgence in faux hairpieces. Elizabeth's closet was rumored to contain over eighty wigs at the time of her death, which would have enabled the queen to sport a fresh hairdo every day for almost three months.[28] In France, Henry III and his successors did their part to popularize the trend for men when they began donning the hairpieces in their twenties and thirties to disguise the effects of early-onset baldness.[29]

The amount of hair needed to produce wigs for royalty and the upper classes in later centuries fueled an illicit hair trade that would explode and span the globe in later centuries. In the sixteenth and early seventeenth centuries, wigs were made from horse hair and sometimes the hair of lower ranked individuals. Catherine de' Medici allegedly paid a woman for her daughter's hair.[30] Marguerite de Valois, Queen of Navarre and of France, is rumored to have kept blonde servants to provide hair for her ever-expanding collection of golden-hued wigs. The demand for wig hair grew so high at the end of the sixteenth century that English moralist Phillip Stubbes issued a blanket warning to the lower classes to guard themselves against hair thievery:

> And if there be any poore women (as nowe and then, we see God doeth blesse them with beautie as well as the rich) that hath faire haire, these nice Dames will not rest, till they haue bought it. Or if any children haue faire haire, they wil intice them into a secrete place, and for a pennie or two they wil cut off their haire: as I heard that one did in the city of London of late, who meeting a little childe with verie faire haire, inueighled her into a house, promised her a pennie, and so cut off her haire.[31]

The shock value of Stubbes's social critique lies in the claim that the most privileged members of the community prey upon the youngest and most vulnerable to further their own vanity. While Stubbes's proclivity toward exaggeration means that we need to take what he says with a grain of salt, Emily Cockayne gives some credence to his claim when she notes that before the mid-seventeenth century, hair from country women was preferred for wigs because it was not perceived to be "sullied by the pollutants of the city."[32] Regardless of the extent of the practice, wigs made from the hair of the lower classes represents a form of social subordination by taking away one group's identifying symbol and using it to build up another's.

While it is tempting to see wigs as a clear-cut example of top-down socioeconomic repression, London diarist Samuel Pepys reminds us in a journal entry dated September 3, 1665, that the wig is a fluid symbol and the statements that it makes about class are a two-way street. Having just returned from the barber—who shaved his head and fit him with a new periwig—Pepys expresses considerable anxiety about wearing it:

> Up, and put on my coloured silk suit, very fine, and my new periwig, bought a good while since, but durst not wear it because the plague was in Westminster when I bought it; and it is a wonder what will be the fashion after the plague is done, as to periwigs, for nobody will dare to buy any hayre for fear of the infection, that it had been cut off the heads of people dead of the plague.[33]

Pepys's trepidation over wearing his new hairpiece stems from the worry that the hair used to make it may have come from plague victims. Public health concerns aside, Pepys implicitly acknowledges that if his wig is made from another human's hair, then that person was likely a member of a lower class. "The nature of wigs," Lynn Festa says, "sometimes makes it difficult to decide where one person's parts end and another's begin."[34] If one of the ways that the upper class subjugates the lower is by wearing the latter's body parts on top of their heads, then the act of doing so simultaneously (and literally) binds the groups together in an intimate and inexorable way. The ease with which wigs are mobilized simultaneously to reinforce and blur the distinctions between classes reminds us, in Angela Rosenthal's terms, that hair "always serves to communicate," regardless of its form.[35] In the next section, I extend Rosenthal's definition of form to include absence. Specifically, I examine the signifying potential of the practice of genital grooming, showing how the removal of pubic hair challenges the social order constructed by sumptuary discourse at the same time as it works to revise it. While the appearance of some individuals' head hair may mark them as prostitutes or peasants, their hairless pudenda make a compelling case for including them in the same social categories as women belonging to higher social classes.

THE DEMOCRATIZING POWER OF PUBIC HAIRLESSNESS

Like everything in this world, pubic hair has friends and allies, but Terry Eagleton is not one of them. The literary theorist famously likened the scholarly study of pubes to scraping the bottom of an intellectual barrel. "Not all students are blind to the Western narcissism involved in working in the history of pubic hair," he writes, "while half the world's population lacks adequate sanitation and survives on less than two dollars a day."[36] Scholars of early modern pudenda need not worry about disappointing Eagleton or his followers because there is no pubic hair in this era to study.[37] I am joking of course, but as many scholars have observed, pubic hair is nothing short of an endangered species in Renaissance art.[38]

One of the reasons why pubic hair is so hard to find is because it fails to conform to contemporaneous artistic standards of beauty. As Anne Hollander bluntly puts it, European nudes in the fifteenth century were "virtually shapeless, tending to resemble long, lumpy sausages with no strongly marked bodily diversions."[39] Within this artistic paradigm, the triangular tuft of moss is an undesirable protrusion that disrupts the seamless flow of the female form. In antiquity, female beauty was embodied in the form of the Three Graces, a trio of minor goddesses who often were portrayed nude and without any discernable body hair. Through preserving this corporeal representation of the goddesses, Renaissance artists ranging from Raphael to Lucas Cranach the Elder also preserve the hairless feminine ideal to important ideological ends (Figure 8.4).

In every era, art influences practice. I follow Jill Burke in holding that there is "no way to make a neat causal connection between the visual art of this period and female bodily identity."[40] Although we do not know how widespread the practice of pubic hair removal was in early modern Europe, the sheer number of descriptions of the practice that survive seem to suggest that if genital depilation was not common, it was not uncommon either.[41] According to the sixteenth-century Spanish novel *The Portrait of Lozana*, there was a thriving market for hair removal services in many cities in Europe. The titular character even gets into the act when she starts earning a living by plucking eyebrows and shaving off the "female hair" of local women.[42] There is also some indication that members of the royal household may have removed their body hair, or at least wanted the fawning public to think that they did. *The Queen's Closet Opened*—a kind of textual tour of the royal household—was first printed in 1655 and includes a recipe for removing unwanted hair.[43] Similarly, Caterina Sforza's *Experimenti* contains a whopping nine recipes for depilation.[44] While these texts do not specify that their recipes are intended for pubic hair removal, notably they also do not specify that they should or could not be used on this region of the body either.

Despite or because of the *Experimenti* and *The Queen's Closet Opened*, a slew of depilatory how-to guides hit the streets in the sixteenth and seventeenth centuries which promoted everything from tweezing to destroying hair follicles with hot needles to using strips of fabric dipped in sticky and smelly pitch.[45] One of the go-to sources for

FIGURE 8.4 Raphael, *The Three Graces* (ca. 1504–1505). Musée Condé, Chantilly. Photo: public domain via Wikimedia Commons.

CLASS AND SOCIAL STATUS 137

depilatory guidance was the *Tortula*, a compendium of three texts on women's medicine that was first published in the twelfth century and circulated widely in Europe throughout subsequent ones. Included among its recipes is one designed for use on all of a woman's "hairs from her head down."[46] Another recipe—targeted to noblewomen—is designed specifically to remove pubic hair:

> When the woman has anointed herself all over with this depilatory, let her sit in a very hot steambath, but she should not rub herself because her limbs will be excoriated. But when she has stayed there a little while, try to pull out the hairs from the pubic area. If they do not fall out easily, let her have hot water be poured over her and let her wash herself all over, drawing her palm [over her skin] gently.[47]

We find a visual image of the finished product of the depilatory process in a print made by German artist Sebald Beham (ca. 1530–1550) (Figure 8.5). The image shows a naked woman sitting in a public bathhouse. She makes no attempt to cover her genitals but, rather, strategically positions her legs in a way to highlight her fully exposed hairless pudendum. On the wall next to the woman is a container filled with grooming instruments—including scissors and tweezers—whose very presence implies recent use. Whether this scene reflects common practice or is exemplary in nature, however, is less important than the broader claims that the image makes, namely that

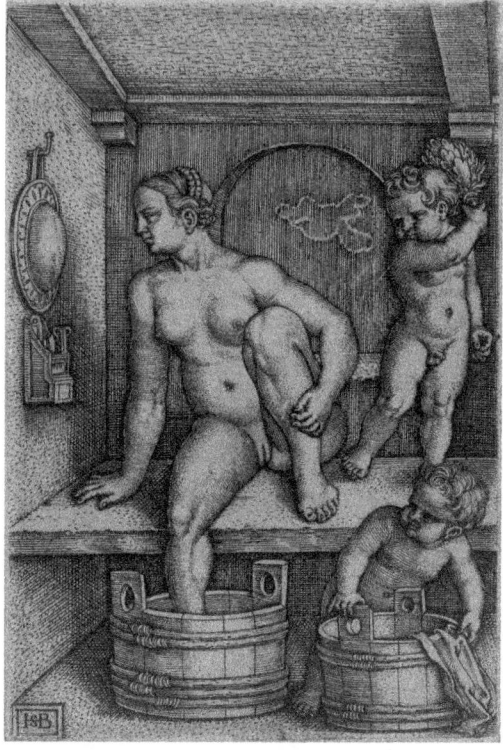

FIGURE 8.5 After Barthel Beham, print made by Sebald Beham, *Woman with Two Children in the Bath House* (ca. 1530–1550). British Museum Collection Database 1853, 0709.77. www.britishmuseum.org/museum. Photo: Courtesy British Museum, London.

many women from lower classes had access to depilatory techniques and instruments and that they had the agency to use them if they so desired. That the naked *mons pubis* serves as the image's focal point—upstaging the woman's head hair—gestures to the body part's signifying potential. Specifically, it suggests that the hairless pudendum has the ability to articulate a claim about an individual's identity that may compete with or openly contradict that made by her head hair.

We see an example of the authoritative tension that exists between the head and pubic regions in Giuseppe Cesari's early seventeenth-century *Diana and Actaeon* (ca. 1602–1603) (Figure 8.6). In this animated scene from Ovid's *Metamorphoses*, the unlucky hunter Actaeon stumbles across the goddess Diana bathing in a wooded spring with her consort of nymphs. The painting captures the moment of embarrassed surprise at the invasion of the naked women's privacy; some reach for towels; others scramble to cover exposed body parts; one furiously splashes water on the hunter. Diana is distinguished from the group and marked as socially superior by a small crescent moon crown that she wears on her head. But what Diana's hair says about her class above the neck is challenged by what appears below it. What is most notable about the rest of Diana's body is how similar it is—down to the hairless genital region—to the bodies of her nymphs. The implication that the painting invites the reader to consider is provocative: take away the goddess's crown, and one of the highest ranking deities in Roman mythology becomes indistinguishable from and, by extension, interchangeable with a glorified servant. While Cesari's painting does not go as far as to neutralize class distinctions completely, it raises the specter of its possibility.

The idea that pubic hairlessness can serve as a democratizing agent becomes less of a hermeneutic stretch when positioned within the era's new narrative of baldness.

FIGURE 8.6 Giuseppe Cesari, *Diana and Actaeon* (ca. 1602–1603). Museum of Fine Arts, Budapest. Photo: public domain via Wikimedia Commons.

Traditionally taken as a sign of loss and infirmity, Anu Korhonen demonstrates how the absence of male head hair evolved in early modern literary culture to constitute an alternative version of esteemed masculine identity.[48] This claim is strengthened during the sixteenth and seventeenth centuries when membership in the upper class was signaled in part by the wearing of wigs, and the only way one could wear a wig properly was with a shaved head.

Circulating in the same period, texts like Poggio Bracciolini's mid-fifteenth-century *Facetia Erotica* work to make similar claims about female pubic baldness. In one of the joke book's most memorable tales, a courtesan sues her barber for giving her a bad haircut:

> There exists in Florence a court of public morals, which is chiefly concerned with matters affecting the rights of prostitutes, and which seeks to protect them against hindrance in the performance of their public function. Before this court, there once appeared a courtesan to lay claim for damages against a certain barber, whom she had called in to shave her lower parts. It appeared that the latter had so cut her about the loins with his razor, that for many days she was unable to ply her trade. On this ground she claimed damages in accordance with the number of patrons she had lost. I wonder what was the verdict of the court?[49]

The funniest jokes often are those whose underlying truths hit closest to home, and this is no exception. The humor that is the imaginary trial for the crime of pubic hair assault gives way to the recognition of the legitimacy of the courtesan's case. The basis of the woman's complaint is that her marketability directly correlates with the appearance of her pubic mound. She loses income not because her injuries prevent her from performing the clinical part of her job, but because the cuts, scrapes, and scabs generated by the grooming session gone awry shatter the illusion of the type of person that she and all other courtesans present themselves to be, namely a more sensuous version of the rich girl next door. In the story, pubic baldness emerges not only as a requisite physical feature of the category of woman that the courtesan professionally imitates but as the defining one. Put another way, the hairless *mons pubis* serves as the key that unlocks the gate to the world of the upper class, and the courtesan cannot pass as one without it.

The theory of identity construction floated in Bracciolini's story—that pretending is a form of being—takes on some weight when it is situated alongside the narrative of another group of marginalized women. Erasmus's *Praise of Folly* takes aim at a wide swath of society, but it reserves some of its most vitriolic criticism for the category of women who are past reproductive age yet continue to act on their desires:

> But it is even more amusing to see these old women, so ancient they might as well be dead and so cadaverous they look as if they had returned from the grave, yet they are always mouthing the proverb "life is sweet." They are as hot as bitches in heat, or (as the Greeks say) they rut like goats. They pay a good price for the services of some handsome young Adonis. They never cease smearing their faces with makeup. They can't tear themselves away from the mirror. They pluck and thin their pubic bush.[50]

While the author makes it abundantly clear that he is not aroused by the final product, what is notable about the women's strategy to tap into the fountain of youth is its effectiveness. In the same way that the lower classes use hats, hairstyles, and hair accessories to wiggle their way into social groups higher than their own, older women borrow the genital hairstyles of their younger counterparts to similar ideological and practical ends. Having pudenda that look like they belong to much younger women grants older women access to a privileged social sphere from which they would otherwise be barred by virtue of their age. By successfully attracting much younger men and mating with them, older women figuratively and literally displace younger women from their designated spots within the traditional sexual economy.

If Erasmus's tale of woe presents what might be the most tabloidish example of class confusion and social conflation, then the most compelling might be Peter Floetner's cryptically titled woodcut *The Allegory of Truth* (Figure 8.7). The scene features a woman, wearing not much more than her birthday suit and flamboyant hat, trimming her pubic hair with an enormous pair of pruning shears. The woman's appearance and the unconventional setting for such an intimate act of personal grooming lead Jolly and Malcolm Jones to read the woman respectively as a prostitute and/or a mercenary's whore.[51] *Washington Post* art critic Blake Gopnik's interpretation of the woman's identity is more generous; using the same contextual clues, he proposes that she is perhaps an allegorical embodiment of *vanitas* or *nude veritas*.[52] The inability of scholars to reach a consensus on the social status of the woman—she is read simultaneously as a prostitute and an embodiment of the most deeply esteemed classical virtue—opens up the intriguing possibility that everyone may be right. Throughout the early modern era, the personification of naked truth takes a diverse array of forms, including a companion of Father Time and Death.[53] In Floetner's image, the personification also may be recruited to playfully expose another kind of inevitable reality. The woodcut captures the woman in a moment of physical transition; she does not have a full pubic bush but is not completely bare down there

FIGURE 8.7 Peter Floetner, *Allegory of Truth* (ca. first half of the sixteenth century). Graphische Sammlung, Nürnberg. Photo: public domain via Wikimedia Commons.

either. Immortalized in a state of eternal in-betweenness, the woman is caught between two corporeal states and the class and social identities that are affiliated with them. What this image conveys through the woman's actions then is possibility and confidence in the belief that the more hair that she shears off, the higher up the social ladder she has the potential to ascend.

CONCLUSION

One of sumptuary law's overarching aims was to control contemporary fashion trends. It is appropriate then that, in the end, sumptuary legislation proved itself to be a fleeting fad. This genre of law fizzled in popularity in the second half of the seventeenth century in Europe and largely went the way of the dinosaur by the end of the eighteenth. Between 1450 and 1650, however, sumptuary culture was in its apex. Legislators capitalized on the legal mode's popularity by actively attempting to convert head hair into a reliable marker of class and social status. The law and its supporting culture fell short of its aspiration in part by failing to account for the competing narratives of personal identity constructed by the hairless pubic region. Going hairless "down there" constituted a form of both symbolic and physical resistance to the reigning social hierarchy in that it blurred the distinctions between upper- and lower-class bodies beyond recognition. When viewed alongside one another, two works of art produced at opposite ends of the early modern timeline expand the range of signification of the hairless pudendum. Specifically, they portray it not just as a mode of class resistance, but also as an agent in the construction of an alternative social order.

Albrecht Dürer's *The Women's Bath* (1496) features a group of six women in a bathhouse, engaged in various acts of grooming themselves and each other (Figure 8.8). The women's pubic regions are obscured from view by strategically placed body parts and pitchers of water. Importantly, the body's other hirsute marker of class—head hair—also is mostly obscured from the viewer. Half of the women's heads in the scene are covered by shower caps or wrapped up in scarves, the head hair that is shown is undressed, unadorned with decorative accessories, and otherwise devoid of any material signifying markers of class as defined by sumptuary law. A parallel scene is staged in *A Tepidarium with Female Nudes* (Figure 8.9), with one notable difference. One woman's body out of the group is fully exposed, revealing a hairless pubic region. The message that the absence of pubic hair communicates does not compete with but rather complements that made by the woman's head hair. Specifically, the image captures the woman in the process of covering her head with a towel. When she is finished with the job, her head hair will be fully covered, rendering her entire body visibly hairless.

The presentation of hairless or almost hairless bodies in these images thwarts one's ability to distinguish the individuals represented in them based on class and social status. But this is precisely the point. In both images, the public bath house is portrayed as a sanctuary from sumptuary culture and a place where the law is rendered irrelevant because the objects that it governs—hair and clothes—either do not take a form over which it has jurisdiction, or are entirely absent. At the same time as the images figure the bath house as an escape from the long arm of the law, they also imagine the space as an alternative social sphere governed by democratic ideals of identity construction. The women's bodies—which self-consciously appear in a variety of shapes and sizes—are not interchangeable, but they are not able to be classified by rank and degree either. As bold

FIGURE 8.8 Albrecht Dürer, *The Women's Bath* (ca. 1496). Kunsthalle Bremen. Photo: public domain via Wikimedia Commons.

FIGURE 8.9 *A Tepidarium with Female Nudes* by manner of French (Fontainebleau) School CMS_PCF_593145 Collections-Public, National Trust Images.

as this vision of a classless social order is, the seventeenth-century painting reminds us that the image is, at least in the era of its production, still a fantasy. The specter of reality lurks in the background of the painting and aptly takes the form of a fully clothed figure, wearing a sumptuary law-prescribed headdress.

CHAPTER NINE

Cultural Representations

LYN BENNETT

Longing for more than a glimpse of the locks he first spied on April 6, 1327, the Italian poet Petrarch complained that "I have not seen you, lady, / leave off your veil in sun or shadow" (lines 1–2).[1] Developing the sonnet form in immortalizing tribute to his beloved, Petrarch claimed the young Laura as the impetus and focus of his influential *Canzoniere*. Yet the "scattered rhymes" of 366 *rime sparse* songs and sonnets produced over four decades are as invested in poetry as they are in love; the result is that Petrarch's sequence centers less on a coherent and knowable woman than on an abstract ideal defined only by the collection of tropes that give her shape. Thus informing "the Renaissance norm of a beautiful woman" among countless imitators who proved no more interested in representing feminine reality, Petrarch's Laura set the standard for a poetic tradition featuring an idealized beloved who seldom achieves even the sum of her attributes.[2] This is not to say, however, that the "composite of details" of Petrarchan convention are equally admired or given equal weight.[3] Though only one among the eyes, brows, cheeks, and lips that also define her, it is her long, blonde, golden, crisp, and curling locks that may be the most significant of the blazoned woman's metaphorically rendered parts.

As the natural attribute thought most to distinguish women from men, hair figures prominently in the work of Petrarch's many imitators.[4] Following the lead of their Italian predecessor, the English poets who are the focus of this chapter likewise proved less concerned with faithful representation than finding in the impossibly idealized "an enduring monument for the beloved" and, in the suffering of the courting lover, "a total metaphor for the human condition."[5] Thus addressing an audience beyond the admired and unattainable, the Petrarchan mode that became firmly established in English convention served likewise as a vehicle for displaying the "eloquence and wit" that might advance the hopes of an aspiring courtier.[6] A means of courtly display in two senses, then, the verse of Petrarch's English imitators is equally poetry about poetry, and its mode is one in which hair—in an age when women were expected to wear it long and in increasingly elaborate styles—may have been most amenable to the poet's creative powers.[7] Whether celebrating or warning against those it adorns, poetic representations of hair thus work to purposes sometimes as complex, contradictory, and wide-ranging as the medium itself. Whether bringing together hair and earthly riches, hair and classical mythology, hair and Christian morality, hair and human mortality, or hair and poetry, Petrarch's locks prove most useful not in celebrating women or the love they are supposed to represent but in affirming the mastery of an eloquent wit over both nature and art.

PETRARCH'S LOCKS

Credited along with Sir Thomas Wyatt for bringing the Petrarchan mode to English poetry, the early sixteenth-century poet and Earl of Surrey, Henry Howard, gained notoriety with the 1557 posthumously published volume *Songs and Sonnets*, popularly known as *Tottel's Miscellany*. Included in this anthology is Surrey's "Complaint that his ladie after she knew of his loue kept her face alway hidden from him."[8] Imitating Petrarch's verse in both form and content, the poem opens by lamenting the beloved's insistence on wearing a "cornet black" to conceal the antithetically blonde hair he longs to see. That she does so "in cold nor yet in heate" (line 2) is read as a perverse attempt to thwart the speaker's attentions with no regard for other necessity, for "Sins that she knew I did her loue and serue," the speaker explains, "Her golden tresse is clad alway with blacke" (lines 8–9). The subsequent poem, "Request to his loue to ioyne bountie with beautie," features the speaker further appealing to his addressee not to hide "The golden gift that nature did thee geue" (line 1), but to choose instead to feed her friends with the "fourme" and the "fauour" (line 3) its willing display would represent.[9] In a later song, "A description of such a one as he would loue," Surrey's speaker further confirms the importance of hair to the love-worthy woman, who need possess not only "A Face that should content me wonderous wel" (line 1) but locks of "crisped gold" (line 6).[10] For Surrey as for Petrarch, the value of hair to the idealized love object is affirmed by the precious metal from which her locks are spun.

Figured through a metaphor perhaps dying but far from dead, the golden tresses of the Renaissance ideal further imply that hair functioned also as a marker of "social privilege."[11] Thus likening all of the blazoned woman's parts to the earthly riches that enable and represent privilege, Edmund Spenser's late sixteenth-century *Amoretti* features in Sonnet 15 a catalogue of mercantile metaphors that, as well as sapphire eyes, ruby lips, pearly teeth, ivory forehead, and silver hands, include "locks" akin to the "finest gold on ground" (line 11).[12] William Drummond of Hawthornden later echoes Spenser in a 1616 sonnet that culminates in a blazon truncated to a mere two lines of parallel equivalence: "Pearle, Iuorie, Corrall, Diamond, Sunnes, Gold, / Teeth, Necke, Lips, Heart, Eyes, Haire, are to behold" (lines 13–14). Appealing to the familiarity of convention, Drummond's poem confirms the requisite perfections "to bee had" (line 12) in the love-worthy woman and ends in asserting over a mere two lines the nature-exceeding, "all (more faire)" (line 12) parts Spenser had elaborated over fourteen.[13]

A testament to worth beyond the earthly, golden hair sometimes elevates the female subject to the heavenly and celestial. In his 1593 *Parthenophil and Parthenophe*, Barnabe Barnes opens "Sonnet LXXI" praising "Those haires of Angels gold" (line 1).[14] Likewise, William Smith may indulge in sustained *paralepsis* in his 1596 *Chloris*, where the speaker begins Sonnet 47 by refusing to "tell thee of the lilly white" but goes on to itemize, while paradoxically declining to do so, a blazon that includes "golden haires like *Phoebus* bright" (lines 1–3).[15] In Barnes's figuring, the beloved's hair is not akin to the earthly gold specified by Surrey and Drummond but is of the kind belonging also to "Angels" and, in Smith's, is akin to the "*Phoebus* bright" rays cast by the classical god of sun and light. Reversing the formula in his celebration of the momentous 1613 Valentine's Day marriage of Princess Elizabeth, daughter of King James, to the Elector Palatine, Henry Peacham figures a Phoebus who appears in a more usually "Snowtress'd" winter to "threw about his golden hayre" to honor the occasion with a more promising green.[16]

As Peacham's tribute suggests, hair maintained its figurative value even in accounts of love requited. Celebrating the same event, Thomas Heywood's epithalamium depicts starlight as the constellation Cassiopeia "who spreads her glistering hair" and bids Hymen also to "spread thy golden haire."[17] Like Peacham's Phoebus casting the golden rays of his metaphorical locks upon the nuptials, Heywood's god of weddings reflects the virginal and "blushing Bride" who similarly "comes with her haire" spread out and "Disheuel'd 'bout her shoulders."[18] In his *Epithalamion*, the marriage hymn resolves the longing of the *Amoretti* sonnets that precede it as Spenser's verse moves "from a narrowly defined Petrarchan register to a Canticle register."[19] Even so, the focus on hair remains in a bride who is distinguished by "long loose yellow locks lyke golden wyre" (line 154) as much as her white attire.[20] In his 1629 *Argalus and Parthenia*, an admittedly weak imitation of Sir Philip Sidney's earlier *Arcadia*, Francis Quarles recounts a dream wedding featuring "a princely Bride, with robes befitting / The state of Maiesty," whose "Nymphlike haire" was worn "Loosely disshueul'd."[21] Her hair anticipates the later bride Parthenia's hair, which "Hung loosely downe, and vayl'd the backer part," in an image that also nods to the celestial with tresses that spread over "her skyresembling robes."[22]

Like Quarles, sonneteers were also interested in imitating the work of the renowned poet and statesman, whose *Astrophel and Stella* served as testament to Sidney's originality even as it met the "traditionally learnt expectations and demands" of Elizabethan love poetry.[23] Published in 1595 but circulated in manuscript from the 1580s, Sidney's sequence was purportedly inspired by the unattainable Penelope Rich, the married woman thought to have served as the later poet's Laura. Given that "Astrophel" connotes "lover of a star," Stella is often figured as belonging to the celestial world her name implies. Accordingly, his Sonnet 13 features a Phoebus who sets out to judge which of Jove's, Mars's, and Love's "armes the fairest were" (line 1). Last to present, the Cupid who is Love personified "smiles" in anticipation of his assured win, "for on his crest there lies / *Stellas* faire haire" (lines 9–10), in response to which Phoebus "drew wide the curtaines of the skies, / To blaze these last" (lines 12–13) ever among the firmament. Stella and her hair shine so brightly, it turns out, that the other competitors were not even in the running: "The first, thus matcht," the poem concludes, "were scantly gentlemen" (line 14).[24] Defeating the hopes of others while serving the heraldic arms emblazoned on an armament of self-defense, Stella's hair also implies that even the fairest, most golden, and brightest of hair may be as powerful and threatening as it is wondrous to gaze upon.

Frequently figured also as an instrument of capture, the locks of the admired beloved can enthrall even the most unwilling. The imprisonment implied by a word that also connotes an instrument of containment Sidney's speaker warns against in the preceding Sonnet 12, an apostrophe to Cupid complaining "That from her locks thy day-nets none scapes free" (lines 1–2).[25] The "locks" of hair thus become the "nets" of capture in an equally familiar metaphor not exclusive to male poets. In her 1613 closet drama, *The Tragedie of Mariam*, Elizabeth Cary explores hair's Petrarchan possibilities with an exchange that sees husband Herod declare that "on the brow of Mariam hangs a Fleece" composed of that "Whose slenderest twine is strong enough to bind / The hearts of kings." That hair, he goes on, exceeds even "the pride and shame of Greece," for "Troy flaming Helen's not so fairly shin'd" (4.7.413–16) as Mariam's. More beautiful than Helen's "'Tis true indeed," responds the antagonist Salome, but the twines of Mariam's hair also serve as the "nets" with which she catches the unwitting "hearts that do not shun a bait." Her "very tresses hide deceit" (4.7.417–20), Salome therefore insists, but Herod rejects the familiar trope with the insistence that he "never saw a net that show'd so fair" (4.7.424) as the locks of his yet beloved Mariam.[26]

Sometimes even more positive representations invoke the wires—or, in Herod's case, twine—of which nets are also made. In his Sonnet 37, Spenser at least alludes to hair's darker purpose in admiring the "golden tresses" his beloved suggestively "doth attire vnder a net of gold" (lines 1–2).[27] What is implied here Spenser also makes explicit later, as the speaker of Sonnet 73 laments being "self captyued" by a heart whose "seruile bands" are tied only by the locks of an addressee that are, he explains, "the fayre tresses of your golden hayre" (lines 1–3).[28] Addressing "Those amber locks" of semi-precious gemstone, Sonnet 14 of Samuel Daniel's 1592 *Delia* also describes hair as constituting "those same nets," here metaphorically imprisoning a speaker whose "libertie," the speaker laments, "thou didst surprize" (lines 1–2).[29] In the later lyric "Loves Hue and Cry" (pub. 1646), poet and playwright James Shirley brings together images of light and capture in hair whose "net of beams," the speaker is certain, "would prove / Strong enough to imprison Jove" (lines 7–8), while Thomas Jordan's "A vow to his inestimable Mistresse" (pub. 1637) takes a bodily tour that includes hair fit "To catch a Cupid in" (line 13), a metaphor for which the speaker asks "pardon sweetest if I terme a snare" (lines 12).[30]

Even the "wanton winds" (line 5) of Sidney's Sonnet 103, an apostrophe admiring how "happie" must be the River Thames "that didst my *Stella* beare!" (line 1), are so taken with Stella's "beauties so divine" (line 6) that "Ravisht, staid not, till in her golden haire / They did themselues (O sweetest prison) twine" (lines 7–8). Captivating it may be, but Stella's hair does not quite comprise the net that can hold the wind, and it turns out that neither her locks nor the poet's art can forever contain the breeze "forst by Nature still to flie" (line 10). Even so, the allure of Stella's "golden haire" had been too much even for "Æols youth" (line 9) to resist, who did first "with puffing kisse those Lockes display" (line 11).[31] Akin to that of Petrarch's Laura, whose "blonde, curling hair," Snook observes, "is defined not just by its color but also by being so fine it can be stirred and scattered by the breeze," Stella represents the "idealized, beautiful, virtuous, elite women" of an English tradition that also celebrates "hair notable for its abundance, movement, and slight, natural curl or wave."[32]

Inspiring not only the wind's puffing kisses, the alluring yet entrapping locks of poetic convention can lead also to the worst of human temptations. Maintaining that his "hart is damnd in Loues sweet fire" (line 14), the speaker of Henry Constable's 1594 *Diana* itemizes in Sonnet 6 the ways his adoration renders him guilty of all the seven deadly sins. Fittingly enough, the "*covetous*" of his love is specifically attached to the sight-pleasing "gold" that "it never would remove from her faire haire" (lines 9–10).[33] Hair's beauty evidently commands such power to enthrall that the speaker of Barnes's Sonnet 68 even wishes that it were something else altogether:

> Would God (when I beheld thy bewteous face,
> And golden tresses, rich with pearle, and stone)
> Medusaes visage had appear'd in place,
> With snakie lockes, looking on me alone:
> Then had her dreadfull charming lookes me changed
> Into a sencelesse stone, oh were I sencelesse! (lines 1–6)[34]

In this case, "golden tresses" have led the pining lover to so much grief that he would rather have met the "snakie lockes" of a Medusa to become "sencelesse stone" than suffer love unrequited.

Poetic representations of hair's beauty and allure are not, however, exclusive to idealized or dangerous women. In his 1599 "Epigram 22: *Ad Gulielmum Shakespeare*," John Weever equally admires the titular "Adonis with his amber tresses" of hair that recall the familiar gold of the Petrarchan mistress. In Shakespeare's *Venus and Adonis* those "Faire firehot" locks work equally well as on a goddess of love smitten with the young hunter and intent on "charming him to love her" (lines 5–6).[35] The Venus of Shakespeare's poem may command both "windy sighs and golden hairs" (line 51) that elsewhere prove irresistible, but it is the envious wind that contrives to blow off Adonis's bonnet and, like the breeze lured by the hair of Sidney's Stella, "Play with his locks" (line 1090).[36] Likewise, Christopher Marlowe's "Hero and Leander," though extolling "Hero the fair," who was even by "young Apollo courted for her hair" (1.6–7), proves more interested in the "Amorous Leander" (1.51) whose desire for Hero inspired his swim across the Hellespont.[37] The "beautiful and young" (1.51) lover is distinguished in particular by "dangling tresses that were never shorn," for "Had they been cut, and unto Colchos borne, / Would have allur'd the vent'rous youth of Greece, / To hazard more, than for the Golden Fleece" (1.55–58).[38] As beautiful and valuable as the "fleece" common also to Cary's Mariam, his hair is Leander's finest feature, drawing the attention even of gods as he makes his way across waters separating him from a beloved adorned by tresses barely mentioned. Vowing to protect Leander, Neptune "put Helle's bracelet on his arm, / And swore the sea should never do him harm" (2.179–80). On the contrary, the god in his element, "smiling wantonly, his love bewray'd" (2.182) as he slides between Leander's "arms" (2.184) while caressing his "his breast, his thighs, and every limb" (2.189). The exploration of Leander's parts begins, however, with a Neptune who first "clapp'd his plump cheeks" and "with his tresses play'd" (2.181) as beautiful hair yet proves primary in the language of love.[39]

THE POETICS OF HAIR

No matter how vivid, alluring, and memorable, however, the hyperbolized hair of Elizabethan love poetry did not go unchallenged. The most famous of the anti-Petrarchan offerings is, of course, found in Shakespeare's well-known Sonnet 130. Not only are this mistress's eyes nothing like the sun, her locks are far from gold, but "If hairs be wires, black wires grow on her head" (line 4). Offering a revisionist contribution to a poetic trend whose peak had passed by the time his sonnets were published in 1609, Shakespeare's sequence "assails Petrarchism for strained comparisons and unoriginal rhetoric," challenging not only specific tropes with the wiry black hair of the mysterious "dark lady" but also a tradition that offered idealized and impossible representations of women and all of their parts.[40] Hence the poem's famous last lines, "And yet by heaven I think my love as rare, / As any she belied with false compare" (line 14), present a well-known and suggestively ambiguous "she" that can serve, on the one hand, as a pronoun representing the mistress who has indulged in belying comparisons and, on the other, as a noun pointing to "any she" poetically rendered from comparisons impossible for a woman who—as all women must—merely "treads on the ground" (line 12).[41] Her anti-idealized form may render Shakespeare's as incoherent and unknowable as the more familiar golden mistress but, in claiming to represent a concrete reality and not an abstract ideal, the poem critiques as it competes with the tradition it ostensibly rejects. The black hair of "Sonnet 130" thus functions less as tribute to an actual woman (or to the reality she might represent) than it is invoked in service to revisionist and therefore poetic purpose.

Hair's usefulness to the poet Shirley likewise confirms in the distinctly anti-Petrarchan lyric, "One that loved none but deformed Women," a poem engaging in what Heather Dubrow dubs the satirical "ugly beauty" tradition.[42] Shirley's salvo opens with what seems to be a rhetorical question, "What should my Mistris do with hair?" (line 1) that is quickly answered by the rejection of art, the "frizzling" and "curling" the speaker will happily "spare" (line 2) and urges the "deformed" woman also to leave off her head covering, insisting instead that "No dressing should conceal her ear, / Which I would have at length appear" (lines 5–6). The poem does not, however, reject artifice with the aim of championing a more realistic and less-than-perfect woman. As it turns out, Shirley's speaker favors the "deformed" not to women's advantage but as a means of ensuring that a future wife will "in wedlock better agree" (line 17) by not indulging in otherwise certain cuckoldry.[43] In a less satirical mode, Michael Drayton's 1619 *Idea* deflates the transitory ideal of Petrarchan creation by taking pleasure in the declining beauty of age. Eagerly anticipating in Sonnet 8 the time when "Thy dainty hair, so curl'd and crisped now" comes to more closely to resemble "grizzled moss upon some aged tree" (lines 7–8), Drayton's poetic art asserts his own as well as nature's triumph over impossible beauties and the conventions their crisp and curling hair represents.[44]

In a similar vein, Thomas Carew's "A Divine Mistress" (pub. 1640) considers the art that writes upon nature in figuring a mistress in whose "peeces still I see / Some errour, that might mended bee" (lines 1–2). Because the woman of whom Carew writes was made not by the "Nature that made me," the poet "cannot spare, / From her just shape the smallest haire" (lines 11–12). The otherworldly mistress, in other words, is a product of "every beauteous line" (line 6) from which both she and poetic tradition are comprised. Thus "fram'd by hands farre more divine" (line 5), such a mistress "hath too much divinity for mee" (line 15), the speaker laments as he ends by calling upon the "Gods" to "teach her some more humanitie" (lines 16).[45] The poem's closing line could, of course, be read as a complaint about the haughtiness of a woman too self-important even to acknowledge the speaker's existence, a reading that (as we know from Surrey's face and hair-hiding mistress) is certainly conventional. But the attention given to the scornful mistress and her every detail has, the poet complains, focused poetry's attention on impossible minutiae at the expense of a mimetic mode interested in more faithful representation. Unlike many of his predecessors, Carew does not champion but questions both the divine powers claimed in the fashioning of ever more impossible ideals and the nature of poetry that is therefore neither true nor purposeful.[46] Carew's divine mistress, in other words, should be properly "taught" by the poetic "Gods" who created her to be more human and less impossibly divine, a woman from whom the "smallest haire" could be spared without any lamentable or even discernible loss.

The problems with taking poetic exercise to an extreme so crucially dependent on even the "smallest haire" playwright John Ford dramatizes in his 1633 over-the-top tragedy, *'Tis Pity She's a Whore*. Featuring the incestuous love of Giovanni for his sister Annabella, Ford's best-known play considers the dangers in misunderstanding the hyperbole of poetic art gone too far. Giovanni describes his sister Annabella in fourteen blazonic lines centered on a world of variety that allude also to Shakespeare's Cleopatra. Annabella has, he says, the "threads of purest gold" for "Hair" (2.5.52–3).[47] For Giovanni, whose madness is made fully manifest when he later harvests his sister's actual heart as proof of his winning it, Annabella does not possess hair that is like gold but is instead crowned with "threads of purest gold" that are like hair. Reversing the usual equation literalizes the metaphor, and enjambing the line so that "Hair" is forced apart from the precious metal of which it is composed further highlights the break from reality Giovanni's poetic (mis)understanding represents. Reversing as well the culturally understood role of art as mirroring an already extant nature, Giovanni's words suggest that nature comes into creation by art: in the madness of his skewed vision, nature merely mirrors the art he has come to understand as reality.

Barnes's Sonnet 71 likewise extolls "Those haires of Angels gold" (line 1) that Giovanni celebrates but proceeds to highlight the artificiality of what the poem's opening in part aims to create. The idealized "she" the tresses of heavenly gold are understood to represent the speaker goes on to address directly—and tellingly—with the parenthetical "(For thou by nature Angellike art framed)" (line 2).[48] Alluding also to an art that overwrites nature, the graphic framing of parentheses enacts in form what the line describes in content, and that content is suggestively ambiguous: here, "art" can be read as the second-person verbal form of the infinitive *to be* (as in "thou art") or as the poetic "art" that can alone frame and thus properly display—and even create—the subject's "Angellike" nature. The line's ambiguity may aim to champion art's capacity to create another nature, but it also implies ambivalence about the very art the poem represents. In an age of Christian belief and a poetic tradition in which even Petrarch "chastises Laura for a narcissism that is the poetic reflection of his own self-absorption," the poem may also warn against not only excessive adoration but also the potentially damning hubris of poetic creation.[49]

As a vehicle for poetic prowess, hair is fully on display in Drummond's apostrophe addressing that "Haire, precious Haire which Midas Hand did straine" (line 1). A sonnet in Petrarchan form, the poem establishes hair's fatal allure in the desire of the king whose lust for gold led to death by starvation, and takes up a familiar metaphor in describing "the Wreathe of Gold that crownes those Browes" (line 2). This mistress's hair may shine brilliantly enough to outdo the "Lillie" (line 4) and even "Winters whitest White in Whitenesse staine" (line 3) but, given the funereal flower's renown as an emblem of death and winter's as the definitively dead season, both comparisons also suggest that the oft-admired "Haire" of Petrarchan convention does indeed embody the "(fatall Present)" that, the speaker goes on to explain "first caus'd my Woes" (line 5), and

> When loose yee hang like Danaës golden Raine,
> Sweet Nettes, which sweetly doe all Hearts enchaine,
> Strings, deadly Strings, with which Loue bends his Bowes.
> How are yee hither come? tell me, O Haire,
> Deare Armelet, for what thus were yee giuen·
> I know a Badge of Bondage I you weare,
> Yet Haire for you, ô that I were a Heauen!
> Like Berenices Locke that yee might shine
> (But brighter farre) about this Arme of mine. (lines 6–14)[50]

Danaë was, of course, the mythological woman locked in a subterranean chamber in response to a prophecy predicting that her son would kill her father, thus rendered childless until fruitfully showered with Zeus' "golden Raine" (line 6). The image of imprisonment invoked with "Danaës golden Raine," however, soon becomes the more familiar metaphor of hair that is also the "Sweet Nettes" enchaining "all Hearts," hair that supplies the "deadly Strings" of Cupid's bow, and the hair that is a "Badge of Bondage" encircling the speaker's arm. Now removed from the woman it once crowned, the celebrated hair is capable of shining "brighter farre" in the hypothetical "Heaven" of the speaker's body than the shorn amber tresses of Berenice, the wife of Ptolemy of Egypt whose enviable locks were set in constellation by the admiring Jupiter. The hair now firmly in the speaker's possession may constitute a "Dear Armelet" capable of outdoing even the stars, yet the utter absence of the once-idealized beloved from whom her hair is now irrevocably detached suggests its greater usefulness to the poet's overtly intertextual enterprise.

As Drummond's hyperbolic and deeply self-conscious apostrophe recognizes, the Petrarchan mode is an art of extravagant comparison that sees poets ever striving to outdo one another. It is no accident that the "laurel potential" suggested by Laura's name alludes also to the poet's crown, nor is it by chance that the anagrammatic ideal of Daniel's Delia is only one letter removed from the poet's own name.[51] In its very extravagance, though, Drummond's poem may also constitute another of "the anti-Petrarchan poems" that "allow their authors to lay claim to many types of success," and sometimes that success is asserted particularly through the "agency and autonomy" implied in rejecting—or, like Drummond, outdoing—the many and familiar "boilerplate imitations of Petrarch."[52] It is no secret, either, that the sequence credited with inspiring so many imitators, Sidney's *Astrophel and Stella*, emulated but, in "reworking the terms of Petrarchism," also revised the conventions earlier poets had more closely followed.[53] Even in its attempt "to claim a more sincere originality" for the poet and his verse, *Astrophel and Stella* may scrutinize the sequence's own Petrarchism as much as it critiques Astrophel's excessive adulation and pursuit of a woman unavailable to him.[54]

The purpose of art is, of course, a well-known preoccupation of Sidney's evident also in the poetic awareness we have seen in Sonnet 13, a display of heraldic arms that blazons even while calling "attention to the act of blazoning itself."[55] But Sidney is especially interested in art and its relationship with the nature it purports to represent. "There is no Art," as he insists in his *Defence of Poesie*, "delivered unto mankind that hath not the workes of nature for his principall object." At the same time affirming the freedom of his art to create, Sidney also argues that the poet alone is granted special license to indulge "the vigor of his own invention," to "grow in effect into another nature: in making things either better then nature bringeth foorth, or quite a new."[56] Granted, Sidney may have declared nature's world merely "brazen," while "the Poets only deliver a golden," yet he also believed that poetry must reflect the reality of "the general nature" in making art "by practice" seem to be nature.[57] Here Sidney advocates the ideal of *sprezzatura* promoted by Baldassare Castiglione in his influential *Book of the Courtier*, a sixteenth-century conduct manual for courtly behavior advocating, among other things, making seem easy and effortless that which was acquired only through diligent effort.

A natural attribute but also signifier of "elite identity," as Snook argues of Sidney's *Arcadia*, hair serves to champion the "aesthetic knowledge" necessary "to gracefully hide one's art."[58] Hence, upon meeting whom he perceives to be the Amazon Zelmane but is really the disguised Pyrocles, the *Arcadia*'s questing Palladius (who is actually Musidorus), "Well might" also

> perceaue the hanging of her haire in fairest qua[n]titie, in locks, some curled & some as it were forgotten, with such a carelesse care, & an arte so hiding arte, that she seemed she would lay them for a paterne, whether nature simply, or nature helped by cunning, be more excellent: the rest whereof was drawne into a coronet of golde richly set with pearle, and so ioyned all ouer with gold wiers, and couered with feathers of diuers colours, that it was not vnlike to an helmet, such a glittering shew it bare, & so brauely it was held vp fro[m] the head.[59]

Invoking the language of Petrarchan love poetry in depicting a cross-dressed man, the description proposes in hair's arrangement an ideal of art and nature. Skillfully "drawne into a coronet of golde" enhanced with "pearle" and held together with the requisite "gold wiers," the hair is at once of art and nature, with some of its locks deliberately "curled" and others apparently "forgotten." Both naturally easy and artfully arranged, the disguised Pyrocles's hair offers "a paterne," its oxymoronic "careless care" representing the ideal of "an arte so hiding arte" that it becomes impossible to determine where "nature simply, or nature helped by cunning" art "be more excellent." That Palladius/Musidorus "could not perfectly see her face" when he first spied the "Amazon" later revealed as the young prince and his lost cousin, suggests much about hair's usefulness to the poet: unlike the potentially identity-revealing but obscured face, hair has the capacity to make art seem nature.[60]

Hair analogous to the poetic ideal appears also in the twelfth chapter of *Arcadia*'s first book, which features "The painted muster of an eleven conquered beauties," the eighth of whom turns out to be "the excelle[n]tly-faire Queene Helen." Her locks are, as we have come to expect, featured prominently, her "lacinth haire curled by nature, & intercurled by arte (like a fine brooke through golde sa[n]ds) had a rope of faire pearles, which now hiding, now hidden by the haire, did as it were play at fast or loose, each with other, mutually giuing & receiuing riches." Helen is so perfect, in fact, that if she "had not bene know[n], some would rather have judged it the painters exercise," an attempt to "to shew what he could do" in "the cou[n]terfaiting of any living pattern: for no fault the most fault finding wit could have found."[61] In Book Three, we find a description of the sad princess and star-crossed lover, Philoclea who, though "like rainein Sunshile" weeping, "In the dressing of her haire and apparell," the "suttle Cecropia" properly could not espy "neither a careful arte, nor an arte of carelesnesse, but euen left to a neglected chaunce, which yet coulde no more vnperfect her perfections, then a Die anie way cast, could loose his squarenesse."[62] Expressed in the rhetorical figure *antimetabole*, which sees words (or their alternative forms) repeated in reverse order, the "careful arte" and "arte of carelessness" (in the sense of done without fuss) suggest a reciprocity of ease and attentiveness, affirming their interdependence and equal importance in a circular form that may contrast with the cubed rigidity of dice but is alike in balanced and assured reliability.

Hair figures even more prominently in the prose romance of Lady Mary Wroth, Sidney's niece and the author of *The Countess of Montgomery's Urania*. Pamphilia is the lover of the unattainable Amphilanthus (brother to the titular Urania's beloved Leonius) and the speaker of a now well-known sequence of poems addressed to or about him. A sonnet writer herself, Pamphilia is described in decidedly Petrarchan terms as she appears, though not for the first time,

> apparreld in a Gowne of light Tawny or Murrey, embrodered with the richest, and perfectest Pearle for roundnesse and whitenes, the work contriued into knots and Garlands; on her head she wore a crowne of Diamonds, without foiles, to shew her clearenesse, such as needed no foile to set forth the true brightnesse of it: her haire (alas that plainely I must call that haire, which no earthly riches could value, nor heauenly resemblance counterfeit) was prettily intertwind betweene the Diamonds in many places, making them (though of the greatest value) appeare but like glasse set in gold.[63]

In a work that aims, Snook suggests, "to develop the theory that hair is a reliable sign of class identity" and thus challenge the "sexual difference" that was "a central proposition of what constitutes natural hair," Pamphilia's serves in part to affirm an aristocratic nature on full display in a decidedly Petrarchan blazon.[64] Denying authorship of a "Sonnet" she had earlier finished carving into the bark of an ash, Pamphilia remarks that identity could not here be discerned by the character of handwriting offering "no proofe against me," given that "many Poets write as well by imitation, as by sence of passion."[65] At once distinct and imitative, Wroth's depiction of her poetess revises the terms so familiar in the work of her male counterparts in an anti-comparison that does them one better. Pamphilia's hair may be adorned with pearls and crowned with diamonds but, given that it already exceeds what may be comparable to the "earthly riches" or the "heavenly resemblance" on which the male poet so often relies, neither her diamonds nor her hair requires the foil of comparison otherwise necessary to making both shine brighter.[66]

As Wroth's outdoing comparison further suggests, hair offers a particularly malleable vehicle for revising the "boilerplate" terms of Petrarchism. Known for the plain style that aimed to redress poetic and rhetorical excess, poet and playwright Ben Jonson draws on the Petrarchan in the blazon that makes up his "A Celebration of Charis: 4. Her Triumph," a poem urging its audience to "Do but look on her hair" for "it is bright / As Love's star when it riseth!" (lines 13–14).[67] In his "Simplex Munditiis" from his 1609 drama, *Epicoene*, the poet explicitly advocates an easy nature over the forced artifice of art, bidding his addressee to

Give me a look, give me a face,
That makes simplicity a grace;
Robes loosely flowing, hair as free:
Such sweet neglect more taketh me
Than all the adulteries of art;
They strike mine eyes, but not my heart.
(lines 7–12)[68]

The admired "sweet neglect" with "hair as free" as "Robes loosely flowing" Jonson describes comes to the forefront in Robert Herrick, who finds in his "Delight in Disorder" an admirably "wild civility" (line 12) that can "bewitch" more "than when art / Is too precise in every part" (lines 13–14).[69] Though Herrick's poem does not specifically mention hair (an omission that may itself constitute an anti-Petrarchan move), it does respond to that tradition with a blazon more careless than contrived in a poem that may have fourteen lines but is clearly not a sonnet. Likewise, in "Corinna's Going a-Maying," Herrick's speaker urges the subject of his poem to rise and greet the day, and "Take no care" and "Fear not" the absence of "jewels for your gown or hair," for "the leaves will strew / Gems in abundance upon you" (lines 17–20).[70] In "Art Above Nature: To Julia," however, Herrick's speaker confesses that when, among all of the parts of attire that make up "all of those airy silks" (line 15) set in flowing motion by "wild civility" (line 14), he first beholds "a forest spread / With silken trees upon thy head" (lines 1–2), he can end only with the confession that "mine eye and heart" thus "Dotes less on Nature than on Art" (lines 17–18).[71] Though advocating a less rigid aesthetic than his Petrarchan predecessors, Herrick fashions himself a poet whose art yet improves nature.

Famously rearranging Petrarchan convention in his Elegy 2, "The Anagram," John Donne rewrites nature as he blazons a Flavia who, "though her cheeks be yellow, her hair's red" (line 7), is thus composed of parts not "in th' usual place" (line 15).[72] His notoriously colonizing Elegy 19, "To His Mistress Going to Bed," resists glorifying hair with the voice of a speaker who matter-of-factly bids his mistress to "Off with that wiry coronet and shew / The hairy diadem which on you doth grow" (lines 15–16).[73] In this case, the "wiry" and "hairy" adjectives do not extoll the beauty of hair but serve merely to modify the more important "coronet" and "diadem" that cover it; hair for Donne seems most useful as a means of asserting his own autonomy and agency. Urging the casting off of deceptive head coverings but refusing to dwell on the characteristics of the locks they conceal, Donne rejects the familiar while affirming the transcendent power of the "masculine persuasive force" he explicitly asserts elsewhere.[74]

Hair plays a different role in "The Funeral," however, a poem voiced by what Theresa M. DiPasquale identifies as one of Donne's "most stubbornly Petrarchan personae."[75] Yet Donne's speaker remains firmly in charge of another's locks as he implores that, upon his death, "Whoever comes to shroud me" should neither "harm / Nor question much" (lines 1–2) the memento that is a "subtle wreath of hair, which crowns my arm" (line 3). A token of a love that defies description, the circle of hair is a "mystery" as well as "the sign you must not touch" (line 4). Yet the bracelet's symbolism turns out to be less important than its function as "the sinewy thread" (line 9) that does "make me one of all" by pulling together the speaker's many "parts" (line 11). Though the speaker admits "strength and art" (line 12) that come "from a better brain / Can better do't" (lines 13–14), the hair token nevertheless accomplishes what it cannot while adorning the enduringly fragmented woman of Petrarchan convention.[76] Firmly possessed by the speaker, the token given so "that I / By this should know my pain" (lines 15–16) may be only "an empty sign" on the part of the unknown woman who killed him, but it is also the means of a poet's triumph and a lover's revenge: "for since you would have none of me," the poem decisively concludes, "I bury some of you" (line 24).[77] Asserting the power of the poet to destroy as well as create, hair is thus apotheosized in tribute to a persuasive force decisively triumphing over nature as well as poetic convention.

CONCLUSION

The wreath that becomes "A bracelet of bright haire about the bone" (line 6) serves yet another purpose in Donne's "The Relic." A token encouraging any future digger to believe "that there a loving couple lies" (line 8), the beloved's locks provide the means for an imagined age to be "by this paper taught" (line 21) of the "miracles we harmless lovers wrought" (line 22). Aiming forever to immortalize the mistress who will prove another "Mary Magdalen" (line 17) in "The Relic" while permanently burying another in "The Funeral," hair's opposing purposes serve a poetic and rhetorical exercise no less significant even when "All measure, and all language, I should pass, / Should I tell what a miracle she was" ("The Relic," lines 32–33).[78] For the "monarch of anti-Petrarchist wit," art may fall short of meeting a nature that ever exceeds it but, as Dubrow puts it, even the rejection of its immortalizing claims render the poet both "resident and alien in the realms of Petrarchism."[79] Donne thus offers in a single author a little world of representations that, taken together, prove less interested in the nature of hair or in those it represents than its usefulness as a persuasive and poetic device. For English verse more broadly, hair in all its infinite variety proves useful even when put to opposing purposes—ever made cunningly, Petrarch's locks turn out to be much more art than nature.

NOTES

Introduction

1. Brush (1600–1619), silver, pierced and engraved, height 16.8 cm, length 12 cm maximum, width 9 cm. Victoria and Albert Museum, London. M.51-1955; Comb (1530–1550), carved elephant ivory, height 12 cm, width 16.2 cm, depth 0.6 cm. Victoria and Albert Museum, London. 468-1869. The V&A has multiple combs in its collection.
2. Comb (1500–1600), boxwood, height 9.3 cm, width 11.7 cm, diameter 3.5 cm. Victoria and Albert Museum, London. 236-1872.
3. Casket (1575–1600), softwood with beech wood veneers, height 23.5 cm, width 43.5 cm, depth 30.5 cm. Victoria and Albert Museum, London. 7901-1861.
4. Comb case and lid (1400–1500), moulded leather, tooled, carved, and stamped, height 12 cm, width 12 cm, depth 3 cm. Victoria and Albert Museum, London. 15-1891.
5. Keith Thomas, *Religion and the Decline of Magic: Studies in Popular Beliefs in Sixteenth and Seventeenth Century England* (Oxford: Oxford University Press, 1971), 437–8. Jeffrey R. Watt, "Love Magic and the Inquisition: A Case from Seventeenth-Century Italy," *Sixteenth Century Journal* 41, no. 3 (2010): 675–89, describes the case of the bewitchment of one Laura Coccapani by Fra Valerio Trionfanti in 1628 in the town of Carpi in Italy. They had fallen in love, but the relationship had broken down in 1627 when Coccapani married. Within months, however, Laura claimed to feel the effects of a powerful spell. When she was with her husband, blood flowed from her breasts, demons tormented her and moved objects and furniture within her house, and she felt like she was eating rags. Coccapani reported to the inquisitor that when she was in bed with her husband, the bed would be covered with hair the same color as her own, which the maid would need to clean up by burning it—a testimony confirmed by the maid herself. When Trionfanti was investigated by the inquisitor of Modena, the investigators found letters, a braid of her hair, another lock of hair, and short curly hairs, which turned out to be pubic hairs that Coccapani had given Trionfanti, along with the braid. It was then suspected that the hair was used in casting the spell. In the end, however, while the priest was incarcerated for three months, he was ultimately found innocent of the charges—perhaps, Watt suggests, because the church was by this time more concerned with the misuse of sacramental objects in magic or conjuring demons, and Trionfanti had been merely engaging in "body magic." Guido Ruggiero, *Binding Passions: Tales of Magic, Marriage, and Power at the End of the Renaissance* (New York: Oxford University Press, 1993), 195–6, tells the story of another practitioner of body magic, a sixteenth-century priest from Siena named Aurelio who became known as the fortune-telling friar and was accused of using hair to cast love spells, having been found with packets of hair in his possession.
6. Ring (mid-seventeenth century to late seventeenth century), enameled gold with hair, depth 0.5 cm, diameter 2.3 cm. Victoria and Albert Museum, London. M.2821-1931. On

love tokens and hair, see Pamela S. Hammons, *Gender, Sexuality, and Material Objects in English Renaissance Verse* (Farnham: Ashgate, 2010), 16, 18.

7. Richard Corson, *Fashions in Hair: The First Five Thousand Years* (1965, rpt., London: Peter Owen, 1980).
8. Jane Ashelford, *A Visual History of Costume: The Sixteenth Century* (London: BT Batsford, 1983); Valerie Cumming, *A Visual History of Costume: The Seventeenth Century* (London: BT Batsford, 1984); Herbert Norris, *Tudor Costume and Fashion* (Mineola, NY: Dover, 1997); Evelyn Welch, "Signs of Faith: The Political and Social Identity of Hair in Renaissance Italy," in *La fiducia secondo i linguaggi del potere*, ed. Paolo Prodi (Bologna: Il Mulino, 2008), 371–86; Evelyn Welch, "Art on the Edge: Hair and Hands in Renaissance Italy," *Renaissance Studies* 23, no. 3 (2008): 241–68.
9. Margaret Pelling, *The Common Lot: Sickness, Medical Occupations and the Urban Poor in Early Modern England* (London: Longman, 1998), 215; Annemarie Kinzelbach, "Erudite and Honoured Artisans? Performers of Body Care and Surgery in Early Modern German Towns," *Social History of Medicine* 27, no. 4 (2014): 668–88; Sandra Cavallo, *Artisans of the Body in Early Modern Italy: Identities, Families and Masculinities* (Manchester: Manchester University Press, 2007), 38–41.
10. Jean-Marie Le Gall, *Un Idéal Masculin? Barbes et moustaches XVe-XVIIIe siècles* (Paris: Payot, 2011).
11. Anu Korhonen, "Strange Things Out of Hair: Baldness and Masculinity in Early Modern England," *Sixteenth Century Journal* 41, no. 2 (2010): 371–91.
12. Merry Wiesner-Hanks, *The Marvelous Hairy Girls: The Gonzales Sisters and their Worlds* (New Haven, CT: Yale University Press, 2009).
13. M.A. Katritzky, "'A Wonderful Monster Borne in Germany': Hairy Girls in Medieval and Early Modern German Book, Court and Performance Culture," *German Life and Letters* 67, no. 4 (2014): 469.
14. Sefy Hendler, "*Pelo sopra pelo*: Sculpting Hair and Beards as a Reflection of Artistic Excellence During the Renaissance," *Sculpture Journal* 24, no. 1 (2015): 7–21.
15. Will Fisher, *Materializing Gender in Early Modern English Literature and Culture* (Cambridge: Cambridge University Press, 2006), 83–158; Mark Albert Johnston, *Beard Fetish in Early Modern England: Sex, Gender, and Registers of Value* (Surrey: Ashgate, 2011).
16. Elliott Horowitz, "The New World and the Changing Face of Europe," *Sixteenth Century Journal* 28, no. 4 (1997): 1181–201.
17. Sherry Velasco, "Women with Beards in Early Modern Spain," in *The Last Taboo: Women and Body Hair*, ed. Karín Lesnik-Oberstein (Manchester: Manchester University Press, 2006), 181–90.
18. On Milton's *Samson Agonistes*, see Will Fisher, "'The Ornament of their Sex': Hair and Gender," in *Materializing Gender*, 129–58; on Milton's *Paradise Lost*, see Stephen B. Dobranski, "Clustering and Curling Locks: The Matter of Hair in *Paradise Lost*," *PMLA* 125, no. 2 (2010): 337–53; on Shakespeare, see Edward J. Geisweidt, "Horticulture of the Head: The Vegetable Life of Hair in Early Modern English Thought," *Early Modern Literary Studies* 19 (2009): n.p., and Gustav Ungerer, "Sir Andrew Aguecheek and His Head of Hair," *Shakespeare Studies* 16 (1983): 101–33. On Anne Clifford and Margaret Cavendish, see Edith Snook, *Women, Beauty and Power in Early Modern England: A Feminist Literary History* (Basingstoke: Palgrave Macmillan, 2011), 115–79.
19. Alf Hiltebeitel and Barbara D. Miller, eds., *Hair Its Power and Meaning in Asian Cultures* (Albany: State University of New York Press, 1998); Ayana B. Byrd and Lori L. Tharps,

Hair Story: Untangling the Roots of Black Hair in America (New York: St. Martin's Press, 2001).

20. Judith A. Carney, "'With Graines in Her Hair': Rice in Colonial Brazil," *Slavery and Abolition* 25, no. 1 (2004): 1–27.
21. John Calvin, "The 17. Sermon upon the Second Chapter," in *The Sermons of M. John Calvin*, trans. Laurence Tomson (London: G. Bishop, 1579), 198–211.
22. John Milton, *Samson Agonistes*, in *The Complete Poetry and Essential Prose of John Milton*, eds. William Kerrigan, John Rumrich, and Stephen M. Fallon (New York: Modern Library, 2007), 58–9.
23. Peter Paul Rubens, *Samson and Delilah* (ca. 1609–1610), painting, 185 × 205 cm. The National Gallery, London. Available online in ARTstor Collections.
24. For another example of a short-haired Samson having his hair cut, see Lucas Cranach the Elder, *Samson and Delilah* (ca. 1528–1530), painting, 57.2 × 37.8 cm. The Metropolitan Museum of Art, New York. Available online in ARTstor Collections.
25. Dirck Volkertsz, *Samson and Delilah* (1551), engraving, 24.8 × 19.7 cm. *The Illustrated Bartsch*. Available online in ARTstor Collections; Philips Galle, *Delilah Shaves Off the Seven Locks of Samson's Hair* (n.d.), engraving, diameter 25.9 cm. *The Illustrated Bartsch*. Available online in ARTstor Collections.
26. Anton Woensam of Worms, *Samson and Delilah* (1529), engraving, 16.4 × 22.1 cm. *The Illustrated Bartsch*. Available online in ARTstor Collections.
27. See Corson, *Fashions in Hair*, pl. 46, style S.
28. Richard Corson documents shoulder-length and longer hairstyles on Italian, English, German, Hungarian, French, and Dutch men in the last quarter of the fifteenth century and in the 1630s and after. *Fashions in Hair*, pl. 37–40, 45, 56–8.
29. Ashelford, *A Visual History*, 79.
30. Cumming, *A Visual History*, 67, 71, 81, 82.
31. Ibid., 81.
32. Phillis Cunnington and Catherine Lucas, *Occupational Costume in England* (London: Adam & Charles Black, 1967), 302–4.
33. Johnston, *Beard Fetish*, 108.
34. Corson, *Fashions in Hair*, 159–71.
35. Elizabeth Ewing, *History of Children's Costume* (New York: Scribner, 1977), discusses breeching (30–2).
36. Phillis Cunnington and Anne Buck, *Children's Costume in England: From the Fourteenth Century to the end of the Nineteenth Century* (London: Adam and Charles Black, 1965), 36, 69, 95.
37. After Gerrit van Honthorst, *The Duke of Buckingham and His Family* (1628), oil on canvas, 145.4 × 198.1 cm. National Portrait Gallery, London. NPG 711.
38. See also the portrait of the Capel Family by Cornelius Johnson (ca. 1640). National Portrait Gallery, London. NPG 4759.
39. *William Cecil, 1st Baron Burghley* (after 1587), oil on panel, 113 × 91.1 cm. National Portrait Gallery, London. NPG 362. See also Roy Strong, *Tudor and Jacobean*, vol. 2 (London: HMSO, 1969), figs. 50–61.
40. Jacopo Tintoretto, *Old Man and a Boy* (ca. 1565), oil on canvas, 103 × 83 cm. Kunsthistorisches Museum, Vienna. Available online in ARTstor Collections.
41. Korhonen, "Strange Things," 375–8.
42. Albrecht Dürer, *Vanitas* (old woman with a bag of coins; vanity; reverse side of the portrait of a young man) (1507), painting, 35 × 29 cm. Kunsthistorisches Museum, Vienna. Available online in ARTstor Collections.

43. *Age* (seventeenth century), relief, 10 × 8.1 cm. Victoria and Albert Museum, London. A.68-1938.
44. Erin J. Campbell, "Prophets, Saints, and Matriarchs: Portraits of Old Women in Early Modern Italy," *Renaissance Quarterly* 63, no. 3 (2010): 807–49.
45. Jan van Belcamp (attr.), *The Great Picture Triptych* (1646), oil on canvas, centre panel 254 × 254 cm, side panels 254 × 119.38 cm. Abbott Hall Art Gallery, Kendal. https://www.abbothall.org.uk/great-picture. For more on this portrait, see Snook, *Women, Beauty and Power*, 152–5.
46. Margo Hendricks, "Race: A Renaissance Category?" in *A Companion to English Renaissance Literature and Culture*, ed. Michael Hattaway (Oxford: Blackwell Publishing, 2002). Blackwell Reference Online; Ania Loomba, *Shakespeare, Race and Colonialism* (Oxford: Oxford University Press, 2002), 22–44.
47. Philip Sidney, *The Countess of Pembroke's Arcadia, 1590: The New Arcadia*, ed. Victor Skretkowicz (Oxford: Clarendon Press, 1987), 190.
48. William Shakespeare, *Titus Andronicus*, in *William Shakespeare: The Complete Works*, eds. Stanley Wells and Gary Taylor (Oxford: Clarendon Press, 1988), 125–52.
49. Galen, *Mixtures*, in *Galen: Selected Works*, ed. P.N. Singer (Oxford: Oxford University Press, 1997, EBSCOhost eBook), 253; Helkiah Crooke, *Microcosmographia: A Description of the Body of Man* (London: William Jaggard, 1615), 68.
50. Edith Snook, "Beautiful Hair, Health, and Privilege in Early Modern England," *Journal for Early Modern Cultural Studies* 15, no. 4 (2015): 22–51.
51. Shane White and Graham White, *Stylin': African American Expressive Culture from Its Beginnings to the Zoot Suit* (Ithaca, NY: Cornell University Press, 1998), 37–62.
52. Mark Albert Johnston, "Bearded Women in Early Modern England," *Studies in English Literature, 1500–1900* 47, no. 1 (2007): 1–28, 19.
53. Ilse E. Friesen, *The Female Crucifix: Images of St. Wilgefortis Since the Middle Ages* (Waterloo, ON: Wilfrid Laurier University Press, 2001), 112.
54. Ibid., 2, 4.
55. Michelle Moseley-Christian, "From Page to Print: The Transformation of the 'Wild Woman' in Early Modern Northern Engravings," *Word & Image* 27, no. 4 (2011): 429–42.
56. Wiesner-Hanks, *The Marvelous Hairy Girls*, 32–5.
57. Ibid., 110.
58. Alan Stewart, "Humanity at a Price: Erasmus, Budé, and the Poverty of Philology," in *At the Borders of the Human: Beasts, Bodies and Natural Philosophy in the Early Modern Period*, eds. Erica Fudge, Ruth Gilbert, and Susan Wiseman (Houndmills: Palgrave, 1999), 9.

Chapter 1

1. Merry Wiesner-Hanks, *The Marvelous Hairy Girls: The Gonzales Sisters and their Worlds* (New Haven, CT: Yale University Press, 2009), 42–3.
2. Merry Wiesner-Hanks, "Women," in *Oxford Encyclopedia of the Reformation*, ed. Hans J. Hillerbrand, 4 vols. (Oxford: Oxford University Press, 1996), 4: 390–8.
3. Martin Luther, *Commentaries on I Corinthians 7; I Corinthians 15; Lectures on I Timothy*, vol. 28 of *American Edition of Luther's Works*, ed. Hilton C. Oswald (St. Louis, MO: Concordia Publishing, 1973), 274.
4. Ibid., 275.

5. Martin Luther, *The Babylon Captivity of the Church*, vol. 36 of *American Edition of Luther's Works*, 152; also Luther, *Commentaries on I Corinthians*, 276.
6. Martin Luther, *Notes on Ecclesiastes, Lectures on the Song of Solomon, Treatise on the Last Words of David*, vol. 15 of *Luther's Works*, ed. Jaroslav Pelkian (St. Louis, MO: Concordia Publishing, 1972), 228.
7. Ibid., 241.
8. Ibid., 251.
9. Online edition of Calvin's commentaries, Christian Classics Ethereal Library, Calvin College: http://www.ccel.org/ccel/calvin/calcom43.iii.iv.iii.html (Accessed April 23, 2018).
10. Ibid., http://www.ccel.org/ccel/calvin/calcom39.xviii.i.html (Accessed April 23, 2018).
11. Ibid.
12. See Mirjam van Veen et al., eds., *Sisters: Myth and Reality of Anabaptist, Mennonite, and Doopsgezind Women ca 1525–1900* (Leiden: Brill, 2014); also C. Arnold Snyder and Linda H. Hecht, eds., *Profiles of Anabaptist Women: Sixteenth-Century Reforming Pioneers* (Waterloo, ON: Wilfrid Laurier University Press, 1996).
13. Menno Simons, "Reply to Martin Micron, 1556," in *The Complete Writings of Menno Simons, c.1496–1561*, ed. J.C. Wenger, trans. Leonard Verduin (Scottdale, PA: Herald Press, 1956 [1984]), 851.
14. See Gary K. Waite, "A Reappraisal of the Contribution of Anabaptists to the Religious Culture and Intellectual Climate of the Dutch Republic," in *Religious Minorities and Cultural Diversity in the Dutch Republic: Studies Presented to Piet Visser on the Occasion of his 65th Birthday*, ed. August den Hollander et al. (Leiden: Brill, 2014), 6–28.
15. As cited in Joris's earliest known tract, "Of the Wonderful Working of God," in *The Anabaptist Writings of David Joris, 1535–1543*, ed. Gary K. Waite (Scottdale, PA: Herald Press, 1994), 116–17.
16. David Joris, "David Joris's Response to Johannes Eisenburg, 1537," in *The Anabaptist Writings*, 162.
17. See "The Anonymous Biography of Joris," in *The Anabaptist Writings*, 31–103, esp. 89.
18. Gary K. Waite, "Talking Animals, Preserved Corpses and Venusberg: The Sixteenth-Century Worldview and Popular Conceptions of the Spiritualist David Joris (1501–1556)," *Social History* 20 (1995): 147–8.
19. Wiesner-Hanks, *The Marvelous Hairy Girls*, 37.
20. William Prynne, *The vnlouelinesse, of loue-lockes. Or, A summarie discourse, proouing: the wearing, and nourishing of a locke, or loue-locke, to be altogether vnseemely, and vnlawfull vnto Christians....* (London, 1628), fol. A3r–v.
21. Ptolemy, *The Compost of Ptolomeus* (London: M. Parsons, 1638[?]), H7; see also Keith Thomas, *Religion and the Decline of Magic* (New York: Scribners, 1971), 567.
22. Thomas, *Religion and the Decline of Magic*, 567. Here he is paraphrasing John Gaule, *Select Cases of Conscience Touching Witches and Witchcraft* (London: Printed by W. Wilson, 1646), 4–5.
23. Christopher S. Mackay, ed., *The Hammer of Witches: A Complete Translation of the Malleus Maleficarum* (Cambridge: Cambridge University Press, 2006 [2009]), 417.
24. Pierre de Lancre, *On the Inconstancy of Witches: Pierre de Lancre's Tableau de l'inconstance des mauvais anges et demons (1612)*, ed. Gerhild Scholz Williams (Tempe, AZ: ACMRS, 2006), 61.
25. Thomas, *Religion and the Decline of Magic*, 437–8.
26. Emmanuel LeRoy Ladurie, *Montaillou: The Promised Land of Error*, trans. Barbara Bray (New York: Random House, 1979), 31.

27. Ibid., 31–2.
28. On popular beliefs related to saints, see Aron Gurevich, *Medieval Popular Culture: Problems of Belief and Perception*, trans. János M. Back and Paul A. Hollingsworth (Cambridge: Cambridge University Press, 1988), 39–77.
29. We now know that hair only appears to grow after death during the process of decay. Paul Barber, *Vampires, Burial, and Death: Folklore and Reality* (New Haven, CT: Yale University Press, 2010), vii, 6–7, 42, 119.
30. Ibid., 31–2.
31. Ibid., 52, 62.
32. Wiesner-Hanks, *The Marvelous Hairy Girls*, 35. See also M.A. Katritzky, "'A Wonderfull Monster Borne in Germany': Hairy Girls in Medieval and Early Modern German Book, Court and Performance Culture," *German Life and Letters* 67, no. 4 (2014): 467–80.
33. Wiesner-Hanks, *The Marvelous Hairy Girls*, 39.
34. Ibid., 39–40.
35. Ibid., 196.
36. Mackay, *The Hammer of Witches*, 119.
37. Jean Bodin, *On the Demon-Mania of Witches*, trans. Randy A. Scott (Toronto: CRRS, 1995), 171.
38. Ibid., 139.
39. Ibid., 139; George Mora, ed., *Witches, Devils, and Doctors in the Renaissance: Johann Weyer, "De praestigiis daemonum"* (Binghamton, NY: Medieval & Renaissance Texts & Studies, 1991), bk. 4, chap. 9, 302–3.
40. Bodin, *On the Demon-Mania of Witches*, 153.
41. Jacqueline Van Gent, *Magic, Body and the Self in Eighteenth-Century Sweden* (Leiden: Brill, 2009), 8.
42. Ibid., 121–2.
43. Ibid., 71.
44. P.G. Maxwell-Stuart, ed. and trans., *Martín del Rio: Investigations into Magic* (Manchester: Manchester University Press, 2000), 120.
45. Still the best introduction to medieval magic is Richard Kieckhefer, *Magic in the Middle Ages* (Cambridge: Cambridge University Press, 1989 [2000]), esp. 8–17.
46. Danielle Régnier-Bohler, "Imagining the Self," in *A History of Private Life: Revelations of the Medieval World*, ed. Georges Duby (Cambridge, MA: Belknap Press, 1985), 362.
47. Charles Zika, *The Appearance of Witchcraft: Print and Visual Culture in Sixteenth-Century Europe* (London: Routledge, 2007) and *Exorcising our Demons: Magic, Witchcraft and Visual Culture in Early Modern Europe* (Leiden: Brill, 2003). See also Van Gent, *Magic, Body and the Self*, 82.
48. Zika, *Appearance of Witchcraft*, 12, 15.
49. Ibid., 21; Ulric Molitor, *Des Sorcières et des Devineresses* (Paris: Librairie Critique Emile Nourry, 1926).
50. Zika, *Appearance of Witchcraft*, 21.
51. Ibid., 22–3.
52. Ibid., 35.
53. Ibid., 82; Zika, *Exorcising our Demons*, 247; see also Jane Davidson, *The Witch in Northern European Art, 1470–1750* (Freren: Luca Verlag, 1987), 18.
54. Zika, *Appearance of Witchcraft*, 84.
55. Ibid., 181.
56. Wiesner-Hanks, *The Marvelous Hairy Girls*, 42.

57. Gary K. Waite, *Eradicating the Devil's Minions: Anabaptists and Witches in Reformation Europe, 1535–1600* (Toronto: University of Toronto Press, 2007).
58. Gary K. Waite, "Naked Harlots or Devout Maidens? Images of Anabaptist Women in the Context of the Iconography of Witches in Europe, 1525–1650," in Van Veen, *Sisters*, 17–51. The images are available at http://dpc.uba.uva.nl/doopsgezindeprenten, as are the Luyken images cited below.
59. Ibid., 17–51.
60. Zika, *Exorcising our Demons*, 247.
61. On the transition, see Gary K. Waite, "Sixteenth-Century Religious Reform and the Witch-Hunts," in *The Oxford Handbook of Witchcraft in Early Modern Europe and Colonial America*, ed. Brian Levack (Oxford: Oxford University Press, 2013), 485–506.
62. On the witch-hunts, see Brian P. Levack, *The Witch-Hunt in Early Modern Europe*, 4th ed. (New York: Routledge, 2016).
63. Francesco Maria Guazzo, *Compendium Maleficarum*, ed. Montague Summers (1608, New York: Dover, 1988), 57.
64. Mackay, *The Hammer of Witches*, 545.
65. Ibid., 548, 552–3.
66. Ibid., 554.
67. Zika, *Appearance of Witchcraft*, 196.
68. Stuart Clark, *Thinking with Demons: The Idea of Witchcraft in Early Modern Europe* (Oxford: Oxford University Press, 1997).

Chapter 2

1. See Geraldine Biddle-Perry and Sarah Cheang, "Introduction: Thinking about Hair," in *Hair: Styling, Culture and Fashion*, eds. Geraldine Biddle-Perry and Sarah Cheang (London: Bloomsbury, 2008), 7.
2. *The Problemes of Aristotle* (London: Arn. Hatfield, 1607), sig. A4r–A6r.
3. Levinus Lemnius, *The Touchstone of Complexions* (London: Thomas Marsh, 1581), fol. 90v, 112r, 129r–129v, 147v.
4. Ibid., fol. 36r–43r, 90v, 112r, 129r–129v, 147v; Will Fisher, *Materializing Gender in Early Modern English Literature and Culture* (Cambridge: Cambridge University Press, 2006), 132–3, 139; Edith Snook, *Women, Beauty and Power in Early Modern England* (Basingstoke: Palgrave Macmillan, 2011), 116–19.
5. Snook, *Women, Beauty and Power*, 143.
6. Edward Herbert, *The Life of Edward, First Lord Herbert of Cherbury*, ed. J.M. Shuttleworth (London: Oxford University Press, 1976), 2.
7. Quoted in Snook, *Women, Beauty and Power*, 149.
8. Anne Fanshawe, *Memoirs of Lady Fanshawe* (London: Henry Colburn, 1829), 4.
9. Oliver Heywood, *His Autobiography, Diaries, Anecdote and Event Books*, ed. J. Horsfall Turner (Brighouse: Privately printed, 1882), 1: 35.
10. Hugh Cholmley, *The Memoirs and Memorials of Sir Hugh Cholmley of Whitby 1600–1657*, ed. Jack Binns (Woodbridge: Yorkshire Archaeological Society and Boydell Press, 2000), 65–6, 70, 78.
11. Nicholas Breton, *An Olde Mans Lesson* (London: Edward White, 1605), sig. D2r.
12. Leonard Wright, *A Summons for Sleepers* ([London: E. Aggas?], 1589), 31.
13. James Melville, *Memoirs of Sir James Melville of Halhill 1535–1617*, ed. Frances A. Steuart (London: George Routledge & Sons, 1929), 95.

14. Fynes Moryson, *Unpublished Chapters of Fynes Moryson's Itinerary*, ed. Charles Hughes (London: Sherratt & Hughes, 1903), 297, 347.
15. Robin Bryer, *The History of Hair: Fashion and Fantasy Down the Ages* (London: Philip Wilson, 2000), 31–2.
16. Herbert, *The Life*, 79.
17. Snook, *Women, Beauty and Power*, 11.
18. See e.g. Eduardo Lopez, *A Report of the Kingdome of Congo, a Region of Africa* (London: Iohn Wolfe, 1597), 14, 76–86; Richard Hakluyt, *The Principal Navigations* (London: George Bishop, Ralph Newberie, & Robert Barker, 1599), 2:19–23; Snook, *Women, Beauty and Power*, 139–41.
19. For ugly hair, see e.g. Mary Wroth, *The Countess of Mountgomeries Urania* (London: [Augustine Mathewes?], 1621), 113.
20. Thomas Cogan, *The Haven of Health* (London: John Norton, 1605), 6.
21. Michael C. Schoenfeldt, *Bodies and Selves in Early Modern England: Physiology and Inwardness in Spenser, Shakespeare, Herbert, and Milton* (Cambridge: Cambridge University Press, 1999), 17.
22. Sandra Lee Bartky, *Femininity and Domination: Studies in the Phenomenology of Oppression* (New York: Routledge, 1990), 85.
23. Snook, *Women, Beauty and Power*, 146.
24. Juan Luis Vives, *Instruction of a Christen Woman* (London: Thomas Berthelet, 1541), fol. 28r–28v.
25. Tuke, *A Treatise against Painting and Tincturing* (London: Edward Merchant, 1616), sig. G3r.
26. Robert Greene, "Alcida," in *Life and Complete Works in Prose and Verse of Robert Greene*, ed. Alexander B. Grosart (1617, repr., London: Privately printed, 1881–1883), 9: 27.
27. Phillip Stubbes, *The Anatomie of Abuses* (London: Richard Iones, 1583), fol. 33r–35v; Anthony Fletcher, *Gender, Sex and Subordination in England, 1500–1800* (New Haven, CT: Yale University Press, 1995), 60–1. Adam Martindale's sister, for example, when fallen on hard times in the 1620s, contemplated selling her hair. Adam Martindale, *The Life of Adam Martindale*, ed. Richard Parkinson (Manchester: The Chetham Society, 1845), 8.
28. Thomas Bentley, *The Fift Lampe of Virginitie* (London: H. Denham, 1582), 3; Arthur Dent, *The Plaine Mans Path-way to Heaven* (1601, repr., Amsterdam: Theatrum Orbis Terrarum, 1974), 45.
29. James Cleland, *Hero-Paideia* (Oxford: Joseph Barnes, 1607), 216; Anu Korhonen, *Silmän ilot: Kauneuden kulttuurihistoriaa uuden ajan alussa* (Jyväskylä: Atena, 2005), 42–3; Fisher, *Materializing Gender*, 141–2.
30. Lewis Wager, *The Life and Repentaunce of Marie Magdalene*, ed. Frederick Ives (1566, repr., Chicago: University of Chicago Press, 1902), 26–7.
31. Alice Thornton, *The Autobiography of Mrs. Alice Thornton, of East Newton, Co. York* (Durham: Surtees Society, 1875), 87–8, 157–8.
32. Korhonen, *Silmän ilot*, 17–18.
33. Rose Thurgood, "A Lecture of Repentance," in *Scripture Women*, ed. Naomi Baker (Nottingham: Trent Editions, 2005), 19.
34. Linda Pollock, *With Faith and Physic. The Life of a Tudor Gentlewoman Lady Grace Mildmay, 1552–1620* (New York: St. Martin's Press, 1995), 44–5.
35. Fisher, *Materializing Gender*, 142; Amanda Flather, *Gender and Space in Early Modern England* (Woodbridge: The Royal Historical Society, 2007), 126–7; see also Georgine De Courtais,

Women's Headdress and Hairstyles in England from AD 600 to the Present Day (London: B.T. Batsford, 1973), 49–56; Penny Howell Jolly, "The Fashionable Man," in *Hair: Untangling a Social History*, ed. Penny Howell Jolly (Saratoga Springs, NY: The Frances Young Tang Teaching Museum, 2004), 49; Victoria Sherrow, *Encyclopedia of Hair: A Cultural History* (Westport, CT: Greenwood Press, 2006), 115; Snook, *Women, Beauty and Power*, 120–1.

36. Evelyn Welch, "Art on the Edge: Hair and Hands in Renaissance Italy," *Renaissance Studies* 23, no. 3 (2008): 245–6.
37. Flather, *Gender and Space*, 24–5.
38. Roland du Jardin, *A Discourse of the Married and Single Life* (London: Ionas Man, 1621), 61–2; Stefano Guazzo, *The Civile Conversation* (London: Thomas East, 1586), fol. 33v–34r; see also Mary Rogers, "The Decorum of Women's Beauty: Trissino, Firenzuola, Luigini and the Representation of Women in Sixteenth-Century Painting," *Renaissance Studies* 2, no. 1 (1988): 69.
39. Stubbes, *The Anatomie of Abuses*, fol. 33r–35v.
40. See Annibale Romei, *The Courtiers Academie* (London: Valentine Sims, 1598), 27–30.
41. See William Prynne's *The Unloveliness of Lovelocks* (1628) and Thomas Hall's *Loathsomeness of Long Haire* (1653).
42. William Fiston, *Schoole of Good Manners* (London: William Ihones, 1595), sig. C1v.
43. Baldassare Castiglione, *The Book of the Courtier* (1561, London: J.M. Dent & Sons, 1974), 39, 47.
44. See e.g. Anon., *Hæc-Vir* (London: John Trundle, 1620), sig. C1r–C1v; Anon., *Hic Mulier* (London: John Trundle, 1620), sig. A4r–A4v, B3r–B3v.
45. Erasmus, *A Lytell Booke of Good Maners for Children* (London: Wynkyn de Worde, 1532), sig. A7v–A8r.
46. Paul Griffths, *Youth and Authority: Formative Experiences in England 1560–1640* (Oxford: Clarendon Press, 1996), 222.
47. Jolly, "The Fashionable Man," 21–3; Fisher, *Materializing Gender*, 142.
48. James I, *Basilikon Doron* (Edinburgh: Robert Walde-graue, 1603), 112–13.
49. Thomas Dekker, *The Guls Horne-booke* (London: Nicholas Okes, 1609), 16–17.
50. Quoted in Paul Griffiths, *Youth and Authority*, 228–9; see also Amanda Bailey, *Flaunting. Style and the Subversive Male Body in Renaissance England* (Toronto: University of Toronto Press, 2007), 33–4.
51. Frances Parthenope Verney, *Memoirs of the Verney Family During the Civil War* (London: Longmans, Green, and Co, 1892), 1:160–1.
52. Will Fisher, "The Renaissance Beard: Masculinity in Early Modern England," *Renaissance Quarterly* 54, no. 1 (2001): 168–75; see also Annette Drew-Bear, *Painted Faces on the Renaissance Stage: The Moral Significance of Face-Painting Conventions* (Lewisburg, PA: Bucknell University Press, 1994), 31; Fisher, *Materializing Gender*, 98–9, 108–11.
53. Anu Korhonen, "Strange Things Out of Hair: Baldness and Masculinity in Early Modern England," *Sixteenth Century Journal* 41, no. 2 (2010): 385–8.
54. The four volumes of the fifteenth-century collection of secrets attributed to Alessio Piemontese, printed in English in the mid-sixteenth century, have a large number of these recipes. See Alessio Piemontese, *The Secretes of the Reverende Maister Alexis of Piemovnt* (1558, Repr., Amsterdam: Theatrum Orbis Terrarum, 1975), passim. Recipes for hair were also published by William Bullein, Thomas Lupton, John Partridge, Thomas Vicary, Hugh Platt, and others.
55. Negative emotions and psychological disorders, too, could be displayed through hair and gestures relating to it. For example, carelessly arranged hair signified depression, anguish,

or fear, and pulling at one's hair signified despair or extreme anger. See Alan C. Dessen, "The Body of Stage Directions," *Shakespeare Studies* 29 (2001): 29–30.
56. Korhonen, *Silmän ilot*, 118–23.
57. See for example Dorothy Osborne's letters of January 28, and February 11, 1653/54. *The Letters of Dorothy Osborne to William Temple*, ed. G.C. Mooore Smith (Oxford: Clarendon Press, 1928), 137, 146.
58. Dekker, *The Guls Horne-booke*, 16; Elizabeth Cary, *The Tragedie of Mariam* (London: Thomas Creede, 1613), sig. G2r.
59. Jane Anger, *Jane Anger Her Protection for Women* (London: Richard Iones and Thomas Orwin, 1589), sig. C1.
60. Lucy Hutchinson, *Memoirs of the Life of Colonel Hutchinson*, ed. James Sutherland (London: Oxford University Press, 1973), 63.
61. Welch, "Art on the Edge," 243.
62. Peter Erondell, *The French Garden* (London: Edward White, 1605), sig. E1v.
63. Anon., *The Lady Falkland, Her Life*, ed. Richard Simpson (London: Catholic Publishing, 1861), 14–15.
64. Ibid.
65. Margaret Pelling, "Appearance and Reality: Barber-Surgeons, the Body and Disease," in *London 1500–1700: The Making of the Metropolis*, eds. A.L. Beier and Roger Finlay (London: Longman, 1986), 87, 94–5; Mark Albert Johnston, "'To What Bawdy House Doth Your Maister Belong?': Barbers, Bawds, and Vice in the Early Modern London Barbershop," in *Masculinity and the Metropolis of Vice, 1550–1650*, eds. Amanda Bailey and Roze Hentschell (New York: Palgrave Macmillan, 2010), 116; Snook, *Women, Beauty and Power*, 120.
66. Patrick Hannay, *A Happy Husband* (London: Richard Redmer, 1618), sig. B2v–B3v.
67. Phillip Stubbes, *The Second Part of the Anatomie of Abuses* (London: William Wright, 1583), sig. G8r–H1r.
68. Fisher, *Materializing Gender*, 142–3; Snook, *Women, Beauty and Power*, 146–7.
69. Hutchinson, *Memoirs*, 31.

Chapter 3

1. One late nineteenth-century author lists the various colors of blonde hair desired by the dyeing process in Renaissance Italy: from a brilliant blonde (*rutilis*) and tawny color (*lionato*), to a honey blonde, or the French *cendré* (ash blonde). See Theodore Child's *Wimples and Crisping Pins: Being Studies in Coiffure and Ornaments of Women* (New York: Harper and Brothers, 1895), 125–6.
2. Richard Corson, *Fashions in Hair: The First Five Thousand Years* (London: Peter Owen, 1980).
3. See John Jeffries Martin, *Myths of Renaissance Individualism* (London: Palgrave Macmillian, 2004) for a nuanced discussion of the *mentalité* of this time period, vis-à-vis our modern or postmodern definition of what signals a display of "individualism."
4. This fine (*multa*) was noted among the fifteenth-century *sentenze dei podestà milanese*, cited in Rosita Levi-Pisetzky, *Il costume e la moda nella società italiana* (Turin: Giulio Einaudi editore, 1978), 175.
5. Carole Collier Frick, "Cappelli e copricapi nella Firenze del Rinascimento. L'emergere dell'identità sociale attraverso l'abbigliamento," in *Moda e Moderno. Dal Medioevo al Rinascimento*, ed. Eugenia Paulicelli (Rome: Meltemi Press, 2006), 103.

6. Jane Bridgeman, "Dates, Dress, and Dosso: Some Problems of Chronology," in *Dosso's Fate: Painting and Court Culture in Renaissance Italy*, eds. Luisa Ciammitti, Steven R. Ostrow, and Salvatore Settis (Los Angeles: The Getty Research Institute for the History of Art and the Humanities, 1998), 176–7.
7. Jane Bridgeman, "'Troppi belli e troppo eccellenti': Observations on Dress in the Work of Piero della Francesca," in *The Cambridge Companion to Piero della Francesca*, ed. Jeryldene Wood (Cambridge: Cambridge University Press, 2002), 79–80. See also Isabella Campagnol Fabretti, "Mode e tessuti veneziani negli *Habiti Antichi* di Cesare Vecellio," in *Il vestito e la sua immagine. Atti del convegno in omaggio a Cesare Vecellio nel quarto centenario della morte*, ed. Jeannine Guérin Dalla Mese (Belluno: Provincia di Belluno Editore, 2002), 28 (n. 7); see also Giovanna Sapori, *Il costume e l'immagine pittorica nel Seicento umbro* (Florence: Centro Di della Edifimi srl, 1984), 134; and finally, Joanna Woods-Marsden, "Piero della Francesca's Ruler Portraits," in *The Cambridge Companion to Piero della Francesca*, 197.
8. Giorgio Vasari, *The Lives of the Artists* (New York: Penguin, 1965), 228 as cited in Frick, "Cappelli e copricapi," 104–5.
9. J. C. Flugel, *The Psychology of Clothes* (London: Hogarth Press, 1950), 110–12, 118–19.
10. Alison Lurie, *The Language of Clothes* (New York: Random House, 1981), 25.
11. Patricia Simons has counted at least forty portraits in the Ghirlandaio frescoes as a whole in Santa Maria Novella. Patricia Simons, "Portraiture and Patronage in Quattrocento Florence with Special Reference to the Tornaquinci and Their Chapel in S. Maria Novella" (Unpublished PhD diss., University of Melbourne, 1985), 265–316. Also see Jean Cadogan, *Domenico Ghirlandaio: Artist and Artisan* (New Haven, CT: Yale University Press), 2000.
12. Lawrence Langner, *The Importance of Wearing Clothes* (New York: Hastings House Publishers, 1959), 98–9.
13. Flugel, *The Psychology*, 50–2.
14. Possibly made from a life-size wax image taken after the violence of the Pazzi Conspiracy of 1478 almost killed him. (National Gallery of Art: The Collection: *Lorenzo de' Medici*, www.nga.gov [Accessed August 18, 2016].)
15. A letter from Margherita Datini to her husband Francesco relates in part, "ch'lo non vorei il mantello nuovo e 'l chapuccio vechio." "Le lettere di Margherita Datini a Francesco di Marco," ed. Valeria Rosati. *Archivio storico pratese* 52 (1976): 140.
16. The fashioning of *cappucci* was a job for tailors, not hat-makers, as it was complicated to craft and was tailored of the same fabric as a person's cloak. Tailors were kept subordinate to the ruling class for whom they toiled. Their fees for tailoring in Florence were regulated by communal statute under Rubric LXXI of the 1415 Statuta Populi ("Quod sartores debeant subesse offitialibus grasciae, et satisdare, et recipere pretia infrascripta").
17. For *cassone* decorations, see Cristelle L. Baskins, *Cassone Painting, Humanism, and Gender in Early Modern Italy* (Cambridge: Cambridge University Press, 1998).
18. See, for example, the Adimari-Ricasoli wedding *cassone* (1450) by Giovanni di Ser Giovanni (called "lo Scheggia"), L'Accademia, Florence.
19. See Levi Pisetzky, *Il costume*, 174.
20. Parenti Ricordanze, in the Archivio di Stato di Firenze (ASF), Carte Strozziane, 2nd ser., 17 bis, fols. 6r, 7r–v. However, we have little visual evidence of these highly adorned *cappucci* for women, as they do not appear in the formal artwork of the Quattrocento. See Simons, "Portraiture and Patronage," 146.

NOTES 167

21. Ghirlandaio's *The Calling of Saint Peter* in the Sistine Chapel shows this new fashion in 1481, one man in the right foreground among the Florentine delegation wearing a *cappello* on his head. The detached *becchetto* of the *cappuccio* has become a nonchalant *stola* draped elegantly across his arm. One diarist writing in 1533 said of the *cappuccio* dismissively that people had stopped wearing it in the city and that by 1532, not a one was to be seen. Luca Landucci, *Diario fiorentino dal 1450 al 1516*, ed. Iodoco De Badia (Florence, 1883, repr., Florence: Studio Biblos, 1969), 371.
22. See Quentin Bell, *On Human Finery* (London: Hogarth Press, 1947), 37. For an example of too-large headwear on a man, see Artemisia Gentileschi's 1622 *Portrait of a Condottiero*, Palazzo d'Accursio, Bologna.
23. Simonetta Prosperi Valenti Rodinò, in *Il costume e l'immagine pittorica nel Seicento umbro*, 28. A scudo was worth about four-fifths of a ducat or florin.
24. San Bernadino da Siena, *Le prediche volgari di San Bernardino da Siena nel 1427*, ed. Orazio Bacci (Siena: Tip edit. All' inseg di. S. Bernadino, 1895), 33–4. Communal officials approved new sumptuary laws in 1433, noting that it realized "the great desire of these officials to restrain the barbarous and irrepressible bestiality of women." See ASF, Deliberazioni dei Signori and Collegi, ordinaria autorita, 42, fols. 5v–6r, cited in ed. Gene Brucker, *The Society of Renaissance Florence: A Documentary Study* (New York: Harper & Row, 1971), 180–1.
25. See the profile portrait of Beatrice d'Este in the *Sforza Altarpiece*, Master of the Pala Sforzesca (ca. 1494–1495).
26. ASF, Catasto (CAT) Reg. 24, fol. 314, for archival records of female embroiderers working in Florence in 1427.
27. See Carole Collier Frick, *Dressing Renaissance Florence: Family, Fortunes and Fine Clothing* (Baltimore: Johns Hopkins University Press, 2002), 466–8.
28. In the fresco by Filippo Lippi, *Banquet of Herod*, 1452–1466, in the Cathedral of San Stefano, Prato, a blonde female figure attending the banquet is given such an ornate hair treatment.
29. See Antonio del Pollaiuolo's *Profile Portrait of a Young Woman* (ca. 1475), Metropolitan Museum of Art, New York, which depicts such an intricate formal hair treatment on a serious, dutiful-looking young woman.
30. Janet Cox-Rearick, *Splendors of the Renaissance: Princely Attire in Italy; Reconstructions of Historic Costumes from King Studio, Italy* (New York: Art Gallery of the Graduate Center, the City University of New York, 2004), 9–11.
31. See Jane Bridgeman, who attributes the taste for earrings to changes in hairstyles and head coverings in "Dates, Dress, and Dosso," 195.
32. A Pisanello drawing of a *balzo* on a dancing woman entitled *Costume illustration*, from ca. 1438–1440, is in the collection of the Ashmolean Museum, Oxford.
33. See Roberta Milliken, *Ambiguous Locks: An Iconology of Hair in Medieval Art and Literature* (Jefferson, NC: McFarland and Co., 2012), 51.
34. Marie Vibbert, "Headdresses of the 14th and 15th Centuries," *The Compleat Anachronist* no. 133, SCA monograph series (August 2006).
35. One style of veiling that was popular in the north until the 1460s was the *kruseler*, which added a row or rows of gathered frills to the borders of a linen coif or veil. It was worn widely in Bohemia, Hungary, Poland, Scandinavia, and the Holy Roman Empire. See Carl Köhler, *A History of Costume*, trans. Alexander K. Dallas (Philadelphia: David McKay Company, 1928), 191–2.

36. Janet Arnold, *Queen Elizabeth's Wardrobe Unlock'd* (Leeds: W. S. Maney and Son Ltd., 2001), 110–11, 204–5.
37. Jane Ashelford, *The Art of Dress: Clothing and Society 1500–1914* (New York: Abrams, 1996).
38. Jill Condra, ed., *The Greenwood Encyclopedia of Clothing Through World History: 1501–1800* (Westport, CN: Greenwood Press, 2008), 75.
39. Grazietta Butazzi, "Il modello spagnolo nella moda europea," in *Le Trame della moda*, eds. Anna Giulia Cavagna and Grazietta Butazzi (Rome: Bulzoni, 1995), 82–4.
40. For the codpiece, see Carole Collier Frick, "Boys to Men: Codpieces and Masculinity in Sixteenth-Century Europe," in *Gender and Early Modern Constructions of Childhood*, eds. Naomi J. Miller and Naomi Yavneh (Farnham: Ashgate Publishing, 2011), 169–70.
41. Corson, *Fashions in Hair*, 161–9.
42. Military garments served as inspiration for fashion at the time, a testament to the ongoing contact the general public had with war. In addition to short hair and beards, military clothing included the sleeveless tabard, shorter half-tabard, the cuirass (which eventually took the "peasecod belly" shape), the beret, and the flat, square-toed shoes (*scarpe punta quadrata*) first seen at court as slippers and then fashioned into shoes with leather soles, like those worn by mercenary soldiers. See Grazietta Butazzi, "Un paio di pianelle cinquecentesche delle Civiche Raccolte di Arte Applicata di Milano," in *Il costume nell'età del Rinascimento*, ed. Dora Liscia Bemporad (Florence: Edifir, 1980), 341.
43. ASF, MAP, CXXXII. Wardrobe of Duke Lorenzo de' Medici, 1515–1516.
44. See Theodore Child, *Wimples and Crisping-pins: Being Studies in the Coiffure and Ornaments of Women* (1895) (Repr., Whitefish, MT: Kessinger Publishing, 2007), 133–8.
45. Ostrich plumes were worn as hat decorations in 1590s Venice but were called "decadent" by social critics of the time. Fabretti, "Mode e tessuti veneziani," 30.
46. Paola Goretti, "La regolamentazione delle apparenze: vesti e ornamenti nella legislazione suntuaria bolognese del XVI secolo," *Schede umanistiche* 2 (1996): 126–7.
47. See *Portrait of Antoine, Bastard of Burgundy* by Rogier van der Weyden (ca. 1460) for the "sugarloaf hat" in the collection of the Royal Museums of Fine Arts of Belgium, Brussels.
48. See Janet Arnold, *Patterns of Fashion: The Cut and Construction of Clothes for Men and Women 1560–1620*, rev. ed. (New York: Macmillian, 1986).
49. Blair Worden, *The English Civil Wars 1640–1660* (London: Penguin Books, 2009), 52.

Chapter 4

1. Among the many studies, see most recently Caroline van Eck, Joris van Gastel, and Elsje van Kessel, eds., *The Secret Lives of Artworks: Exploring the Boundaries between Art and Life* (Leiden: Leiden University Press, 2014) and Nebahat Avcıoğlu, Allison Sherman, and Deborah Howard, eds., *Artistic Practices and Cultural Transfer in Early Modern Italy: Essays in Honour of Deborah Howard* (Farnham: Ashgate, 2015).
2. For the value of beards in England, see Mark Albert Johnston, *Beard Fetish in Early Modern England: Sex, Gender, and Registers of Value* (Farnham: Ashgate, 2011), 9–102.
3. Patricia Rubin, "Understanding Renaissance Portraiture," in *The Renaissance Portrait from Donatello to Bellini*, eds. Dale Tucker and Margaret Aspinwall (New York: Metropolitan Museum of Art, 2011), 4–5; Tarnya Cooper, *Citizen Portrait: Portrait Painting and the Urban Elites of Tudor and Jacobean England and Wales* (New Haven, CT: Yale University Press, 2012), 41–64.
4. Phillip Stubbes, *The Anatomie of Abuses Containing a Description of such Notable Vices and Enormities, as Raigne in many Countries of the World, but especiallie in this Realme*

of England..., 4th ed. (London: Richard Iohnes, 1595), 39–40. These examples seem to contradict Sandra Cavallo's statement that attention to hairstyle increased in the seventeenth century. See Sandra Cavallo, *Artisans of the Body in Early Modern Italy: Identities, Families and Masculinities* (Manchester: Manchester University Press, 2007), 55. For a very short discussion of Stubbes's book see Tarnya Cooper, "Elizabethan Theatre," in *Searching for Shakespeare: Catalogue*, ed. Tarnya Cooper (New Haven, CT: Yale University Press, 2006), 98.

5. Marguerite Droz-Emmert, *Catharina van Hemessen Malerin der Renaissance* (Basel: Schwabe, 2004), 81, 101, 115, 117, 119, 121, 137.
6. Amanda E. Herbert, *Female Alliances: Gender, Identity, and Friendship in Early Modern Britain* (New Haven, CT: Yale University Press, 2014), esp. 78–115; Nadine Akkerman and Birgit Houben, eds., *The Politics of Female Households Ladies-in-Waiting Across Early Modern Europe* (Leiden: Brill, 2014).
7. For the spread of the wig-fashion in Europe, see Cavallo, *Artisans*, 56, n. 80.
8. Stubbes, *Anatomie*, 40–1.
9. For an overview, see Sharon T. Strocchia, "Introduction: Women and Healthcare in Early Modern Europe," *Renaissance Studies* 28, no. 4 (2014): 496–514. See also Elaine Leong, "Making Medicines in the Early Modern Household," *Bulletin of the History of Medicine* 82 (2008): 145–68; Alisha Rankin, "Exotic Materials and Treasured Knowledge: The valuable Legacy of Noblewomen's Remedies in Early Modern Germany," *Renaissance Studies* 28, no. 4 (2014): 533–55; Jane Stevens Crawshaw, "Families, Medical Secrets and Public Health in Early Modern Venice," *Renaissance Studies* 28, no. 4 (2014): 597–618.
10. Tessa Storey, "Face Waters, Oils, Love Magic and Poison: Making and Selling Secrets in Early Modern Rome," in *Secrets and Knowledge in Medicine and Science, 1500 – 1800*, eds. Elaine Leong and Alisha Rankin (Farnham: Ashgate, 2011), 143–65; Montserrat Cabré, "Keeping Beauty Secrets in Early Modern Iberia," in Leong and Rankin, *Secrets*, 167–90.
11. Ruprechts-Karls-Universität Heidelberg, Universitäts-Bibliothek, Bibliotheca Palatina, *Codex Palatinus Germanicus* (Cod. Pal. germ.) 192, fol. 5r–7r.
12. Matthias Miller, "Wissenschaftlicher Kommentar zu Cod. Pal. germ. 192," Universitäts Bibliothek Heidelberg, 2005.
13. *Cod. Pal. germ.* 192, fol. 5r.
14. *Cod. Pal. germ.* 192, fol. 5v.
15. *Cod. Pal. germ.* 192, fol. 6r.
16. *Cod. Pal. germ.* 192, fol. 5v; an Italian example from 1476 shows that making hair grow again became a promise in medical contracts. See Gianna Pomata, *La Promessa di Guarigione: Malati e Curatori in Antico Regime* (Rome: Laterza, 1994), 353.
17. *Cod. Pal. germ.* 192, fol. 6r, 6v.
18. *Cod. Pal. germ.* 192, fol. 6r.
19. Johann Bürtzel, *Ein Schönes vnd bewertes Artzneybüch* (1565), Western MS 166, Wellcome Library, London, fol. 1–8, 27–38. Only scarce information about Bürtzel is available, but in 1549 an arithmetic book was published in Augsburg. See Johannes Burkhardt, "Altökonomik und Handelsliteratur in den Augsburger Druckmedien," in *Augsburger Buchdruck und Verlagswesen von den Anfängen bis zur Gegenwart*, eds. Helmut Gier, Johannes Janota, and Hans Jörg Künast (Wiesbaden: Harrassowitz, 1997), 439.
20. For a general study on Bock, see Brigitte Hoppe, *Das Kräuterbuch des Hieronymus Bock* (Stuttgart: Hiersemann, 1969).
21. Hieronymus Bock, *New Kreütter Buch von Underscheydt, Würckung und Namen der Kreütter* (Straßburg: Rihel, 1539), fol. 13r, 24v–25r. Such signs on head and skin were

feared because of serious consequences. See Annemarie Kinzelbach, "Infection, Contagion, and Public Health in Late Medieval and Early Modern German Imperial Towns," *Journal of the History of Medicine and Allied Sciences* 61 (2006): 369–89.

22. Johannes G. Mayer, "Die Wahrheit über den *Gart der Gesundheit* (1485) und sein Weiterleben in den Kräuterbüchern der Frühen Neuzeit," in *A Passion for Plants: Materia Medica and Botany in Scientific Networks from the 16th to 18th centuries*, eds. Sabine Anagnostou, Florike Egmond, and Christoph Friedrich (Stuttgart: Wissenschaftliche Verlagsgesellschaf, 2011), 119–28.

23. Adam Lonitzer, *Kreuterbuch, Künstliche Conterfeyung der Bäume, Stauden, Kräuter...* (Frankfurt: Egenolf, 1557), *Vorrede* (preface). A Latin "natural history" containing much of the German version was published twenty-seven years earlier.

24. Sandra Cavallo and Tessa Storey, *Healthy Living in Late Renaissance Italy* (Oxford: Oxford University Press, 2013), 13–47.

25. Johann Baptist Fickler "*pro uso domestico*," Lonitzer *Kreuterbuch*, Bayerische Staatsbibliothek (BSB), Digitale Bibliothek, 2 L.impr.c.n.mss.72.

26. Margaret Pelling, *The Common Lot: Sickness, Medical Occupations and the Urban Poor in Early Modern England* (Harlow: Longman, 1998).

27. Signaled already by the illustrations, Lonitzer, *Kreuterbuch*, 1–13.

28. Lonitzer, *Kreuterbuch*, 1–14, 87.

29. Annemarie Kinzelbach, *Gesundbleiben, Krankwerden, Armsein in der Frühneuzeitlichen Gesellschaft: Gesunde und Kranke in den Reichsstädten Überlingen und Ulm, 1500–1700* (Stuttgart: Steiner, 1995), 103–8; Carole Rawcliffe, *Urban Bodies: Communal Health in Late Medieval English Towns and Cities* (Woodbridge: Boydell Press, 2013), 176–228; Janna Coomans and Guy Geltner, "On the Street and in the Bathhouse: Medieval Galenism in Action? En la calle y en los baños públicos: Â¿galenismo medieval en acción?" *Anuario de Estudios Medievales* 43, no. 1 (2009): 58–62.

30. Bettina Borgemeister, *Die Stadt und ihr Wald: Eine Untersuchung zur Waldgeschichte der Städte Göttingen und Hannover vom 13. bis zum 18. Jahrhundert* (Hannover: Hahn, 2005), 127–57, 188–92; Paul Warde, "Waldnutzung, Landschaftsentwicklung und Staatliche Reglementierung in der Frühen Neuzeit," in *Landnutzung und Landschaftsentwicklung im Deutschen Südwesten*, eds. S. Lorenz and P. Rückert (Stuttgart: W. Kohlhammer, 2009), 199–217.

31. On Hoogstraten, see Thijs Weststeijn, *The Visible World: Samuel van Hoogstraten's Art Theory and the Legitimation of Painting in the Dutch Golden Age* (Amsterdam: Amsterdam University Press, 2008).

32. Celeste Brusati, *Artifice and Illusion: The Art and Writing of Samuel van Hoogstraten* (Chicago: University of Chicago Press, 1995),138–68; Weststeijn, *Visible World,* 171–216, 285–304.

33. Moritz Landgraf von Hessen, *Tax-Ordnung aller Wahren und Victualien* (Kassel: Wessel, 1622), 38, 85.

34. He, of course, might have had an opportunity to borrow. See Sheilagh Ogilvie, Markus Küpker, and Janine Maegraith, "Household Debt in Early Modern Germany: Evidence from Personal Inventories," *The Journal of Economic History* 72 (2012): 134–67.

35. Cavallo, *Artisans*; Annemarie Kinzelbach, "Erudite and Honoured Artisans? Performers of Body Care and Surgery in Early Modern German Towns," *Social History of Medicine* 27 (2014): 668–88.

36. For calendars in general, see Kevin Birth, "Calendars: Representational Homogeneity and Heterogeneous Time," *Time & Society* 22 (2013): 216–36; for calendars written

by physicians, see Sabine Schlegelmilch, "Vom Nutzen des Nebensächlichen-Paratexte in den Kalendern des Arztes Johannes Magirus (1615–1697)," in *Astronomie-Literatur-Volksaufklärung: Der Schreibkalender der Frühen Neuzeit mit seinen Text- und Bildbeigaben*, ed. Klaus-Dieter Herbst (Bremen: Ed. Lumière, 2012), 393–411.

37. Jeremias Brotbeihel, *Kalender, auff das Jar M.D.LXI* (Dillingen: Mayer, 1560); Anne Liewert, *Die meteorologische Medizin des Corpus Hippocraticum* (Berlin: de Gruyter, 2015); Jonathan Green, *Printing and Prophecy: Prognostication and Media Change, 1450 – 1550* (Ann Arbor: University of Michigan Press, 2012).

38. Thomas Murner, *Ein andechtig geistliche Badenfart* ([Straßburg], 1514) urn:nbn:de:bvb:12-bsb00083105-1. The heading "*Das haubt waschen,*" illustration and text, is discussed in the context of Figure 4.5.

39. Nunneries even had specific rooms for bloodletting, according to the prioress Clara Staiger, who described her life during the Thirty Years War, "Verzeichnis und beschreibung wenn ich S[chwester] Clara Staigerin geborn. Jn das kloster komen Vnd was sich die jar fürnemns begeben. Vnd verloffen," in *Klara Staigers Tagebuch. Aufzeichnungen während des Dreißigjährigen Krieges im Kloster Mariastein bei Eichstätt*, ed. Ortrun Fina (Regensburg: Pustet, 1981), 44–5; on baths and bathing in hospitals, see Kinzelbach, *Gesundbleiben*, 88, 326, 376; and Annemarie Kinzelbach and Patrick Sturm, "Der Siechenhauskomplex vor den Toren Nördlingens: Entwicklung, Funktion und bauliche Gestalt vom 13. bis zum 18. Jahrhundert," *Jahrbuch d. Historischen Vereins für Nördlingen und Umgebung* 33 (2011), 34, 41.

40. Kinzelbach, *Gesundbleiben*, 94–5.

41. BSB, *Einblattdrucke der frühen Neuzeit, Dissen Kallender […]* (Augsburg: Hofer, [1547]), http://bsbipad.bsb.lrz.de/nas/einblattdrucke/330000389_0_r.pdf.

42. Hubert Steinke, "Medizinische Karriere im städtischen Dienst," in *Jakob Ruf, Leben, Werk und Studien: Mit der Arbeit seiner Hände: Leben und Werk des Zürcher Stadtchirurgen und Theatermachers Jakob Ruf (1505–1558)*, ed. Hildegard E. Keller, 2nd ed. (Zürich: Verl. Neue Zürcher Zeitung, 2008), 97–8; more generally see Sabine Griese, "Gebrauchsformen und Gebrauchsräume von Einblattdrucken des 15. und frühen 16. Jahrhunderts," in *Einblattdrucke des 15. und frühen 16. Jahrhunderts: Probleme, Perspektiven, Fallstudien*, eds. Volker Honemann, Sabine Griese, Falk Eisermann, and Marcus Ostermann (Tübingen: Niemeyer, 2000) and Nikolaus Henkel, "Schauen und Erinnern: Überlegungen zu Intentionalität und Appellstruktur illustrierter Einblattdrucke," in *Einblattdrucke*, 209–43.

43. Schlegelmilch, "Vom Nutzen," 396–406.

44. Johann J. Butzlin, *Kalender sampt der Practick vff das Jar M.D.LXXVII* (Zurich: Froschower, 1576); Bartholomäus Scultetus, *New und Alter Römischer Allmanach und Schreib Kalender auffs Jahr Chri. MDCV* (Prague: Straus, 1605).

45. Jeremias Graf, *Nach der alten und neuen Zeit deutlicher und wolgefaster Haußhaltungs Calender auff das Jahr Christi M DC LIX* (Altenburg, Meißen: Bauer, 1659); *Hauß- Garten- und Land- Calender: vor Sr. Königl. Maijest. in Pohlen, und Churfürstl. Durchl. zu Sachsen, Auff das Jahr Christi 1712* (Leipzig: n.p.), Digitale Bibliothek BSB, urn:nbn:de:bsz:14-db-id3677207606.

46. This is shown for parts of the Holy Roman Empire by Annemarie Kinzelbach, "Zur Sozial- und Alltagsgeschichte eines Handwerks in der frühen Neuzeit: 'Wundärzte' und ihre Patienten in Ulm," *Ulm und Oberschwaben* 49 (1994): 111–44; Kinzelbach, "Erudite"; Annemarie Kinzelbach, *Chirurgen und Chirurgiepraktiken* (Mainz: Donata Kinzelbach, 2016), 3–13, 20–9. Different developments describe, for example, French cities, Susan

Broomhall, *Women's Medical Work in Early Modern France* (Manchester: Manchester University Press, 2004), 16–43; the Italian region, Cavallo, *Artisans*, 1–15; London, Celeste Chamberland, "Honor, Brotherhood, and the Corporate Ethos of London's Barber-Surgeons' Company, 1570–1640," *Journal of the History of Medicine and Allied Sciences* 64, no. 3 (2009): 300–32; cities in Aragon, Carmel Ferragud, "Barbers in the Process of Medicalization in the Crown of Aragon during the Late Middle Ages," in *Medieval Urban Identity: Health, Economy and Regulation*, ed. Flocel Sabaté (Newcastle upon Tyne: Cambridge Scholars, 2015), 143–65; and Britain, Margaret Pelling, "Barber-Surgeons' Guilds and Ordinances in Early Modern British Towns—the Story so Far," *The Medical World of Early Modern England, Wales and Ireland, 1500–1715: Working Paper, Centre for Medical History, University of Exeter: 2014*, http://practitioners.exeter.ac.uk/wp-content/uploads/2014/11/Pelling_BarberSurgeonsOrds-2.pdf.

47. *Deutsches Rechtswörterbuch* (DRW), s.v. "Badgeld" http://drw-www.adw.uni-heidelberg.de/drw-cgi/zeige?index=lemmata&term=badgeld (Accessed September 30, 2014). For specific examples see Robert Hoffmann, "Die Augsburger Bäder und das Handwerk der Bader," *Zeitschrift des Historischen Vereins für Schwaben und Neuburg* 12 (1885): 1–35, 3–4; Kinzelbach, *Gesundbleiben*, 89–91.

48. Jeremias Grienewaldt, *Ratispona oder Summarische Beschreibung der Stadt Regensburg* (Regensburg, 1615), fol. 474; BSB Cgm 5529, online.

49. Kinzelbach, *Gesundbleiben*, 88–95, 326, 376; Annemarie Kinzelbach, "Bordell, Gesundbrunnen, alltäglicher Luxus? Bäder und Badende-ein Gang durch die Jahrhunderte," *Damals* 38, no. 4 (2006): 60–7; Cavallo, *Artisans*, 38–57; Kinzelbach and Sturm, "Der Siechenhauskomplex," 34, 41; Robert Büchner, *Im städtischen Bad vor 500 Jahren: Badhaus, Bader und Badegäste im alten Tirol* (Vienna: Böhlau, 2014), 46.

50. Hoffmann, "Die Augsburger Bäder," 3; Alfred Martin, *Deutsches Badewesen in vergangenen Tagen: Nebst einem Beitrage zur Geschichte der deutschen Wasserheilkunde* (Jena: Diederichs 1906), 184; Kinzelbach, *Gesundbleiben*, 91.

51. Kinzelbach, *Gesundbleiben*, 90.

52. Drawing from diverse sources see, for example, (concerning imperial cities) Hoffmann, "Die Augsburger Bäder"; Hermann Frickinger, "Beiträge zur Medizinalgeschichte der Stadt Nördlingen. Fortsetzung und Schluß," *Jahrbuch d. Historischen Vereins für Nördlingen und Umgebung* 8 (1920/21): 83–8; August Jegel, "Bäder, Bader und Badesitten im alten Nürnberg," *Reichsstadt Nürnberg Altdorf und Hersbruck* 6 (1954): 21–63; Kinzelbach, *Gesundbleiben*, 88–95, 103, 106, 132, 230, 265, 306, 314, 316, 326, 359–60, 367–8, 376–80.

53. Murner, *Ein andechtig*; for information on Murner, see Hedwig Heger, *Thomas Murner Mönch, Dichter, Gelehrter* (Karlsruhe: Badische Bibliotheksgesellschaft, 1983).

54. A similarly odd Latin quotation "et cinerem imposuerunt capiti suo" occurs in various prints of the Lutheran *Biblia Sacra* and was translated in a (later) Greek-Latin-German Bible as "they spread ash on their heads." See David Wolder and Martin Luther, *Biblia Sacra Graece, Latine & Germanice: Evangelia Quatuor* (Hamburg: Jacobus Lucius, 1596), (1 Macc. 3: 47).

55. A barber-surgeon's suggestions for preparations of lye and soap see, for example, in Joseph Schmid, *Speculum chirurgicum* (Augsburg: Hermsdorff, 1675), 321–5, 464–5. Detailed descriptions of lye and soap preparations were published later even by female citizens of imperial cities. See Anna J. Endter, *Die so Kluge als Künstliche von Arachne und Penelope Getreulich Unterwiesene Hauß-Halterin* (Nürnberg: Endter, 1703), 456–66, 480–6, 681–2, 686.

56. Prices and values for comparison come from Christoph Schorer, *Memminger Chronick... von Ao. 369. biß 1660* (Ulm: Balthasar Kuehn, 1660), 114; and from archival manuscript evidence *Obligations-Protokoll* (1568–1614) (throughout); *Kontraktenprotokoll* (1589, 1618) (throughout); *Ratsprotokoll* (1587), fol. 571v; all in Stadtarchiv Überlingen (from here: StadtAUe).
57. Mss *No. 1044*, *[contract] Hanns Khuon Schlosser* (1581); *Vergleichung dess Newen Bads* (1581); *Ratsprotokolle* (1579), fol. 214v (315 fl for the house) StadtAUe.
58. Leah L. Otis, *Prostitution in Medieval Society: The History of an Urban Institution in Languedoc* (Chicago: University of Chicago Press, 1985), 89–99; Jacques Rossiaud, *La prostitution médiévale* (Paris: Flammarion, 1988), chap. 5.
59. Cavallo, *Artisans*, 38–41.
60. Well known are Paracelsus 1562 and Paracelsus 1571 [1535] but there were many more publications, including that by Gallus Etschenreuter, *Aller Heilsamen Bäder und Brunnen Natur* (Straßburg, 1571); Johann P. Zangmaister, *Instruction Vonn Arth, Aigenschafft, und nutzlichem Gebrauch deß köstlichen Badwassers, nahend bey Saltzburg gelegen* (Salzburg: Kürner, 1601); Johann Remmelin, *Ferinae Weltzheimenses. Das ist, Gründliche erforschung, von Natur, Eigenschafften, vnd Gebrauch, deß heilsamen Wildbrunnens zu Weltzen, das Thier- oder Wildbad ...* (Augsburg: Michelspacher, 1619) and many more in the following decades. For the tradition of such publications in Italy, see Katharine Park, "Natural Particulars: Medical Epistemology, Practice, and the Literature of Healing Springs," in *Natural Particulars: Nature and the Disciplines in Renaissance Europe*, eds. Anthony Grafton and Nancy G. Siraisi (Cambridge, MA: MIT Press, 1999), 347–67; from a perspective of knowledge-transfer Frank Fürbeth, "Adaption gelehrten Wissens für laikale Zwecke in der Bäderheilkunde der frühen Neuzeit," in *Wissenschaftsgeschichte und Geschichte des Wissens im Dialog: Connecting Science and Knowledge*, eds. Kaspar von Greyerz, Silvia Flubacher, and Philipp Senn (Göttingen: V&R unipress, 2013), 211–32.
61. Etschenreuter, *Bäder*, 31. Mss *No. 1044* (contracts concerning baths and barbers 1581, 1609, 1615); *No. 141, Schaffer- und Bestallbuch*, (1580–1583) fol. 153–88; *Ratsprotokolle* (1573), fol. 4v, 8v; (1585), fol. 434v; (1587), fol. 581v; (1602), fol. 332v; Jakob Reutlinger, *Historische Collectaneen von Überlingen*, 10, fol. 1, 111; 16, 1, fol. 195v; 16, 2, fol. 362v; all in StadtAUe.
62. Benno Schmidt "1. Frankfurter Zunfturkunden bis zum Jahre 1612," in *VI. Frankfurter Amts- und Zunfturkunden bis zum Jahre 1612* (Frankfurt: Veröffentlichungen der Historischen Kommission der Stadt Frankfurt am Main, 1914), 65–86; Gustav A. Wehrli, *Die Wundärzte und Bader Zürichs als Zünftige Organisation* (Zürich: Antiquarische Gesellschaft, 1931), 8–10, 56–97; Sabine Sander, "Bader und Barbiere," in *Lexikon des alten Handwerks. Vom Spätmittelalter bis ins 20. Jahrhundert*, ed. Reinhold Reith (Munich: Beck, 1990), 200–43; Kinzelbach, "Erudite," 672–6, 679–81, 683–7.
63. Hans Sachs and Jost Amman, *Eygentliche Beschreibung aller Stände auff Erden* (Frankfurt: 1568), illustration and text 58, 60.
64. Sachs and Amman, *Eygentliche*, illustration and text 60.
65. Free translation of Sachs and Amman, *Eygentliche*, illustration and text 58.
66. Annemarie Kinzelbach, "'Böse Blattern' oder 'Franzosenkrankheit': Syphilis-konzept, Kranke und die Genese des Krankenhauses in oberdeutschen Reichsstädten der frühen Neuzeit," in *Neue Wege in der Seuchengeschichte*, eds. Martin Dinges and Thomas Schlich (Stuttgart: Steiner, 1995), 43–69, 54–5.
67. Kinzelbach, "Böse Blattern," 56–65; Claudia Stein, *Negotiating the French Pox in Early Modern Germany* (Aldershot: Ashgate, 2009), 147–73.

68. Mss *Akten R39, F2,* N01; *R39, F2,* N43; *Lazarett unverzeichnet, Lasarets Ordnung* (n.d.); *Siechenhaus unverzeichnet, Leprosorium* (1487, 1515); all in Stadtarchiv Nördlingen [from here StadtANoe]. Mss *Akten und Urkunden N001,* 1424; *N108,* 1604; *N109,* 1624; *N112,* 1545–1616; all in Spitalarchiv Überlingen. Mss *Akten Reichsstadt A [4394]* 1471–1486; *A [9585]*; all in Stadtarchiv Ulm [from here StadtAU]. Schmidt "Zunfturkunden," 67, 68; Susanne Kremmer and Hans E. Specker, *Repertorium der Policeyordnungen der Frühen Neuzeit: Reichsstädte 3: Ulm* (Frankfurt: Klostermann, 2007), 159, 168, 251. See also Kinzelbach, *Gesundbleiben,* 99, 233, 335, 353–77.
69. Trade-regulations are an issue of their own. For more on recent discussions including general juridical implications, see Peter Fleischmann, "Die Kodifizierung des Handwerksrechts in der Reichsstadt Nürnberg: Entstehung und Folgen," in *Ökonomie und Recht: Historische Entwicklungen in Bayern,* ed. C. Becker (Berlin: Lit-Verlag, 2009), 21–36l; on limited trade regulation, see Karel Davids and Bert De Munck, eds., *Innovation and Creativity in Late Medieval and Early Modern European Cities* (Farnham: Ashgate, 2014).
70. Hoffmann, "Die Augsburger Bäder," 20.
71. Margaret Pelling, "Apprenticeship, Health and Social Cohesion in Early Modern London," *History Workshop* 37, no.1 (1994): 33–56; Kinzelbach, "Zur Sozial-und Alltagsgeschichte," 120–7; Karel Davids, "Apprenticeship and Guild Control in the Netherlands, c. 1450–1800," in *Learning on the Shop Floor: Historical Perspectives on Apprenticeship,* eds. Bert De Munck, Steven L. Kaplan, and Hugo Soly (New York: Berghahn Books, 2007), 65–84, 66–7; Cavallo, *Artisans,* 136–59; Kinzelbach, *Chirurgen,* 48–55.
72. Mss *Reichsstadt A 3530,* 21, 301; 95, 175, 228v; *A 3533; Akten Reichsstadt A [1085]; A [6634]* for example 3.8.1627; 18.5.1629; 28.9.1629; all in StadtAU. Schmidt "Zunfturkunden," 65–85. See Cavallo, *Artisans,* 136–221 (Italy); Pelling, "Barber-Surgeons," 9, 14 (England); Kinzelbach, *Chirurgen,* 41–4, 48–55, 97 (imperial cities).
73. For status, social and political opportunities of these artisans and the interrelation with general changes in parts of the Holy Roman Empire and Switzerland see especially Hoffmann, "Die Augsburger Bäder," 22–4; Wehrli "Wundärzte," 58–98; Sabine Sander, *Handwerkschirurgen. Sozialgeschichte einer verdrängten Berufsgruppe* (Göttingen: Vandenhoeck & Ruprecht, 1989), 125–34, 204–15, 241; Sabine von Heusinger, *Die Zunft im Mittelalter: Zur Verflechtung von Politik, Wirtschaft und Gesellschaft in Straßburg* (Stuttgart: Steiner, 2009), 125–31; Kinzelbach, "Erudite." For other parts of Europe see, for example, Cavallo *Artisans,* 202–51; Pelling, "Barber-Surgeons"; Ferragud, "Barbers" 2015.
74. Cavallo, *Artisans,* 89–111; Kinzelbach, "Erudite."
75. Kinzelbach, *Chirurgen,* 3–7, 14–34, 37–41, 56–60.
76. Ulm Museum Inv. Nr. 1928.6026. Kinzelbach, *Chirurgen,* 3–34, 67–8.
77. Mss *Akten Reichsstadt A [3103]* 13.5.1729, 20.5.1729, 17.2.1735, 21.2.1735; all in StadtAU; *Bestand Reichsstadt Rst N E 5/2 N20* Nuremberg Stadtarchiv.
78. Johann Dietz "Meister Johann Dietz, Das ist: die getreue, von ihm selbst gemachte Beschreibung seines Lebens [1666–1738], " in *Meister Johann Dietz, des Großen Kurfürsten Feldscher und Königlicher Hofbarbier,* ed. Ernst Consentius (Munich: Langewiesche-Brandt, 1915), 11–312, 200–4, 218–22; Knut Schulz and Christiane Schuchard, *Handwerker Deutscher Herkunft und ihre Bruderschaften im Rom der Renaissance: Darstellung und Ausgewählte Quellen* (Rome: Herder, 2005), 40–9; Cavallo, *Artisans,* 244.

Chapter 5

1. For an introduction to early modern medical culture, see Harold J. Cook, "Medicine," in *The Cambridge History of Science, vol. 3 Early Modern Science*, eds. Katharine Park and Lorraine Daston (Cambridge: Cambridge University Press, 2006), 407–34.
2. Thomas Winston, *Anatomy Lectures at Gresham College* (London: R. Daniel, 1659), 210.
3. Aristotle, *History of Animals*, trans. D'Arcy Wentworth Thompson (Raleigh, NC: Generic NL Freebook Publisher, n.d., EBSCOhost ebook), 85–8.
4. See Aristotle, *On the Generation of Animals*, trans. Arthur Platt (Raleigh, NC: Generic NL Freebook Publisher, n.d., EBSCOhost ebook), 86–91.
5. Galen, *Mixtures*, in *Galen: Selected Works*, ed. P.N. Singer (Oxford: Oxford University Press, 1997, EBSCOhost eBook), 251.
6. Ibid., 252.
7. Ibid., 251–2. Galen, *On the Usefulness of the Parts of the Body*, trans. Margaret Tallmadge May (Ithaca, NY: Cornell University Press, 1968), likens eyebrows to the small hard plants growing in rocky soil, while the longer hair growing on the head, armpits, and pudenda grows in moister parts (2:534).
8. Galen, *Mixtures*, 249–50.
9. Galen, *The Art of Medicine*, in *Galen: Selected Works*, ed. P.N. Singer (Oxford: Oxford University Press, 1997, EBSCOhost eBook), 354–6.
10. Ibid., 352.
11. Ibid., 353.
12. Ibid., 358–61
13. Thomas Vicary, *A Profitable Treatise of the Anatomy of Man's Body* (London: Henry Bamforde, 1577), sig. Ciii.
14. Ibid., sig. eiv–eii.
15. Thomas Vicary, *The English Mans Treasure* (London: Thomas Creede, 1613), 10.
16. Helkiah Crooke, *Microcosmographia: A Description of the Body of Man* (London: William Jaggard, 1615), 70.
17. Ibid., 66–7.
18. Jean Riolan, *A Sure Guide, or, The Best and Nearest Way to Physick and Chyrurgery*, trans. Nicholas Culpeper (London: Peter Cole, 1657), 120.
19. Galen, *Mixtures*, 253–4.
20. Levinus Lemnius, *Touchstone of Complexions*, trans. Thomas Newton (London: Thomas Marsh, 1576), 41v.
21. Ibid., 41v.
22. Ibid., 41v.
23. Galen, *Usefulness*, 530–1.
24. Crooke, *Microcosmographia*, 70.
25. Galen, *Mixtures*, 251–2.
26. Ibid., 253.
27. Ibid., 253.
28. Crooke, *Microcosmographia*, 68.
29. Ibid., 68, 69.
30. Edith Snook, "Beautiful Hair, Health, and Privilege in Early Modern England," *Journal for Early Modern Cultural Studies* 15, no. 4 (2015): 22–51.
31. Vicary, *Profitable Treatise*, sig. Eiv.

32. Thomas Elyot, *The Castle of Health* (London: Printed for the Company of Stationers, 1610), 3–5. Elyot also directly links hair color to humors: black hair comes of choler or "adustion of bloud," red hair of heat, gray of melancholy, and white hair by "a lack of naturall heate, and by occasion of flegme putrified" (17).
33. Lemnius, *Touchstone*, 33v. Lemnius considers the hair resulting from a cold (64v), dry (69v), and moist (80) complexion and of compound complexions (90v, 112, 127v, 129v, 130, 147v).
34. Ibid., 35–35v.
35. Ibid., 36v.
36. Ibid., 37v.
37. Ibid., 39v.
38. Ibid., 80.
39. Thomas Chamberlayne, *The Compleat Midwifes Practice* (London: Nathaniel Brooke, 1656), 8–9.
40. Jane Sharp, *The Midwives Book* (London: Simon Miller, 1671), 42.
41. Margaret Pelling, *The Common Lot: Sickness, Medical Occupations, and the Urban Poor in Early Modern England: Essays* (London: Longman, 1998), 204.
42. Sandra Cavallo, *Artisans of the Body in Early Modern Italy: Identities, Families and Masculinities* (Manchester: Manchester University Press, 2007), 39.
43. Ibid., 40.
44. Galen, *On the Usefulness*, 531.
45. William Bullein, *The Government of Health* (London: Valentine Sims, 1595), 23v–24.
46. On the importance of linen and perfumes in sixteenth- and seventeenth-century France, see Georges Vigarello, *Concepts of Cleanliness: Changing Attitudes in France Since the Middle Ages*, trans. Jean Birrell (Cambridge: Cambridge University Press, 1988), 58–89.
47. Victoria Sherrow, "Renaissance Europe," in *Encyclopedia of Hair: A Cultural History* (Westport, CN: Greenwood Press, 2006), 328; Katherine Ashenburg, *The Dirt on Clean: An Unsanitized History* (New York: North Point Press, 2007), 101.
48. Douglas Biow, *The Culture of Cleanliness in Renaissance Italy* (Ithaca, NY: Cornell University Press, 2006).
49. Ashenburg, *Dirt on Clean*, 94–5, 98–9, 101. See Caspar Netscher, *Interior with a Mother Combing her Child's Hair* (1669), painting, 44.5 × 61 cm. Rijksmuseum, Amsterdam. ARTstor; Gerard ter Borch, *Mother Combing Her Child's Hair* (1652–1653), painting, 33.5 × 29 cm. Mauritshuis, The Hague. ARTstor.
50. Michael Sweerts, *Sleeping Old Man and Girl* (1650), painting, 44.5 × 32.5 cm. Museum Boijmans van beauningen, Rotterdam.
51. William Drage, *Physical Experiments: Being a Plain Description of the Causes, Signs, and Cures of Most Diseases Incident to the Body of Man* (London: Simon Miller, 1668), 393.
52. Ibid., 394–5.
53. Riolan, *A Sure Guide*, 121–2.
54. Giovanni Vigo, "Of Additions," in *The Whole Worke of that Famous Chirurgion Master John Vigo*, trans. by men skillful in that art (London: Thomas East, 1586), 367v.
55. Frances Catchmay, *A booke of medicens*, (1625), MS 184a, Wellcome Library, London, f.13.
56. Peter Levens, *A Right Profitable Booke for all Diseases, called The Path-way to Health* (London: John Beale, 1632), A4.
57. Culpeper, *The English Physician* (London: William Bentley, 1652), 5, 38, 114, 153, 214, 215.

NOTES 177

58. Nicholas Culpeper, *A Physicall Directory or a Translation of the London Dispensatory* (London: Peter Cole, 1649), 36.
59. Jane Jackson, *A Very Shorte and Compendious Method of Phisicke and Chirurgery* (1642), MS 373, Wellcome Library, London, f. 60v, 98v, 102.
60. Elizabeth Digby's *Housebook* (1650), Egerton MS 2197, British Library, London. f. 25v, 42.
61. On women's medical recipes, see Elaine Leong, "Making Medicines in the Early Modern Household," *Bulletin of the History of Medicine* 82 (2008): 145–68; Elaine Leong, "Collecting Knowledge for the Family: Recipes, Gender and Practical Knowledge in the Early Modern English Household," *CNT Centaurus* 55 (2013): 81–103; Elaine Leong and Sara Pennell, "Recipe Collections and the Currency of Medical Knowledge in the Early Modern Medical 'Marketplace,'" in *Medicine and the Market in England and Its Colonies, c. 1450–1850*, eds. Mark S. Jenner and Patrick Wallace (London: Palgrave, 2007), 133–53.
62. Drage, *Physical*, 378–97.
63. Crooke, *Microcosmographia*, 70.
64. Drage, *Physical*, 382, 384, 385.
65. John Gerard, *The Herball or Generall Historie of Plantes* (London: Adam Islip, Joice Norton and Richard Whitakers, 1636), sig. Bbbbbbb.
66. Ibid., 1146, 1180.
67. Culpeper, *A Physicall Directory*, 4–5, 25, 65, 69, 71.
68. Ibid., 73.
69. Ibid., sig. Aviv–Aviii.
70. Levens, *A Right Profitable*, sig. A3.
71. Ibid., sig. A4.
72. Nicholas Culpeper, *Culpeper's School of Physick* (London: Printed for N. Brook, 1659), 112.
73. Drage, *Physical*, 381–2 [misnumbered as 383–2] outlines cures of propriety for excess hair that used ashes of horseleeches, the blood of a bat, and pigeon's dung. *A Physical Dictionary* (London: G. Dawson, 1657), defines propriety: "a pain by propriety is when the cause of the pain is in the part pained, as when the head-ach comes from the humors in the head it's called a pain by propriety" (sig. L2).
74. Thomas Brugis, *The Marrow of Physicke* (London: Pronte by Richard Hearne, 1640), 2:22.
75. Charles Butler, *The Feminine Monarchie* (Oxford: Joseph Barnes, 1609), sig. M4.
76. Salvator Winter, *A Pretious Treasury: Or a New Dispensatory* (London: Thomas Harper, 1649), 15.
77. [W.M.], *The Queen's Closet Opened* (London: Nathaniel Brook, 1655), 100, 270.
78. Pope John XXI, *The Treasury of Health* (London: Thomas East, 1585), sig. Aviii–B.
79. Drage, *Physical*, 381–2 [misnumbered as 383–2]; Giambattista Della Porta, *Natural Magick* (London: Thomas Young and Samuel Speed, 1658), 236.
80. Levens, *Right Profitable*, sig. A4.
81. William Langham, *The Garden of Health* (London: Printed by the deputies of Christopher Barker, 1598), sig. b5.
82. Ibid., 397.
83. Ibid., 187–8.
84. Porta, *Natural Magick*, 238.

85. Peter Temple, *Medical, Cookery and Other Recipes* (1656), Stowe MS 1077, British Library, London, f. 47.
86. Ibid., f. 10.
87. Ibid., f. 47.
88. Ambrose Paré, "Of the Faculties of Simple Medicines," in *The Workes of that Famous Chirurgion Ambrose Parey*, trans. Thomas Johnson (London: Th. Cotes and R. Young, 1634), 1081–2.
89. Ibid., 1082.
90. Culpeper, *English Physician*, 18; Levens, *A Right Profitable*, sig. A3v
91. Levens, *A Right Profitable*, 235.
92. Ibid., 236.
93. Winter, *A Pretious Treasury*, 13, 17, 238.
94. Drage, *Physical*, 391.
95. Lucrezia Marinella, *The Nobility and Excellence of Women, and the Defects and Vices of Men*, trans. and ed. Anne Dunhill (Chicago: University of Chicago Press, 1999), 168.
96. Porta, *Natural Magick*, 233.
97. Ibid., 233.
98. Mikhail Bakhtin, *Rabelais and His World*, trans. Hélène Iswolsky (Bloomington: Indiana University Press, 1984), 313, 316.
99. Stephen Greenblatt, "Filthy Rites," *Daedalus* 111 (1982): 2.

Chapter 6

1. The influential work of Michel Foucault and subsequent gender and queer theorists suggests that the latter term is anachronistic as a reference to sexual identity in early modernity since the concepts of hetero-, homo-, and bisexuality are subsequent constructions. I thus use the term *sexuality* throughout this chapter to refer to erotic inclinations, desires, and functions rather than to specific sexual identities.
2. Alexandra Shepard, *Meanings of Manhood in Early Modern England* (Oxford: Oxford University Press, 2003).
3. See Thomas Laqueur, *Making Sex; Body and Gender from the Greeks to Freud* (Cambridge, MA: Harvard University Press, 1992).
4. See for instance, Leviticus 19:27: "neither shalt thou marre the tuftes of thy beerd" (fol. xlvii^v); Ezekiel 44:20: "they shall not shave theyr heades, nor nouryshe the bushe of theyr heare, but rounde theyr heades onely" (fol. cviv); 1 Corinthians 11:14: "Doth not nature it selfe teach you, that it is a shame for a man, yf he have long here and a prayse to a woman: yf she have longe here. For hyr heer is geven her to cover her wythall" (fol. lxix). Biblical citations are from *The Byble in Englyshe* (London, 1541).
5. In *Fashions in Hair: The First Five Thousand Years* (London: Peter Owen, 1965), Richard Corson depicts hair fashions for early modern women as long and straight, often formed into braids, twists, rolls, or chignons, and frequently interwoven with ribbons. Before the reign of Henry VIII, men appear beardless, with shoulder length, banged hair; afterward, men appear wearing short hair and beards.
6. Judith Butler, *Bodies That Matter: on the Discursive Limits of "Sex"* (New York: Routledge, 1993); Valerie Traub, *The Renaissance of Lesbianism in Early Modern England* (Cambridge: Cambridge University Press, 2002).
7. Thomas Hill, *The contemplation of mankinde containing a singular discourse after the art of physiognomie, on all the members and partes of man, as from the heade to the foote, in a more ampler maner than hitherto hath beene published of any* (London, 1571), [2]15.

NOTES   179

8. Hill, *Contemplation*, 4.
9. Ambroise Paré, *Des Monstres, Des Prodiges, Des Voyages* (1585, repr. Paris: Livre Club, 1964), 194.
10. Translation quoted from Dudley Wilson, *Signs and Portents: Monstrous Births from the Middle Ages to the Enlightenment* (London: Routledge, 1993), 76–7. In *The Complete Works of Montaigne: Essays, Travel Journals, Letters* (London: Hamish Hamilton, 1948), Donald M. Frame translates the same passage, "I have just seen a shepherd in Médoc, thirty years old or thereabouts, who has no sign of genital parts. He has three holes by which he continually makes water. He is bearded, has desire, and likes to touch women" (539).
11. John Bulwer, *Anthropometamorphosis: Man Transform'd: or, the Artificiall Changling* (London, 1650), sig. A1.
12. Bulwer, *Anthropometamorphosis*, sig. B1v.
13. Ibid., sig. B4v.
14. Hill, *Contemplation*, 6–7.
15. Ibid., 5–5v.
16. Ibid., 5v–6, 6–6v.
17. Ibid., 8v, 11v.
18. Ibid., 9v.
19. Ibid., 10–10v.
20. Ibid., 11.
21. Ibid., 17.
22. Bulwer, *Anthropometamorphosis*, sig. K2v.
23. Ibid., sig. K3, K3v.
24. Ibid., sig. K3v, K4.
25. William Prynne, *The Unlovelinesse, of Loue-Lockes. Or, A Summarie Discourse, Proouing: The Wearing, and Nourishing of a Locke, or Loue-Locke, to be Altogether Vnseemely, and Vnlawfull vnto Christians* (London, 1628), sig. A2.
26. Ibid., 8, 10.
27. Ibid., 35–6.
28. Phillip Stubbes, *The Second Part of the Anatomie of Abuses* (London: Printed by R. Ward, 1583), H1v.
29. Thomas Hall, *Comarum akosmia the loathsomenesse of long haire, or, A treatise wherein you have the question stated, many arguments against it produc'd, and the most materiall arguguments [sic] for it refell'd and answer'd* (London: Printed by J.G[rismond], 1654), 7.
30. Ibid., 11.
31. Will Fisher, *Materializing Gender in Early Modern English Literature and Culture* (Cambridge: Cambridge University Press, 2006), 142.
32. Hill, *Contemplation*, 15–15v.
33. Ibid., 19v.
34. Bulwer, *Anthropometamorphosis*, sig. L2.
35. Ibid., sig. Ff4, Ff4v.
36. Hill, *Contemplation*, 149v.
37. Bulwer, *Anthropometamorphosis*, sig. O1v, O3–O3v.
38. Hill, *Contemplation*, 45, 45v.
39. Bulwer, *Anthropometamorphosis*, sig. O2–O2v.
40. Ibid., sig. P2.

41. John Stowe, *The Annals of England: Faithfully Collected Out of the Most Authenticall Authors, Records, and Other Monuments of Antiquitie* (London: Printed by Eliot's Court Press and F. Kingston, 1600), 962–3.
42. Hill, *Contemplation*, 145v, 145v–146.
43. Bulwer, *Anthropometamorphosis*, sig. Ff1v.
44. Ibid., sig. Ee1.
45. Hill, *Contemplation*, 146.
46. Bulwer, *Anthropometamorphosis*, sig. Ff3v.
47. Ben Jonson, *The Alchemist*, in *Ben Jonson: Four Comedies*, ed. Helen Ostovich (London: Longman, 1997).
48. William Shakespeare, *Much Ado About Nothing*, in *The Riverside Shakespeare*, eds. G. Blakemore Evans et al. 2nd ed. (Boston, MA: Houghton-Mifflin, 1997), 361–98.
49. Robert Greene, *A Quip for an Upstart Courtier* (London: Printed by John Wolfe, 1592), sig. D3.
50. Benjamin Rudyerd, *Le Prince d'Amour, or the Prince of Love. With a collection of several ingenious poems and songs by the wits of the age* (London: Printed by William Leake, 1660).
51. Hill, *Contemplation*, 147, 149.
52. Ibid., 149–149v.
53. Anonymous, "The Ballad of the Beard," in *Satirical Songs and Poems on Costume: From the 13th to the 19th Century*, ed. F.W. Fairholt, vol. 27 of *Early English Poetry, Ballads, and Popular Literature of the Middle Ages* (London: Percy Society, 1849). For both Fairholt's reprint and John Phillip's version "On the Beard" in *Sportive Wit*, see Mark Albert Johnston, *Beard Fetish in Early Modern England: Sex, Gender, and Registers of Value* (Farnham: Ashgate, 2013), 257–8.
54. For a more detailed discussion of beard qualities and values, see Johnston, *Beard Fetish*, esp. 56–97.
55. Stubbes, *The Second Part of the Anatomie of Abuses*, sig. H1v.
56. Bulwer, *Anthropometamorphosis*, 198.
57. Ibid., sig. Dd2, Dd4v–Ee1.
58. Ibid., sig. Dd3.
59. Ibid., sig. Dd3.
60. Ibid., sig. Ee1.
61. Ibid., sig. Ee1v.
62. Ibid.
63. Ibid., 58.
64. *Hic Mulier: or, the Man-Woman: Being a Medicine to Cure the Coltish Disease of the Staggers in the Masculine-Feminines of Our Times* (London: Printed by I. T[rundle], 1620), sig. A3v, A4v, B3.
65. Thomas Wall, *God's Holy Order in Nature, Which Man and Woman were Created in, Truly Stated and Explained* (London: Printed by William Marshall, 1690), sig. B2. Two years earlier, Wall made the same case for the proprieties of gendered hair lengths in *Spiritual Armour to Defend the Head from the Superfluitie of Naughtiness…* (London: William Marshall, 1688).
66. Richard Brathwaite, *Natures Embassie: or, The Wilde-mans Measures: Danced Naked by Twelve Satyres* (London: Printed by Richard Field, 1621), 203.
67. Prynne, *The Unlovelinesse, of Love-Lockes*, sig. A3.
68. Ibid., 35–6.
69. Ibid., 39, 10.

70. Hill, *Contemplation*, 147v.
71. Ibid., 11v.
72. Ibid., 148.
73. Bulwer, *Anthropometamorphosis*, sig. Gg1.
74. Alexander Read, *The Chirurgicall Lectures of Tumors and Vlcers* (London: Printed by John Haviland, 1635), 253.
75. Thomas Hill, *The Moste Pleasuante Arte of the Interpretacions of Dreames* (London: Printed by Thomas Marsh, 1576), sig. I3.
76. Ibid.
77. Ibid., 147–147v. Although the *OED* cites no instance of Hill's term "frowte," it likely derives from the same root as "forward" (adj. A1), meaning unreasonable, obstinate, ungovernable, and evilly disposed.
78. Ibid., ([2]21v).
79. William Shakespeare, *Macbeth*, in *The Riverside Shakespeare*, eds. G. Blakemore Evans et. al., 2nd ed. (Boston, MA: Houghton Mifflin), 1355–90.
80. John Evelyn, *The Diary of John Evelyn*, ed. Guy de la Bédoyère (Dorchester: Dorset Press, 1994), 114.
81. Rev. J. Granger, *A Biographical History of England, from Egbert the Great to the Revolution*, 5th ed. (London: William Baynes and Son, 1824), 4:98.
82. Henry Wilson and James Caufield, *The Book of Wonderful Characters: Memoirs and Anecdotes of Remarkable and Eccentric Persons in All Ages and Countries* (London: John Camden Hotten, [1869?]).
83. John Evelyn, *Memoirs Illustrative of the Life and Writings of John Evelyn*, ed. William Bray (1819, Rprt., London: Murray, 1871), 253 n.1.
84. For the two more youthful images of Barbara, and for further discussions of the cultural significances of bearded women in early modern England, see my "Bearded Women in Early Modern England," *Studies in English Literature* 47, no. 1 (2007): 1–28, and *Beard Fetish*, chap. 4.
85. Samuel Pepys, *The Diary of Samuel Pepys*, ed. Harry B. Wheatley (London: George Bell, 1900), 8:174.

Chapter 7

1. See José Piedra's "The Black Stud's Spanish Birth," *Callaloo* 16, no. 4 (1993): 820–46. Piedra's powerful essay offers insightful and provocative readings of the various ways in which medieval and early modern Spanish writers depicted blackness as paradoxical and hyper-genitalized.
2. Jeremy Lawrance, "Black Africans in Renaissance Spanish Literature," in *Black Africans in Renaissance Europe*, eds. T.F. Earle and Kate Lowe (Cambridge: Cambridge University Press, 2005), 72.
3. Sebastián de Covarrubias Horozco, *Tesoro de la lengua castellana o española*, eds. Ignacio Arellano and Rafael Zafra (Vervuert: Universidad de Navarra, 2006), 1395.
4. John Florio, *A Worlde of Wordes*, ed. Hermann W. Haller (Toronto: University of Toronto Press, 2013 [1598]), 545.
5. Real Academia Española: *Diccionario de la Autoridades* (1726–1739). http://web.frl.es/DA.html (Accessed on September 3, 2016).
6. María Elena Martínez, "The Language, Genealogy, and Classification of 'Race,'" in *Race and Classification: The Case of Mexican America*, eds. Ilona Katzew and Susan Deans-Smith (Stanford, CA: Stanford University Press, 2009), 26.

7. Covarrubias, *Tesoro*, 473.
8. Martínez, "Language," 29.
9. Ibid.
10. Ibid.
11. Ibid.
12. Ibid.
13. David M. Goldenberg's *The Curse of Ham: Race and Slavery in Early Judaism, Christianity, and Islam* (Princeton, NJ: Princeton University Press, 2003) examines the ancient link between black skin color and slavery. See also Bernard Lewis's *Race and Slavery in the Middle East: An Historical Enquiry* (New York: Oxford University Press, 1990).
14. Sweet, "Iberian," 152. For additional information on Alfonso's contributions to the culture of Castile, see Robert I. Burns, ed., *Emperor of Culture: Alfonso X the Learned of Castile and His Thirteenth-Century Renaissance* (Philadelphia: University of Philadelphia Press, 1990) and Joseph F. O'Callaghan's *The Learned King: The Reign of Alfonso X of Castile* (Philadelphia: University of Philadelphia Press, 1993).
15. Ibid., 152.
16. Bernard Lewis, *Race and Slavery in Islam: An Historical Enquiry* (Oxford: Oxford University Press, 1990), 36.
17. Francisco de Quevedo, *Poesía varia*, ed. James O. Crosby (Madrid: Cátedra, 2007), 409–15.
18. Juan Huarte de San Juan, *Examen de ingenios para las ciencias*, ed. Guillermo Serés (Madrid: Cátedra, 1989), 613, 617.
19. Ibid., 614–16.
20. Ibid., 616–17.
21. Ibid., 617.
22. Cortés cited in Nelson I. Madera, "La relación entre fisionomía y el carácter de los personajes en *Don Quijote de la* Mancha" (PhD diss., Florida State University, 1992), 211.
23. Emilio Cotarelo y Mori, ed., *Colección de entremeses, loas, bailes y mojigangas desde fines del siglo XVI a mediados del XVIII, tomos I y II* (Madrid: Nueva Biblioteca de Autores Españoles, 1911), 1: clxxi.
24. Lope de Rueda, *Comedia Eufemia*, in *Las cuatro comedias*, ed. Alfredo Hermenegildo (Madrid: Cátedra, 2001), 117.
25. Ibid., 118.
26. Ibid., 121.
27. Ibid., 118.
28. Baltasar Fra-Molinero has written most on black women in early modern Spanish literature. He defines Eulalla as "La negra enamorada adquiere mayor refinamiento en el personaje de Eulalla, en la comedia *Eufemia* de Lope de Rueda. De lo cómico se pasa a lo patético, ya que el galán de esta esclava, Polo, es un rufián de cuidado que quiere seducirla y venderla a las primeras de cambio. En Eulalla aparece plenamente desarrollada la ridiculización de las pretensiones de ascenso social de una esclava negra. En su lengua de negro explica sus esfuerzos por aclarar su cara y cabellos—«¿no tengo yo cabeyo como la otro?—, haciendo suya la fíbula de Esopo representada en los *Emblemata* de Alciato." (The easily infatuated black woman acquires the utmost refinement in the character of Eulalla in Lope de Rueda's *Comedia Eufemia*. Her comical nature overruns with pathetic behavior, for this slave's *galán*, Polo, is a ruffian *par excellence* who from the start wants to seduce her and sell her for anything possible. Developed in Eulalla's role is the

ridiculing of a black female slave's pretensions at social climbing. In her Black language, she explains her efforts by lightening her face and hair—"I don't have hair like the other [white] woman?"—making her own Aesop's fable represented in the Alciato's *Book of Emblems*). Baltasar Fra-Molinero, *La imagen de los negros en el teatro del Siglo do Oro* (Madrid: Siglo Veintiuno, 1995), 30–1.

29. Referencing current studies on women, recipes, and science in Spain, see work by Montserrat Cabré, particularly "Women or Healers? Household Practices and the Categories of Health Care in Late Medieval Iberia," *Bulletin of the History of Medicine* 82, no. 1 (2008): 18–51. Also on women, recipes, and science, see Elaine Leong, "Collecting Knowledge for the Family: Recipes, Gender and Practical Knowledge in the Early Modern English Household," *Centaurus 55* (2013): 81–103. On women, science, and cosmetic recipes see the first chapter of Edith Snook's *Women, Beauty, and Power* or (the same essay) "The Beautifying Part of Physic": Women's Cosmetic Practices in Early Modern England," *Journal of Women's History* 20, no. 3 (2008): 10–33, for an examination of products to make the skin fair.
30. Frantz Fanon, *Black Skin, White Masks* (New York: Grove Press, 1967).
31. Rueda, *Comedia Eufemia*, 118.
32. Pierre Bourdieu, *Language and Symbolic Power*, ed. John B. Thompson, trans. Gino Raymond and Matthew Adamson (Cambridge, MA: Harvard University Press, 1991).
33. Rueda, *Comedia Eufemia*, 120.
34. Ibid., 119–29.
35. Patricia Hill Collins, *Black Feminist Thought: Knowledge, Consciousness, and the Politics of Empowerment* (New York: Routledge, 1990), 78.
36. Shirley Anne Tate, *Black Beauty: Aesthetics, Stylization, Politics* (New York: Routledge, 2009), 129.
37. Ibid.
38. Ibid.
39. See Ingrid Banks, *Hair Matters: Beauty, Power, and Black Women's Consciousness* (New York: New York University Press, 2000) and Noliwe M. Rooks, *Hair Raising: Beauty, Culture, and African American Women* (New Brunswick, NJ: Rutgers University Press, 1997).
40. Tate, *Black Beauty*, 130.
41. Pauli Murray, "The Liberation of Black Women," in *Voices of the New Feminism*, ed. Mary Lou Thompson (Boston, MA: Beacon, 1970), 106.
42. Collins, *Black Feminist*, 93.

Chapter 8

1. R. Lightbown, *Piero della Francesca* (New York: Abbeville Press, 1992), 237; J. Sorabella, "Portraiture in Renaissance and Baroque Europe," Heilbrunn Timeline of Art History, The Metropolitan Museum of Art, 2007. http://www.metmuseum.org/toah/hd/port/hd_port.htm (Accessed July 4, 2016).
2. Frances Baldwin, *Sumptuary Legislation and Personal Regulation in England*, Johns Hopkins Studies in Historical and Political Science 44 (Baltimore: Johns Hopkins University Press, 1926), 10.
3. For the pervasiveness of sumptuary law, see Catherine Killerby, *Sumptuary Law in Italy: 1200–1500* (Oxford: Clarendon Press, 2002), 5; Julia Emberley, *Venus and Furs: The Cultural Politics of Fur* (London: I.B. Tauris, 1998), 43, and Kim Phillips, "Masculinities and the Medieval Sumptuary Laws," *Gender & History* 19 (2007): 23.

4. Anthony Synnott, "Shame and Glory: A Sociology of Hair," *The British Journal of Sociology* 38, no. 3 (1987): 395.
5. A. Cassa, *Funerali, pompe, conviti* (Brescia, 1887), 61–2.
6. Claire Sponsler, "Narrating the Social Order: Medieval Clothing Laws," *Clio* 21, no. 3 (1992), 279.
7. Maria Muzzarelli, "Reconciling the Privilege of a Few with the Common Good: Sumptuary Laws in Medieval and Early Modern Europe," *Journal of Medieval and Early Modern Studies* 39 (2009): 600.
8. Alan Hunt, *Governance of the Consuming Passions: A History of Sumptuary Law* (New York: St. Martin's Press, 1996), 115.
9. Victoria L. Sherrow, *The Encyclopedia of Hair: A Cultural History* (Westport, CT: Greenwood Press, 2006), 2.
10. Mark Albert Johnston, "Bearded Women in Early Modern England," *Studies in English Literature, 1500–1900* 47 (2007): 1.
11. Johnston, "Bearded Women in Early Modern England," 1. See also Will Fisher, "The Renaissance Beard: Masculinity in Early Modern England," *Renaissance Quarterly* 54 (2001): 175; and Will Fisher, *Materializing Gender in Early Modern English Literature and Culture* (Cambridge: Cambridge University Press, 2006).
12. Cited in Hunt, *Governance of the Consuming Passions*, 154.
13. Cited in Sherrow, *The Encyclopedia of Hair*, 2.
14. K. Greenfield, "Sumptuary Law in Nürnberg: A Study in Paternal Government," *Johns Hopkins University Studies in Historical and Political Science* (Baltimore: Johns Hopkins Univeristy Press, 1918), 262.
15. Greenfield, "Sumptuary Law in Nürnberg," 258.
16. Killerby, *Sumptuary Law in Italy*, 2.
17. Cited in Wilifred Hooper, "The Tudor Sumptuary Laws," *The English Historical Review* 30 (1915): 436.
18. Emberley, *Venus and Furs*, 46.
19. Ben Jonson, *Cynthia's Revels*, eds. E. Rasmussen and M. Steggle, in vol. 1 of *The Cambridge Edition of the Works of Ben Johnson*, eds. D. Bevington, M. Butler, and I. Donaldson (Cambridge: Cambridge University Press, 2012), 2.4: 48–58.
20. Ben Jonson, *Volpone, or the Fox*, ed. R. Dutton, in vol. 3 of *The Cambridge Edition of the Works of Ben Johnson*, 3.4: 10–12.
21. Ben Jonson, *Volpone*, 3.4. 32–5.
22. See Sherrow, *The Encyclopedia of Hair*, 155.
23. C. Vecellio, *The Clothing of the Renaissance World*, eds. Margaret F. Rosenthal and Ann Rosalind Jones (London: Thames & Hudson, 2008), 145.
24. Killerby, *Sumptuary Law in Italy*, 117.
25. Peter Erondell, *The French Garden: For English Ladyse and Gentlewomen to Walke in* (London: William White, 1605), Dialogue 1.
26. "Medals: The Renaissance Calling Card," *Italian Renaissance Learning Resources*, Oxford University and The National Gallery of Art. http://italianrenaissanceresources.com/units/unit-4/essays/medals-the-renaissance-calling-card/ (Accessed July 5, 2016). See also Evelyn Welch, "Art on the Edge: Hair and Hands in Renaissance Italy," *Renaissance Studies* 23 (2008): 245–6.
27. Welch, "Art on the Edge," 245–6.
28. H. Norris, *Costume & Fashion: The Tudors*. Vol. 3.2 (New York: E.P. Dutton and Co., 1938), 636.

NOTES

29. Ibid., 655.
30. Ibid., 172.
31. Philip Stubbes, *Anatomie of Abuses*, in M. Kidnie, "A Critical Edition of Philip Stubbes's *Anatomie of Abuses*" (PhD diss., University of Birmingham, 1996), 157.
32. Emily Cockayne, *Hubbub: Filth, Noise and Stench in England 1600–1770* (New Haven, CT: Yale University Press, 2007), 66.
33. Cited in Richard Corson, *Fashions in Hair: The First Five Thousand Years* (New York: Hillary House Publishers, 1971), 218.
34. Lynn Festa, "Personal Effects: Wigs and Possessive Individualism in the Long Eighteenth Century," *Eighteenth-Century Life* 29 (2005): 48.
35. Angela Rosenthal, "Raising Hair," *Eighteenth-Century Studies* 38 (2004): 1.
36. Terry Eagleton, *After Theory* (New York: Penguin, 2004), 6.
37. For a response to Eagleton, see L. Tondeur, "A History of Pubic Hair, or Reviewers' Responses to Terry Eagleton's *After Theory*," in *The Last Taboo: Women and Body Hair*, ed. K. Lesnik-Oberstein (Manchester: Manchester University Press, 2006), 48–65. For a discussion of the signifying features of the female "pubic beard," see Johnston, "Bearded Women," 3–4, and Mark Albert Johnston, Beard Fetish in Early Modern England: Sex, Gender, and Registers of Value (Farnham: Ashgate, 2013), 159–212; Fisher, "The Renaissance Beard," 155–8. For pubic hair removal trends over time, see Amanda Hess, "For Women, a New Look Down Under," *New York Times Magazine*, December 1, 2013, http://tmagazine.blogs.nytimes.com/2013/12/01/on-beauty-for-women-a-new-look-down-under/?_r=0 (Accessed July 5, 2016); Ashley Fetters, "The New Full Frontal: Has Pubic Hair in America Gone Extinct?" The *Atlantic*, December 13, 2011, http://www.theatlantic.com/health/archive/2011/12/the-new-full-frontal-has-pubic-hair-in-america-gone-extinct/249798/ (Accessed July 5, 2016) and Roger Friedland, "Looking through the Bushes: The Disappearance of Pubic Hair," *The Huffington Post*, June 13, 2011, http://www.huffingtonpost.com/roger-friedland/women-pubic-hair_b_875465.html (Accessed July 5, 2016).
38. Anne Hollander, *Seeing Through Clothes* (New York: Viking, 1978), 96–100; Penny Jolly, "Pubics and Privates: Body Hair in Late Medieval Art," in *The Meanings of Nudity in Medieval Art*, ed. S. Lindquist (Farnham: Ashgate, 2012), 187–201.
39. Hollander, *Seeing Through Clothes*, 100.
40. Jill Burke, "Did Renaissance Women Remove their Body Hair?" *Jill Burke's Blog*, December 9, 2012. https://renresearch.wordpress.com/2012/12/09/did-renaissance-women-remove-their-body-hair/ (Accessed May 17, 2016).
41. Burke, "Did Renaissance Women Remove their Body Hair?"
42. F. Delicado, *Portrait of Lozana: The Lusty Andalusian Woman*, trans. Bruno M. Damiani (Potomac, MD: Scripta Humanistica, 1987), 18, 208.
43. [W.M.], *The Queen's Closet Opened* (London: Nathaniel Brooks, 1659), 55.
44. *Making Up the Renaissance*. https://sites.eca.ed.ac.uk/renaissancecosmetics/cosmetics-recipes/hair/ (Accessed June 6, 2016).
45. See P. Braunstein, "Toward Intimacy: The Fourteenth and Fifteenth Centuries," in *A History of Private Life*, ed. G. Duby, trans. A. Goldhammer (Cambridge: Belknap Press, 1988), 2: 600; Virginia Smith, *Clean: A History of Personal Hygiene and Purity* (Oxford: Oxford University Press, 2007), 161–5 and Jolly, "Pubics," 190.
46. Monica Green, ed., *The Trotula: A Medieval Compendium of Women's Medicine* (Philadelphia: University of Pennsylvania Press, 2001), 167.
47. Green, *The Trotula*, 169.
48. Anu Korhonen, "Strange Things Out of Hair: Baldness and Masculinity in Early Modern England," *The Sixteenth-Century Journal* 41 (2010): 373.

49. Poggio Bracciolini, *Facetia Erotica of Poggio Fiorentino* (New York: privately printed, 1930), 39.
50. Desiderius Erasmus, *The Praise of Folly*, trans. Clarence H. Miller (New Haven, CT: Yale University Press, 1979), 48–9.
51. Jolly, "Pubics," 189; M. Jones, *The Secret Middle Ages* (Westport, CT: Praeger, 2002), 250.
52. Blake Gopnik, "Acomocliticism," *Cabinet Magazine* 40 (2010–2011), http://www.cabinetmagazine.org/issues/40/gopnik.php (Accessed July 7, 2016).
53. Marina Warner, *Monuments & Maidens: The Allegory of the Female Form* (Berkeley: University of California Press, 2000), 310–19.

Chapter 9

1. From Petrarch, "Sonnet 11: '*Lassare Il Velo O Per Sole O Per Ombra*'," in *The Complete Canzoniere*, trans. A.S. Kline (Poetry in Translation, 2001), www.poetryintranslation.com.
2. Nancy Vickers, "Diana Described: Scattered Woman and Scattered Rhyme," in *Writing and Sexual Difference*, ed. Elizabeth Abel (Chicago: University of Chicago Press, 1982), 95.
3. Ibid., 97.
4. In *Materializing Gender in Early Modern English Literature and Culture* (Cambridge: Cambridge University Press, 2006), 129–31, Will Fisher explains how writers from Ovid to Montaigne to William Prynne—who was known for penning, among other things, a treatise entitled *The Unlovelinesse of Love-lockes*—suggest that a change in sex also involved "a change in the length of the individual's hair." Prynne's treatise, Fisher notes, also suggests that physicians' discourse uphold the idea that the female sex is endowed with "fine" hair and the male with "coarse." More generally, women's hair was also thought "naturally longer than men's" (18).
5. Jane Hedley, *Power in Verse: Metaphor and Metonymy in the Renaissance Lyric* (University Park: Pennsylvania State University Press, 1988), 127. As Hedley's comments imply, the experience recounted by the requisite pining lover is correspondingly more universal than specific, and therefore not meant to express the reality of a particular individual. Gary Waller, "Acts of Reading: The Production of Meaning in Astrophil and Stella," *Studies in the Literary Imagination* 15, no. 1 (1982): 25, makes a similar point in suggesting that the *Canzoniere*'s speaker may thus be read as offering its "poems to an audience of sympathetic listeners as a mirror" that reflects "less of his own experiences than theirs" and more "of his experiences as paradigmatic of theirs."
6. Natasha Distiller, *Desire and Gender in the Sonnet Tradition* (Basingstoke: Palgrave Macmillan, 2008), 48.
7. Fisher, *Materializing Gender,* 130, notes that hair became particularly important from about 1590, when "a well-developed discourse on hair in England" began to emerge. Focused especially on gender, that discourse overwhelmingly argued "that women should have long locks and men should have short." Moreover, "Fashion historians note that over the course of the sixteenth and seventeenth centuries, women slowly abandoned the wimple and the other headdresses," bringing about a "shift in hair fashions" that "changed dramatically" from about the mid-sixteenth century and well into the seventeenth "as women gradually came to wear their tresses uncovered" (137, 142). Edith Snook, *Women, Beauty and Power in Early Modern England: A Feminist Literary History* (New York: Palgrave Macmillan, 2011), 120, further points out that hair may have been "imagined to grow according to nature's beckoning," but was also conceived as "wildly open to

8. In *Songes and Sonettes, Written by the Right Honorable Lorde Henry Haward Late Earle of Surrey, and Other* (London: Richard Tottel, 1557), n.p.
9. Ibid.
10. Ibid.
11. Edith Snook, "Beautiful Hair, Health, and Privilege in Early Modern England," *Journal for Early Modern Cultural Studies* 15, no. 4 (2015): 25.
12. Edmund Spenser, *Amoretti and Epithalamion* (Eugene: University of Oregon, Renascence Editions, 2005), 10.
13. William Drummond, *Poems: by William Drummond, of Hawthorne-denne, The Second Impression* (Edinburgh: Andro Hart, 1616), n.p.
14. Barnabe Barnes, *Parthenophil and Parthenophe Sonnettes, Madrigals, Elegies and Odes* (London: J. Wolfe, 1593), 47.
15. William Smith, *Chloris, Or the Complaint of the Passionate Despised Shepheard* (Eugene: University of Oregon, Renascence Editions, 2006), 19.
16. Henry Peacham, "Part 4," in *The Period of Mourning, with Nuptiall Hymnes: In Honor of this Happy Marriage* (London: T.S., 1613), Gv.
17. Thomas Heywood, *A marriage triumphe Solemnized in an epithalamium, in memorie of the happie nuptials betwixt the high and mightie Prince Count Palatine. And the most excellent princesse the Lady Elizabeth* (London: Edward Merchant, 1613), sig. B3v, C3r.
18. Ibid., sig. B2r.
19. Theresa M. Krier, "Generations of Blazons: Psychoanalysis and the *Song of Songs* in the *Amoretti*," *Texas Studies in Literature and Language* 40, no. 3 (1998): 306. Distiller, *Desire and Gender*, 73, notes "the sequence's highly unusual use of Petrarchan postures" that finds resolution in the closing *Ephithalamion*. The closing marriage hymn thus represents a marked departure from what Krier, "Generations," 306, describes as the "Petrarchan tempests" of the earlier sonnets. Petrarchism is, however, clearly on display in Spenser's epic *The Faerie Queene*, especially in a description of Belphoebe (whose name alone is suggestive), with "yellow lockes crisped, like golden wyre" that "About her shoulders weren loosely shed" (2.3.30) are not dissimilar to Spenser's bride's. Mary Villeponteaux, "*Semper Eadem*: Belphoebe's Denial of Desire," in *Renaissance Discourses of Desire*, eds. Claude J. Summers and Ted-Larry Pebworth (Columbia: University of Missouri Press, 1993), 33, finds in the "elaborate blazon" of Belphoebe, which includes no fewer than "nine stanzas of physical description," a "political Petrarchism" that "poses a threat to masculine power" (45), while Edward J. Geisweidt, in "Horticulture of the Head: The Vegetable Life of Hair in Early Modern English Thought," *Early Modern Literary Studies* 19 (2009): 6.1–24, argues that her hair in particular suggests a strong connection with the natural world. Representations of hair in Spenser, in other words, can be read as equally serving desire, resolution, politics, and nature.
20. It was conventional for brides to wear their hair loose. Though women increasingly wore their heads uncovered from the mid-sixteenth century onward, Fisher notes that it had always been married women who most "frequently concealed" their hair (*Materializing Gender*, 142). Fisher explains, given that hair began increasingly to be referred to as a "covering" as headdresses were abandoned, it may also be that the bride's long loose hair functioned also to signify her modesty (*Materializing Gender*, 137).

21. Francis Quarles, *Argalus and Parthenia: The Argument of the History* (London: John Marriot 1629), 26.
22. Ibid., 107.
23. Waller, "Acts of Reading," 28. Among those demands are the Petrarchan poet's "perpetual longings" that "provide subject matter for his poetry and the occasion for his assuming the vocation of poet" explains Lauren Silberman, "Singing Unsung Heroines," in *Rewriting the Renaissance: The Discourses of Sexual Difference in Early Modern Europe*, eds. Margaret W. Ferguson, Maureen Quilligan, and Nancy Vickers (Chicago: University of Chicago Press, 1986), 260.
24. Sir Philip Sidney, *The Oxford Authors: Sir Philip Sidney*, ed. Katherine Duncan-Jones (New York: Oxford University Press, 1989), 157–8.
25. Ibid., 157.
26. Elizabeth Cary, *The Tragedy of Mariam, the Fair Queen of Jewry*, eds. Barry Weller and Margaret W. Ferguson (Berkeley: University of California Press, 1994).
27. Spenser, *Amoretti and Epithalamion*, 19.
28. Ibid., 35. For Spenser, this is not necessarily a bad thing. His *Amoretti* was written to Elizabeth Boyle, whom he eventually married, and the sequence is exceptional in ending with the lovers' resolution and in the closing *Ephithalamion*'s consummation; hence the sequence "is constructed—and should be read—as poetry of courtship, written by a real historical figure," argues Ilona Bell, *Elizabethan Women and the Poetry of Courtship* (Cambridge: Cambridge University Press, 1998), 168.
29. Samuel Daniel, *Delia. Contayning Certayne Sonnets: With the Complaint of Rosamond* (Eugene: University of Oregon, Renascence Editions, 1998), 10. Bell notes, given that the poet "mentions but does not describe Delia's voice, hand, and eye," that Daniel chooses to describe the hair of an anagrammed ideal does suggest something of its particular significance to Petrarchan rhetoric (*Courtship*, 135).
30. James Shirley, *Poems, &c. by James Shirley* (London: Humphrey Moseley, 1646), 7; Thomas Jordan, *Poeticall varieties: or, Varietie of fancies* (London: T.C. for Humphry Blunden, 1637), 16–17.
31. Sir Philip *Sidney*, "Sonnet 103," in *The Oxford Authors*, 208.
32. Snook, "Beautiful Hair," 24–5.
33. Henry Constable, *Diana: Or, The excellent conceitful Sonnets of H. C.* (Eugene: University of Oregon, Renascence Editions, 1998), 5.
34. Barnes, *Parthenophil and Parthenophe*, 46.
35. John Weever, *Epigrammes in the Oldest Cut, and Newest Fashion* (London: V.S. for Thomas Bushell, 1599), n.p.
36. William Shakespeare, "Venus and Adonis," in *The Norton Shakespeare*, eds. Stephen Greenblatt et al. (New York: Norton, 1997), 608, 632.
37. Christopher Marlowe, "Hero and Leander," in *Christopher Marlowe: Complete Plays and Poems*, ed. E.D. Pendry (London: Everyman, 1976), 401–2. Snook, "Beautiful Hair," 34, points out that "While lovely Leander's hair might be long and never shorn, texts invested in gender difference—in a way perhaps that Marlowe's poem is not—tend to allow the same texture and curl to denote beautiful hair in men and women but then distinguish it by length." In his verse romance, for example, Quarles's extended blazon of the titular Parthenia includes hair that falls "raught downe beneath her yuory knees" (*Argalus and Parthenia*, 2), while the goddess Ceres later helps to celebrate the nuptials with "Her golden Tresses dangled to the ground" (*Argalus and Parthenia*, 116).
38. Marlowe, "Hero and Leander," 402.

NOTES

39. Ibid., 417.
40. Heather Dubrow, *Echoes of Desire: English Petrarchism and Its Counterdiscourses* (Ithaca, NY: Cornell University Press, 1995), 130.
41. Shakespeare, "Sonnet 130," in Greenblatt et al., eds., *The Norton Shakespeare*, 1040–1.
42. This is a mode Dubrow, *Echoes of Desire*, 163–4, describes as comprising "poems that describe, generally in ostensibly favorable terms, a woman with qualities that are seldom the subject of praise." This counter-tradition is equally centered on the nature and use of poetry as its standards of beauty "occupy marginalized spaces in a generic system that itself was prone both to establish and to flout generic standards," thus allowing "poets to practice genre criticism by example rather than precept."
43. James Shirley, *Poems, &c. by James Shirley* (London: Humphrey Moseley, 1646), 33–4.
44. Michael Drayton, *Idea* (1619), Luminarium Editions, www.luminarium.org/editions/idea.
45. Thomas Carew, *Poems* (London: I.D. for Thomas Walkley, 1640), 8.
46. Anthony Low, "Thomas Carew: Patronage, Family, and New-Model Love," in *Renaissance Discourses of Desire*, eds. Claude J. Summers and Ted-Larry Pebworth (Columbia: University of Missouri Press, 1993), 93, highlights the poem's revisionist intent in arguing that Carew revises convention to the extent that "the discourse of desire undergoes a fundamental change," for "None of Carew's lovers stays faithful to a haughty, refusing mistress, none pines away with unsatisfied desire, none is killed, even in jest, by submission to superior disdain."
47. John Ford, *'Tis Pity She's a Whore*, ed. Brian Morris (1968, Repr., The New Mermaids; London, 1990; New York: A & C Black and W.W. Norton, 1995). Cleopatra is famously described in *Antony and Cleopatra, The Norton Shakespeare*, 2648, by the admiring Enobarus, who insists that

> Age cannot wither her, nor custom stale
> Her infinite variety. Other women cloy
> The appetites they feed, but she makes hungry
> Where most she satisfies. (2.2.240–3)

48. Barnes, *Parthenophil and Parthenophe*, 47.
49. Bell, *Courtship*, 131.
50. Drummond, *Poems*, F2v.
51. Distiller, *Desire and Gender*, 48.
52. Dubrow, *Echoes of Desire*, 85–6.
53. Distiller, *Desire and Gender*, 63.
54. Hedley, *Power in Verse*, 16. See also Tom W.N. Parker, *Proportional Form in the Sonnets of the Sidney Circle* (Oxford: Clarendon Press, 1998), which argues that "there are too many tricks that turn on artifice to take anything at face value" (49) and that the sequence's first poems "may be read as a thorough condemnation of Astrophil's understanding of love" (45). Given what we know about Sidney, a dedicated statesman and eventual martyr to the Protestant cause, it may be that the entire sequence means to question the Petrarchism it so skillfully—and distractingly—represents.
55. Moira P. Baker, "'The Uncanny Stranger on Display': The Female Body in Sixteenth- and Seventeenth-Century Love Poetry," *South Atlantic Review* 56, no. 2 (1991): 10.
56. Sir Philip Sidney, *Defence of Poesie* (Posonby, 1595, Repr., Eugene: University of Oregon, Renascence Editions, 1995), 14.
57. Ibid., 32–4.
58. Snook, *Women, Beauty and Power*, 130.

59. Sir Philip Sidney, *Book I, The Countess of Pembroke's Arcadia (1590)* (Eugene: University of Oregon, Renascence Editions, 2005), 75.
60. Ibid., 74.
61. Ibid., 102.
62. Philip Sidney, *Book III, The Countess of Pembroke's Arcadia (1590)* (Eugene: University of Oregon, Renascence Editions, 2005), 20. Written in expressed admiration of Sidney's romance, Quarles's includes a like description of the bride Parthenia featuring "Her dissheueld hayre" that "Hung downe behind, as if the onely care / Had bin to reconcile neglect and Art" (*Argalus and Parthenia*, 107).
63. Lady Mary Wroth, *The Countesse of Mountgomeries Urania* (London: John Marriot and John Grismand, 1621), 141.
64. Snook, *Women, Beauty and Power*, 125–33.
65. Wroth, *Urania*, 77.
66. Snook, *Women, Beauty and Power*, 115, also points to Wroth's revisionist intent, arguing that her prose romance offers in another of its many stories "a vision of female identity dependant on the construction of hair as a visceral instrument of privilege."
67. Ben Jonson, in *Ben Jonson and the Cavalier Poets*, ed. Hugh MacLean (New York: W.W. Norton & Co., 1974), 48.
68. Ibid., 91–2.
69. Robert Herrick, "'Delight in Disorder' in 'Robert Herrick'," in *Ben Jonson and the Cavalier Poets*, ed. MacLean, 109.
70. Robert Herrick, "'Corinna's Going a-Maying,' in 'Robert Herrick'," in MacLean, ed., *Ben Jonson and the Cavalier Poets*, 113–15.
71. Robert Herrick, "'Art Above Nature: To Julia,' in 'Robert Herrick'," in MacLean, ed., *Ben Jonson and the Cavalier Poets*, 135.
72. John Donne, "Elegy 2," in *Selected Poetry and Prose*, eds. T.W. Craik and R.J. Craik (London: Methuen, 1986), 71–3.
73. John Donne, "Elegy 19," in Craik and Craik, eds., *Selected Poetry and Prose*, 85–6.
74. Donne, "Elegy 17," line 4 in *Poems of John Donne*, vol. 1, ed. E.K. Chambers (London: Lawrence & Bullen, 1896, Repr., www.luminarium.org), 139–41.
75. Theresa M. DiPasquale, "Donne's Catholic Petrarchans: The Babylonian Captivity of Desire," in Summers and Pebworth, eds., *Renaissance Discourses of Desire*, 78. DiPasquale, 78–81, also describes Donne's Petrarchism as "reminiscent of specifically Roman piety" that marks the "tradition-bound faith" of Catholicism and Petrarchism more generally as "a discourse that perpetuates the dubious pleasure of unconsummated longing."
76. Mary Villeponteaux, "*Semper Eadem*: Belphoebe's Denial of Desire," in Summers and Pebworth, eds., *Renaissance Discourses of Desire*, 34, accounts for the blazon as the "dismemberment of the woman in response to her perceived power to dismember the man who views her." In "The Funeral," the metaphorical becomes the literal through a speaker who shifts the focus to his own potential but thwarted dismemberment as he pulls his own potentially scattered parts into a cohesive whole and does so with means provided by the woman who, willingly parted from at least some of her hair, works to dismember herself.
77. DiPasquale, "Donne's Catholic Petrarchans," 84; John Donne, "The Funeral," in Craik and Craik, eds., *Selected Poetry and Prose*, 41–2.
78. John Donne, "The Relic," in *Selected Poetry and Prose*, eds. Craik and Craik, 58–9. Though the connection has been challenged, critics generally agree that the poem intends to commend the virtues of Magdalen Herbert, mother of the poet George.
79. Dubrow, *Echoes of Desire*, 205–7.

FURTHER READING

Primary Texts

Anger, Jane. *Jane Anger Her Protection for Women*. London: Richard Jones and Thomas Orwin, 1589.
Anon, A *Discourse of the Married and Single Life*. London: Jonas Man, 1621.
Anon. *Hæc-Vir*. London: John Trundle, 1620.
Aristotle. *History of Animals*. Translated by D'Arcy Wentworth Thompson. Raleigh, NC: Generic NL Freebook Publisher, n.d. EBSCOhost ebook.
Aristotle. *On the Generation of Animals*. Translated by Arthur Platt. Raleigh, NC: Generic NL Freebook Publisher, n.d. EBSCOhost ebook.
Barnes, Barnabe. *Parthenophil and Parthenophe Sonnettes, Madrigals, Elegies and Odes*. London: [J. Wolfe], 1593.
Bentley, Thomas. *The Fift Lampe of Virginitie*. London: H. Denham, 1582.
Bock, Hieronymus. *New Kreütter Buch von Underscheydt, Würckung und Namen der Kreütter so in Teütschen Landen wachsen*. Straßburg: Rihel, 1539.
Bodin, Jean. *On the Demon-Mania of Witches*. Translated by Randy A. Scott. Toronto: Centre for Reformation and Renaissance Studies, 1995.
Brathwaite, Richard. *Natures Embassie: or, The Wilde-mans Measures: Danced Naked by Twelve Satyres*. London: Richard Field, 1621.
Breton, Nicholas. *An Olde Mans Lesson*. London: Edward White, 1605.
Brotbeihel, Jeremias. *Kalender, auff das Jar M.D.LXI*. Dillingen: Mayer, [1560]. Digitale Bibliothek Bayerische Staatsbibliothek (from here: BSB) urn: nbn:de:bvb:12-bsb00087945-0.
Brugis, Thomas. *The Marrow of Physicke*. London: Richard Hearne, 1640.
Bullein, William. *The Government of Health*. London: Valentine Sims, 1595.
Bulwer, John. *Anthropometamorphosis: Man Transform'd: or, the Artificiall Changling ....* London: William Hunt, 1653.
Burke, Jill. "Making up the Renaissance." https://sites.eca.ed.ac.uk/renaissancecosmetics/cosmetics-recipes/hair/(Accessed June 6, 2016).
Butzlin, Johann J. *Kalender sampt der Practick vff das Jar M.D.LXXVII*. Zurich: Froschower, 1576. Digitale Bibliothek BSB urn: nbn:de:bvb:12-bsb10174557-7.
Carew, Thomas. *Poems*. London: J. D. for Thomas Walkley, 1649.
Cary, Elizabeth. *The Tragedie of Mariam*. London: Thomas Creede, 1613.
Cary, Elizabeth. *The Lady Falkland, Her Life*. Edited by Richard Simpson. London: Catholic Publishing, 1861.
Cary, Elizabeth. *The Tragedy of Mariam, the Fair Queen of Jewry*. Edited by Barry Weller and Margaret W. Ferguson. Berkeley: University of California Press, 1994.
Cassa, A. *Funerali, pompe, conviti*. Brescia: n.p., 1887.
Castiglione, Baldassare. *The Book of the Courtier*. 1561. London: J.M. Dent & Sons, 1974.
Chamberlayne, Thomas. *The Compleat Midwifes Practice*. London: Nathaniel Brooke, 1656.

Cholmley, Hugh. *The Memoirs and Memorials of Sir Hugh Cholmley of Whitby 1600–1657*. Edited by Jack Binns. Woodbridge: Yorkshire Archaeological Society & Boydell Press, 2000.

Cleland, James. *Hero-Paideia*. Oxford: Joseph Barnes, 1607.

Cogan, Thomas. *The Haven of Health*. London: John Norton, 1605.

Colonna, Francesco. *Hypnerotomachia*. 1592. Amsterdam: Theatrum Orbis Terrarum, 1969.

Constable, Henry. *Diana*. 1594. University of Oregon, Renascence Editions, 2005. PDF e-book.

Cotarelo Y Morí, Emilio, ed. *Colección de entremeses, loas, bailes y mojigangas desde fines del siglo XVI a mediados del XVIII, tomos I y II*. Madrid: Nueva Biblioteca de Autores Españoles, 1911.

Covarrubias Horozco, Sebastián de. *Tesoro de la lengua castellana o española. Edición integral e ilustrada*. Edited by Ignacio Arellano and Rafael Zafra. Vervuert: Universidad de Navarra, 2006.

Crooke, Helkiah. *Microcosmographia: A Description of the Body of Man*. London: William Jaggard, 1615.

Culpeper, Nicholas. *A Physicall Directory or a Translation of the London Dispensatory*. London: Peter Cole, 1649.

Culpeper, Nicholas. *Culpeper's School of Physick*. London: N. Brook, 1659.

Daniel, Samuel. *Delia: Contayning Certayne Sonnets: with the Complaint of Rosamond*. 1592. University of Oregon, Renascence Editions, 1998. PDF e-book.

Dekker, Thomas. *The Guls Horne-booke*. London: Nicholas Okes, 1609.

Delicado, F. *Portrait of Lozana: The Lusty Andalusian Woman*. Translated by Bruno M. Damiani. Potomac, MD: Scripta Humanistica, 1987.

Dent, Arthur. *The Plaine Mans Path-way to Heaven*. 1601. Amsterdam: Theatrum Orbis Terrarum, 1974.

Dietz, Johann. "Meister Johann Dietz, Das ist: die getreue, von ihm selbst gemachte Beschreibung seines Lebens [1666–1738]." In *Meister Johann Dietz, des Großen Kurfürsten Feldscher und Königlicher Hofbarbier*. Edited by Ernst Consentius, 11–312. Munich: Langewiesche-Brandt, 1915.

Donne, John. *Selected Poetry and Prose*. Edited by T.W. Craik and R.J. Craik. London: Methuen, 1986.

Drage, William. *Physical Experiments: Being a Plain Description of the Causes, Signs, and Cures of Most Diseases Incident to the Body of Man*. London: Simon Miller, 1668.

Drayton, Michael. *Idea*. 1619. Luminarium Editions, 2000. PDF e-book.

Drummond, William. *Poems: by William Drummond, of Hawthorne-denne, The Second Impression*. Edinburgh: Andro Hart, 1616.

Endter, Anna J. *Die so Kluge als Künstliche von Arachne und Penelope Getreulich Unterwiesene Hauß-Halterin*. Nuremberg: Endter, 1703.

Erasmus, Desiderius. *A Lytell Booke of Good Maners for Chyldren*. London: Wynkyn de Worde, 1532.

Erondell, Peter. *The French Garden*. London: Edward White, 1605.

Etschenreuter, Gallus. *Aller Heilsamen Bäder und Brunnen Natur*. Straßburg, 1571, urn:nbn:de:bvb:12-bsb00034062-2.

Evelyn, John. *Memoirs Illustrative of the Life and Writings of John Evelyn*. Edited by William Bray. 1819. Reprint, London: Murray, 1871.

Evelyn, John. *The Diary of John Evelyn*. Edited by Guy de la Bédoyère. Dorchester: Dorset Press, 1994.

Fairholt, F.W., ed. *Satirical Songs and Poems on Costume: From the 13th to the 19th Century*. Vol. 27 of *Early English Poetry, Ballads, and Popular Literature of the Middle Ages*. London: Percy Society, 1849.

Fanshawe, Anne. *Memoirs of Lady Fanshawe*. London: Henry Colburn, 1829.

Fiston, William. *Schoole of Good Manners*. London: William Ihones, 1595.

Ford, John. *'Tis Pity She's a Whore*. Edited by Brian Morris. 1968. Reprint, The New Mermaids. London, 1990; and New York: A & C Black and W.W. Norton, 1995.

Galen. *On the Usefulness of the Parts of the Body*. Translated by Margaret Tallmadge May. Ithaca, NY: Cornell University Press, 1968.

Galen. *The Art of Medicine*. In *Galen: Selected Works*. Edited by P.N. Singer, 345–96. Oxford: Oxford University Press, 1997. EBSCOhost eBook.

Galen. "Mixtures." In *Galen: Selected Works*. Edited by P.N. Singer, 202–89. Oxford: Oxford University Press, 1997. EBSCOhost eBook.

Gerard, John. *The Herball or Generall Historie of Plantes*. London: Adam Islip, Joice Norton, and Richard Whitakers, 1636.

Graf, Jeremias. *Nach der alten und neuen Zeit deutlicher und wolgefaster Haußhaltungs Calender auff das Jahr Christi M DC LIX*. Altenburg: Bauer, 1659. urn:nbn:de:urmel-452fd8b3ff4f-4d61-b7f4-cdf4cf1895065-00170133-018.

Granger, Rev. J. *A Biographical History of England, from Egbert the Great to the Revolution*. 5th ed. London: William Baynes and Son, 1824.

Greene, Robert. *A Quip for an Upstart Courtier*. London: John Wolfe, 1592.

Greene, Robert. "Alcida." 1617. In *Life and Complete Works in Prose and Verse of Robert Greene*, vol. 9. Edited by Alexander B. Grosart, 1–113. London: privately printed, 1881–1883.

Guazzo, Francesco Maria. *Compendium Maleficarum*. 1608. Edited by Montague Summers. New York: Dover, 1988.

Guazzo, Stefano. *The Civile Conversation*. London: Thomas East, 1586.

Hakluyt, Richard. *The Principal Navigations*. London: George Bishop, Ralph Newberie, and Robert Barker, 1599.

Hall, Thomas. *Comarum akosmia the Loathsomenesse of Long Haire*. London: J. G[rismond], 1654.

Hannay, Patrick. *A Happy Husband*. London: Richard Redmer, 1618.

Hauß- Garten- und Land- Calender: vor Sr. Königl. Maijest. in Pohlen, und Churfürstl. Durchl. zu Sachsen, Auff das Jahr Christi 1712. Leipzig, n.d. Digitale Bibliothek BSB urn: nbn:de:bsz:14-db-id3677207606.

Herbert, Edward. *The Life of Edward, First Lord Herbert of Cherbury*. Edited by J.M. Shuttleworth. London: Oxford University Press, 1976.

Heywood, Oliver. *The Rev. Oliver Heywood, B. A. 1630–1702: His Autobiography, Diaries, Anecdote and Event Books*. 4 vols. Edited by J. Horsfall Turner. Brighouse: privately printed, 1882.

Heywood, Thomas. *A Marriage Triumphe Solemnized in an Epithalamium, in Memorie of the Happie Nuptials Betwixt the High and Mightie Prince Count Palatine. And the Most Excellent Princesse the Lady Elizabeth*. London: Edward Merchant, 1613.

Hic Mulier: or, the Man-Woman: Being a Medicine to Cure the Coltish Disease of the Staggers in the Masculine-feminines of our Times. London: John Trundle, 1620.

Hill, Thomas. *The Contemplation of Mankinde Containing a Singular Discourse after the Art of Physiognomie*. London: Henry Denham, 1571.

Hill, Thomas. *The Moste Pleasuante Arte of the Interpretacions of Dreames*. London: Thomas Marsh, 1576.

Horstius, Johann D. *Kurtze Beschreibung der Sauer-Brunnen Zu Langen-Schwalbach vnd Dönningstein*. Frankfurt: Fickwirth, 1659. urn:nbn:de:bvb:12-bsb1ß287004-4.

Huarte De San Juan, Juan. *Examen de ingenios para las ciencias*. Edited by Guillermo Serés. Madrid: Cátedra, 1989.

Hutchinson, Lucy. *Memoirs of the Life of Colonel Hutchinson*. Edited by James Sutherland. London: Oxford University Press, 1973.

James I. *Basilikon Doron*. Edinburgh: Robert Walde-graue, 1603.

John XXI, Pope. *Treasury of Health*. London: Thomas East, 1585.

Jonson, Ben. *The Alchemist*. In *Ben Jonson: Four Comedies*. Edited by Helen Ostovich, 369–536. London: Longman, 1997.

Jonson, Ben. *Cynthia's Revels*. Edited by E. Rasmussen and M. Steggle. In *The Cambridge Edition of the Works of Ben Johnson*. Edited by D. Bevington, M. Butler, and I. Donaldson, 1:427–537. Cambridge: Cambridge University Press, 2012.

Jonson, Ben. *Volpone, or the Fox*. Edited by R. Dutton. In *The Cambridge Edition of the Works of Ben Jonson*. Edited by D. Bevington, M. Butler, and I. Donaldson, 3:25–191. Cambridge: Cambridge University Press, 2012.

Jordan, Thomas. *Poeticall Varieties: or, Varietie of Fancies*. London: T.C. for Humphry Blunden, 1637.

Klarwill, V. *Queen Elizabeth and Some Foreigners*. Translated by T.H. Nash. London: Butler and Tanner. 1928.

La Tour Landry, Geoffrey de. *The Book of the Knight of La Tour Landry*. Edited by Thomas Wright. EETS orig. series 33. London: Early English Text Society, 1906.

Lancre, Pierre de. *On the Inconstancy of Witches: Pierre de Lancre's Tableau de l'inconstance des mauvais anges et demons (1612)*. Edited by Gerhild Scholz Williams. Tempe: Arizona Center for Medieval and Renaissance Studies, 2006.

Langham, William. *The Garden of Health*. London: Printed by the deputies of Christopher Barker, 1598.

Lemnius, Levinus. *Touchstone of Complexions*. Translated by Thomas Newton. London: Thomas Marsh, 1576.

Lemnius, Levinus. *The Touchstone of Complexions*. London: Thomas Marsh, 1581.

Levens, Peter. *A Right Profitable Booke for all Diseases, called The Path-way to Health*. London: John Beale, 1632.

Lives and Letters of the Devereux, Earls of Essex, in the Reign of Elizabeth, James I, and Charles I, 1540–1656. Edited by Walter Bourchier Devereux. London: John Murray, 1853.

Lonitzer, Adam. *Kreuterbuch: Kunstliche Conterfeijtunge der Bäume, Stauden, Hecken, Kreuter, Getreyde, Gewürtze*. 6th ed. Frankfurt: Egenolff, 1578.

Lopez, Eduardo. *A Report of the Kingdome of Congo, a Region of Africa*. London: John Wolfe, 1597.

[M.,W] *The Queens Closet Opened*. London: Nathaniel Brook, 1655.

Mackay, Christopher S., ed. *The Hammer of Witches: A Complete Translation of the Malleus Maleficarum*. Cambridge: Cambridge University Press, 2009.

Marinella, Lucrezia. *The Nobility and Excellence of Women, and the Defects and Vices of Men*. Edited and translated by Anne Dunhill. Chicago: University of Chicago Press, 1999.

Marlowe, Christopher. "Hero and Leander." In *Complete Plays and Poems*. Edited by E.D. Pendry, 401–20. London: Everyman, 1976.

Martindale, Adam. *The Life of Adam Martindale*. Edited by Richard Parkinson. Manchester: The Chetham Society, 1845.

Maxwell-Stuart, P.G., ed. and trans. *Martín del Rio: Investigations into Magic*. Manchester: Manchester University Press, 2000.

Melville, James. *Memoirs of Sir James Melville of Halhill 1535–1617*. Edited by Frances A. Steuart. London: George Routledge & Sons, 1929.

Milton, John. *Samson Agonistes*. In *The Complete Poetry and Essential Prose of John Milton*. Edited by William Kerrigan, John Rumrich, and Stephen M. Fallon, 707–61. New York: Modern Library, 2007.

Montaigne, Michel de. *The Complete Works of Montaigne: Essays, Travel Journals, Letters*. Translated by Donald M. Frame. London: Hamish Hamilton, 1948.

Mora, George, ed. *Witches, Devils, and Doctors in the Renaissance: Johann Weyer*, De praestigiis daemonum. Binghamton, NY: Medieval & Renaissance Texts & Studies, 1991.

Moritz, Landgraf van Hessen. *Tax-Ordnung aller Wahren und Victualien*. Kassel: Wessel, 1622. urn:nbn:de:bvb:12-bsb10510805-6.

Moryson, Fynes. *Unpublished Chapters of Fynes Moryson's Itinerary*. Edited by Charles Hughes. London: Sherratt & Hughes, 1903.

Murner, Thomas. *Ein andechtig geistliche Badenfart*. 1514. urn:nbn:de:bvb:12-bsb00083105-1.

Nashe, Thomas. "The Unfortunate Traueller." 1594. In *The Works of Thomas Nashe*. Vol. 2. Edited by Ronald B. McKerrow, 199–328. Oxford: Basil Blackwell, 1958.

Osborne, Dorothy. *The Letters of Dorothy Osborne to William Temple*. Edited by G.C. Moore Smith. Oxford: Clarendon Press, 1928.

Paracelsus. *Baderbüchlin Sechs köstliche Tractat, Armen vnd Reychen, Nutzlich vnd Notwendig, von Wasserbädern*. Mülhausen: Schmid, 1562, urn:nbn:de:bvb:12-bsb00086379-9.

Paracelsus. *Von dem Bad Pfeffers, Gelegen in ober Schweitz*, Von *seinen tugenten*. 1535. Straßburg: Müller, 1571. urn:nbn:de:bvb:12-bsb10191353-9.

Paré, Ambroise. "Of the Faculties of Simple Medicines." In *The Workes of that Famous Chirurgion Ambrose Parey*. Translated by Thomas Johnson, 1027–83. London: Th. Cotes and R. Young, 1634.

Paré, Ambroise. *Des Monstres, Des Prodiges, Des Voyages*. 1585. Reprint, Paris: Livre Club, 1964.

Peacham, Henry. *The Period of Mourning, with Nuptiall Hymnes: In Honor of this Happy Marriage*. London: T.S., 1613.

Pepys, Samuel. *The Diary of Samuel Pepys*. Edited by Harry B. Wheatley. London: George Bell, 1900.

Petrarch. *The Complete Canzoniere*. Translated by A.S. Kline. Poetry in Translation, 2001. PDF e-book.

Piemontese, Alessio. *The Secretes of the Reverende Maister Alexis of Piemovnt*. 1558. Amsterdam: Theatrum Orbis Terrarum, 1975.

Porta, Giambattista della. *Natural Magick*. London: Thomas Young and Samuel Speed, 1658.

Prynne, William. *The Unlovelinesse, of Love- lockes. Or, A Summarie Discourse, Proouing: the Wearing, and Nourishing of a Locke, or Loue-locke, to be Altogether Vnseemely, and Vnlawfull vnto Christians*. London, 1628.

Quarles, Francis. *Argalus and Parthenia: The Argument of the History*. London: John Marriot, 1629.

Read, Alexander. *The Chirurgicall Lectures of Tumors and Ulcers*. London: J[ohn] H[aviland], 1635.

Recipe Books Digital Collection. Wellcome Library, London.

Remmelin, Johann. *Ferinae Weltzheimenses*. Augsburg: Michelspacher, 1619.

Kingsford, C.L., ed. *Report on the Manuscripts of Lord de L'Isle & Dudley Preserved at Penshurst Place*, vol. 2, 99–619. London: Royal Commission on Historical Manuscripts, 1934.

Reusner, Hieronymus. *Eygentliche und gründtliche Beschreibung ... Minerischen Wildtbadts ... Wembdingen, 1618*. Reprint, Augsburg: Morhardt, 1627.

Rich, Barnabe. *The Honestie of This Age*. London: T.A., 1615.

Riolan, Jean. *A Sure Guide, or, The Best and Nearest Way to Physick and Chyrurgery*. Translated by Nicholas Culpeper. London: Peter Cole, 1657.

Rodocanachi, E. *La femme italienne à l' époque de la Renaissance*. Paris, 1907.

Romei, Annibale. *The Courtiers Academie*. London: Valentine Sims, 1598.

Rudyerd, Benjamin. *Le Prince d'Amour, or the Prince of Love. With a Collection of Several Ingenious Poems and Songs by the Wits of the Age*. London: William Leake, 1660.

Rueda, Lope de. *Comedia llamada Eufemia*. In *Las cuatro comedias*. Edited by Alfredo Hermenegildo, 73–127. Madrid: Cátedra, 2001.

Sachs, Hans, and Jost Amman. *Eygentliche Beschreibung aller Stände auff Erden*. Frankfurt, 1568.

Schmidt, Benno. "1. Frankfurter Zunfturkunden bis zum Jahre 1612." In *VI. Frankfurter Amts- und Zunfturkunden bis zum Jahre 1612*. Frankfurt: Veröffentlichungen der Historischen Kommission der Stadt Frankfurt am Main, 1914.

Schmid, Joseph. *Speculum chirurgicum*. Augsburg: Hermsdorff, 1675. urn:nbn:de:bvb:12-bsb10888179-1.

Schorer, Christoph. *Memminger Chronick, Oder Kurtze Erzehlung vieler denckwürdigen Sachen ... von Ao. 369. biß 1660*. Ulm: Balthasar Kuehn: 1660. urn:nbn:de:bvb:12-bsb10003306-2.

Scultetus, Bartholomäus. *New und Alter Römischer Allmanach und Schreib Kalender auffs Jahr Chri. MDCV: Gericht auff d. New Corrigirte und Alte Rechnung ...*. Prague: Straus, 1605. urn:nbn:de:bvb:12-bsb10392683-6.

Shakespeare, William. *Titus Andronicus*. In *William Shakespeare: The Complete Works*. Edited by Stanley Wells and Gary Taylor, 125–52. Oxford: Clarendon Press, 1988.

Shakespeare, William. *Macbeth*. In *The Riverside Shakespeare*. Edited by G. Blakemore Evans et. al., 1355–90. 2nd ed. Boston, MA: Houghton Mifflin, 1996.

Shakespeare, William. *Antony and Cleopatra*. In *The Norton Shakespeare*. Edited by Stephen Greenblatt et al., 2619–708. New York: Norton, 1997.

Shakespeare, William. *Much Ado About Nothing*. In *The Riverside Shakespeare*. Edited by G. Blakemore Evans et. al., 361–98. 2nd ed. Boston, MA: Houghton-Mifflin, 1997.

Shakespeare, William. "Sonnets." In *The Norton Shakespeare*. Edited by Stephen Greenblatt et. al., 1923–76. New York: Norton, 1997.

Shakespeare, William. "Venus and Adonis." In *The Norton Shakespeare*. Edited by Stephen Greenblatt et. al., 601–34. New York: Norton, 1997.

Sharp, Jane. *The Midwives Book*. London: Simon Miller, 1671.

Shirley, James. *Poems, &c. by James Shirley*. London: Humphrey Moseley, 1646.

Sidney, Sir Philip. "Astrophil and Stella." In *The Oxford Authors: Sir Philip Sidney*. Edited by Katherine Duncan-Jones, 153–211. New York: Oxford University Press, 1989.

Sidney, Sir Philip. *Defence of Poesie*. 1595. Eugene, OR: Renascence Editions, 1995. PDF e-book.

Sidney, Sir Philip. *The Countess of Pembroke's Arcadia*. 1590. Eugene, OR: Renascence Editions, 2005. PDF e-book.

Smith, William. *Chloris*. 1596. Eugene, OR: Renascence Editions, 2006. PDF e-book.

Spenser, Edmund. *Amoretti and Epithalamion*. 1595. Eugene, OR: Renascence Editions, 1996. PDF e-book.

Spenser. *The Faerie Queene*. 1596. Eugene, OR: Renascence Editions, 1995. PDF e-book.

Staiger, Clara. "Verzaichnus und beschreibung: wenn ich schwester Clara Staigerin geborn, in das closter komen nd was sich die jar fürnem begeben und verloffen." In *Eichstätt im Schwedenkriege. Tagebuch der Augustinernonne Clara Staiger, Priorin des Klosters Mariastein über die Kriegsjahre 1631 bis 1650*. Edited by Joseph Schlecht. Eichstätt: Brönner'sche Buchhandlung, 1889.

Staiger, Klara. "Verzeichnis und beschreibung wenn ich S[chwester] Clara Staigerin geborn. Jn das kloster komen Vnd was sich die jar fürnemns begeben. Vnd verloffen." In *Klara Staigers Tagebuch. Aufzeichnungen während des Dreißigjährigen Krieges im Kloster Mariastein bei Eichstätt*. Edited by Ortrun Fina. Regensburg: Pustet, 1981.

Stowe, John. *The Annales of England: Faithfully Collected out of the most Autenticall Authors, Records, and Other Monuments of Antiquitie*. London: Eliot's Court Press and F. Kingston, 1600.

Stubbes, Phillip. *The Anatomie of Abuses*. London: Richard Jones, 1583.

Stubbes, Phillip. *The Second Part of the Anatomie of Abuses*. London: William Wright, 1583.

Stubbes, Phillip. *A Chrystal Glasse for Christian Women*. London: John Wright, 1632.

Temple, Peter. *Medical, Cookery and Other Recipes*. Stowe MS 1077. London: British Library, 1656.

The Problemes of Aristotle. London: Arn. Hatfield, 1607.

Thornton, Alice. *The Autobiography of Mrs. Alice Thornton, of East Newton, Co. York*. Durham: Surtees Society, 1875.

Thurgood, Rose. "A Lecture of Repentance." In *Scripture Women*. Edited by Naomi Baker, 1–27. Nottingham: Trent Editions, 2005.

Tottel, Richard, ed. *Songes and Sonettes, written by the right honorable Lorde Henry Haward late Earle of Surrey, and other*. London: Richard Tottel, 1557.

Tuke, Thomas. *A Treatise against Painting and Tincturing*. London: Edward Merchant, 1616.

Vasari, Giorgio. *The Lives of the Artists*. Translated by George Bull. New York: Penguin, 1965.

Verney, Frances Parthenope. *Memoirs of the Verney Family During the Civil War*. London: Longmans, Green, and Co., 1892.

Vicary, Thomas. *A Profitable Treatise of the Anatomy of Man's Body*. London: Henry Bamforde, 1577.

Vicary, Thomas. *The English Mans Treasure*. London: Thomas Creede, 1613.

Vigo, Giovanni. "Of Additions." In *The Whole Worke of that Famous Chirurgion Master John Vigo*. Translated by men skillful in that art, 350–79. London: Thomas East, 1586.

Vives, Juan Luis. *Instruction of a Christen Woman*. London: Thomas Berthelet, 1541.

Wager, Lewis. *The Life and Repentaunce of Marie Magdalene*. 1566. Edited by Frederick Ives. Chicago: University of Chicago Press, 1902.

Waite, Gary K., ed. *The Anabaptist Writings of David Joris, 1535–1543*. Scottdale, PA: Herald Press, 1994.

Wall, Thomas. *God's Holy Order in Nature, Which Man and Woman were Created in, Truly Stated and Explained*. London: Printed for the author, and sold by William Marshal, 1690.

Weever, John. *Epigrammes in the Oldest Cut, and Newest Fashion*. London: V. S[ims], 1599.

Weigel, Marsilius. *Beschreibung des Vortrefflichen … Warmen Bads Emß*. Frankfurt: Beyer, 1627.

Wilson, Henry, and James Caufield. *The Book of Wonderful Characters: Memoirs and Anecdotes of Remarkable and Eccentric Persons in All Ages and Countries*. London: John Camden Hotten, [1869?].
Winston, Thomas. *Anatomy Lectures at Gresham College*. London: R. Daniel, 1659.
Winter, Salvator. *A Pretious Treasury: or a New Dispensatory*. London: Tho. Harper, 1649.
Wolder, David, and Martin Luther. *Biblia Sacra Graece, Latine & Germanice: Evangelia Quatuor*. Hamburg: Jacobus Lucius, 1596.
Wright, Leonard. *A Summons for Sleepers*. London: J. Wolfe, 1589.
Wroth, Lady Mary. *The Countesse of Mountgomeries Urania*. London: John Marriot and John Grismand, 1621.
Zangmaister, Johann P. *Instruction Vonn Arth, Aigenschafft, und nutzlichem Gebrauch deß köstlichen Badwassers, nahend bey Saltzburg gelegen*. Salzburg: Kürner, 1601.

Secondary Sources

Akkerman, Nadine, and Birgit Houben, eds. *The Politics of Female Households: Ladies-in-Waiting Across Early Modern Europe*. Leiden: Brill, 2014.
Arnold, Janet. *Patterns of Fashion: The Cut and Construction of Clothes for Men and Women 1560–1620*. Rev. ed. New York: Macmillian, 1986.
Arnold, Janet. *Queen Elizabeth's Wardrobe Unlock'd*. Leeds: W.S. Maney and Son Ltd., 2001.
Ashelford, Jane. *A Visual History of Costume: The Sixteenth Century*. London: B.T. Batsford, 1983.
Ashelford, Jane. *The Art of Dress: Clothing and Society 1500–1914*. New York: Abrams, 1996.
Avcıoğlu, Nebahat, Allison Sherman, and Deborah Howard, eds. *Artistic Practices and Cultural Transfer in Early Modern Italy: Essays in Honour of Deborah Howard*. Farnham: Ashgate, 2015.
Bailey, Amanda. *Flaunting: Style and the Subversive Male Body in Renaissance England*. Toronto: University of Toronto Press, 2007.
Baker, Moira P. "'The Uncanny Stranger on Display': The Female Body in Sixteenth- and Seventeenth-Century Love Poetry." *South Atlantic Review* 56, no. 2 (1991): 7–25.
Baldwin, F. *Sumptuary Legislation and Personal Regulation in England*. Johns Hopkins Studies in Historical and Political Science 44. Baltimore: Johns Hopkins University Press, 1926.
Banks, Ingrid. *Hair Matters: Beauty, Power, and Black Women's Consciousness*. New York: New York University Press, 2000.
Barber, Paul. *Vampires, Burial, and Death: Folklore and Reality*. New Haven, CT: Yale University Press, 2010.
Bartky, Sandra Lee. *Femininity and Domination: Studies in the Phenomenology of Oppression*. New York: Routledge, 1990.
Bartlett, R. "Symbolic Meanings of Hair in the Middle Ages." *Transactions of the Royal Historical Society* 4 (1994): 43–60.
Baskins, Cristelle L. *Cassone Painting, Humanism, and Gender in Early Modern Italy*. Cambridge: Cambridge University Press, 1998.
Bell, Ilona. *Elizabethan Women and the Poetry of Courtship*. Cambridge: Cambridge University Press, 1998.
Bell, Quentin. *On Human Finery*. London: Hogarth Press, 1947.
Bhabha, Homi K. *The Location of Culture*. New York: Routledge, 1994 (2002).
Biddle-Perry, Geraldine, and Sarah Cheang. "Introduction: Thinking about Hair." In *Hair: Styling, Culture and Fashion*. Edited by Geraldine Biddle-Perry and Sarah Cheang, 3–12. London: Bloomsbury, 2008.

Biow, Douglas. *The Culture of Cleanliness in Renaissance Italy*. Ithaca, NY: Cornell University Press, 2006.

Biow, Douglas. *On the Importance of Being an Individual in Renaissance Italy: Men, their Professions, and their Beards*. Philadelphia: University of Pennsylvania Press, 2015.

Birth, Kevin. "Calendars: Representational Homogeneity and Heterogeneous Time." *Time & Society* 22 (2013): 216–36.

Borgemeister, Bettina. *Die Stadt und ihr Wald: Eine Untersuchung zur Waldgeschichte der Städte Göttingen und Hannover vom 13. bis zum 18. Jahrhundert*. Hannover: Hahn, 2005.

Bourdieu, Pierre. *Language and Symbolic Power*. Edited by John B. Thompson. Translated by Gino Raymond and Matthew Adamson. Cambridge, MA: Harvard University Press, 1991.

Braunstein, P. "Toward Intimacy: The Fourteenth and Fifteenth Centuries." In *A History of Private Life*. Edited by G. Duby. Translated by A. Goldhammer, 2: 535–630. Cambridge: Belknap Press. 1988.

Bridgeman, Jane. "Dates, Dress, and Dosso: Some Problems of Chronology." In *Dosso's Fate: Painting and Court Culture in Renaissance Italy*. Edited by Luisa Ciammitti, Steven R. Ostrow, and Salvatore Settis, 176–200. Los Angeles: The Getty Research Institute for the History of Art and the Humanities.

Bridgeman, Jane. "'Troppi belli e troppo eccellenti': Observations on Dress in the Work of Piero della Francesca." In *The Cambridge Companion to Piero della Francesca*. Edited by Jeryldene Wood, 76–90. Cambridge: Cambridge University Press, 2002.

Broomhall, Susan. *Women's Medical Work in Early Modern France*. Manchester: Manchester University Press, 2004.

Brusati, Celeste. *Artifice and Illusion: The Art and Writing of Samuel van Hoogstraten*. Chicago: University of Chicago Press, 1995.

Bryer, Robin. *The History of Hair: Fashion and Fantasy Down the Ages*. London: Philip Wilson, 2000.

Büchner, Robert. *Im städtischen Bad vor 500 Jahren: Badhaus, Bader und Badegäste im alten Tirol*. Vienna: Böhlau, 2014.

Burke, J. "Did Renaissance Women Remove their Body Hair?" *Jill Burke's Blog*. December 9, 2012. https://renresearch.wordpress.com/2012/12/09/did-renaissancewomen-remove-their-body-hair/ (Accessed May 17, 2016).

Burkhardt, Johannes. "Altökonomik und Handelsliteratur in den Augsburger Druckmedien." In *Augsburger Buchdruck und Verlagswesen von den Anfängen bis zur Gegenwart*. Edited by Helmut Gier, Johannes Janota and Hans Jörg Künast, 423–45. Wiesbaden: Harrassowitz, 1997.

Burns, Robert I., ed. *Emperor of Culture: Alfonso X the Learned of Castile and his Thirteenth-Century Renaissance*. Philadelphia: University of Pennsylvania Press, 1990.

Butazzi, Grazietta. "Il modello spagnolo nella moda europea." In *Le Trame della moda*. Edited by Anna Giulia Cavagna and Grazietta Butazzi, 80–94. Rome: Bulzoni, 1995.

Butler, Judith. *Bodies that Matter: On the Discursive Limits of Sex*. New York: Routledge, 1993.

Byrd, Ayana B., and Lori L. Tharps. *Hair Story: Untangling the Roots of Black Hair in America*. New York: St. Martin's Press, 2001.

Cabré, Montserrat. "Keeping Beauty Secrets in Early Modern Iberia." In *Secrets and Knowledge in Medicine and Science, 1500 – 1800*. Edited by Elaine Leong and Alisha Rankin, 167–90. Farnham: Ashgate, 2011.

Campbell, Erin J. "Prophets, Saints, and Matriarchs: Portraits of Old Women in Early Modern Italy." *Renaissance Quarterly* 63 (2010): 807–49.

Carney, Judith A. "'With Graines in Her Hair': Rice in Colonial Brazil." *Slavery and Abolition* 25, no. 1 (2004): 1–27.
Cavallo, Sandra. *Artisans of the Body in Early Modern Italy: Identities, Families and Masculinities*. Manchester: Manchester University Press, 2007.
Cavallo, Sandra, and Tessa Storey. *Healthy Living in Late Renaissance Italy*. Oxford: Oxford University Press, 2013.
Chamberland, Celeste. "Honor, Brotherhood, and the Corporate Ethos of London's Barber-Surgeons' Company, 1570–1640." *Journal of the History of Medicine and Allied Sciences* 64, no. 3 (2009): 300–32.
Child, Theodore. *Wimples and Crisping Pins: Being Studies in Coiffure and Ornaments of Women*. New York: Harper and Brothers, 1895.
Clark, Stuart. *Thinking with Demons: The Idea of Witchcraft in Early Modern Europe*. Oxford: Oxford University Press, 1997.
Cockayne, E. *Hubbub: Filth, Noise & Stench in England 1600–1770*. New Haven, CT: Yale University Press, 2007.
Condra, Jill, ed. *The Greenwood Encyclopedia of Clothing Through World History: 1501–1800*. Westport, CN: Greenwood Press, 2008.
Coomans, Janna, and Guy Geltner. "On the Street and in the Bathhouse: Medieval Galenism in Action? En la calle y en los baños públicos: Â¿galenismo medieval en acción?" *Anuario de Estudios Medievales* 43, no. 1 (2013): 53–82.
Cooper, Tarnya. *Citizen Portrait: Portrait Painting and the Urban Elites of Tudor and Jacobean England and Wales*. New Haven, CT: Yale University Press, 2012.
Cooper, W. "The Tudor Sumptuary Laws." *The English Historical Review* 30 (1915): 433–49.
Corson, Richard. *Fashions in Hair: The First Five Thousand Years*. New York: Hillary House Publishers, 1971.
Courtais, Georgine de. *Women's Headdress and Hairstyles in England from AD 600 to the Present Day*. London: B.T. Batsford, 1973.
Cox-Rearick, Janet. *Splendors of the Renaissance: Princely Attire in Italy; Reconstructions of Historic Costumes from King Studio, Italy*. New York: Art Gallery of the Graduate Center, the City University of New York, 2004.
Crawshaw, Jane Stevens. "Families, Medical Secrets and Public Health in Early Modern Venice." *Renaissance Studies* 28, no. 4 (2014): 597–618.
Cumming, Valerie. *A Visual History of Costume: The Seventeenth Century*. London: B.T. Batsford, 1984.
Cunnington, Phillis, and Anne Buck. *Children's Costume in England: From the Fourteenth Century to the End of the Nineteenth Century*. London: Adam and Charles Black, 1965.
Cunnington, Phillis, and Catherine Lucas. *Occupational Costume in England*. London: Adam & Charles Black, 1967.
Davids, Karel. "Apprenticeship and Guild Control in the Netherlands, c. 1450–1800." In *Learning on the Shop Floor: Historical Perspectives on Apprenticeship*. Edited by Bert De Munck, Steven L. Kaplan, and Hugo Soly, 65–84. New York: Berghahn Books, 2007.
Davids, Karel, and Bert De Munck, eds. *Innovation and Creativity in Late Medieval and Early Modern European Cities*. Farnham: Ashgate, 2014.
Davidson, Jane. *The Witch in Northern European Art, 1470–1750*. Freren: Luca Verlag, 1987.
Dessen, Alan C. "The Body of Stage Directions." *Shakespeare Studies* 29 (2001): 27–35.
DiPasquale, Theresa M. "Donne's Catholic Petrarchans: The Babylonian Captivity of Desire." In *Renaissance Discourses of Desire*. Edited by Claude J. Summers and Ted-Larry Pebworth, 77–92. Columbia: University of Missouri Press, 1993.

Distiller, Natasha. *Desire and Gender in the Sonnet Tradition*. Basingstoke: Palgrave Macmillan, 2008.
Dobranski, Stephen. "Clustering and Curling Locks: The Matter of Hair in *Paradise Lost*." *PMLA* 125 (2010): 337–53.
Drew-Bear, Annette. *Painted Faces on the Renaissance Stage: The Moral Significance of Face-Painting Conventions*. Lewisburg, PA: Bucknell University Press, 1994.
Droz-Emmert, Marguerite. *Catharina van Hemessen Malerin der Renaissance*. Basel: Schwabe, 2004.
Dubrow, Heather. *Echoes of Desire: English Petrarchism and Its Counterdiscourses*. Ithaca, NY: Cornell University Press, 1995.
Eagleton, Terry. *After Theory*. New York: Penguin, 2004.
Van Eck, Caroline, Joris van Gastel, and Elsje van Kessel, eds. *The Secret Lives of Artworks: Exploring the Boundaries between Art and Life*. Leiden: Leiden University Press, 2014.
Emberley, Julia. *Venus and Furs: The Cultural Politics of Fur*. London: I.B. Tauris, 1998.
Enders, Lieselott. "Bader- und Barbiergilden in der frühneuzeitlichen Kurmark." *Jahrbuch für Brandenburgische Landesgeschichte* 59 (2008): 50–71.
Erasmus, Desiderius. *The Praise of Folly*. Translated by Clarence H. Miller. New Haven, CT: Yale University Press, 1979.
Ewing, Elizabeth. *History of Children's Costume*. New York: Scribner, 1977.
Ferragud, Carmel. "Barbers in the Process of Medicalization in the Crown of Aragon during the Late Middle Ages." In *Medieval Urban Identity: Health, Economy and Regulation*. Edited by Flocel Sabaté, 143–65. Newcastle upon Tyne: Cambridge Scholars, 2015.
Festa, Lynn M. "Personal Effects: Wigs and Possessive Individualism in the Long Eighteenth Century." *Eighteenth-Century Life* 29 (2005): 47–90.
Fetters, Ashley. "The New Full Frontal: Has Pubic Hair in America Gone Extinct?" *The Atlantic*, December 13, 2011. http://www.theatlantic.com/health/archive/2011/12/the-new-full-frontal-has-pubic-hair-in-america-gone-extinct/249798/.
Firth, Raymond. *Symbols: Public and Private*. London: Allen & Unwin, 1973.
Fisher, Will. *Materializing Gender in Early Modern English Literature and Culture*. Cambridge: Cambridge University Press, 2006.
Fisher, Will. "The Renaissance Beard: Masculinity in Early Modern England." *Renaissance Quarterly* 54, no. 1 (2001): 155–87.
Flather, Amanda. *Gender and Space in Early Modern England*. Woodbridge: The Royal Historical Society, 2007.
Fleischmann, Peter. "Die Kodifizierung des Handwerksrechts in der Reichsstadt Nürnberg: Entstehung und Folgen." In *Ökonomie und Recht: Historische Entwicklungen in Bayern*. Edited by Christoph Becker, 21–36. Berlin: Lit-Verlag, 2009.
Fletcher, Anthony. *Gender, Sex and Subordination in England, 1500–1800*. New Haven, CT: Yale University Press, 1995.
Flugel, J.C. *The Psychology of Clothes*. London: Hogarth Press, 1950.
Foyster, Elizabeth. "A Laughing Matter? Marital Discord and Gender Control in Seventeenth-Century England." *Rural History* 1, no. 4 (1993): 5–21.
Fra-Molinero, Baltasar. *La imagen de los negros en el teatro del Siglo de Oro*. Madrid: Siglo Veintiuno, 1995.
Freud, Sigmund. "Fetishism." In *On Sexuality*. Vol. 1, *The Pelican Freud Library*. Edited by Angela Richards. Translated by James Strachey. 1977. Reprint, New York: Penguin, 1981.

Frick, Carole Collier. "Cappelli e copricapi nella Firenze del Rinascimento. L'emergere dell'identità sociale attraverso l'abbigliamento." In *Moda e Moderno. Dal Medioevo al Rinascimento*. Edited by Eugenia Paulicelli, 103–28. Rome: Meltemi Press, 2006.

Frickinger, Hermann. "Beiträge zur Medizinalgeschichte der Stadt Nördlingen. Fortsetzung und Schluß." *Jahrbuch d. Historischen Vereins für Nördlingen und Umgebung* 8 (1920/1921): 35–90.

Friedland, Roger. "Looking through the Bushes: The Disappearance of Pubic Hair." *The Huffington Post*, June 13, 2011. http://www.huffingtonpost.com/roger-friedland/women-pubic-hair_b_875465.html.

Friesen, Ilse E. *The Female Crucifix: Images of St. Wilgefortis Since the Middle Ages*. Waterloo, ON: Wilfrid Laurier University Press, 2001.

Fürbeth, Frank. "Adaption gelehrten Wissens für laikale Zwecke in der Bäderheilkunde der frühen Neuzeit." In *Wissenschaftsgeschichte und Geschichte des Wissens im Dialog: Connecting Science and Knowledge*. Edited by Kaspar von Greyerz, Silvia Flubacher, and Philipp Senn, 211–32. Göttingen: V&R unipress, 2013.

Geisweidt, Edward J. "Horticulture of the Head: The Vegetable Life of Hair in Early Modern English Thought." *Early Modern Literary Studies* 19 (2009): 1–24.

Van Gent, Jacqueline. *Magic, Body and the Self in Eighteenth-Century Sweden*. Leiden: E.J. Brill, 2009.

Gopnik, Blake. "Acomocliticism." *Cabinet Magazine* 40 (2010/2011). http://www.cabinetmagazine.org/issues/40/gopnik.php.

Green, Jonathan. *Printing and Prophecy: Prognostication and Media Change, 1450 – 1550*. Ann Arbor: University of Michigan Press, 2012.

Greenblatt, Stephen. "Filthy Rites." *Daedalus* 111 (1982): 1–16.

Greenfield, K. "Sumptuary Law in Nürnberg: A Study in Paternal Government." In *Johns Hopkins University Studies in Historical and Political Science*. Baltimore: Johns Hopkins University Press, 1918.

Griese, Sabine. "Gebrauchsformen und Gebrauchsräume von Einblattdrucken des 15. und frühen 16. Jahrhunderts." In *Einblattdrucke des 15. und frühen 16. Jahrhunderts: Probleme, Perspektiven, Fallstudien*. Edited by Volker Honemann, Sabine Griese, Falk Eisermann, and Marcus Ostermann, 179–208. Tübingen: Niemeyer, 2000.

Griffiths, Paul. *Youth and Authority: Formative Experiences in England 1560–1640*. Oxford: Clarendon Press, 1996.

Gurevich, Aron. *Medieval Popular Culture: Problems of Belief and Perception*. Translated by János M. Back and Paul A. Hollingsworth. Cambridge: Cambridge University Press, 1988.

Hammons, Pamela S. *Gender, Sexuality, and Material Objects in English Renaissance Verse*. Farnham: Ashgate, 2010.

Hedley, Jane. *Power in Verse: Metaphor and Metonymy in the Renaissance Lyric*. University Park: Pennsylvania State University Press, 1988.

Heger, Hedwig. *Thomas Murner Mönch, Dichter, Gelehrter*. Karlsruhe: Badische Bibliotheksgesellschaft, 1983.

Hendler, Sefy. "*Pelo sopra pelo*: Sculpting Hair and Beards as a Reflection of Artistic Excellence During the Renaissance." *Sculpture Journal* 24, no. 1 (2015): 7–21.

Hendricks, Margo. "Race: A Renaissance Category?" In *A Companion to English Renaissance Literature and Culture*. Edited by Michael Hattaway. Oxford: Blackwell Publishing, 2002. Blackwell Reference Online.

Henkel, Nikolaus. "Schauen und Erinnern: Überlegungen zu Intentionalität und Appellstruktur illustrierter Einblattdrucke." In *Einblattdrucke des 15. und frühen 16. Jahrhunderts:

Probleme, Perspektiven, Fallstudien. Edited by Volker Honemann, Sabine Griese, Falk Eisermann, and Marcus Ostermann, 209–43. Tübingen: Niemeyer, 2000.

Herbert, Amanda E. *Female Alliances: Gender, Identity, and Friendship in Early Modern Britain.* New Haven, CT: Yale University Press, 2014.

Hess, A. "For Women, a New Look Down Under." *New York Times Magazine*, December 1, 2013. http://tmagazine.blogs.nytimes.com/2013/12/01/on-beauty-for-women-a-new-look-down-under/?_r=0.

Hill, Ruth. "Entering and Exiting Blackness: A Color Controversy in Eighteenth-Century Spain." *Journal of Spanish Cultural Studies* 10, no. 1 (2009): 43–58.

Hill Collins, Patricia. *Black Feminist Thought: Knowledge, Consciousness, and the Politics of Empowerment.* New York: Routledge, 1990.

Hiltebeitel, Alf, and Barbara D. Miller, eds. *Hair: Its Power and Meaning in Asian Cultures.* Albany: State University of New York Press, 1998.

Hoffmann, Robert. "Die Augsburger Bäder und das Handwerk der Bader." *Zeitschrift des Historischen Vereins für Schwaben und Neuburg* 12 (1885): 1–35.

Hollander, Anne. *Seeing Through Clothes.* New York: Viking, 1978.

Hoppe, Brigitte. *Das Kräuterbuch des Hieronymus Bock.* Stuttgart: Hiersemann, 1969.

Horowitz, Elliott. "The New World and the Changing Face of Europe." *The Sixteenth Century Journal* 28 (1997): 1181–201.

Hunt, A. *Governance of the Consuming Passions: A History of Sumptuary Law.* New York: St. Martin's Press, 1996.

Jegel, August. "Bäder, Bader und Badesitten im alten Nürnberg." *Reichsstadt Nürnberg Altdorf und Hersbruck* 6 (1954): 21–63.

Johnston, Mark Albert. "Bearded Women in Early Modern England." *Studies in English Literature, 1500–1900* 47 (2007): 1–28.

Johnston, Mark Albert. "'To What Bawdy House Doth Your Maister Belong?': Barbers, Bawds, and Vice in the Early Modern London Barbershop." In *Masculinity and the Metropolis of Vice, 1550–1650.* Edited by Amanda Bailey and Roze Hentschell, 115–35. New York: Palgrave Macmillan, 2010.

Johnston, Mark Albert. *Beard Fetish in Early Modern England: Sex, Gender, and Registers of Value.* London: Routledge, 2011; and Farnham: Ashgate, 2011.

Jolly, P. "Pubics and Privates: Body Hair in Late Medieval Art." In *The Meanings of Nudity in Medieval Art.* Edited by S. Lindquist, 183–206. Farnham: Ashgate, 2012.

Jolly, Penny Howell. "The Fashionable Man." In *Hair: Untangling a Social History.* Edited by Penny Howell Jolly, 20–6. Saratoga Springs, NY: The Frances Young Tang Teaching Museum, 2004.

Jones, M. *The Secret Middle Ages.* Westport, CT: Praeger, 2002.

Katritzky, M.A. "'A Wonderfull Monster Borne in Germany': Hairy Girls in Medieval and Early Modern German Book, Court and Performance Culture." *German Life and Letters* 67 (2014): 467–80.

Kieckhefer, Richard. *Magic in the Middle Ages.* Cambridge: Cambridge University Press, 1989, 2000.

Killerby, Catherine Kovesi. *Sumptuary Law in Italy: 1200–1500.* Oxford: Clarendon Press, 2002.

Kinzelbach, Annemarie. "Zur Sozial-und Alltagsgeschichte eines Handwerks in der frühen Neuzeit: 'Wundärzte' und ihre Patienten in Ulm." *Ulm und Oberschwaben* 49 (1994): 111–44.

Kinzelbach, Annemarie. "'Böse Blattern' oder 'Franzosenkrankheit': Syphilis-konzept, Kranke und die Genese des Krankenhauses in oberdeutschen Reichsstädten der frühen Neuzeit." In

Neue Wege in der Seuchengeschichte. Edited by Martin Dinges and Thomas Schlich, 43–69. Stuttgart: Steiner, 1995.

Kinzelbach, Annemarie. *Gesundbleiben, Krankwerden, Armsein in der Frühneuzeitlichen Gesellschaft: Gesunde und Kranke in den Reichsstädten Überlingen und Ulm, 1500–1700*. Stuttgart: Steiner, 1995.

Kinzelbach, Annemarie. "Bordell, Gesundbrunnen, alltäglicher Luxus? Bäder und Badende-ein Gang durch die Jahrhunderte." *Damals* 38, no. 4 (2006): 60–7.

Kinzelbach, Annemarie. "Infection, Contagion, and Public Health in Late Medieval and Early Modern German Imperial Towns." *Journal of the History of Medicine and Allied Sciences* 61 (2006): 369–89.

Kinzelbach, Annemarie, and Patrick Sturm. "Der Siechenhauskomplex vor den Toren Nördlingens: Entwicklung, Funktion und bauliche Gestalt vom 13. bis zum 18. Jahrhundert." *Jahrbuch d. Historischen Vereins für Nördlingen und Umgebung* 33 (2011): 25–54.

Kinzelbach, Annemarie. "Erudite and Honoured Artisans? Performers of Body Care and Surgery in Early Modern German Towns." *Social History of Medicine* 27 (2014): 668–88.

Kinzelbach, Annemarie. *Chirurgen und Chirurgiepraktiken. Wundärzte als Reichsstadtbürger, 16. bis 18. Jahrhundert*. Mainz: Donata Kinzelbach, 2016.

Köhler, Carl. *A History of Costume*. Translated by Alexander K. Dallas. Philadelphia: David McKay Company, 1928.

Korhonen, Anu. *Silmän ilot. Kauneuden kulttuurihistoriaa uuden ajan alussa*. Jyväskylä: Atena, 2005.

Korhonen, Anu. "Strange Things Out of Hair: Baldness and Masculinity in Early Modern England." *Sixteenth Century Journal* 41, no. 2 (2010): 371–91.

Kremmer, Susanne, and Hans E. Specker. *Repertorium der Policeyordnungen der Frühen Neuzeit: Reichsstädte 3: Ulm*. Frankfurt: Klostermann, 2007.

Krier, Theresa M. "Generations of Blazons: Psychoanalysis and the Song of Songs in the Amoretti." *Texas Studies in Literature and Language* 40, no. 3 (1998): 293–327.

Langner, Lawrence. *The Importance of Wearing Clothes*. New York: Hastings House Publishers, 1959.

Laqueur, Thomas. *Making Sex: Body and Sex from the Greeks to Freud*. Cambridge, MA: Harvard University Press, 1992.

Lawrence, Jeremy. "Black Africans in Renaissance Spanish Literature." In *Black Africans in Renaissance Europe*. Edited by T.F. Earle and Kate Lowe, 70–93. Cambridge: Cambridge University Press, 2005.

Leach, Edmund. "Magical Hair."*Journal of the Royal Anthropological Institute of Great Britain and Ireland* 88 (1958): 147–64.

Le Gall, Jean-Marie. *Un Idéal Masculin? Barbes et moustaches XVe–XVIIIe siècles*. Paris: Payot, 2011.

Leong, Elaine. "Making Medicines in the Early Modern Household." *Bulletin of the History of Medicine* 82 (2008): 145–68.

Levi-Pisetzky, Rosita. *Il costume e la moda nella società italiana*. Turin: Giulio Einaudi editore, 1978.

Lewis, Bernard. *Race and Slavery in the Middle East: An Historical Enquiry*. Oxford: Oxford University Press, 1990.

Liewert, Anne. *Die meteorologische Medizin des Corpus Hippocraticum*. Berlin: de Gruyter, 2015.

Lightbown, R. *Piero della Francesca*. New York: Abbeville Press, 1992.

Loomba, Ania. *Shakespeare, Race and Colonialism*. Oxford: Oxford University Press, 2002.
Low, Anthony. "Thomas Carew: Patronage, Family, and New-Model Love." In *Renaissance Discourses of Desire*. Edited by Claude J. Summers and Ted-Larry Pebworth, 93–106. Columbia: University of Missouri Press, 1993.
Lowe, Scott. *Hair*. New York: Bloomsbury Academic Press, 2016.
Lurie, Alison. *The Language of Clothes*. New York: Random House, 1981.
MacLean, Hugh, ed. *Ben Jonson and the Cavalier Poets*. New York: W.W. Norton & Co., 1974.
Martin, Alfred. *Deutsches Badewesen in vergangenen Tagen: Nebst einem Beitrage zur Geschichte der deutschen Wasserheilkunde*. Jena: Diederichs, 1906.
Martínez, María Elena. "The Language, Genealogy, and Classification of 'Race'." In *Race and Classification: The Case of Mexican America*. Edited by Ilona Katzew and Susan Deans-Smith, 25–42. Stanford, CA: Stanford University Press, 2009.
Marx, Karl. *Capital: A Critique of Political Economy*. Vol. 1. Edited by Frederick Engels. Translated by Samuel Moore and Edward Aveling. 1906. Reprint, London: Lawrence and Wishart, 2003.
Maurer, Rudolf. *Baden, schröpfen, amputieren: Die Geschichte der Bader in Baden bei Wien*. Vienna: Verl.-Haus der Ärzte, 2004.
Mayer, Johannes G. "Die Wahrheit über den *Gart der Gesundheit* (1485) und sein Weiterleben in den Kräuterbüchern der Frühen Neuzeit." In *A Passion for Plants: Materia Medica and Botany in Scientific Networks from the 16th to 18th Centuries*. Edited by Sabine Anagnostou, Florike Egmond, and Christoph Friedrich, 119–28. Stuttgart: Wissenschaftliche Verlagsgesellschaf, 2011.
Miller, Matthias. "Wissenschaftlicher Kommentar zu Cod. Pal. germ. 192." Universitäts Bibliothek Heidelberg, 2005. http://digi.ub.uni-heidelberg.de/diglit/cpg192.
Milliken, Roberta. *Ambiguous Locks: An Iconology of Hair in Medieval Art and Literature*. Jefferson, NC: McFarland and Co., 2012.
Mills, Charles W. *The Social Contract*. Ithaca, NY: Cornell University Press, 1999.
Morris, D. *The Naked Woman: A Study of the Female Body*. New York: Macmillan, 2007.
Moseley-Christian, Michelle. "From Page to Print: The Transformation of the 'Wild Woman' in Early Modern Northern Engravings." *Word & Image* 27 no. 4 (2011): 429–42.
Murray, Pauli. "The Liberation of Black Women." In *Voices of the New Feminism*. Edited by Mary Lou Thompson, 87–102. Boston, MA: Beacon, 1970.
Muzzarelli, M. "Reconciling the Privilege of a Few with the Common Good: Sumptuary Laws in Medieval and Early Modern Europe." *Journal of Medieval and Early Modern Studies* 39 (2009): 597–619.
Nicholl, C. *The Lodger Shakespeare: His Life on Silver Street*. New York: Viking, 2008.
Norris, H. *Costume & Fashion: The Tudors*. Vol. 3. New York: E.P. Dutton and Co. 1938.
O'Callaghan, Joseph F. *The Learned King: The Reign of Alfonso X of Castile*. Philadelphia: University of Pennsylvania Press, 1993.
Ogilvie, Sheilagh, Markus Küpker, and Janine Maegraith. "Household Debt in Early Modern Germany: Evidence from Personal Inventories." *Journal of Economic History* 72 (2012): 134–67.
Oldstone-Moore, Christopher. *Of Beards and Men: The Revealing History of Facial Hair*. Chicago: University of Chicago Press, 2015.
Omi, Michael, and Howard Winant, eds. *Racial Formation in the United States: From the 1960s to the 1980s*. New York: Routledge, 1989.

Otis, Leah L. *Prostitution in Medieval Society: The History of an Urban Institution in Languedoc.* Chicago: University of Chicago Press, 1985.

Park, Katharine. "Natural Particulars: Medical Epistemology, Practice, and the Literature of Healing Springs." In *Natural Particulars: Nature and the Disciplines in Renaissance Europe.* Edited by Anthony Grafton and Nancy G. Siraisi, 347–67. Cambridge, MA: MIT Press, 1999.

Parker, Tom W.N. *Proportional Form in the Sonnets of the Sidney Circle.* Oxford: Clarendon Press, 1998.

Payne, B., G. Winakor, and J. Farrell-Beck. *The History of Costume from Ancient Mesopotamia Through the Twentieth Century.* New York: Harper Collins, 1992.

Pelling, Margaret. "Appearance and Reality: Barber-Surgeons, the Body and Disease." In *London 1500–1700: The Making of the Metropolis.* Edited by A.L. Beier and Roger Finlay, 82–112. London: Longman, 1986.

Pelling, Margaret. "Apprenticeship, Health and Social Cohesion in Early Modern London." *History Workshop* 37, no. 1 (1994): 33–56.

Pelling, Margaret. *The Common Lot: Sickness, Medical Occupations, and the Urban Poor in Early Modern England: Essays.* London: Longman, 1998.

Pelling, Margaret. "Barber-Surgeons' Guilds and Ordinances in Early Modern British Towns—the Story so Far." *The Medical World of Early Modern England, Wales and Ireland, 1500–1715: Working Paper,* Centre for Medical History, University of Exeter, 2014, http://practitioners.exeter.ac.uk/wp-content/uploads/2014/11/Pelling_BarberSurgeonsOrds-2.pdf.

Phillips, Kim M. "Masculinities and the Medieval Sumptuary Laws." *Gender & History* 19 (2007): 22–42.

Piedra, José. "The Black Stud's Spanish Birth." *Callaloo* 16, no. 4 (Autumn, 1993): 820–46.

Pollock, Linda. *With Faith and Physic: The Life of a Tudor Gentlewoman Lady Grace Mildmay, 1552–1620.* New York: St. Martin's Press, 1995.

Pomata, Gianna. *La Promessa di Guarigione: Malati e Curatori in Antico Regime.* Rome: Laterza, 1994.

Powell M., and J. Roach. "Big Hair." *Eighteenth-Century Studies* 38, no. 1 (2004): 79–99.

Rákóczi, Katalin. "Eine 'Badenfahrt' im 16. Jahrhundert." In *"Ohne Wasser ist ein Heil": Medizinische und kulturelle Aspekte der Nutzung von Wasser.* Edited by Sylvelyn Hähner-Rombach, 83–92. Stuttgart: Steiner, 2005.

Rankin, Alisha. "Exotic Materials and Treasured Knowledge: The Valuable Legacy of Noblewomen's Remedies in Early Modern Germany." *Renaissance Studies* 28, no. 4 (2014): 533–55.

Rawcliffe, Carole. *Urban Bodies: Communal Health in Late Medieval English Towns and Cities.* Woodbridge: Boydell Press, 2013.

Régnier-Bohler, Danielle. "Imagining the Self." In *A History of Private Life: Revelations of the Medieval World.* Edited by Georges Duby, 311–93. Cambridge, MA: Belknap Press, 1985.

Rogers, Mary. "The Decorum of Women's Beauty: Trissino, Firenzuola, Luigini and the Representation of Women in Sixteenth-Century Painting." *Renaissance Studies* 2, no. 1 (1988): 47–88.

Rooks, Noliwe M. *Hair Raising: Beauty, Culture, and African American Women.* New Brunswick, NJ: Rutgers University Press, 1997.

Rosenthal, A. "Raising Hair." *Eighteenth-Century Studies* 38, no. 1 (2004): 1–16.

Rossiaud, Jacques. *La prostitution médiévale.* Paris: Flammarion, 1988.

Rubin, Patricia. "Understanding Renaissance Portraiture." In *The Renaissance Portrait from Donatello to Bellini.* Edited by Dale Tucker and Margaret Aspinwall, 2–25. New York: Metropolitan Museum of Art, 2011.

Ruggiero, Guido. *Binding Passions: Tales of Magic, Marriage, and Power at the End of the Renaissance*. New York: Oxford University Press, 1993.

Sander, Sabine. *Handwerkschirurgen. Sozialgeschichte einer verdrängten Berufsgruppe*. Göttingen: Vandenhoeck & Ruprecht, 1989.

Sander, Sabine. "Bader und Barbiere." In *Lexikon des alten Handwerks. Vom Spätmittelalter bis ins 20. Jahrhundert*. Edited by Reinhold Reith, 17–22. Munich: Beck, 1990.

Schlegelmilch, Sabine. "Vom Nutzen des Nebensächlichen-Paratexte in den Kalendern des Arztes Johannes Magirus (1615–1697)." In *Astronomie-Literatur-Volksaufklärung: Der Schreibkalender der Frühen Neuzeit mit seinen Text- und Bildbeigaben*. Edited by Klaus-Dieter Herbst, 393–411. Bremen: Ed. Lumière, 2012.

Schoenfeldt, Michael C. *Bodies and Selves in Early Modern England: Physiology and Inwardness in Spenser, Shakespeare, Herbert, and Milton*. Cambridge: Cambridge University Press, 1999.

Schulz, Knut, and Christiane Schuchard. *Handwerker deutscher Herkunft und ihre Bruderschaften im Rom der Renaissance: Darstellung und ausgewählte Quellen*. Rome: Herder, 2005.

Shepard, Alexandra. *Meanings of Manhood in Early Modern England*. Oxford: Oxford University Press, 2003.

Sherrow, Victoria. *Encyclopedia of Hair: A Cultural History*. Westport, CN: Greenwood Press, 2006.

Silberman, Lauren. "Singing Unsung Heroines." In *Rewriting the Renaissance: The Discourses of Sexual Difference in Early Modern Europe*. Edited by Margaret W. Ferguson, Maureen Quilligan, and Nancy Vickers, 259–71. Chicago: University of Chicago Press, 1986.

Smith, Virginia. *Clean: A History of Personal Hygiene and Purity*. Oxford: Oxford University Press, 2007.

Snook, Edith. *Women, Beauty and Power in Early Modern England: A Feminist Literary History*. New York: Palgrave Macmillan, 2011.

Snook, Edith. "Beautiful Hair, Health, and Privilege in Early Modern England." *Journal for Early Modern Cultural Studies* 15, no. 4 (2015): 22–51.

Sorabella, J. "Portraiture in Renaissance and Baroque Europe." Heilbrunn Timeline of Art History, The Metropolitan Museum of Art, 2007, http://www.metmuseum.org/toah/hd/port/hd_port.htm.

Sponsler, Claire. "Narrating the Social Order: Medieval Clothing Laws." *Clio* 21, no. 3 (1992): 265–83.

Stein, Claudia. *Negotiating the French Pox in Early Modern Germany*. Aldershot: Ashgate, 2009.

Steinke, Hubert. "Medizinische Karriere im städtischen Dienst." In *Jakob Ruf, Leben, Werk und Studien: Mit der Arbeit seiner Hände: Leben und Werk des Zürcher Stadtchirurgen und Theatermachers Jakob Ruf (1505–1558)*. Edited by Hildegard E. Keller, 91–102. 2nd ed. Zürich: Verl. Neue Zürcher Zeitung, 2008.

Storey, Tessa. "Face Waters, Oils, Love Magic and Poison: Making and Selling Secrets in Early Modern Rome." In *Secrets and Knowledge in Medicine and Science, 1500 – 1800*. Edited by Elaine Leong and Alisha Rankin, 143–65. Farnham: Ashgate, 2011.

Strocchia, Sharon T. "Introduction: Women and Healthcare in Early Modern Europe." *Renaissance Studies* 28, no. 4 (2014): 496–514.

Sweet, James H. "The Iberian Roots of American Racist Thought." *William and Mary Quarterly* 54, no. 1 (1997): 143–66.

Synnott, A. "Shame and Glory: A Sociology of Hair." *British Journal of Sociology* 38, no. 3 (1987): 381–413.

Tate, Shirley Anne. *Black Beauty: Aesthetics, Stylization, Politics*. New York: Ashgate, 2009.

Green, Monica, ed. *The Trotula: A Medieval Compendium of Women's Medicine*. Philadelphia: University of Pennsylvania Press, 2001.

Thomas, Keith. *Religion and the Decline of Magic*. New York: Scribners, 1971.

Tondeur, L. "A History of Pubic Hair, or Reviewers' Responses to Terry Eagleton's *After Theory*." In *The Last Taboo: Women and Body Hair*. Edited by K. Lesnik-Oberstein, 48–65. Manchester: Manchester University Press, 2006.

Trasko, M. *Daring Do's: A History of Extraordinary Hair*. Paris: Flammarion, 1994.

Traub, Valerie. *The Renaissance of Lesbianism in Early Modern England*. Cambridge: Cambridge University Press, 2002.

Udry, Susan. "Robert de Blois and Geoffroy de la Tour Landry on Feminine Beauty: Two Late Medieval French Conduct Books for Women." *Essays in Medieval Studies* 19 (2002): 90–102.

Ungerer, Gustav. "Sir Andrew Aguecheek and His Head of Hair." *Shakespeare Studies* 16 (1983): 101–33.

Vecellio, C. *The Clothing of the Renaissance World*. Edited by Margaret F. Rosenthal and Ann Rosalind Jones. London: Thames & Hudson, 2008.

Velasco, Sherry. "Women with Beards in Early Modern Spain." In *The Last Taboo: Women and Body Hair*. Edited by Karín Lesnik-Oberstein, 181–90. Manchester: Manchester University Press, 2006.

Vickers, Nancy. "Diana Described: Scattered Woman and Scattered Rhyme." In *Writing and Sexual Difference*. Edited by Elizabeth Abel, 95–108. Chicago: University of Chicago Press, 1982.

Vigarello, Georges. *Concepts of Cleanliness: Changing Attitudes in France Since the Middle Ages*. Translated by Jean Birrell. Cambridge: Cambridge University Press, 1988.

Villeponteaux, Mary. "*Semper Eadem*: Belphoebe's Denial of Desire." In *Renaissance Discourses of Desire*. Edited by Claude J. Summers and Ted-Larry Pebworth, 29–45. Columbia: University of Missouri Press, 1993.

Von Heusinger, Sabine. *Die Zunft im Mittelalter: Zur Verflechtung von Politik, Wirtschaft und Gesellschaft in Straßburg*. Stuttgart: Steiner, 2009.

Waite, Gary K. "Talking Animals, Preserved Corpses and Venusberg: The Sixteenth-Century Worldview and Popular Conceptions of the Spiritualist David Joris (1501–1556)." *Social History* 20 (1995): 137–56.

Waite, Gary K. "Naked Harlots or Devout Maidens? Images of Anabaptist Women in the Context of the Iconography of Witches in Europe, 1525–1650." In *Sisters: Myth and Reality of Anabaptist, Mennonite, and Doopsgezind Women ca 1525–1900*. Edited by Mirjam van Veen et al., 17–51. Leiden: E.J. Brill, 2014.

Walker, Garthine. *Crime, Gender and Social Order in Early Modern England*. Cambridge: Cambridge University Press, 2003.

Waller, Gary F. "Acts of Reading: The Production of Meaning in *Astrophil and Stella*." *Studies in the Literary Imagination* 15, no.1 (1982): 23–35.

Warde, Paul. "Waldnutzung, Landschaftsentwicklung und Staatliche Reglementierung in der Frühen Neuzeit." In *Landnutzung und Landschaftsentwicklung im deutschen Südwesten: Zur Umweltgeschichte im Späten Mittelalter und in der Frühen Neuzeit*. Edited by Sönke Lorenz and Peter Rückert, 199–217. Stuttgart: W. Kohlhammer, 2009.

Watt, Jeffrey R. "Love Magic and the Inquisition: A Case from Seventeenth-Century Italy." *Sixteenth Century Journal* 41, no. 3 (2010): 675–89.

Wehrli, Gustav A. "Die Bader, Barbiere und Wundärzte im alten Zürich." *Mitteilungen der Antiquarischen Gesellschaft in Zürich* 30, no. 3 (1927): 5–100.

Wehrli, Gustav A. *Die Wundärzte und Bader Zürichs als zünftige Organisation*. Zürich: Antiquarische Gesellschaft, 1931.

Welch, Evelyn. "Art on the Edge: Hair and Hands in Renaissance Italy." *Renaissance Studies* 23, no. 3 (2008): 241–68.

Welch, Evelyn. "Signs of Faith: The Political and Social Identity of Hair in Renaissance Italy." In *La fiducia secondo i linguaggi del potere*. Edited by Paolo Prodi, 371–86. Bologna: Il Mulino, 2008.

Weststeijn, Thijs. *The Visible World: Samuel van Hoogstraten's Art Theory and the Legitimation of Painting in the Dutch Golden Age*. Amsterdam: Amsterdam University Press, 2008.

White, Shane, and Graham White. *Stylin': African American Expressive Culture from Its Beginnings to the Zoot Suit*. Ithaca, NY: Cornell University Press, 1998.

Wiesner-Hanks, Merry. "Women." In *Oxford Encyclopedia of the Reformation*. 4 vols. Edited by Hans J. Hillerbrand, 4:390–8. Oxford, Oxford University Press, 1996.

Wiesner-Hanks, Merry. *The Marvelous Hairy Girls: The Gonzales Sisters and their Worlds*. New Haven, CT: Yale University Press, 2009.

Wiesner, Merry. E. *Women and Gender in Early Modern Europe*. 3rd ed. Cambridge: Cambridge University Press, 2008.

Wilson, Dudley. *Signs and Portents: Monstrous Births from the Middle Ages to the Enlightenment*. London: Routledge, 1993.

Zika, Charles. *Exorcising our Demons: Magic, Witchcraft and Visual Culture in Early Modern Europe*. Leiden: E.J. Brill, 2003.

Zika, Charles. *The Appearance of Witchcraft: Print and Visual Culture in Sixteenth-Century Europe*. London: Routledge Press, 2007.

CONTRIBUTORS

Lyn Bennett is Associate Professor of English at Dalhousie University, Canada. She is the author of two monographs, *Women Writing of Divinest Things: Rhetoric and the Poetry of Pembroke, Wroth and Lanyer* (2004) and *Rhetoric, Medicine, and the Woman Writer, 1600–1700* (2018). Her work appears in publications as diverse as *Christianity and Literature*, *Genre*, and the *Journal of Medical Humanities*. Her current research focuses on the self-fashioning rhetoric of the professions and, in collaboration with Edith Snook of the University of New Brunswick, on the circulation and production of recipes in early modern Atlantic Canada.

Carole Collier Frick is Professor of History and Chair, Department of Historical Studies, Southern Illinois University Edwardsville, USA. She writes on material culture, gender relations, the needle trades, and construction of social and cultural identity in Renaissance Europe. Her publications include: *Dressing Renaissance Florence: Families, Fortunes, and Fine Clothing* (2003); "The Florentine '*Rigattiere*': Second Hand Clothing Dealers and the Circulation of Goods in the Renaissance," in *Old Clothes, New Looks: Second-hand Fashion*, edited by Alexandra Palmer and Hazel Clark (2005); "Gendered Space in Renaissance Florence: Theorizing Public and Private in the 'Rag Trade'," in *Fashion Theory* (2005); "Cappelli e copricapi nella Firenze del Rinascimento" in *Moda e modern*, edited by Eugenia Paulicelli (2006); "Boys to Men: Codpieces and Masculinity in Sixteenth-century Europe," in *Gender and Early Modern Constructions of Childhood*, edited by Naomi Yavneh and Naomi Miller (2011).

Mark Albert Johnston is Associate Professor of English at the University of Windsor, Canada, and is the author of *Beard Fetish in Early Modern England: Sex, Gender, and Registers of Value* (2011). His critical essays have appeared in the journals *English Literary History*, *Studies in English Literature*, *English Literary Renaissance*, and *Modern Philology* as well as in the collections *Masculinity and the Metropolis of Vice: London 1550–1650* (2010), *Thunder at a Playhouse: Essaying Shakespeare and the Early Modern Stage* (2010), and *Queering Childhood in Early Modern English Drama and Culture* (2018), which he coedited with Jennifer Higginbothom.

Nicholas Jones is Assistant Professor of Spanish and Africana Studies at Bucknell University, PA, USA. He researches the agency, subjectivity, and performance of black diasporic identities in early modern Iberia, Cuba, and Mexico. He is coeditor of *Early Modern Black Diaspora Studies: A Critical Anthology* (2018) with Cassander L. Smith and Miles P. Grier. His first book, entitled *Lumbe, Lumbe!: Radical Performances of Habla de negros in Early Modern Spain*, is under contract. Jones has also published articles in the *Journal for Early Modern Cultural Studies*, *Arizona Journal of Hispanic Cultural Studies*, *Hispanic Review*, and *Postmedieval*.

CONTRIBUTORS

Annemarie Kinzelbach has recently joined the research team at the Department of History and Ethics of Medicine at TUM (Technical University of Munich), Germany. In the past she has been associated with the universities of Ulm, Berlin, Erlangen-Nürnberg, and Heidelberg. She has published widely on the social and cultural history of medicine in premodern imperial cities. Her recent publications include *Chirurgen und Chirurgie-Praktiken: Wundärzte als Reichsstadtbürger, 16. bis 18. Jahrhundert* (2016); together with Andrew Mendelssohn, "Common Knowledge: Bodies, Evidence, and Expertise in Early Modern Germany," in *Isis* 108 (2017): 259–79; and "Dissecting Pain: Patients, Families and Medical Expertise in Early Modern Germany," in *Pathology in Practice: Diseases and Dissections in Early Modern Europe*, edited by Silvia de Renzi, Marco Bresadola, and Maria Conforti (2018): 170–87.

Anu Korhonen is Lecturer in European Cultural Studies at the University of Helsinki, Finland. She has published widely on early modern English cultural history both in English and in Finnish, and has been interested in themes such as gender and the body, humor and laughter, and historical theory. Among her latest publications is a special issue on early modern time and temporality in the *Journal of Early Modern Studies* 2017, coedited with Alessandro Arcangeli, which includes her essay "'The several hours of the day had variety of employments assigned to them': Women's Timekeeping in Early Modern England."

Jana Mathews is Associate Professor of English at Rollins College, USA, Florida's oldest liberal arts institution. Her teaching and research focus on the intersection of literature and law in medieval and early modern Europe. Her academic essays on the topic have appeared in several edited collections as well as *The Journal of Religion and Popular Culture*, *The Journal for the Study of British Cultures*, and *Fragments: Interdisciplinary Approaches to the Study of Ancient and Medieval Pasts*.

Edith Snook is Professor of English at the University of New Brunswick, Fredericton, Canada. Her research focuses on women's writing in early modern England, as well as health and beauty practices and recipes. She is the author of two books: *Women, Beauty and Power in Early Modern England: A Feminist Literary History* (2011, 2015) and *Women, Reading, and the Cultural Politics of Early Modern England* (2005). Among her other publications are essays on children's diseases, recipes, and women's knowledge in *Social History of Medicine* and an essay on hair, health, and privilege in *The Journal for Early Modern Cultural Studies*.

Gary K. Waite is Professor of early modern European history at the University of New Brunswick, Fredericton, Canada. Author and editor of several books, he has published widely in a number of fields relating to religion and culture in the Low Countries and Europe, including on Anabaptism and spiritualism, the unconventional spiritualist David Joris, Dutch drama guilds, witchcraft and demonology, and seventeenth-century Dutch views of Jews and Muslims, with a book forthcoming titled, *Jews and Muslims in Seventeenth-Century Discourse: From Religious Enemies to Allies and Friends*. He is now working on a funded research project on religious nonconformists and the early Enlightenment.

INDEX

Absalom (character in the Bible) 4–7
Africa 3, 10–11, 15, 43, 115–25
age 7–12, 14, 40, 42, 47–8, 51, 58, 85–7, 89–90, 96, 99, 104–6, 139–40, 150
Alfonso X of Castile 118
Americas 3, 11, 53, 103, 109, 116–17
Anger, Jane 49
Anne [Boleyn], queen of England 3, 63
Anne of Austria, queen of Spain 64
apprentices, the hair of 7, 13, 48, 106, 129
apprenticeship, barbers 81–3
Arabs 15, 88, 117–18
Aristotle 14, 85–9, 104
armpit hair 9, 87, 175 n.7

Bakhtin, Mikhail 97
Baldung, Hans 24, 29–33
Baldwin, Frances Elizabeth 128
Banks, Ingrid 124
Barber, Paul 26
barbers and barber-surgeons 2, 4–5, 13–14, 22–3, 28, 50, 71, 75–84, 90, 95, 101, 106–10, 112, 135, 139
barbershops 13–14, 50, 78–84, 107
Barnes, Barnabe 146, 148, 151
Bateman, Stephen 7
bathhouses 14, 78–83, 137, 141–3
bathing 14, 73–80, 91, 138
beauty 5–7, 11, 15–16, 19, 23, 40–3, 46–51, 73–4, 87, 96, 102, 109, 119–25, 135–6, 148–50, 155
Beham, Sebald 137
Bell, Quentin 57
Bentley, Thomas 45
Bhabha, Homi 124
biblical dictates and exemplars 2, 4–7, 17–20, 44, 46, 79, 99–100, 104
Biow, Douglas 3, 91
blackface 15, 120–1, 125
Bock, Hieronymus 74
Bodin, Jean 28
body hair 2–3, 11–12, 26–7, 36, 40, 48–9, 85–90, 111, 119, 124, 136–7, 141. See also armpit hair; pubic hair

Borgia, Lucrezia 46
Botticelli, Sandro 4, 55, 69, 72–3, 131
Bracciolini, Poggio 139
braids 7, 15, 17–19, 45–6, 49–50, 53, 58, 60, 69, 72, 120, 125, 129, 132
Brandt, Isabella 67
Breton, Nicholas 42
Brotbeihel, Jeremias 76–8
Bullein, William 90
Bulwer, John 101–12
Burke, Jill 136
Butler, Charles 94
Butler, Judith 100
Butts, Margaret, Lady 63
Bützel, Johann 74
Byrd, Ayana B. and Lori L. Tharps 3

Calvin, John 4, 12, 17–19
Campbell, Erin J. 9
Carew, Thomas 150
Carney, Judith 3
Cary, Elizabeth, Viscountess Falkland 50, 147–9
Castiglione, Baldassare 16, 47, 152
Catalina Micaela, infanta of Spain 66
Catchmay, Frances, Lady 92
Catherine of Aragon, queen of England 64, 105–6
Cavallo, Sandra 2, 90
Cavendish, Margaret, Duchess of Newcastle upon Tyne 3
Cecil, William, first Baron Burghley 9
Cesari, Giuseppe 138
Charles V, Holy Roman Emperor and king of Spain 4, 53, 64
children's hair 7–9, 45, 47–8, 58, 73, 87, 91–2, 96, 101, 134
  boys' hair 7–9, 40, 47–8, 58, 99–101, 106, 109–10, 114
  girls' hair 3, 8–9, 19, 23, 28, 58–60, 91
Cholmley, Hugh 41
civility 11–12, 88–90, 96–7, 103, 109, 154
cleanliness 44, 47, 51, 80, 90–2, 94–5, 116
Cleland, James 45

Clifford, Anne, Countess of Pembroke, Dorset, and Montgomery 9, 41
climate, influence of 10–11, 42, 53, 88, 103, 118
Cockayne, Emily 134–5
College of Physicians 93
Collins, Patricia Hill 123
complexion 1, 13, 40–2, 85–90, 92, 94–7, 102, 104, 111
Constable, Henry 16, 148
Corson, Richard 2, 110, 178 n.5
Cortés, Jerónimo 119
Cotarelo y Mori, Emilio 120
Council of Trent 18, 53, 65
Cromwell, Oliver 4, 67–8
Crooke, Helkiah 11, 86–8, 93
Culpeper, Nicholas 92–4

Daniel, Samuel 148, 152, 188 n.29
da Toledo, Eleonora 60
da Vinci, Leonardo 50
d'Este, Isabella, Marchesa of Montua 46, 60–1, 133–4
de Cervantes Saavedra, Miguel 122
de Covarrubias y Horozco, Sebastián 115–17, 125
de Lancre, Pierre 23–4
de' Medici, Catherine 134
de' Medici, Lorenzo 56
de Montaigne, Michel 101
de Quevedo, Francisco 119
de Rueda, Lope 15, 115, 120–5
de Valois, Marguerite, queen of Navarre and France 134
Dekker, Thomas 48
del Pollaiuolo, Piero 131–3
del Rio, Martin 28–9
della Francesca, Piero 127
demons 17, 23–5, 27–31, 34–5, 37, 156 n.5
Dent, Arthur 45
Digby, Elizabeth 92
DiPasquale, Theresa M. 155
Dircksz, Barend 33
distinction 3–12, 100–3, 106, 128–43
Donne, John 154–5
Drage, William 91–4, 96
Drayton, Michael 150
Drummond, William of Hawthornden 146, 151–2
Dubrow, Heather 150, 155, 189 n.42
Dürer, Albrecht 9, 24, 30–1, 33–5, 71–2, 141–3

Eagleton, Terry 135
Egypt 11, 88, 152
Elizabeth I, queen of England 4, 42, 64, 68, 134
Elizabeth of York, queen of England 63
Elyot, Thomas 86, 89, 176 n.32
Emberley, Julia 130
England 2–3, 7–11, 13–16, 23, 37, 39–52, 60, 63–9, 72–3, 82, 85–97, 99–114, 122, 129–31, 134–6, 145–55
Erasmus 47, 139–40
Erondell, Peter 49–50, 132–3
Eve (character in the Bible) 4, 11, 25
Evelyn, John 112–13
excrement, hair as 2, 14, 23, 48, 85–7, 89–92, 94, 97, 104

facial hair
    beards 3, 7, 9–12, 14, 18, 20–3, 41–2, 48, 50, 53–4, 64–6, 68, 71, 75, 80, 82, 84, 87–9, 95–6, 100–1, 104–14, 119, 129
        on women 3, 11–12, 31, 110–14, 119
    eyebrows 47, 53, 85, 87, 89, 95, 105, 136, 175 n.7
    eyelashes 87
    mustaches 64, 67, 71, 108
false hair. *See also* prosthetic hair
    false beards 14, 101
    hairpieces 15, 58, 60, 69–70, 72, 134
    wigs 14–15, 42, 69, 72, 101, 109–10, 120, 133–5, 139
family identity 8–10, 13, 19, 21, 25, 40–1, 43, 46, 59–60, 70
Fanon, Frantz 122
Fanshawe, Ann, Lady Fanshawe 41
fashions 1–4, 8–9, 13, 17, 23–4, 37, 42–51, 53–70, 105–8, 130–5, 141
femininity 23, 44–7, 102, 109–14, 131–41
Festa, Lynn 135
Fisher, Will 3, 48, 104, 186 n.4, 186 n.7, 187 n.20
Floetner, Peter 140
Florio, John 116
Ford, John 150–1
foreignness 43–4, 54, 103, 107–9, 112, 120–1, 123
France 3, 7, 12, 19, 23, 25–6, 28, 43, 50, 56, 58, 60–5, 80, 95, 101, 104, 134
fur 11–12, 15, 119

Galen 2, 10, 14, 85–8, 90, 99–100, 119
gender 2–10, 13–15, 17–23, 25, 37, 39–40, 43–9, 51, 85, 87, 90, 99–114, 117, 120–5. *See also* femininity; masculinity

gender difference 3–5, 8, 37, 47
Gentileschi, Artemisia 70
Gerard, John 93–4
Germany 2–3, 5–7, 18–19, 23, 26–8, 33, 36, 43, 58, 62, 74, 79–80, 88, 113, 130, 137. *See also* Holy Roman Empire
Gonzales, Petrus 12, 26
Gonzales sisters (Maddalena, Francesca, and Antonietta) 3, 12, 26
Gopnik, Blake 140
Greenblatt, Stephen 97
Greene, Robert 45, 106–7
Grien, Hans Baldung 24, 29–33
Grienewaldt, Jeremias 78
Guazzo, Francisco Maria 34–6

hair care equipment 75–8
   brush 1, 45, 47, 74
   comb 1, 47, 94, 96
   curling iron 45, 95
   pads 9, 122–3
   razor 4–5, 75–6, 139
   scissors 4–5, 75–6, 109, 137
   tweezers 137
hair care practices. *See also* hair removal
   braiding 7, 15, 17–19, 45–6, 49–50, 53, 58, 60, 69, 72, 120, 124–5, 129, 132, 178 n.5
   brushing 1
   coloring 1, 14–15, 44–5, 49, 64, 73–4, 85, 93, 95–7, 99, 101, 104–5, 109, 120–4, 131–2, 165 n.1
   combing 14, 44, 47–50, 75–6, 90–2, 94–5
   curling or crisping 12, 23, 45–7, 49–50, 53, 64, 68, 72, 74, 94–5, 103–4, 110, 150, 152–3
   perfuming 44, 49–50, 64, 176 n.46
   powdering 50, 64, 91
   sociability of 49–51
   straightening 122
   washing 14, 43, 73–4, 76–81, 84, 91, 95, 108, 133
hair care practitioners 78–84. *See also* barbers; servants, role in hair care
hair characteristics
   abundance 5, 7, 14, 41, 48, 51, 74, 85–6, 88–9, 94–5, 102–4, 107, 114, 148
   color 14, 39–43, 45, 49, 53, 85–7, 92, 95–6, 100, 102–4, 107, 128, 131–2, 148, 156 n.5, 176 n.32
      black 9–10, 16, 19, 40–1, 43, 48, 74, 86–9, 95–6, 102, 149
      blonde 10, 15, 40–3, 45, 48, 53, 64, 68–9, 71, 74, 86, 95–6, 104, 115, 120–5, 131–2, 134, 145–53
      brown 8, 9, 40–2, 48, 67, 74, 104
      flaxen 41–2
      gray/white 9–10, 40, 48, 86–7, 93, 95–6, 104–5
      red 21–2, 26, 41–2, 62, 86, 88–9, 95, 104, 107, 154
   curliness 7–12, 14–15, 19, 23, 39–43, 45–7, 49–50, 53, 54, 60, 64, 66–9, 71–2, 74, 86, 88–9, 92, 94–5, 102–4, 131, 145, 148, 150, 152–3
   hardness/softness 40, 85, 87–9, 95, 102–3
   length 4–5, 7–9, 12, 14–15, 17–19, 21, 23–4, 30, 37, 40–1, 43, 46–8, 51, 54, 58, 60, 62, 64–5, 67–8, 72, 88–9, 94–5, 100, 103–6, 109–11, 113, 145, 147, 158 n.28, 175 n.7, 178 n.4, 186 n.4, 186 n.7
   straightness 8–9, 56, 69, 86, 88, 95, 104
   texture 14, 43, 49, 100–2, 118–20
   wool, hair described as 10–11, 43, 118
hair covering 1–2, 4, 7–10, 12–13, 17–20, 25, 29–31, 34, 37, 45–6, 53–70
hair maladies 14, 92–6. *See also* remedies
   alopecia 14, 85, 92–3
   excess hair 11–12, 26–7, 47, 85, 94, 96, 103, 119, 177 n.73
   hair loss 2–3, 9, 14, 48, 85–6, 92–4, 97, 134, 138–9
   hypertrichosis universalis 3, 26
   lice 14, 47, 74–5, 80, 85, 91–2, 97
   scurf 44, 74, 93
hair removal 14–15, 48–9, 94, 97, 101, 105, 109, 135–41
   cutting 1–2, 4–7, 12, 14, 17–18, 20, 22–3, 25, 37, 46–51, 53–4, 64, 66–8, 71–3, 75–84, 90–1, 99–100, 103, 109–10, 134–5, 139
   plucking 53, 58, 60, 90, 105, 109, 136, 139
   shaving 12, 14, 81, 83–4, 99–100
      of eyebrows 105
      of facial hair 7, 20, 54, 82, 100, 106–9
      of head 4, 17–19, 24, 35–7, 53, 94–5, 100, 103–4, 135, 139
      of pubic hair 36–7, 135, 139
Hall, Thomas 104
headwear 7–10, 13, 53–70, 127–35
health 3, 11, 13–14, 39–40, 43, 46, 50–1, 71–84, 85–97, 102, 112, 135
Hendler, Sefy 3

INDEX

Hendricks, Margo 10
Henrietta Maria, queen of England 68
Henry II, king of France 12
Henry III, king of France 64–5, 134
Henry V, king of England 105
Henry VIII, king of England 3, 63–5, 105–7, 178 n.5
Herbert, Edward, first Lord Herbert of Cherbury 41, 43
Herrick, Robert 16, 154
Heywood, Oliver 41
Heywood, Thomas 147
Hic Mulier 109–10
Hill, Thomas 101–8, 110–12
Hiltebeitel, Alf and Barbara D. Miller 3
Holbein, Hans 63–4
Hollander, Anne 135–6
Hollar, Wenceslaus 7
Holy Roman Empire 4, 14, 53, 62, 78, 82–4. See also Germany
Horowitz, Elliott 3
Hortensius, Lambertus 33–4
household 13, 48–9, 72–5, 84, 99, 133, 136
Howard, Henry, Earl of Surrey 15, 146, 150
Huarte de San Juan, Juan 119
humors 1–2, 14, 40–4, 51, 76, 81, 85–97, 99–102, 104, 106–7, 114, 118–19, 176 n.32
Hunt, Alan 129
Hutchinson, Lucy 49, 51

identity 1–3, 7, 11, 13–15, 22, 39–53, 55, 68, 85–8, 90, 97, 102, 120–5. *See also* family identity; gender; national identity; race; religious identity
India 88
Inns of Court 7, 106
Italy 2–3, 9, 13, 23, 34–6, 46, 50, 53–60, 66, 68, 72, 82–3, 91, 95–6, 112, 116, 130–1, 145, 156 n.5, 158 n.28, 165 n.1

Jackson, Jane 92–3
James I, king of England 47–8
Johnston, Mark Albert 129
Jonson, Ben 16, 106, 109, 130–1, 154
Jordan, Thomas 148
Joris, David 4, 12, 18, 20–3
Juliana Nassau-Dillenburg, Countess 73–4

Killerby, Katherine 132
Knox, John 64
Kramer, Heinrich 23–4, 27, 36–7

Ladurie, Emmanuel LeRoy 25
Laqueur, Thomas 100
law 15, 35–7, 60, 64, 104, 127–32, 141, 143
Le Gall, Jean-Marie 2
Lemnius, Levinus 40, 86–7, 89
Levens, Peter 94–5
Lonitzer, Adam 74–6
Loomba, Ania 10
loose hair 11, 15, 29–32, 34, 45, 46, 64, 68, 113, 147
lovelocks 47–8
Ludwig VI, Count Palatine 73–4
Luther, Martin 5–6, 12, 17–19
Luyken, Jan 34

magic 1, 12, 23–9, 31, 34–5, 37, 156 n.5
Marinella, Lucrezia 96
Marlowe, Christopher 16, 149, 188 n.37
marriage 8, 13, 26, 57, 59–60, 78, 106, 117, 131, 146–7
Martínez, María Elena 116–17
Mary, queen of Scots 42, 134
masculinity 2–3, 5–7, 9, 12, 18, 22–3, 47–9, 99–109, 114, 119, 139
Micron, Martin 20
Mildmay, Grace 46
Milton, John 3–4
mimicry 15, 115, 124–5
Molitor, Ulrich 29–30
monstrosity 26, 37, 104, 107–8, 111
morality 1, 4, 9, 13, 17–18, 23, 30, 37, 39, 42, 45–52, 58, 60, 72–3, 80, 89, 100–3, 111, 117, 128, 134, 145
Moseley-Christian, Michelle 11
Murner, Thomas 79–80
Murray, Pauli 124
Muzzarelli, Maria 129

national identity 2, 10, 13–14, 39, 42–4, 103–4, 109, 131
nature 3–4, 12, 14, 16, 18–19, 25, 55, 88, 90, 96, 99–114, 122, 130, 145–55
Netherlands 3, 18, 20–3, 33–7, 62

order 1, 3–4, 7, 11–12, 14–15, 19, 91–2, 94, 96–7, 99, 100–5, 107, 110, 112, 114, 117, 129, 135, 141, 143
Ovid 138, 186 n.4

Paré, Ambrose 95, 101
Peacham, Henry 146–7
Pelling, Margaret 2, 50, 90

Pepys, Samuel 114, 135
Petrarch (Francesco Petrarca) 4, 15–16, 54, 145–55
Phillips, Kim 128
physicians, the hair of 7
physiology 85–90
Platter, Felix 26
poetics 149–55
politics 2–4, 12–14, 39, 42, 48, 51, 54–5, 64, 70, 83, 88, 99, 104, 116. *See also* Roundheads
   class politics 4, 7, 12–13, 15, 39, 70, 123, 127–43
   gender politics 99–114
   racial politics 10–11, 15, 42–4, 109, 115–25
power of hair
   erotic power 16, 24, 29–35, 49, 146–9
   patriarchal power 12, 22–3, 64, 105–9
   political power 3–5, 42–4, 54–8, 64
   preternatural power 23–9
   social power 9, 41, 48, 52, 87–90, 99–103, 115–25, 127–43
   spiritual power 17, 20, 22
priests, the hair of 7, 19, 22–4, 156 n.5
prosthetic hair 14, 101, 109, 133. *See also* false hair
prostitution 13, 18, 46, 53, 58, 80, 117, 135, 139–40
Prynne, William 23, 103–4, 109–10, 186 n.4
pubic hair 15, 29, 36, 86, 89, 128, 135–43, 156 n.5

Quarles, Francis 147, 188 n.37
Queen's Closet Opened 94, 136

race 3, 10–11, 13, 15, 23, 39, 88, 115–25
   blackness 3, 10–11, 15, 43, 88, 115–25
   whiteness 3, 10–11, 15, 42–3, 88–9, 115, 118, 120–4
Raphael 136
Read, Alexander 112
Reformation 2, 17–23, 33–5, 65, 100, 105–6, 112
religion 3, 4–7, 10, 12–13, 17–37, 39, 45–6, 50–2, 70, 101, 104, 116–19
   Catholicism 7, 11–12, 18, 22–3, 26–7, 37, 65–6, 112, 117
   Islam 118
   Judaism 17, 19, 116–19
   Protestantism 14, 18–23, 33, 37, 53, 65–8, 106
      Anabaptist 12, 17, 20–3, 33–5

Puritan 23, 37, 51, 67–8, 104
   Quaker 37
religious identity 2, 12
remedies and recipes 13–14, 48–9, 73–5, 85, 90–6, 121–3, 136–7
revenants 26
Riolan, Jean 87, 92
Romania 26
Rooks, Noliwe 124
Rosenthal, Angela 135
Roundheads 4, 51, 67–8, 104
Rubens, Peter Paul 4–5, 67–8
Rudyerd, Benjamin 107
Russell, John, first Earl of Bedford 9

Sa'id al-Andalusi 118
Sachs, Hans and Jost Amman 80–2
saints 11–12, 26–7, 112–14
Samson (character in the Bible) 4–7, 12, 17, 20
San Bernardino of Siena 58
satire 2, 9, 47–8, 50, 119, 130, 150
Scotland 42, 64, 130, 134
selling of hair 73, 134, 163 n.27
Serbia 26
servants, hair of 7, 134
servants, role in hair care 49–51
sexual desire 29, 101
sexual difference 3–4, 13–14, 40, 47–8, 85, 88–9, 99–103
sexual maturity 14, 85–7, 89, 100
sexuality 4, 11–12, 14, 17, 19, 24–5, 29–32, 34–5, 37, 43, 45, 49, 89–90, 99–114, 117, 135–41
Sforza, Caterina, Countess of Forlì 136
Sfroza, Battista, Duchess of Urbino 127–8
Shakespeare, William 3, 10, 16, 31, 97, 106, 109, 112, 149–50
Shepard, Alexandra 99
Shirley, James 148, 150
Sidney, Philip 10, 15–16, 147–9, 152, 189 n.54
Sieber, Roy, Frank Herreman, and Niangi Batulukis 3
Simons, Menno 18, 20
slavery 3, 11, 109, 115, 118–25
Smith, William 146
Snook, Edith 148, 152–3, 186–7 n.7, 188 n.37, 190 n.66
Spain 3, 11, 15, 53, 64, 66, 112, 115–25
Spenser, Edmund 15, 146–8, 187 n.19, 188 n.28

INDEX

Sponsler, Claire 129
sprezzatura 16, 152
Stewart, Alan 12
Stowe, John 106
Stubbes, Phillip 45, 72–3, 104, 107–8, 134–5
Sweert, Michael 91
Swetnam, Joseph 49
Switzerland 37, 83
Synnott, Anthony 128

Tate, Shirley Anne 124
"technology of the self" 13, 44–51
Temple, Peter, Sir 95
theft of hair 15, 45, 133–5
Thomas, Keith 23, 25
Thornton, Alice 46
Thurgood, Rose 46
Tintoretto, Jacopo 9
Titian 60–1, 131
Tortula 137
Traub, Valerie 100
Tuke, Thomas 45

"ugly beauty" 150
universities 7, 48, 106
uses of hair
   in lace 1
   as love token 1, 49, 155
   in magic 1, 17, 25–9, 156 n.5

van Beck, Barbara (Barbara Urselin) 112–14
Van Gent, Jacqueline 28
van Hoogstraten, Samuel 75–6
Vasari, Giorgio 54–5
Vecellio, Cesare 131–2
Velasco, Sherry 3
Verney, Edmund 48
Vicary, Thomas 86–7, 89, 164 n.54
Vigo, Giovanni 92
Villiers, George, first Duke of Buckingham 8–9, 68
Vives, Juan Luis 44–5

Wager, Lewis 45
Wall, Thomas 110
Weever, John 149
Welch, Evelyn 2
werewolves 3, 11–12
White, Shane and Graham White 11
Wiesner-Hanks, Merry 3, 12, 26, 31
wild folk (men and women) 3, 11–12, 26–7
Winston, Thomas 85
wit 145, 153, 155
witches 12–13, 17, 23–5, 27–37, 58, 112
Wright, Leonard 42
Wroth, Mary 16, 153–4
Wyatt, Thomas, Sir 146

Zika, Charles 29–30, 37